A FULL SERVICE
════ BANK ════

A FULL SERVICE BANK

How BCCI Stole Billions Around the World

James Ring Adams and Douglas Frantz

S I M O N & S C H U S T E R

LONDON·SYDNEY·NEW YORK·TOKYO·SINGAPORE·TORONTO

First published in Great Britain by
Simon & Schuster Ltd in 1991
A Paramount Communications Company

First published in this edition in 1992

Copyright © 1992 by James Ring Adams

This book is copyright under the Berne Convention.
No reproduction without permission.
All rights reserved.

Simon & Schuster Ltd
West Garden Place
Kendal Street
London W2 2AQ

Simon & Schuster of Australia Pty Ltd
Sydney

British Library Cataloguing-in-Publication Data available
ISBN 0-671-71133-4

Printed and bound in the United States of America

For my mother and the memory of my sister
J.R.A.

For my children, Elizabeth, Nicholas, Rebecca
D.F.

ACKNOWLEDGMENTS

James Ring Adams thanks:

Many people, Pakistani, Arab and American, who prefer not to be mentioned by name. In particular, I appreciate the help of former BCCI employees who were caught in a scandal not of their making and ought to be considered its victims.

Robert Morgenthau, John Moscow and their staffs, models of public integrity.

The personnel of Operation C-Chase: Paul O'Brien, Bonni Tischler, Bob Moore, Steve Cook, Dave Burris and the unsung staff supervised by Tam Audritsh who put in thousands of hours to turn undercover tapes into an exceptionally valuable public record. In spite of the controversy, C-Chase should be remembered as a brilliant episode in federal law enforcement.

Bill Rosenblatt and Dennis Fagan, pioneers of Operation Greenback.

John Hume, Noma Smith, Debra Dunn for indispensable and extremely generous help. Also Sandy Weinberg, Jay Hogan and Michael O'Kane.

Tracy Schilling, a compassionate presence, and good friends Lex Hood and Ken Muzynski.

Mark Jackowski, Robert Merkle, Jerry Sanford, Richard Gregorie, Buddy Parker and the staffs of the Federal District Courts of Tampa, Alexandria and Washington D.C. and of the National Archives.

Jack Blum and Dennis Kane.

Alan Petigny and Shoshana Edelberg of WUSF-FM, Tampa, an outstanding news team. Len Apcar of the *St. Petersburg Times*. Tom Bray of the *Detroit News*. Howard Dickman of the *Reader's Digest*.

Acknowledgments

Christopher Rencki, for great help from across the water.

Robert Bartley of the *Wall Street Journal*, who put me on the story in the first place, and Allen Dodds Frank and Rachel Ehrenfeld, who smelled a rat back in 1986.

Chris Byron, David Asman, John Fund and Melanie Kirkpatrick, for constant gossip and encouragement.

Lois de la Haba and Jane Chelius, for launching the project and keeping it on course.

David Geil, Jr. and Sr., Abram Shulsky, Frank Fukuyama and Virginia Armat. And those who couldn't avoid living with the work, my mother and family, Jared, Jonathan, Abigail and Laurel.

===

Doug Frantz thanks:

The many journalists whose work is cited in the Notes and Sources section. Readers are urged to consult that listing for a far more complete guide to the invaluable work performed by members of the Fourth Estate. Scrutiny by journalists remains one of the surest means of safeguarding the political and financial processes.

For individual mention, *Los Angeles Times* reporters Bob Jackson, Ron Ostrow and Bill Rempel; *Los Angeles Times* Washington bureau librarians Abebe Gessessee and Pat Welch; and David McKean of the staff of Senator John Kerry.

Also, for their support, Jack Nelson and Dick Cooper of the *Times* Washington bureau and Mike Miller, *Times* national editor.

SOME OF THE MAJOR PLAYERS

Agha Hasan Abedi: The visionary Pakistani-born banker founded the Bank of Credit and Commerce International in 1972. He built BCCI into an international power with the help of thousands of loyal employees and a few well-chosen friends.

Emir Abreu: A veteran Customs agent and native of Puerto Rico, he played the critical and dangerous undercover role in C-Chase of picking up drug money from the traffickers.

Kamal Adham: A wealthy businessman and founder of Saudi Arabia's intelligence service, he became a large stockholder in the parent company of First American. He denied accusations by U.S. authorities that he was acting as a front for BCCI and Abedi.

Syed Z. A. Akbar: He was head of BCCI's treasury department when the bank lost $1 billion in bad trades through the department. Yet after he left to join a commodities-trading firm, he still helped the bank try to hide $23 million of General Manuel Noriega's money.

Roberto Baez Alcaino: Known as the Jeweler because he ran a jewelry store in Los Angeles, he turned to drug smuggling and money laundering to finance a lavish life-style.

Robert Altman: A smart young lawyer and the protégé of Clark Clifford, he became president of First American Bankshares and dealt often with Abedi and BCCI officials.

Rudolf Armbrecht: A dashing airline pilot, he found it easier to make a living working for the drug lords of the Medellín cartel. By the time he grew suspicious of the undercover agent, it was too late.

Some of the Major Players

Amjad Awan: The only son of a Pakistani intelligence chief, he was General Manuel Noriega's personal banker at BCCI and eventually became the chief target of the undercover investigation launched by the U.S. Customs Service.

Akbar Ali Bilgrami: Born in Pakistan and educated in California, he worked closely with Amjad Awan in BCCI's Miami office. He was suspicious of the undercover agent but assisted in the agent's money-laundering plans anyway.

Jack Blum: A dogged investigator for Senator John Kerry, he refused to walk away from the BCCI case despite rebuffs from Federal prosecutors. Evidence he took to the New York district attorney set in motion events that helped bring down the bank.

Nazir Chinoy: As general manager of BCCI's operations in France, he assisted the undercover agent and his entourage in opening accounts for various front companies in Paris late in the investigation.

Clark Clifford: Former secretary of defense and an adviser to Democratic presidents from Truman to Carter, he spent thirteen years as chairman of First American Bankshares and BCCI's lawyer, but professed that he never knew that BCCI owned a controlling interest in the Washington bank.

Kathy Ertz: A Customs Service agent in Miami, she was brought into Operation C-Chase to help provide cover for the main undercover agent. She used the name Kathy Erickson.

Syed Aftab Hussain: As a junior officer in BCCI's Panama office, he noticed a strange pattern in the account opened by the undercover agent and eventually introduced the agent to key officers in the bank's Miami office.

Senator John Kerry: The Massachusetts Democrat and Vietnam War hero was a freshman senator when he first started investigating BCCI. He refused to let go, despite pressure from colleagues and assurances from Clifford and others that there was nothing seriously wrong with the bank.

Bert Lance: The former budget director under President Jimmy Carter, he was involved in BCCI's unsuccessful attempt to take over a Washington bank and later introduced Abedi to the former president.

Robert Mazur: Posing as a corrupt financial consultant named Robert Musella, the Customs agent and undercover veteran built a routine money-laundering case into an investigation that brought down BCCI.

Some of the Major Players

Gonzalo Mora, Jr.: A small-time money launderer in Colombia, he saw Mazur as his ticket to the big time. He introduced the undercover agent to representatives of the Medellín cartel.

Swaleh Naqvi: As the right-hand man of Agha Abedi at United Bank in Pakistan and later at BCCI, he executed many of the policies set forth by the boss. When Abedi suffered a heart attack, Naqvi began to run BCCI.

Ghaith Pharaon: A Harvard-educated Saudi Arabian, he amassed a fortune through connections to the kingdom's royal family. Federal authorities said his ownership of banks in Atlanta, Georgia, and Encino, California, was a front for BCCI.

Ghassan Qassem: As an officer in BCCI's fashionable Sloane Street branch in London, he unknowingly became the personal banker to terrorist Abu Nidal. Once he discovered the customer's identity, he spied on him for British and American intelligence services.

Masihur Rahman: Son of an Indian supreme court justice, he was persuaded by Abedi to join BCCI as its chief financial officer in 1975. He later said he had no idea what was really going on inside the bank.

Sheik Zayed bin Sultan al-Nahayan: The ruler of the Persian Gulf state of Abu Dhabi, he befriended Abedi early on and helped him found BCCI. Later, he pumped about $1 billion into the bank to try to keep it afloat.

Credit and Commerce American Holdings, NV

Organization Chart
(As of December 31, 1990)

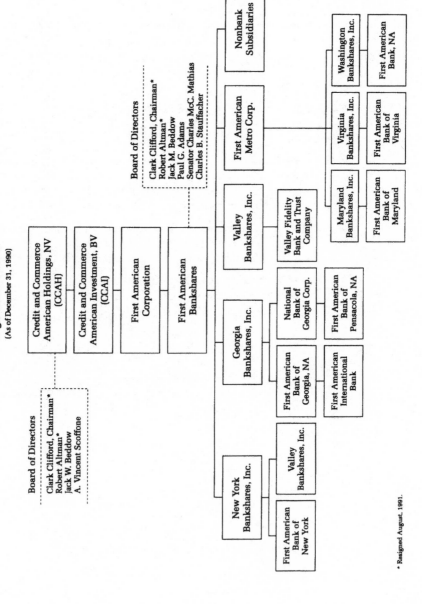

Board of Directors

Clark Clifford, Chairman*
Robert Altman*
Jack W. Beddow
A. Vincent Scoffone

Credit and Commerce American Holdings, NV (CCAH)

Credit and Commerce American Investment, BV (CCAI)

First American Corporation

First American Bankshares

Board of Directors

Clark Clifford, Chairman*
Robert Altman*
Jack M. Beddow
Paul G. Adams
Senator Charles McC. Mathias
Charles B. Stauffacher

Nonbank Subsidiaries

First American Metro Corp.

Valley Bankshares, Inc.

Valley Fidelity Bank and Trust Company

Georgia Bankshares, Inc.

National Bank of Georgia Corp.

First American Bank of Pensacola, NA

First American Bank of Georgia, NA

First American International Bank

New York Bankshares, Inc.

Valley Bankshares, Inc.

First American Bank of New York

Maryland Bankshares, Inc.

First American Bank of Maryland

Virginia Bankshares, Inc.

First American Bank of Virginia

Washington Bankshares, Inc.

First American Bank, NA

* Resigned August, 1991.

Bank of Credit and Commerce International
Shareholders
(1978)

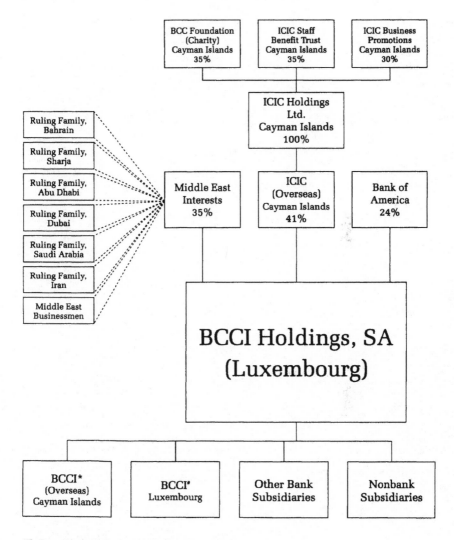

*The Cayman Islands subsidiary established agency offices in Miami, Tampa, and Boca Raton,
Florida, during the 1980s.

' The Luxembourg subsidiary established agency offices in New York, San Francisco, and
Los Angeles during the 1980s.

PART ONE

Building the Bank

Western banks concentrate on the visible,
whereas we stress the invisible.

—Agha Hasan Abedi, founder,
the Bank of Credit and
Commerce International

CHAPTER ONE

A Reverse Robin Hood

At one o'clock in the afternoon on July 5, 1991, officials of the Bank of England marched into the twenty-five branches of the Bank of Credit and Commerce International in Britain and ordered employees to leave. From small offices in the Asian north end of London to the lavish main office in the financial district, the regulators locked the doors and began boxing up thousands of bank records. Simultaneously, regulators swept down on the bank's branches and offices in the United States, France, the Cayman Islands, Spain, and Switzerland.

In Luxembourg, the bank's official headquarters, the tiny duchy's entire judiciary was attending an official picnic in the countryside. Bank regulators had to track them down and find a judge to sign an order to close the bank. While the order was being signed, armed guards stood outside the conference room at the bank's headquarters. Behind the closed doors, representatives of the government of Abu Dhabi, BCCI's principal shareholder, were meeting in a last-ditch attempt to salvage the bank with an infusion of cash and new management, unaware of the drama beginning around the world. So desperate was the Persian Gulf sheikdom to keep the bank open that its officials were meeting on a Friday, the Muslim sabbath. The bank's board members were still inside the conference room when the regulators arrived to seize the bank.

It was eight-thirty that morning on the East Coast of the United States when examiners from the Federal Reserve Board showed up at the bank's office in New York and locked the doors. In the dark hours of predawn in Los Angeles, examiners arrived at the BCCI office downtown and sealed the doors.

These were only the first dominoes to fall. By the end of the weekend, BCCI's operations had been closed in eighteen countries and put under

3

tight supervision or restricted in forty-four others. The coordinated shutdown was a drastic step and a risky one, since the bank's operations were spread around the world and the repercussions within the international financial system could be disastrous, but Robin Leigh-Pemberton, governor of the Bank of England, defended the unprecedented action. The regulators had moved, he said that day, only after being convinced the bank was guilty of "fraudulent conduct on a worldwide scale."

What had been one of the world's largest privately owned banks, with $20 billion in assets and 400 branches spread across seventy-three countries at its zenith, was paralyzed. With near-military precision, banking regulators in seven countries had acted in concert to close down the offices of the Bank of Credit and Commerce International. A bank created explicitly to avoid a central regulator, after nearly two decades of growing like Topsy with scant supervision, was being brought down through the unique cooperation among the regulators of seven nations.

As other countries fell in line, accounts large and small at BCCI branches worldwide were frozen. Depositors faced the loss of their savings. Businesses were paralyzed; ships stranded in ports, unable to deliver cargo. Customers massed outside offices in London, Hong Kong, and a dozen other cities to plead for their money. Hundreds of the bank's 14,000 employees demonstrated against what they labeled a reckless, racist takeover by Western interests.

Some countries resisted the rush to shut down the bank. In Pakistan, the home of the bank's founder and its senior executives, BCCI's three branches remained open on orders from the nation's president, who had once headed a charitable foundation set up by the bank. A sign taped to the front door of the Karachi branch read, "Under State Bank of Pakistan instructions we are operating normally." Across the street, officials at Pakistan's central bank said they were trying to protect the bank's 71,000 depositors in the country.

In Abu Dhabi, home of the ruling family that had bankrolled the bank's beginnings and struggled to save it at the end, it was business as usual. On Sunday, the offices opened for business without a sign of the turmoil engulfing the bank elsewhere. Accounts of the seizures in London and Europe were cut out of foreign newspapers as they arrived. The collapse of the bank was not even reported in Abu Dhabi, where people see only what the government permits.

The shutdown occurred in the midst of a four-day holiday weekend in the United States. That Friday, a county prosecutor named John Moscow was sitting in his cluttered office in lower Manhattan anyway when word came that regulators had taken action against his target. Throughout the day, his phone rang constantly. Present and former bank employees were scurrying forward, offering new information and testimony in hopes of cutting a deal for immunity. They could see the massive global assault on BCCI for what it was, the beginning of the end.

In the midst of the calls came one from Robert Morgenthau, the New York district attorney who was Moscow's boss. As Moscow outlined the calls pouring into the office, one piece of information stood out. A New York–based bank had $30 million in accounts at BCCI when the deposits were frozen. In all probability, the money would be lost. Here was a real victim for the two-year-old investigation that Morgenthau and Moscow had been waging, a loss that would provide compelling evidence of fraud and help complete their indictment.

That same day, on the third floor of the Federal Reserve System headquarters in Washington, D.C., Bill Taylor, the chief of bank supervision and regulation, juggled calls from across the country and around the world. For months, Taylor had been directing the Fed's investigation of BCCI's trail in the United States. It was the most far-reaching and complicated investigation in the history of American bank regulation. Taylor's staff needed more time before confronting the touchy business of shutting down the rogue bank. They were trying to close a major international bank without sending the world's financial system into panic and chaos. Now time had run out.

It had been nearly three years since the public first glimpsed the corruption beneath the surface respectability of the Bank of Credit and Commerce International. In October 1988, the bank and eight of its employees were indicted in Tampa, Florida, on charges of laundering millions of dollars for the Medellín cartel.

The money-laundering charges had been the first fruits of an undercover operation run by the U.S. Customs Service. The federal agents had stumbled onto the bank while pursuing Colombia's Medellín drug cartel. It was one of the luckiest moments in the history of law enforcement, transforming a routine investigation into a case that eventually broke open the world's biggest banking scandal.

That start was small. As a result of the Tampa case, in early 1990, the bank pleaded guilty, paid a record $15 million fine, and then went on about its business. Five employees were tried and convicted of money laundering, with two getting stiff twelve-year prison terms. The bank tried to explain away the incident as the isolated work of lower-level employees, dispatching its army of retainers to smooth the ruffled feathers of customers and regulators alike.

But the Tampa convictions were only the first step in the global unmasking of the secret bank, a bank that thrived in a financial underworld where billions of illicit dollars flow over borders and out of reach of authorities with the press of a computer key.

Much of this dirty money comes from narcotics trafficking, the richest criminal enterprise in history. It generates money by the bag, by the box, by the truckload. Profits accumulate by the ton. Estimates of profits from cocaine sales in the United States alone reach as high as $110 billion a year. The result of this profit is an underground torrent of dollars that oils the machinery of drug corruption.

This river of illegal money does not all spring from drug trafficking. Tributaries flow in from Third World countries, where dictators with names such as Marcos, Duvalier, and Noriega plunder the meager wealth of their people. There is flight capital as rich citizens of unstable countries evade currency restrictions and drain nations of the funds intended to finance their development. There are profits from illegal arms transactions, millions of dollars in American aid siphoned off in Asia and Africa. All finds its way into the flow of hot money. And the customers of the Bank of Credit and Commerce included flotsam from all of these streams.

BCCI appealed to a wide range of customers, among them the U.S. Central Intelligence Agency, which maintained secret accounts at BCCI branches for years. Payments were made to finance covert aid to the Afghan rebels and to bribe General Manuel Antonio Noriega of Panama, himself a favored customer of BCCI. With its operations in most of the world's nastiest corners, BCCI fit the needs of the CIA.

The relationship carried an added benefit. From its vantage as a bank customer, the CIA kept an eye on others who were using the bank—a rogue's gallery of terrorists, corrupt public officials, and arms merchants. Topping the list was the world's most feared and lethal anti-Western terrorist, Abu Nidal. He and his Fatah Revolutionary Council maintained a $60 million account at BCCI's fashionable Sloane Street branch in London to finance terrorism and arms transactions around the world. In cooperation with the branch manager, the CIA, the U.S. State Department's counter-terrorism division, and Britain's MI5 all used the bank as a window on the operations of the Palestinian extremist.

The Bank of Credit and Commerce International was so dirty that the second-ranking official at the CIA described it in 1988 as "the bank of crooks and criminals international."

The doors were open to customers of any stripe, no questions asked. When the government of Peru wanted to hide its cash reserves from creditor banks, BCCI was there. When Iran needed U.S. antitank missiles to fight Iraq, BCCI was there. When General Noriega was indicted by the United States on drug charges and tried to move $23 million out of reach of American authorities, BCCI was there. When

Arab tycoons and Pakistani shipping magnates needed cash to prop up faltering businesses, BCCI was there with loans that were never repaid.

Founded by Pakistanis and financed by Arabs, BCCI had billed itself as a Third World bank, as the financial tool that would help developing countries pull themselves out of poverty and starvation. It had disguised itself through numerous charitable operations, and had hired influence peddlers and respected politicians worldwide to embellish that image. Yet in the end, it was the money of the honest depositors that would disappear in the ruins of the bank. The bank would turn out to be a reverse Robin Hood, stealing from the poor and giving to the rich.

The worst fears of the regulators did not materialize. The shutdown of the bank on July 5 did not disrupt the world's financial system, but it did disrupt the lives and livelihoods of those thousands of people around the world who had trusted the bank.

The failure of a bank is not gauged by the financial markets alone. It must be measured in human terms, as well. And in this case, the costs were steep. Bank accounts were frozen. Life savings were imperiled. Entire national economies were threatened.

In the tiny, impoverished West African nation of Cameroon, the central bank faced the loss of $200 million in BCCI accounts. A palm-oil refinery shut down because its account with BCCI was frozen and $2 million in spare parts sat undelivered. Work on Africa's first pharmaceutical factory stopped because the project was being financed by BCCI. In all, BCCI was the primary banker in eighteen African nations and its insolvency added another layer of misery to the world's most beleaguered continent.

The government of China, always desperate for cash to finance its halting economic progress, had $400 million on deposit when accounts were frozen at BCCI Hong Kong and the adjacent Shenzhen trade zone. Most of the money sat in accounts controlled by the government's financial and trading agencies. For Chinese leaders, the loss was compounded by embarrassment. They had embraced BCCI and its founder, Agha Hasan Abedi, largely because of Abedi's relationship with former U.S. President Jimmy Carter. For years, Carter had accompanied Abedi on trips to China and other developing countries and had provided the banker with invaluable access and respectability.

In fact, Carter was only one of many world leaders and political figures who befriended the charismatic Abedi as he rose from obscurity in Pakistan to the pinnacle of a global financial empire. In Washington, he also was befriended by Clark Clifford, a former presidential adviser and elder statesman of the Democratic Party whose reputation and influence helped Abedi acquire secret control of the biggest banking company in the U.S. capital. Around the world, Abedi and his bank acquired the services of influential people who lent a patina of respectability to the bank. All of them would lose something, too.

And so did people like John Sheehan. On the morning of July 5, 1991, he wrote 200 paychecks to workers at his hauling and labor contracting business in London. The checks were drawn on his BCCI business account, which had a balance of about $1 million. Sheehan had moved his account to BCCI a year earlier because it offered a slightly higher interest rate than his previous bank.

That afternoon, angry employees started showing up at Sheehan's office in Southall, waving paychecks that they had been unable to cash. When BCCI was shut down, no bank in Britain would honor checks drawn on accounts there. Sheehan's accountant finally tracked him down about six o'clock that evening and delivered the news. "At that moment, I thought I was finished," said Sheehan, who had built his business up over the past twenty years and was forced to scramble for new funds to pay the workers and keep his business going.

As many as 55,000 of Britain's small Asian businesses banked with BCCI, among them about sixty percent of the clothing importers and exporters along East London's Whitechapel Road. "The garment trade was already in difficulties because of the recession, but the Bank of England may have put the final nail in the coffin," Hanwantbir Chadha, a clothing trader and president of the local business association on Whitechapel Road, said sadly after the closing. "This is a very big tragedy."

Chadha had learned of BCCI's closing when a small manufacturer returned one of his checks for $50,000 on Friday, July 5. The manufacturer had been unable to cash it because it was drawn on Chadha's BCCI account.

Not just businesses were affected. Throughout May and June of 1991, Spectrum Radio, a station geared to Asian-born listeners, had appealed for donations to construct a shelter in Bangladesh for victims of the recent cyclone. More than 1,000 checks had been mailed in to the station. On July 4, Shafik Rehman, the anchor of Spectrum's broadcasts in Bengali, had deposited the last $80,000 of donations in an account at BCCI. The bank was a natural choice because of its Third World message and strong presence in Bangladesh. When its doors were closed the next day, $55,000 of the contributions could be counted as lost since British deposit insurance would cover only about $25,000.

About sixty local governments in Britain had deposited nearly $200 million in municipal funds with BCCI branches in response to its interest rates, which were as much as a percentage point above those of other British banks. The Western Isles Council in Scotland's Outer

Hebrides had $45 million on deposit with BCCI. The local government had to seek permission to borrow replacement funds. It also suspended its finance director for five days before deciding he was not to blame.

Shipments around the world, involving more than 1,000 vessels, were brought to a halt, with key documents necessary to complete the transactions locked inside the closed offices of BCCI. The documents were letters of credit that allow purchasers to pay for goods on delivery. Without them, the shippers refused to deliver the goods and ships sat unloaded at docks.

The collapse of the Bank of Credit and Commerce International was the world's greatest banking scandal. It has raised serious questions about the effectiveness of bank regulation in an era of international finance. It has cast doubt on the actions of the U.S. Justice Department and banking regulators. And it has left a trail of victims on every continent and touched almost all of the bank's 14,000 employees and 1.3 million depositors. And, as it unfolds, it is an unrivaled story of intrigue, deception, and manipulation.

CHAPTER TWO

True Believers

The beginnings of the Bank of Credit and Commerce International can be traced to three factors. One is a place, the troubled soil of modern Pakistan, a nation created as a refuge for a Muslim minority. Another is the philosophy and heritage of the Muslim religion, a blend of piety, power, and patronage. And the last is a small, intense man named Agha Hasan Abedi, who believed that he was destined for greatness on a global stage.

Abedi was born in 1922 to a Shiite Muslim family in the old Indian city of Lucknow, once the seat of Muslim culture on the subcontinent and home of the decadent Mughul Empire. Old Lucknow teemed with color and court intrigue. Amid its spacious gardens, scented groves, and onion-domed mosques flourished an elegant literature in Urdu, a language derived from the mating of native Hindi with the Persian of the Muslim invaders. As the Mughul emperor in Delhi lost his force, his local agent, the Nawab-Vizir, began to rule in his own right, founding the infamous Kingdom of Oudh.

The British came to Lucknow in force, with a military post nearby that stretched for six miles. One of the great dramas of the Indian mutiny of 1857 was played out against the backdrop of the city's splendid architecture. Muslim rebels beseiged 3,000 British troops and families in the massive residency. After eighty-seven days, only 1,000 of the British emerged when they were finally rescued by more troops. The ruins of the residency still stand untouched in a downtown park, testament to what the British describe as an atrocity and what the Third World celebrates as the first great uprising against Western imperialism.

This was the background that shaped the young Abedi, an atmosphere of culture and romance, not commerce. "Lucknow is a city of poets, painters, and Nawabs," explained a later colleague of Abedi's, "not of

10

businessmen." Abedi's Lucknavi Muslim heritage, remarked another friend, lay behind "his fondness for perfume, gourmet cuisine, fine clothing, art, and the color white, for its purity."

Another Lucknavi tradition had an even more direct influence on Abedi. The city's rulers had been served by courtiers known as *tulekdars*, renowned for their generosity and love of power. The remnants of this system of service and patronage lived on and Abedi's family had served the rajas as administrators and managers since the middle of the nineteenth century. Abedi's father worked as an estate manager for one of Lucknow's princely Muslim families, the Raja of Mahmoodabad. The raja's patronage helped Abedi get into good Indian schools and the university at Lucknow.

Such assistance was necessary in part because the Abedis were Muslims in a country ruled by the British and dominated internally by Hindus. Many Muslims were relegated to menial jobs, and few rose to real power in British India. Early in his life, Abedi learned a lesson he would carry with him throughout his career: There are advantages to be obtained in cultivating richer, more powerful people.

By all accounts, Abedi was a bright student and he graduated with a degree in law from Lucknow University. However, because he had attended a state university, he had a lower social standing than those Indians who were educated in England or in Europe. And because he was Muslim in a country dominated by Hindus, he was doubly an outsider.

Rather than a career in law, the young graduate decided on banking. So in 1946, he went to Bombay, the financial center of British India. There, he took an entry-level position at the newly formed Habib Bank. He also entered comfortably into an arranged marriage.

The bank was the creation of the Muslim Chamber of Commerce, which had been established under the sponsorship of the Muslim nationalist leader Mohammed Ali Jinnah. Banking, too, was dominated by the Hindus in India, and Jinnah wanted to introduce financial power to the Muslim population. Habib Bank soon carved itself a niche catering to the Muslim minority.

Trust is the linchpin of banking. A customer who deposits money in a bank trusts that it will be returned upon demand, presumably with interest. Likewise, the banker who lends money trusts the borrower to repay it, also with interest. Although the banker customarily hedges this trust by demanding some form of collateral, at the bottom line banking is built on trust. Therefore, banks often start out catering to their own kind. This is particularly true among groups of people bonded together by a common oppression. Who better to trust than people with shared beliefs and backgrounds? This was destined to become a guiding tenet for Agha Hasan Abedi, and one that he would exploit in all corners of the globe.

For Muslims, there is yet another binding factor. In the Koran, Mohammed set forth the basis for the Muslim banking system: "Allah hath blighted usury and made alms-giving fruitful." Instead of the traditional debtor-creditor relationship, the two parties become essentially partners in a strict interpretation of the Islamic system. The bank's function, in addition to making a profit, is to help build society. Usury, interpreted as excessive interest, is prohibited. The Islamic code is followed with varying degrees of strictness in banking, but it was a concept that nonetheless offered another common bond between the Muslims who ran Habib Bank and those who patronized it. It was a philosophy adopted by Abedi and BCCI. As the bank grew, Abedi was careful to share his good fortune with others through various foundations, charities, and financing for social programs.

While at Habib Bank, Abedi made friends with another young man, S. M. Fayyaz. "I found him to be very quiet, very unimpressive," Fayyaz recalled years later. "At that time, I used to tell him, 'You look very lazy.' He would not care about his wardrobe. He would not worry about appearance. He was absentminded. He was happy-go-lucky."

The mid-1940s were exciting and dangerous years to be a young man in India. It was a period of great upheaval, drama, and monumental change on the subcontinent. Gandhi was leading the Hindu majority in its push for freedom from Britain, and the Muslims were organizing their own nationalistic drive under Jinnah's charismatic leadership. Jinnah's was a drive that would bear great fruit for Abedi.

For five centuries before the British arrived, the Muslims had dominated India and its majority population of Hindus. Under a century of British control, their position had declined sharply because the British belief in democracy had shifted power to the more populous Hindus. By the 1940s, the Hindus were better educated and better positioned to take control of the country once the British left. Indeed, the British decision to leave behind a parliamentary democracy in India meant almost certain subjugation of the Muslims.

So, under the leadership of the former barrister Jinnah, a movement had been born to establish a separate nation for India's 80 million Muslims. The British, however, wanted to maintain the economic and political unity that they had created in India. The Hindus, too, opposed the new nation, but Jinnah and his nationalist movement prevailed and, on August 15, 1947, India was partitioned and Pakistan came into existence. The new nation, carved out of the northwestern portion of the subcontinent, was for all Muslims in India. While geographically closer to Asia, culturally Pakistan and its people had strong attachments to the Middle East and shared the religion of Islam.

The movement of Muslims to their new homeland, and Hindus out of it, was the greatest mass migration in history. It also was violent and deadly. Some Hindus who were being displaced, such as the ruling class of Kashmir, fought against being included in Pakistan. Similarly, some established Muslims were reluctant to leave India, even though they were immediately subjected to harassment and worse. As the two-way migration took place, there were countless clashes along dusty and crowded roads. A million Hindus and Muslims were killed or starved to death along the migration routes during the postpartition period. Yet from this violence came new opportunities for Abedi and his compatriots.

Habib Bank moved its headquarters from Bombay to Karachi, then only a medium-sized backwater port on the Arabian Sea. Its staff was entirely Muslim, bright young bankers eager to apply their skills to serve the new cause. Among them were Abedi and Fayyaz, both thrilled to be starting their careers anew at this crucial juncture in the history of their people.

"All of us got better chances," said Fayyaz. "There was great excitement. Everyone was going to Karachi."

Habib Bank grew to be Pakistan's largest financial institution, and Abedi climbed steadily through the ranks. Already he was demonstrating leadership qualities, an uncanny knack for persuading staff members to work together.

One day in 1956, Abedi demonstrated what would become characteristic initiative. An agency of the Karachi municipal government wanted to open a bank branch in its main building, but the government-run National Bank was slow to respond. When Abedi heard about the opportunity, he took a few tables and a safe to the building the next day and opened the newest branch of Habib Bank.

In the late fifties, Abedi was ambitious and restless. He met Mian Yusif Saigol, a textile magnate and patron of one of the so-called Twenty-two Families who were coming to dominate Pakistan's economy. A few months after the meeting, Abedi convinced Saigol to finance the start of United Bank Ltd., the first new bank in Pakistan since the creation of the country.

The traits that would carry him onto the world stage were evident even then. Abedi showed a flair for modern banking. United Bank was the first in Pakistan to computerize its records and establish a research section. At the same time, Abedi opened dozens of branches in poor, rural areas that had been ignored by his rivals at Habib Bank and the National Bank.

"These were hardly profitable, but Abedi was keen on serving poor farmers," recalled Saigol's son, Azam. "He was always more interested in deposits than in careful management." Which is not to say that Abedi lacked ideas about management—only that they were rooted in philosophy, not practical application.

At the time, United Bank's headquarters were on the second floor of an office building in downtown Karachi, by this time the business center of Pakistan. On the first floor was the office of Citicorp, the biggest American bank in Pakistan. One day in the mid-1960s, a young Pakistani who had been educated in England and the United States visited Abedi at his office. He was a member of one of the Twenty-two Families and had recently started a small bank of his own. It had been suggested to him that he discuss the banking business with Abedi, who was making a name for himself through the rapid expansion of United Bank. Instead of strategies and business plans, what the novice banker got was a dose of rhetoric intended to be inspirational.

"New management is needed," the man later would recall Abedi telling him. "Not just here at United Bank, but at all banks. The old, hierarchical structures are outmoded. We need new, circular structures." While the rest of the oration has faded beyond the reach of the man's memory, he does remember that he was so stunned by the strange-talking Abedi that he rose abruptly and said he had another appointment. As he left the session with the little man, the young banker thought to himself, "Well, that's enough bullshit for one day."

Abedi was fixated on expansion. With an economy mired in poverty and no welcome mat in India, he trained his sights on a part of the world where his Muslim heritage might open doors. In 1966, he chartered an airplane and flew off to the Middle East, with a single aide in tow.

This was well before the oil embargo of 1973 turned the Persian Gulf into the richest neighborhood in the world. Nonetheless, there was enough oil revenue flowing into the coffers of the ruling families in Saudi Arabia and a host of smaller city-states to create a new class of millionaires and a potentially lucrative new banking market. In addition, these Arab countries were hiring thousands of Pakistani workers and those workers needed a bank to send their hard-earned paychecks to families back home.

Bearing a finely made carpet, Abedi arrived in Abu Dhabi, a tiny sheikdom on the Gulf ruled by Sheik Zayed bin Sultan al-Nahayan. The sheik, a shrewd but illiterate man, had seized power that year from his brother in a coup organized by his British advisers. Zayed's brother had been a backward, mean-spirited man who was rumored to keep the government's treasure beneath his bed in the fortified palace. (After he was replaced, it was said, officials had discovered that rats had eaten $2 million worth of bank notes.) Zayed was far more generous, and over the years he would lavish millions on upgrading the infrastructure of his country. It was that generous streak that Abedi was destined to tap.

After keeping Abedi waiting for several days, Zayed agreed to meet the young banker from Pakistan. The audience was a successful one and Abedi left the country with the sheik's permission to open a branch of United Bank Ltd. in Abu Dhabi. Among the concessions was an agreement that Abedi serve as banker for the sheikdom's Pakistani workers. Their paychecks could be cashed at United Bank and money wired directly back home.

Abedi left Abu Dhabi with another gift. He had learned that the sheik was passionate about the medieval Arab custom of hunting with falcons. So, soon after returning to Pakistan, he began to invite the ruler there for hunting trips in the rugged mountains in search of the country's native bustard, a nearly extinct bird. Abedi made sure that every detail was in place for these trips. There were air-conditioned Jeeps to carry the sheik and his party, lavish hotel rooms, and a constant stream of gifts.

In all his actions, Abedi was polite and solicitous. It made an impression on Zayed, for it was a reception to which the sheiks of the Persian Gulf had not yet grown accustomed. Zayed, who had no money skills himself, was grateful for the assistance and the respect. And in return, he introduced Abedi to the princelings of the other city-states along the Gulf—Bahrain, Kuwait, Oman, Qatar, and the United Arab Emirates, which are seven tiny sheikdoms banded together under the leadership of Zayed's al-Nahayan clan. These Gulf states had a combined population of slightly more than four million and occupied a land area smaller than California, but, on a per capita basis, they would soon become the richest neighborhood in the world. And the richest of them would be Abu Dhabi.

The sheiks, devout Muslims, were perfect customers for Abedi's growing bank. Islamic law prohibited them from earning interest on their bank accounts, so bank officials paid out the interest in favors. Among the favors, according to many reports at the time and later, were harems of willing women for the visiting Arabs. This practice was actually quite similar to that of the *tulekdars* of the Mughul Empire.

These contacts with Zayed and other Arabs were soon to prove essential to Abedi's ambitious dreams, for Pakistan was going through a period of upheaval that set in motion events that would cast Abedi onto the world scene sooner than he had anticipated.

Zulfikar Ali Bhutto was a shrewd politician and theatrical ruler. When he became president of Pakistan in January 1972, after a disastrous war that detached the country's eastern province and created the new nation of Bangladesh, he displaced a discredited military junta. Turning up at rallies attended by as many as half a million people in those first years, he would wave his arms and weep as he preached his message of love and unity.

"Will you work hard? Will you fight? Will you die? Do I have your vow on it?" he asked crowds in Karachi and all across Pakistan. "Yes, Bhutto Sahib, yes," thousands of voices shouted in response.

Behind the rhetoric, Bhutto ruled with a vindictive spirit. Although he talked of eliminating poverty, he worked much harder at avenging old slights, real and imagined. The keystone of both efforts was his plan to nationalize private industry, which to many stood as the symbol of the corruption and privilege of the oligarchy maintained by the influential families. Soon after taking office, Bhutto nationalized such basic industries as steel, automotive assembly, and chemicals. He also pledged to nationalize the banks, which were thought to be corrupt and under the influence of a favored few. Government control of the banks would be slower to pull off, but Bhutto decided to put their executives on notice. In the days after he was sworn in, he ordered several of Pakistan's bankers placed under house arrest. Among them was Agha Hasan Abedi.

This was a watershed event. While restricted to his home under police guard, Abedi hatched his plan for a new bank. The dream that would become the Bank of Credit and Commerce was conceived as a heady mixture of banking and philosophy with an underpinning of nationalism. With Abedi in those critical days was Swaleh Naqvi, a young banker who had worked with him at United Bank and would remain at his side for most of the next two decades.

Among the first outsiders to whom the two men described the plan was a colleague at United Bank named Masihur Rahman. The son of the first Muslim to become chief justice of India's highest court, Rahman had returned to Pakistan in 1961 after obtaining an accounting degree in Britain. He had gone to work for the Pakistan Industrial Development Corporation, which oversaw the nation's heavy industries, and he soon became its chief of finance. In 1966, Abedi and Naqvi had persuaded Rahman to join them at United Bank, where he was made an executive vice president at the age of thirty.

One day in January 1972, Abedi summoned Rahman to his guarded home. It was a Sunday and Rahman, although reluctant to have contact with Abedi while he was under arrest, went to the house. As he sat in the living room sipping tea, he heard Abedi describe his dream of a new, global bank. It would be staffed by Pakistanis, with a sense of family spirit in which profits would go hand in hand with social concerns.

"The few banks that are international are colonial banks from Britain, France, Germany, and lately the United States," Abedi said. "They are really national banks, big national banks of countries. A genuinely global bank could be started to bridge all the Third World countries with the first world. There would be a unique banking structure, which could be very, very useful socially and also very profitable."

Rahman was taken aback by the scope of the scheme. While he believed that Abedi was a man of great vision, this seemed like a fantasy. He said as much to his host, but added, "If it ever materializes, I would certainly like to be part of it."

"Well," said Abedi with a smile, "it's very close to materializing because Sheik Zayed of Abu Dhabi has assured me that he will back such an organization."

Not long after that meeting, the arrest orders against Abedi were lifted. His passport was returned, and he set out on a journey to complete the last step of his dream of creating a new bank.

Transforming vision into reality, Abedi knew, required more than the backing of some Arab sheiks. It required a partnership with an established, international financial organization to provide the instant prestige and access to the broader world that he sought. By late February 1972, he was on an airplane to New York in search of such a partner.

Agha Hasan Abedi was a small man, five feet seven at most, with a broad face and dark hair swept back off his forehead. He had long, wide sideburns, already an out-of-date fashion. Approaching fifty, he wore a dark suit appropriate for the understated propriety demanded in international banking circles. Over the years, he had learned it was necessary for a banker to maintain appearances and to exhibit the most conventional respectability. Back home, however, he would loose the reins on his mystical side and dress all in white, the Muslim color of purity.

On a bitterly cold day that February, he chose a suite at the Waldorf-Astoria in New York City for the most important meeting of his career. The suite suggested accomplishment and financial security without the jarring notes of opulence advertised by less established inns.

His guest was Roy P. M. Carlson. Abedi had gone down to the lobby of the hotel to meet him. On the way back up, the two men had exchanged chitchat about mutual acquaintances in the Middle East and New York's unpleasant weather. Carlson, too, was accustomed to more temperate climes. He was a middle-level executive in San Francisco with the Bank of America. Carlson had been dispatched to New York for this meeting at the recommendation of the bank's man in Pakistan, who had said Abedi had a business proposal worth entertaining. Once the two bankers were in the suite, Abedi wasted no time getting down to the business he had traveled halfway around the world to discuss.

"Mr. Carlson, the banks in Pakistan are going to be nationalized," he

17

said matter-of-factly, as though announcing that the sun would rise in the east tomorrow.

"What?" said the shocked Carlson, whose responsibilities at Bank of America included supervising Pakistan and neighboring India.

"Do not be concerned," said Abedi. "It will be in the pattern of the Indian nationalization. It will not affect foreign branches. Only those banks now owned by Pakistanis, such as the one that employs me."

As often is the case with true believers, Abedi spoke precisely and rapidly, barely stopping for commas and periods. His voice was low and even, with the accented English of his Pakistani countrymen. He was comfortable letting the meaning of his words resonate. He did not need to call attention to them by raising his voice for emphasis.

Without doubt, he had gotten Roy Carlson's attention. And Abedi kept it as he began to describe his dream of creating a new financial empire out of the impending wreckage of Pakistan's largest private banks. He explained that he was the president of United Bank, the second-largest bank in Pakistan. Without providing the details but implying that he had obtained his information from high-ranking officials, Abedi said he had learned about the impending nationalization some weeks earlier. In response, he had set about to create a new opportunity for himself and other Pakistani bankers who would be reluctant to work at government-owned institutions.

Details of Abedi's plan were sketchy. His was a vision. He had a concept, and he had some powerful friends. A group of wealthy Arab sheiks from the Persian Gulf region had already agreed to put up funds for the new bank, he told Carlson. Backed by Arab money and run largely by Pakistani bankers, the institution would cater to the expanding trade and financial needs of the Arab world. That would be just one base.

Plans called for expanding into the world of international banking, particularly in the developing countries. Moreover, he said, thousands of Third World people were forced to go work in developed countries. The new bank would target those communities of people not normally courted by major banks. They were hard-working and saved lots of their pay to send back home. Part of his dream envisioned the creation of an "immigrants' bank."

The exact pattern of growth would be dictated in part by the bank's financial success and in part by its ability to capitalize on Abedi's contacts among the Arabs and leaders of the developing countries. Countries not currently hospitable to foreign banking, especially Western banking, might be persuaded to do business with a bank such as his.

He told the American that he wanted the guidance and financial expertise afforded by partnership with a major international banking organization. He had come to New York, he explained to Carlson, to secure such assistance.

Abedi had first broached the idea of such a partnership a few weeks earlier with American Express, the big U.S. financial services company. American Express was prohibited by U.S. law from owning banks in the United States, but it was interested in acquiring banks in other countries.

Without identifying any companies, Abedi told Carlson that he was discussing possible joint ventures with a number of institutions in New York. But, he confided, talks with the others were not going well. In fact, he suggested, it was possible that he would be free to enter serious negotiations with the Bank of America very soon.

Abedi was being forthright when he said that talks had not been going well. American Express was balking at Abedi's price for a partnership. The Pakistani was demanding total control of all administrative and field operations of the new bank.

When the deal started going sour, Abedi had sought a backup partner. He had approached J. D. Van Oenen, the Bank of America manager in Karachi, Pakistan. Van Oenen, a voluble Dutchman, was intrigued. He had forwarded the proposal to the World Banking Division in San Francisco with a recommendation that it be considered. Carlson's presence in New York meant San Francisco had listened.

In 1972, Bank of America was the world's largest bank, a global giant with assets of $100 billion and nearly 60,000 employees worldwide. But, like the other big Western banks, it barely had a foothold in the Persian Gulf. The oil embargo had not yet flooded the region with wealth, but it was still a potentially lucrative market for international banks. Bank of America's sole presence was a five percent interest in a small bank in Dubai, one of the tiny sheikdoms that formed the United Arab Emirates. At B of A headquarters in the heart of San Francisco's financial district, there was keen interest in getting the bank's formidable foot in the door to the region.

Perhaps Abedi could help, thought Carlson. But he also knew that caution was advised. His employers would not jump into a deal like this without certain understandings and information, no matter how eager they might be to get into the Gulf in a big way. Still, the proposal had more appeal to Bank of America than it did to other major financial institutions because of the bank's own heritage.

Bank of America was started in 1904 by A. P. Giannini, the son of Italian immigrant parents. From its origins, Bank of America had been the bank "for the little fellow," as Giannini had been fond of saying. By the end of World War II, the California bank had become the nation's largest commercial bank, and then the world's largest bank.

Despite its size and power, however, Bank of America had remained an outsider. It was a West Coast institution in a country dominated by East Coast and Midwestern banks. In a world controlled by aristocrats, it was a bank founded by the son of immigrants. To the extent that A. P. Giannini's freewheeling spirit still existed in the bank twenty-three years after his death, Bank of America might just go for Abedi's plan.

"Before we could consider anything seriously, we would have to have a full-blown feasibility study done," Carlson explained to Abedi. "The Bank of America has a very rigid and proscribed format for this sort of thing. But I think there might be some interest in this. I really do."

Abedi promised to get back in touch with Carlson if his other discussions proved unfruitful.

A shrewd businessman never reveals more than necessary. Just as Abedi had failed to mention that he had narrowed his options to American Express and Bank of America, he had concealed the true scope of his vision for the new bank.

Carlson had been granted only a glimpse of Abedi's plan, only the details that would entice the huge American bank. Had Abedi confided his real goal, Carlson might have dismissed him as a hopeless dreamer or a nut. Who would believe that the soft-spoken, intensely polite man from Pakistan dreamed of creating the world's largest bank?

As expected, Abedi's talks with American Express collapsed the day after his first meeting with Roy Carlson, so he contacted the American banker again and agreed to provide a more detailed business plan to the Bank of America auditors.

Over the next several weeks, Abedi and some prospective assistants met with Bank of America officials. The plan they worked out called for the American bank to invest $2.5 million in exchange for a twenty-five percent share of Abedi's institution. Abedi's connections in the Persian Gulf, chiefly Abu Dhabi, had brought promises of sizable deposits and business from a number of Arab rulers and businessmen.

In addition to Sheik Zayed, Abedi had commitments from the likes of Kamal Adham, the chief of intelligence in Saudi Arabia and a close adviser to that nation's royal family, and Faisal Saud al-Fulaij, the chairman of Kuwait Airways and a powerful businessman in that tiny nation. There also were promises of business from a host of other sheiks and businessmen scattered around the oil-rich region. The proposed bank represented but one of the common financial interests of these men, and their businesses would become more entangled as the years went on and their personal wealth mounted.

The value of these relationships cannot be underestimated. The nations of the Persian Gulf are closed societies where, for centuries, outsiders have been viewed with suspicion. This was particularly true of

Westerners, whose religions had been at war with Islam for a thousand years. Even in 1972, the leaders of these city-states were Bedouins who had spent their formative years in goat-hair tents, traveling the desert on camels.

But change was at hand. The world's appetite for oil was growing. Billions in oil revenues were rolling into the region already, and such basic services as water and electricity were coming to the cities. No longer could these royal leaders keep their cash under the bed. Smart international bankers, and there were many at the Bank of America in those days, sensed the opportunities, but they found the region closed to them. Abedi represented the vital entree for the executives of the giant American bank.

In June 1972, Abedi arrived in San Francisco for a series of meetings. They culminated in a luncheon at the Bankers Club, a private restaurant atop the bank's towering three-year-old headquarters in the financial district. In later years, Abedi would refer to it as "the historic lunch." In attendance were Roy Carlson and members of the Bank of America's managing committee, the top executives who would decide whether to invest the bank's money in this venture.

Abedi proved smooth and convincing as he described the concept and dropped the names of Arab associates. A few days after the luncheon, Carlson's recommendation to go ahead was approved by the managing committee. After all, a $2.5 million investment was not much money to the world's largest bank. And it offered enormous leverage value. The new institution would have the Bank of America logo on its stationery. Bank of America loan officers and executives would make business calls alongside Abedi. The California bank would have two spots on the new institution's board of directors. Presumably the two directors plus periodic checks of the new institution's books by the big bank's auditors would provide sufficient control. As for the operation of the bank itself, that would be the sole province of Abedi.

In its quest for access to the oil-producing nations of the Persian Gulf, Bank of America had done something that American Express had refused to do. It had granted Abedi virtually total control over the day-to-day operations of the bank. This was not B of A's bank. It was Agha Hasan Abedi's bank. He was only using the San Francisco bank's prestige, and getting paid for it, too.

The new bank was to be called the Bank of Credit and Commerce International. An imposing name, reflecting the unfettered ambitions of its founder. It would be based initially in Abu Dhabi, a symbol to the Gulf region that the new bank had the blessing of a powerful ruler. But plans were already in the works to move into other countries. And a strategy was being developed to ensure that Abedi's new bank never faced the threat of nationalization that confronted the institution he had founded in Pakistan.

Indeed, it was this desire to escape government control that led Abedi to incorporate his new bank in Luxembourg, a tiny European nation known for its tough bank secrecy laws and lax regulation. The sum of Abedi's life experiences was destined to be reflected in the new bank he had created for himself.

CHAPTER THREE

The Go-Go Years

By November 1972, Agha Hasan Abedi had quit as president of United Bank and started doing business as the Bank of Credit and Commerce International out of offices in Abu Dhabi and Karachi. With him had come Swaleh Naqvi and a handful of other United Bank employees. Masihur Rahman had declined Abedi's offers to join the new bank, despite promises that he would be a millionaire within a decade.

The bank's working capital included the $2.5 million from the Bank of America and an unknown amount of money from its Arab stockholders, such as Zayed and Adham. The Arabs also became the bank's first depositors, providing about $20 million as the bank's initial cash. Abedi had also succeeded in hiring away several of his associates at Habib. They formed the nucleus of the new bank's staff, which would always be predominantly Pakistani.

Some of the early customers also reflected Abedi's heritage. The Saigol family, who had staked him in United Bank, were among the first depositors and borrowers at the new bank. More significant among the first customers were three brothers, Mustafa, Abbas, and Murtaza Gokal.

Like Abedi, the Gokals were Shiite Muslims. They had been born in India but moved with their family to Iraq. When the monarchy was overthrown in Baghdad in the late 1950s, the family had escaped to Karachi. The brothers had set up a company called Gulf Group, and its chief operating arm, Gulf Shipping Lines, had been started in 1969. The company started as little more than a tramp operation carting bulk cargoes through the Arabian Sea out of Karachi. Their first big contract was to haul cement to the Middle East and Africa; Gulf Shipping specialized in shipping to places where others were not interested in doing business.

But the brothers were driven by the vision of creating an international shipping empire and they had quickly expanded beyond the Third World. By the time Abedi founded BCCI, the Gokals were familiar figures in London and Geneva and seemed to have broken free of their confining world in precisely the way that Abedi envisioned for BCCI.

From the outset, Abedi stressed that, no matter how large it became, the bank should be viewed not as a business but as a family. He urged everyone, from tellers to executives, to bring in new business. Everyone would benefit in the end. So junior employees and senior ones alike were prepared to work for comparatively low salaries and were encouraged to work long hours and come in on weekends.

"We gave our all for BCCI," one employee later explained. "We were told it was a family bank which looked after its employees. We were told our sons would come and work for the bank."

Abdur Razzak Sakhia, a Pakistani who became global marketing director for BCCI, describes BCCI in those early days as "a culture of the East." As far as possible, the bank promised lifetime employment. "It was," says Sakhia, "a marriage for life, fitting the Eastern stable society, not Western mobile, transient society."

Abedi was referred to among employees as "Agha Sahib" and "the godfather," the latter phrase used not in the American sense of a mob chieftain, but in the sense that he represented a type of super father.

"He made the other person feel that he, Abedi, was the servant, the other person was a god," said Sakhia. "Although when we sat with him at conferences, we felt we were sitting with a god."

True to his vision, Abedi did not institute a rigidly centralized management structure. Instead, he created a series of committees to oversee the various aspects of the bank's business and development. There was a general committee, which was given the task of promoting the bank's basic concept and its management philosophy. A financial committee supervised credit and lending policies, while the development committee examined ways to expand and the administration committee implemented personnel policies. Only Abedi, as president, had a formal title.

The bank's early growth was concentrated in the Gulf region, where Abedi could take advantage of his contacts. Roy Carlson, who was supervising the Bank of America's investment and trying to develop contacts, often took business trips with Abedi.

"You didn't make calls in offices. That was not the way business was done in the Middle East," Carlson said later. "Mr. Abedi would arrange luncheons, dinners, and receptions at which I would meet some of the bank's customers or potential customers. He had many strong ties there from his previous years. But there also were always new people being courted as well."

These affairs were very Middle Eastern. Often Carlson found himself seated on the floor of an ornate palace, sipping sweet tea from small silver cups. Arrayed around him would be a half dozen or more men dressed in thobes, the long, flowing, shirtlike garment, and ghutras, the traditional Arab headdress. Sometimes during these long sessions the conversation would be pierced by a high-pitched wail: "Allah Akbar"— God is great. With the call to prayer, the men would kick off their sandals and kneel in lines on small rugs, facing Mecca and chanting their prayers.

At any bank in the world, wealthy customers are treated differently from the everyday clientele. In the Arab world, where royal treatment is more than just a phrase, this practice often involved courtesies such as bestowing gifts on valued customers and performing a large number of personal services. Banking was a very personal business.

Carlson had lived in the Middle East himself, so he did not find these gatherings and frequent gifts a strange way to conduct business. Indeed, he was an admirer of the Arab people and their distinct language, dress, behavior, and thoughts. If neither he nor Abedi ever felt quite at home among them, they also never dismissed them simply because they did business in a different way.

The fledgling Bank of Credit and Commerce was positioned perfectly to take advantage of the events of 1973. The Persian Gulf region was about to become the wildest frontier in banking, and Agha Hasan Abedi's vision of a vast banking empire was about to get a jump start.

The riches of the region had been controlled for forty years by such Western companies as Standard Oil and Royal Dutch Shell. They doled out a percentage of the profits to the sheiks who owned the land and retained the bulk of the money for themselves. Perhaps more importantly, the Westerners controlled the quantity and price of the oil that came from the vast reserves beneath Arabia.

Gradually, however, the Arabs had recognized that oil was a weapon they could use. They first tried to exploit it following Israel's victory over Egypt in 1967's Six-Day War, but the efforts to reduce shipments to the West were a dismal failure. The next time, the story was different.

In 1973, when Egypt attacked Israel in an attempt to redeem its honor, Egyptian President Anwar Sadat had the promise of Saudi Arabia's King Faisal, Abu Dhabi's Sheik Zayed, and other potentates that they would assist him by restricting oil. Indeed, it had been Zayed who first advocated the oil embargo as a weapon against the West. Ten days after the war began on October 3, 1973, oil sales to nations supporting Israel were stopped. The oil embargo would last until the spring of 1974.

The embargo exposed the West's critical dependence on Arab oil. Even after the end of the embargo, things were never the same. The Arab nations and Iran, through the Organization of Petroleum Exporting Countries, exploited this dependence and sent the price of crude oil skyrocketing. By the end of 1974, the price had quadrupled to $11.65 a barrel. The Gulf was swimming in money, and its leaders needed sophisticated moneymen to help them spend it.

The entire Gulf became a giant boom town. Foreigners flooded Saudi Arabia and the smaller nations, offering their services for the instant millionaires and billionaires. Virtually all of the money in these feudal countries flowed into the royal treasuries. In the words of Khalid Abu Su'ud, a financial adviser to the crown prince of Kuwait at the time, "Petromoney is government money." And the governments were the members of the royal families. Real opportunities lay with those who had access, men such as Abedi.

As fast as the oil money was flowing in, the Bank of Credit and Commerce was growing even faster. The bank had been only a year old when the oil embargo started, but already it was operating in four Gulf states and had opened its first office in Britain. There, it was intent on catering to the large Pakistani and Asian populations. Its first branches were in Bradford, Birmingham, Wolverhampton, and London's Southall district, all areas with large immigrant populations. The offices were friendly and inviting, a sharp contrast to the aloof British institutions.

But as the Middle Eastern oil producers grew richer, Abedi focused his growth on a different "ethnic" clientele in London, which was becoming a favorite vacation spot for the newly rich Arabs. Between 1973 and 1974, BCCI branches began popping up in much fancier neighborhoods of London, such as a plush premises in Kensington High Street in the West End, a large branch along Cromwell Road, and a marble-and-glass office on Sloane Street in the heart of the fashionable Knightsbridge shopping district. Nearly half a million dollars was spent refurbishing 3,000 square feet of splendid space on Wigmore Street, space that had once belonged to the staid National Westminster Bank. The branches boasted lavish Mediterranean architecture and the signs posted in them were in Arabic and Farsi.

A new unit was formed within the bank to target "HNWs," people with high net worths. Another new division, the one that gathered the deposits that really fueled the growth, was called the "Middle Eastern Mobilisation Unit." It catered to the whims of visiting sheiks, and a fleet of Rolls-Royces from BCCI was often lined up at London's Heathrow Airport waiting for arriving customers.

Rumors began to circulate about the unconventional treatment afforded the bank's wealthy customers. Perhaps they were true. Perhaps they were stoked by resentment toward the Arabs and their dark-skinned bankers. Whatever the truth, many of the bank's competitors complained that BCCI was stealing their biggest customers with its aggressive and questionable business approach.

"If you want five hundred thousand pounds in a suitcase on a Sunday night, a little guy from BCCI will come along with it. You won't get that at Lloyds," said one competitor.

Other rumors were more vicious. There was talk of flight capital transferred clandestinely out of Pakistan, India, and other nations where tight currency restrictions kept wealthy citizens from moving their money abroad. Word spread that BCCI happily provided prostitutes for visiting Arabs. Loans of millions of dollars were supposedly made on a simple request from this or that sheik. An internal bank memo supporting a major loan might read, "Obviously the sheik is good for a million dollars," according to one of the Bank of America executives trying to monitor BCCI's growth.

One of Abedi's lieutenants in London, Ameer Siddiqui, responded to such criticism by telling a Forbes magazine reporter in 1978: "We are attuned to the Arab way of working. Arabs want personal service, Asian courtesy at its zenith. So you visit them at home on occasion. Send them little gifts. They couldn't care less about the gifts. It's the thought. With all due respect to The British Bank of the Middle East or Chartered Bank, they are practicing the English type of banking. Their theory is, 'The customer should come to us.' The theory here is, 'Why should the customer come to us? We should go to the customer.'"

Nowhere was that personal service better exemplified than in Abedi's relationship with Sheik Zayed, his initial patron. It was an association that provided Abedi with much of the illusion central to BCCI's growth for nearly two decades: that BCCI was always solvent because it was backed by seemingly limitless Arab oil money.

Abu Dhabi was among the most feudal of the Persian Gulf emirates. The ruling al-Nahayan controlled all of the wealth that came from oil. When the oil revenues had grown so sharply, Zayed began a major building program, dotting the bleak desert landscape with roads that led to nothing but more desert and grand buildings that often stood empty. He also recognized the necessity of becoming a more sophisticated investor and one of the things he did to further this end was to increase his reliance on Abedi and BCCI. Abedi returned the favor by playing a role in helping the sheik retain power.

Zayed reportedly had fourteen wives and forty-one children plus assorted brothers and other relatives to keep happy. Indeed, staying in power depended in part on sharing the wealth with his relatives. A Pakistani banker who did not work for BCCI later recalled how well-dressed employees of BCCI would be dispatched every month to deliver a briefcase of cash to each of the sheik's brothers.

On New Year's Eve in 1973, Bhutto had delivered a speech praising the private sector and promising that no more industries would be nationalized. The very next day, his government took over Pakistan's banks, nearly two years after Abedi had predicted it would happen. Far from a calamity for Abedi, it proved a boon, for it provided him with a ready pool of able Pakistani bankers for BCCI; since 1974, Abedi had been hiring as many as he could recruit. Even Masihur Rahman finally joined BCCI after the nationalization.

As Abedi assembled his senior staff, a pattern emerged. Abedi came to rely not just on Pakistanis, but on a group called Mohajir, men who, like himself, had immigrated to the new Islamic nation during the partition of British India. Rahman, a Bengali, never really joined the inner circle. The Mohajirs dominated commerce and finance in Pakistan, largely because the country's quota system for native ethnic groups left them little outlet in the civil service or the military. Not fully a part of the new land, they were ripe to transfer their emotional attachment to their employer, a bank that was spreading everywhere but was rooted nowhere.

Abedi's family was growing dramatically. BCCI was becoming a truly international bank. "Mr. Abedi's dream was that we should become the biggest bank of the world in twenty-five years," recalled one of his first aides, Muzaffar Ali Bukhari. "He used to say that in our meetings and conferences. He used to look ahead. Not two years, three years, or five years, but twenty or twenty-five years. And he used to ask questions: 'Where do you see the bank after fifty years?' And the planning was done accordingly."

A symbolic story that swept through the ranks of BCCI in the mid-1970s captured the spirit and arrogance of the bank: According to the story, Abedi supposedly disagreed with a Bank of America manager over the pace of the bank's growth. "You are counting the grains of sand," Abedi reportedly said, "while I am seeing the entire desert."

The Americans were not the only grain counters. The same Pakistani banker who had walked out on Abedi muttering "bullshit" years earlier watched his lavish marketing with great puzzlement. How does Abedi make his money? he wondered aloud in a meeting with Pakistan's minister of finance in the late 1970s. The finance minister said nothing, and one day not long after the conversation the minister's son showed up as a senior officer at BCCI.

The speed of its expansion was alarming to some executives with the

Bank of America as well as to some bankers on the outside. The Bank of England expressed concern as the number of BCCI branches in Britain rose to double figures in 1976, with plans for further expansion announced.

Even though BCCI had moved its corporate offices to London, there was little that the regulators at the British central bank were willing to do. And doing anything would have required a legal stretch by the regulators, for Abedi had foreseen the possibilities of a reaction against his empire and had made arrangements to locate his legal headquarters in two countries known to have the barest of regulatory interference. Control over the British branches, and all of the bank's other branches for that matter, was divided between Luxembourg, a tiny duchy in Europe, and the Cayman Islands in the Caribbean.

Bank of Credit and Commerce International SA was registered in the Caymans in 1975. It functioned as the principal banking subsidiary of BCCI Holdings SA, which had been established in Luxembourg in 1972. Beneath these two umbrella groups, Abedi had begun forming a bewildering array of additional companies and banking entities. The guiding principle seemed to be this: Make BCCI offshore everywhere.

Both Luxembourg and the Cayman Islands were long-time bank secrecy havens, part of a small fraternity of nations that lure financial institutions of all stripes with the promise that their books would be closed to nosy outside regulators and law enforcement officials. In exchange, these countries receive big boosts to their economies. In Luxembourg, the financial services industry had grown so vital to the economy that it accounted for a fifth of the government's revenue and employed more workers than any other sector of the economy. Yet the country has never employed more than fifteen bank examiners, and Luxembourg does not even regulate bank holding companies because they are not considered banks.

There are legitimate reasons for major corporations to set up subsidiaries and affiliates in countries that offer tax and secrecy advantages. What made BCCI highly unusual was that it was a financial institution set up in two offshore countries, which meant that no single regulator could ever see the total picture of the bank's worldwide operations. The possibilities for financial trickery, such as shifting loans between the two holding companies to conceal problems, were quite real. From the point of view of, say, the Bank of England, this situation was cause for alarm. Much of the growth was occurring on the Old Gray Lady's turf.

The Bank of England has never been a lion-hearted regulator. Unlike the Federal Reserve Board or Office of the Comptroller of the Currency in the United States, the British regulator does not have its own staff of examiners. Rather, it must rely on outside auditors, the same firms employed by the banks it is regulating. Furthermore, prior to 1978, the Bank of England had very limited powers to supervise bank operations in any event.

Nonetheless, British law would have allowed the Bank of England to assert control over BCCI's financial operations if the regulators determined that their counterparts in other countries were not doing the job properly. In this case, however, the British chose to defer to Luxembourg and the Cayman Islands despite concerns about the institution's rapid growth.

Hearts were beating a little faster on the other side of the Atlantic, too. Executives at the Bank of America were concerned about the seemingly unchecked growth of their Middle Eastern partner. Huge loans were being made on a signature and a smile. Offices were sprouting in new countries faster than oil wells in the desert. The rumors about the way BCCI conducted its business had been passed along to San Francisco by bank people in the field and, naturally, by a host of competitors eager to cast suspicion on the upstart institution. Unlike the Bank of England, however, the Americans were in a position to act on their growing trepidation.

CHAPTER FOUR

The Odd Couple

The relationship between Agha Hasan Abedi and Thomas Bertram Lance was one of convenience on both sides. Abedi was looking for a way to expand his empire into America, and Lance needed a staggering amount of money to bail himself out of a financial jam. Whether one of these two men wound up taking advantage of the other remains an unanswered question, but in many ways, before the calamities, they seemed made for each other, despite their backgrounds.

Bert Lance was a country boy, a devout Southern Baptist whose father had been an educator in rural Georgia. After starting as a bank teller in 1951, he had married into the family that controlled First National Bank of Calhoun, a small bank in the northwest corner of the state. He was a big, jowly man who spoke with a heavy Georgia drawl. His height, more than six feet, made his ample paunch all the more dramatic, and his heavy-lidded eyes gave Lance the doleful cast of a drowsy hound dog. But he was no dumb cracker. After all, he married the boss's daughter, and later on he was savvy enough to align himself with another country boy from Georgia, a state senator by the name of Jimmy Carter. When Carter was elected governor of the state in 1970, he made Lance director of the highway department. Under state law, Lance was allowed to continue running the Calhoun bank.

When Carter left the governor's office, he picked Lance to run for his spot. Lance mounted an expensive campaign, flying up and down Georgia in his bank's airplane and advertising extensively on television and radio. A big chunk of Lance's campaign funds came from overdrafts written on his accounts at the Calhoun bank. Overdrafts are checks written without enough money in the account to pay for them. Lance and his family had the money in other accounts to cover the checks, but the overdrafts would prove to be a costly mistake.

31

A FULL SERVICE BANK

Lance lost his bid for the governorship in 1974, but his high-profile campaign had elevated him to stardom in Georgia. The following year, he became president of the National Bank of Georgia, an aggressive, fast-growing bank in Atlanta. He took the job on condition that he be allowed to buy a big block of stock in the institution. He did not have the money for the stock, so he borrowed $2.6 million from Manufacturers Hanover Trust in New York. After Lance took over at National Bank of Georgia, the institution switched its bank-to-bank business, or correspondent account, in New York from Citibank to Manufacturers Hanover. That's the way things often work in banking.

With the election of his old patron Jimmy Carter to the presidency of the United States in 1976, Lance moved to Washington as director of the Office of Management and Budget. OMB is the White House agency that monitors financial affairs in the executive branch of the government. Its role in drafting the federal budget makes it one of Washington's most important power centers. The move offered the one-time bank teller a shot at real glory, but there were a couple of hitches.

First, Lance's stock-purchase loan with Manufacturers Hanover required him to remain as chief executive of the bank in Atlanta. But federal regulations required him to resign. Bank stock prices were weak at the time, so he couldn't sell his stock and pay off the loan. Instead, Lance arranged a new loan with The First National Bank of Chicago. The new loan—for about $3.4 million—would pay off Manufacturers Hanover as well as a second loan that Lance had taken out with Chemical Bank of New York. A month before the First National loan was completed, Lance's National Bank of Georgia deposited $200,000 at the Chicago bank. It also took its Chicago correspondent account away from Continental Illinois Bank and gave it to First National.

Second, when the Senate confirmed him for his government job in early 1977, Lance promised not only to resign his bank post but also to sell his stock in the institution. Stock prices were still so low that he would not have netted enough to pay off the First National loan, so he was reluctant to fulfill the pledge. In July, Lance persuaded President Carter to ask the Senate to give him an extension on the stock sale so that he could avoid a ruinous loss on the deal.

Meanwhile, Lance's financial activities had attracted the attention of Congress. Investigators from the Senate Governmental Affairs Committee began asking questions about whether there was a quid pro quo between Lance and First National Bank of Chicago regarding the $3.4 million loan. Perhaps it was not coincidence that had resulted in the opening of the $200,000 account and switching of the correspondent account. Even if there was a connection, this was not a terrible offense and there was no criminal violation involved. But Bert Lance was budget director of the Carter administration and the Senate investigation did not die after just a few headlines.

The U.S. Comptroller's Office, which regulates national banks, issued a report in the middle of August that found no criminal wrongdoing in the relationship between Lance's Georgia bank and First National of Chicago. But the thoroughly neutral document did note an array of what it described as "unsafe and unsound" banking practices. Similar criticism had been expressed in an earlier report by the regulators that criticized Lance and the Calhoun bank for allowing those overdrafts to finance Lance's race for governor, and that document became public, too. Real estate loans made during his tenure at National Bank of Georgia had gone bad, providing more fodder for a gleeful press. Then it was discovered that Lance had pledged his stock in the Atlanta bank as collateral for two loans at once, one from Manufacturers Hanover and the other from Chemical Bank.

On Labor Day, 1977, President Jimmy Carter telephoned Clark M. Clifford, a lawyer who, since the days of Harry Truman, had made a career out of being the man presidents turn to in times of crisis.

"My budget director Bert Lance is in trouble," said the president. "Can you help him?"

Lance was scheduled to testify before the Senate three days later. Clifford accepted the job and assigned the first work to his young protégé, Robert Altman. The young lawyer met with Lance at seven o'clock the next morning and together they crafted an opening statement that would accuse the senators of treating rumor and innuendo as the truth.

The day Lance went to the Senate to testify, Clifford and Altman were at his side. The hearing room was filled to capacity and there was a loud buzzing of conversation and much paper shuffling as Lance prepared to read the opening statement that the two lawyers had drafted for him. Clifford simply raised his hand to the room and it quieted. Such was the respect that Clark Clifford commanded in Washington, even before a potentially hostile panel of U.S. senators. In his statement, Lance defended his actions, claiming that the Calhoun bank had a liberal overdraft policy that was available to all depositors. He claimed that the issue of pledging the stock twice was a technical dispute.

The press made a hero out of Lance, at least for a brief time, portraying him as the victim of a vendetta by the Washington establishment. But the fire would not be doused. A week later, Lance resigned as director of the Office of Management and Budget.

Less than a year after taking over one of the most important jobs in Washington, Bert Lance was nearly broke and out of work. His prospects for a big job in banking seemed bleak at best. About all he had left was his friendship with the President of the United States. That turned out to be enough for Agha Hasan Abedi.

At a Washington hotel in October 1977, the former budget director and the international banker were brought together by Eugene Holley, a former state senator from Augusta, Georgia. Holley had met Abedi the year before while trying to obtain oil rights in the tiny Gulf sheikdom of Qatar. Indeed, he was still trying to get permission when he introduced Abedi to Lance.

Abedi described his growing banking empire to Lance. He told the Georgian that he was interested in making investments in some American banks, perhaps even acquiring one or more banks. Lance, of course, was looking for a buyer for his stock in the National Bank of Georgia and he viewed BCCI as a prospective purchaser. Naturally, Lance downplayed his recent troubles and bragged about his financial acumen. Yes, he said, of course he was still friends with President Carter. Yes, he thought an introduction could be arranged later.

Unfortunately for Lance, BCCI was prohibited by law from buying a major interest in the Georgia bank because of its partnership with the Bank of America. As long as the California bank owned its chunk of BCCI stock the deal would violate a federal ban on interstate banking. That did not mean, however, that Abedi and Lance could not do some business. Abedi suggested that someone from his list of wealthy clients might be interested in acquiring Lance's stock. Also, perhaps Lance had ideas about other institutions that might be available to some of BCCI's shareholders.

So, by the end of the conversation, Abedi had promised to seek a buyer for Lance's stock and Lance had been retained as a financial adviser to help Abedi scout for other investment prospects for BCCI's rich shareholders. In fact, Lance confided to Abedi, he might have a candidate very soon, for the Georgian saw the international banker as a way out of his financial plight.

Abedi had high hopes for this relationship, too. His sights were set on coming to America, and Bert Lance was just one stage in his plans for making that part of the grand dream come true.

As 1977 was drawing to a close, he was touting the Bank of Credit and Commerce International as the world's fastest-growing bank. Its total assets had jumped from $200 million in 1973 to $2.2 billion in 1977. At the same time, its network of banks and branches had soared from 19 branches in five countries to 146 branches in thirty-two countries. BCCI had expanded from Britain and Abu Dhabi to branches throughout the Persian Gulf region, in Egypt, and in other African nations. There were branches in France, West Germany, and Hong Kong. In Switzerland, the bank had bought seventy percent of the Banque de Commerce et de Placements, which had branches in Geneva and Zurich. However, this stake was being challenged by the Swiss government because it violated regulations governing foreign investment in the country.

The pattern of this growth was rooted in the bank's origins and Abedi's style. Sheik Zayed had provided the initial backing in Abu Dhabi and he and members of his family had been rewarded with stock in BCCI and loans on convenient terms. Similarly, each time the bank had opened in another Persian Gulf nation, the rulers received shares in the bank. By 1977 small stakes in BCCI were held by the rulers of Bahrain, Saudi Arabia, and two tiny emirates, Dubai and Sharja. In each location, BCCI had opened branches at a time when the activities of foreign banks were restricted. In another Gulf nation, Oman, BCCI had entered a joint venture with the ruling sultan in 1973 that by 1977 had grown to forty-two branches within the country.

Despite his bad experience with Bhutto's nationalization, Abedi assiduously cultivated the Pakistani government. He helped Bhutto's finance minister float a badly needed foreign bond issue to raise money for the government and was rewarded with the right to open two branches in Pakistan, one in Karachi and one in Lahore. After being forced out by nationalization in 1974, Abedi's reentry into Pakistan added to his legitimacy, and it also furthered his most broadly based service, handling the remittances of his expatriate countrymen. Abedi had concentrated many of his branches in the cities and countries where Pakistan's itinerant workers were located. He was on his way to becoming a figure of influence in his home country.

To attract deposits in its pell-mell push to grow, BCCI opened fancy offices even in impoverished locations. "Walk down the main street of Djibouti and you'll see a building with a marble facade," said a Western banker. "That's BCCI. On the two buildings on either side, the plaster will be breaking and falling."

Pakistani workers and other immigrants around the world found friendly service in the offices of BCCI, so they entrusted their life savings to the bankers who spoke their language. In Britain, with a quarter million Pakistani workers, BCCI had grown to forty-five branches. It was the largest foreign bank in the country in terms of branches. While it still catered to immigrants and continued to promote itself as a Third World bank when it was convenient, the bank also was bent on solidifying its image as a world banking power.

No expense was spared in decorating its new headquarters in London's financial district. Visitors to the headquarters on Leadenhall Street were greeted by staggering opulence. A jade-encrusted Chinese screen, rumored to be worth $100,000, marked off one section. Throughout the offices were deep-pile carpets and polished marble walls. Abedi himself lived in splendor in one of London's richest districts, Harrow-on-the-Hill. It was a world apart from the Pakistani workers and other immigrants who had been his first customers in Britain and who remained his most loyal ones.

In addition to veteran Pakistani bankers, BCCI had hired as top executives people with the sort of influence that could bring in more business. There were the former governors of two central banks and a one-time director of the World Bank. Many of these senior executives were evidence of Abedi's knack for the politically expedient hire. For instance, the founding head of the Nigerian branch of BCCI was Ibrahim Dasuki, an Oxford-educated Nigerian Muslim who had been a leading government official and an associate of the country's political and religious leaders. All of these men were promised generous salaries and bonuses and stock deals that would make them rich, as long as they stayed with the bank.

Muzaffar Ali Bukhari, who spent those early years at Abedi's side, recalled Abedi's orders for the recruitment of top bankers from other organizations and governments.

"He used to say, 'Whenever you come across a good banker—he may be a governor of a central bank of a country or he may be a general manager of another bank—if he's available, you take him.' But we said, 'Sir, there is no work for him.' And he'd say, 'He will generate his own work.' When we go to a developing country in, say, Africa, when we send him, [the new employee] will say, 'With our experience of twenty or thirty years as governor of the central bank of Pakistan or someplace, I will organize your bank.' This is how we expanded."

Loyalty was bought, too, by telling employees at every level that they had an ownership role in the bank through a foundation established in the Cayman Islands. It was called International Credit and Investment Company Holdings, or ICIC, and it was set up to hold stock in the bank on behalf of its employees.

Back in 1974, Abedi had made employee ownership a key part of his appeal to Masihur Rahman that he join BCCI as its general manager for finance, or top accountant. Pakistan's banks had been nationalized and Rahman was chafing under the government's management at United Bank.

"You have lost everything in this abrupt nationalization and so did I," Abedi told Rahman. "I don't want to face this and you shouldn't face this ever again. We are a family and this is like starting a family business. And we all will have a share in this bank."

Abedi was not offering to pay much and the bank was still small, but Rahman was attracted by the chance of owning a piece of the bank. "It gave us," he said later, "something to work for for ourselves."

All members of this family, from the lowliest teller to the most senior executive, were exhorted with evangelical zeal to bring in new deposits and increase business. Annual meetings, which are terminally boring at most institutions, were marathon affairs designed to instill a sense of family and mission. They seemed to have more in common with the Bible-thumping revival meetings of the American South than the banking business. Sometimes they lasted fifteen hours, with Abedi talking for hours about growth and change. Abedi's rhetoric seemed to reflect an obsession with becoming bigger and bigger.

"The extraordinary success we have achieved is primarily due to the power we generate by being both an agent of change and a beneficiary of change at the same time," he explained to the expanding ranks of BCCI executives one year at the annual meeting in Vienna, Austria. "We live with the inevitability of change and we feel it in anticipation. There are times in our lives when change takes on not only a special but an enormous significance. Such is the time for us now."

Going on before the audience of nearly a hundred BCCI executives, board members, and select guests at Vienna's Intercontinental Hotel, he described a business strategy that he called the External Marketing Program, or EMP. Under EMP, the bank's various offices and regional divisions were supposed to generate business for themselves and also for the other operations within the bank at the same time. Doing so, he said, would create new energy to propel BCCI forward.

"We should draw from each other and above all from the infinite and ultimate source, totality, God," he charged. "We shall endeavor our best to experience totality and experience God."

In later years, EMP would take on a new meaning within BCCI. It would come to symbolize the shifting of vast sums of capital between the bank's branches worldwide, moving currency and cash out of one country and into another at the bidding of anyone willing to pay the bank's fees, no questions asked. Here, too, Abedi's strategy reflected his heritage, for the system that he set up, the manner in which BCCI did business, was a modern version of an ancient Pakistani system of transferring money known as hundi.

In hundi, an agent in one city accepts cash from a person and contacts an associate in another city who gives the same amount of cash to a person designated by the initial depositor. These transactions usually occur among friends or relatives and business is done in a very discreet fashion. Even in modern times, hundi serves as a simple, effective, and secret means of transferring money out of countries with tight currency restrictions, such as Pakistan and India.

Alvin Rice was one of the first MBAs hired at the Bank of America. In the 1950s, right after his graduation from Stanford University, Rice had joined a training program at the big bank. Since then, with time out for a brief career in the real estate construction business, he had risen steadily and smoothly at the Bank of America. By 1977, he was in charge of the World Banking Division, which was generating half of the bank's substantial profits. He was viewed as the heir apparent to A. W. "Tom" Clausen, the bank's imposing chairman.

Rice's position also made him the bank's ultimate supervisor over its investment in the Bank of Credit and Commerce International. He even occupied one of the bank's two seats on the BCCI board of directors. The other director designated by the Bank of America was Yves Lamarche, an urbane American who was based in Paris. Lamarche had succeeded Roy Carlson as the Bank of America's officer in charge of the Middle East when Carlson left in 1975.

Rice often traveled to the Persian Gulf with Abedi, making joint calls on government officials and members of various royal families, all of whom seemed thrilled to see their old friend Abedi. In a real way, BCCI served as a calling card for the Bank of America in the region. Rice found Abedi to be a likable business partner.

"Mr. Abedi was a very unusual person and had a very fine leadership style," Rice recalled years later. "He seemed to me to develop loyalty among his people to an extent that was very unusual. He was very thoughtful and quiet. He had a lot of banking experience and he did a good job of corralling very good people."

The five-year-old relationship between the two banks had been profitable for both institutions. Bank of America had built up its book of Middle Eastern business and collected hefty dividends from its BCCI stock. The bank was so satisfied that it had upped its holdings to thirty percent of BCCI's stock and then to more than forty percent. However, the same growth that had fueled the profits and brought in new business was now causing concern. The Bank of America, an orthodox bank despite its freewheeling past, could not monitor the activities of its partner.

The swiftness with which BCCI opened offices in new countries was causing problems with regulators in the States. The Federal Reserve Board, which regulates bank holding companies, had a rule requiring American banks to get permission in advance of opening an office in a foreign country. Because it owned such a hefty chunk of BCCI, the Bank of America was required to obtain the okay from the Fed before BCCI started up in a new country. But BCCI was moving too fast for that, and the result was that the regulators kept pestering the Bank of America. It was more embarrassing than serious, but bankers are notoriously averse to embarrassment, especially when it is generated by regulators.

Of more concern was the sloppy way BCCI was growing. The auditors at Bank of America had long worried over the lack of proper procedures in granting loans at BCCI. There was precious little paper trail—the boring but essential forms, appraisals, and assessments that so warm the heart of a bank auditor or loan officer. Since 1975, Al Rice had been pushing Abedi to improve this part of his operation, and Abedi kept promising to do so.

However, there was so little time for formalities, and business was done a different way in that part of the world. Before he left for a job in Iran with a big conglomerate, Carlson had argued Abedi's case with Rice and other top officials. He explained that all Abedi really needed in the Middle Eastern countries was the ruler's signature, even the ruler's assurance, that a loan would be repaid.

"It is meaningless to go around in those countries asking for forms to be filled out," he said over and over. "These aren't the same standards that are applied by the senior loan committee in San Francisco."

One of BCCI's senior executives, Abdur Razzak Sakhia, later contrasted the bank's methods with those of its Western counterparts this way: "If a client wanted a loan and went to Citibank, they would go by whatever their data processor spit out. We would know him personally. We would understand his business, and we would give him that loan based on our knowledge, not just the computer."

Nonetheless, this was a sometimes unreliable method in the view of the Bank of America officers. Concerns focused sharply on some mega-loans that seemed unsupported by any documents. One example was a series of loans totaling $80 million to the Gokal shipping family, whose fleet of ships was expanding at a dramatic pace as a result of BCCI's generous financing. These loans equaled more than two-thirds of the total capital of BCCI, which meant almost certain catastrophe for the bank should the shippers default. When Rice raised the issue of support for the loans and the unsafe exposure, the answer was unsatisfactory.

"I know these people personally," Abedi told him. "Do not worry."

As in so many of his business decisions, Abedi again reflected common Pakistani and Muslim practices. Loans among friends are common and Abedi was always fast to make them to long-time acquaintances. But a philosophy designed for small-scale, personal transactions does not mesh with the standards of international banking.

Rice had no reason to doubt the integrity of any of BCCI's customers, but he also had no ability to analyze the creditworthiness of many of them. Also, he and others at the bank had been hearing the rumors about the level of "personal service" provided by BCCI to its special customers. International banking is really a small world, and news, especially bad news that could embarrass one's competitors, travels fast on the world wires. Concerns within Bank of America were fueled by a memo written by Tony Tucher, a bank official, on April 27, 1976. In it, Tucher raised the issue of what he called "special patronage" between BCCI and certain Persian Gulf rulers, particularly in Abu Dhabi and neighboring Dubai. He provided a laundry list of questionable activities: bank officers accompanying favored customers on vacations, arranging travel and providing translators and financial advisers around the world, as well as Abedi and others hosting rulers in their homes at lavish parties paid for by the bank. He also expressed concern over what many had told him was a general lack of control over BCCI's actions by Bank of America. He suggested that BCCI officers were withholding information from their American investors and trafficking on the prestige of Bank of America.

The memo summarized the fears and rumors that had been mounting for two years, but Rice and others were reluctant to take action that might sever the profitable relationship. In an internal bank memo a few days later, Rice defended Abedi and his methods.

"On the subject of 'special patronage,' there is no doubt the BCCI organization feels that to maximize the business potential in many of the areas served in the Middle East, it is necessary to remain very close to leading political figures," Rice wrote. "This is particularly true in the Arab Emirates where special attention is given to the ruling sheiks."

He went on to say that the bank had no knowledge of inappropriate patronage and said that his auditors had not uncovered evidence of unusual expenses. He said, however, that BCCI's business development efforts should be monitored closely and added, "Avoiding rumors on the subject is a good idea."

In the area of controls over loans and general growth, Rice was more concerned. He felt that BCCI needed tighter administrative controls. At the time, in an attempt to straighten out the situation, Bank of America was trying to find one of its own executives who could move over to BCCI as chief administrative officer. The problem of lack of controls, Rice thought, would not be solved until someone from the B of A, or someone from the outside whom the bank knew well and trusted, was in place at BCCI. One difficulty with getting someone onboard was that the Bank of America was having a tough time persuading anyone to handle the administration at BCCI. For the proud and slightly disdainful employees of the world's largest bank, the prospect of moving even temporarily to an upstart institution was unappealing, particularly given the rumors that all the key people in Bank of America's international division had heard about the way BCCI did business. Another difficulty was that the California bank had granted extensive control to Abedi in the initial agreement between the two parties.

Rice wrapped up the memo by observing: "The overall relationships between BCCI and the Bank of America continue to improve but are far from what they should be. We are just not operating on the basis of mutual trust and cooperation that make the whole effort and exercise worthwhile. Substantial profits usually have a way of curing problems, but this case is an exception. If we can't make some major breakthroughs in the near future, we will have to consider alternatives, such as divestiture."

To some at Bank of America, it appeared that the Bank of Credit and Commerce wanted to end the relationship. They felt that BCCI had traded on its association with the more prestigious bank to get started and now no longer wanted to be tied to its American partner.

In a conversation with Abedi near the middle of 1976, Rice brought up this sensitive issue. Abedi's response was adamant and angry. He denied that BCCI was trying to end the association.

"All of my officers are very loyal to the Bank of America and they understand that your organization has given them the opportunity for career and personal growth outside of Pakistan," said Abedi. "You can count on our long-term loyalty and on the long-term loyalty of all of my associates."

When Rice raised the possibility that information was being withheld from Bank of America officials, Abedi had a ready answer: "That is not true. But your people might feel that way because our bankers are afraid that they might be criticized by their American colleagues."

Abedi, a charming and persuasive speaker who rarely lost his temper with outsiders, was reassuring. Cultural differences, he explained to Rice, were the root of the problem. His Pakistani employees were trying in their own way to develop the standards of their American partner.

"Your American style of frank criticism is something that Pakistanis are not used to," he told Rice. "Criticism in my culture is taken as a personal affront and for this reason sometimes BCCI officers have not wanted to disclose operating procedures that they know would not meet the Bank of America's high-quality standards. Everyone in my organization admires the quality that you demand everywhere and wants to do everything they can to bring this same type of quality to all aspects of our operations."

Abedi's promises of reform proved hollow, his defenses were lies. In an unguarded moment well after that conversation, a BCCI executive

41

told an American that the Pakistanis felt the Bank of America was holding back BCCI's growth. The American bankers, he said, were too rigid.

"We felt that they were, ah, restricting our growth somewhat because Bank of America is a very established type of bank," the BCCI executive said. "And we wanted to get out and open all over the world."

The one part of the world where BCCI most wanted its own presence, even then, was the United States. However, U.S. banking regulations prohibited BCCI from opening offices in the United States as long as the Bank of America held such a significant portion of its stock.

So Abedi's dream of expanding into the world's richest nation—a dream he had kept secret from the Bank of America—was blocked by the continuing association with the San Francisco banking giant, but that obstacle was about to be removed.

By 1977, the Bank of America's dissatisfaction had increased as financial controls failed to materialize at BCCI. In fact, the auditors found surprisingly serious financial problems that year when they examined BCCI's portfolio of loans. A two-page summary of the loan examination report broke the problems into three areas:

• BCCI's loan-loss reserves, the amount of cash available to cover potential losses on loans, were grossly inadequate. The total reserve was $3 million and it should be increased by almost six times to at least $17 million.

• BCCI had engaged in widespread loans to its own shareholders, a practice known as insider lending. Some of its major Middle Eastern shareholders had received substantial loans.

• BCCI's portfolio of real estate loans was deemed unsatisfactory. Huge loans were concentrated in the Persian Gulf region, opening the bank to major losses in the event of economic or political problems in that area.

These last two items were interconnected in ways that would remain muddy for years. BCCI had paid a price for the patronage of Arab leaders, and the price was millions of dollars worth of loans that were unlikely to be repaid. Perhaps they were never intended to be repaid. As for collateral, many of the loans were backed by suspect parcels of land in sheikdoms where the bank would be prohibited from foreclosing even if it wished to do so.

For instance, Kamal Adham, the Saudi intelligence chief and major BCCI shareholder, had borrowed millions and his total loans from BCCI and its affiliates would eventually top $300 million. Yet auditors one day would discover that many of the loans were backed by unidentified properties in Saudi Arabia. There were no valuations for the properties and, worse, no legal basis for considering them security because mortgages are not routinely enforced in the kingdom. The Federal Reserve would later charge that Adham had even borrowed from BCCI the funds he used to invest in the bank in the first place. Similar discoveries would be made about a series of major bank customers. But that was a long way off.

The Bank of America auditors had caught merely a glimpse of this pattern of reckless and rampant insider dealing. BCCI's regular auditors were seeing even less. At the time, the bank's Luxembourg holding company was being audited by the big accounting firm of Ernst & Whinney; the Cayman Islands unit was audited by Price Waterhouse, another large accounting firm. A Price Waterhouse accountant told a friend a story showing his firm's difficulty in dealing with BCCI. The auditors of the bank's London headquarters discovered that its loan files were written in Urdu. Price Waterhouse employed many Pakistani accountants and one day it assigned one of them to the BCCI account. When the Urdu speaker showed up for work at the bank, however, officials there would not let him in the building. Price Waterhouse agreed to take the accountant off that job.

Outside accountants can earn millions of dollars a year in fees for auditing big businesses, particularly those that are spread across the globe. These audits are supposed to show the public and regulators the true financial picture of the organization. But, as proven in numerous cases in the American savings and loan debacle, even accountants sometimes miss the real story. They don't see key information. They are forced to take the word of management on critical questions. This tendency to accept management's view of the situation is compounded when management itself is intent on hiding the true picture of what is going on inside the organization.

Bank of America had seen enough to get some sense of what was going on inside BCCI. Even more important to the BCCI relationship, by 1977 Alvin Rice had moved up to vice chairman of the bank. He had been replaced as head of world banking by Samuel Armacost, who had no stake in ties to the troublesome partner. Armacost dispatched one of his most trusted aides, Cal Jones, to London to take a look at what was going on with BCCI. Jones soon found that he was not going to get a clear picture of what was happening inside the rapidly expanding bank. Not only was he prohibited from attending key meetings, he also was denied the minutes of those sessions as well as access to the internal working records of the bank. He was, as an associate would later say, put on "a mushroom diet—kept in the dark and fed shit."

Based on the little that its auditors had seen, the sense that they were not getting the whole picture, and the long-standing, unresolved differences over controls, the Bank of America decided to sell its stock in the Bank of Credit and Commerce in late 1977. An agreement would be reached for the orderly sale of the stock over a period of more than two years, so that the price of the shares would not plummet. Abedi arranged for a wealthy Saudi Arabian associate to acquire some of the shares; others were moved into ICIC Holdings, the employee benefit fund.

More critical, the Bank of America had gotten a closer look at BCCI's financial tangle than any regulators, yet the California bankers did not blow the whistle. At least not loudly. One former Bank of America official who was involved with the bank said later that Cal Jones met with Bank of England regulators privately and told them about the poor documentation of loans and the pell-mell growth that were leading his bank to sell its stake in BCCI. No additional evidence has surfaced and there is no record of any report to U.S. banking authorities. Indeed, there was no legal requirement that the B of A describe what its auditors had seen inside BCCI to regulators anywhere. However, had the Bank of America raised an official alarm, authorities in Britain and elsewhere might have been prompted to demand their own examination back in 1978.

But, of course, blowing the whistle could have dropped BCCI's value like a stone just when Bank of America was unloading its shares at a hefty profit. The two institutions were to remain friendly for years to come, with the Bank of America providing a range of correspondent services for BCCI.

From BCCI's standpoint, the Bank of America had served its purpose, midwifing the infant bank into the world. BCCI was now up to operating independently. Whether by design or not, Agha Abedi was freed of the Bank of America at just the right moment. His new friend Bert Lance was on the scene, prepared to open the right doors that would eventually propel Abedi and his empire into the financial capital of the world.

CHAPTER FIVE

Coming to America

O pening a bank in the United States requires a charter, which can be issued by either a state government or the U.S. Comptroller of the Currency. Chartering by a state government is regarded as easier because requirements are less stringent, but national charters offer many advantages and a measure of prestige—sort of like belonging to the country club instead of the public golf course. In either case, the federal banking regulators are supposed to have a say in who is granted a license and who is not.

Bank regulations in the United States are regarded as among the world's most stringent, although their failures in the last two decades have become increasingly spectacular. However, it does make it tougher in the United States than, say, Luxembourg or even England.

Satisfying the regulators falls into two main categories—money and people. It does not take a great deal of the former to start a bank. The minimum requirement usually translates as enough money to cover anticipated normal business losses associated with bad loans or interest rate fluctuations. An investor with $1 million can acquire a bank with assets of $10 million—or $20 million if the regulators are lax. The capital is a cushion in the event the bank fails and the government has to take over. As would be discovered in the savings and loan crisis of the 1980s, too often there is little or no cushion.

As for people, regulators like to see an experienced management team and a board of directors with character and some financial means. For a national charter, the directors must each invest money in the institution, though not a large amount, to show the regulators that the directors will monitor the bank faithfully because they have some of their own wealth at stake.

These regulations apply equally to foreigners who want to start a new bank or buy an existing one on American soil. Starting in 1978, most of these rules were applied for the first time to foreign banks with U.S. branches and agencies, too. So when a foreign bank wants to start full-scale operations in the United States, they must open their books to the American regulators so that capital adequacy and other matters can be demonstrated.

Equally important, U.S. regulators insist that a foreign bank operating here be subject to comprehensive supervision by a home-country regulator. When an institution operates internationally, a review of all its parts is the only way to determine its true financial strength and whether it is operating legally. This is called a consolidated review, and it is the only accurate means of analyzing an international business. If no one is looking at the whole operation, regulators say, it is too easy for a bank to move assets and liabilities from one segment of the institution to another to mask illegal activities or financial problems.

All of these requirements added up to more than a dilemma for Agha Abedi and his Bank of Credit and Commerce International. They were a virtual roadblock, at least to legal and open operation in the United States.

There is some lingering uncertainty about why Abedi split his operation into its Luxembourg and Cayman Islands halves, but he seemed perfectly happy with the result—that no central regulator knew what was happening inside the bank. He certainly chose host countries where the regulators were notoriously lax, and BCCI's financial picture was muddy to begin with. The regulatory arrangement and the secrecy surrounding the Middle Eastern shareholders made it impossible to get a consolidated assessment of the bank's finances. For example, BCCI's annual financial statement in 1976 disclosed that its Hong Kong office maintained $56 million in "confidential" deposits. Such accounts were described as involving money deposited by people known only to top BCCI management.

There also was reason to speculate that the bank's picture was not as rosy as its annual reports indicated by the latter part of the 1970s. The swift worldwide expansion was expensive. As an outsider and newcomer in many locations, BCCI was shut out of the most lucrative consumer and business banking arenas. Instead, it was scrambling for deposits among Third World immigrants and small businesses. These deposits were used to fuel the growth.

And, to a degree unseen by those outside the bank's hierarchy, the deposits of thousands of immigrant workers and small businessmen worldwide were being funneled into sweetheart loans to influential associates and shareholders. The Bank of America auditors had spotted the tip of that iceberg, but it would be a long time before the extent of those ventures was uncovered.

The enigma of the bank's financial standing, however, had not stopped its expansion in Britain. When BCCI's branch network reached forty-five in Britain in 1978, nervous regulators had asked the bank not to open any more offices. However, when it came to examining the underlying finances, the Bank of England contented itself with receiving bits of information from the bank. Not for years would regulators there or anywhere else see a consolidated financial statement.

It would require a different approach to complete the American phase of the grand scheme, as Abedi discovered in 1975 when he tried to slip past American regulators.

Chelsea National Bank, a small, troubled bank in New York that numbered former Mayor Robert Wagner and members of the politically powerful Finley, Kumble law firm as shareholders, was for sale. Abbas Gokal, one of the three brothers in the shipping company, applied to state regulators to buy the bank. He provided a financial statement that showed total assets of $4.5 million, with $3 million of it in the form of a loan he made to his sister on the same date he filled out the statement. His reported annual income for the previous year was $34,000. Financing to buy the bank, he said, would come from his sister, who had returned the favor of his $3 million loan by lending him $4 million. The arrangement puzzled the New York State regulators. "We find it difficult to judge the financial capacity of the applicant," one regulator wrote. In addition, Gokal had no experience as a banker; he was in the shipping business. He indicated that he would rely for advice and counsel on his primary personal and business banker, the Bank of Credit and Commerce International.

Gokal's go-between in filing the application, and the nominee he had selected to run Chelsea, was a senior BCCI executive named Abdus Sami. Born in 1927 in India and educated in the Punjab, Sami had accompanied Abedi at every stage of his career, from Habib Bank to United Bank to the founding of BCCI. The influence of Abedi's rhetoric even showed up on the résumé Sami filed with the New York regulators. His achievements, he wrote, included welding "a large team of executives and officers into a composite personality." Among those identified as prospective board members for the bank was Roy P. M. Carlson.

The financial questions and role of BCCI in the deal did not disqualify Gokal from buying the bank, but since he was relying on BCCI to meet the qualification of experience, New York State regulators needed to learn what they could about that organization. They found a lot of rumors about special relationships with Arab moneymen, about currying favor in certain countries to win bank licenses, but rumors are not facts. However, the fact that dismayed the regulators was that there was no primary regulator with responsibility for overseeing the bank's worldwide activities.

Several times, Abedi went personally to meet with New York State banking regulators, including the superintendent of banking, John Heimann. On each occasion, he expressed BCCI's desire to enter the United States market. And each time, he tried to convince Heimann and senior regulators that BCCI was financially secure and operating legally. It was, Abedi insisted, one of the world's best banks and it deserved to be in the American market. Each time, Heimann replied that he was worried because BCCI did not have a primary regulator. He was, Heimann told Abedi, reluctant to permit BCCI into banking in New York.

"What we had determined was that BCCI was an international banking organization so structured as to have more than one regulator," says Heimann, who went on to become U.S. comptroller of the currency. "Part of the function of regulators is to try to curtail activities of those who try to take advantage of our open system of banking. There is no way to know of criminal intent before an acquisition. But you try to weed them out in advance through regulatory scrutiny."

This advance scrutiny had convinced Heimann that Abedi and his bank should not be involved in operating Chelsea National, or any other American bank for that matter.

"It was critical that BCCI not be involved in Chelsea because they were not fit and proper to operate a bank in the United States," explains Heimann. "BCCI had always been shrouded in mystery. There was no primary regulator. There was a lot of gossip and rumor."

Abbas Gokal was informed by New York authorities that his application was deficient, and a short time later Chelsea National Bank was sold to another buyer.

Obviously, Abedi had discovered that BCCI would get nowhere in the United States using its own name. He had made a mistake in being so open. More importantly, he had learned a lesson. Next time, he would do things differently. That was where Bert Lance and the former budget director's powerful friends fitted in.

Without question, Abedi was a man who knew the value of friends in high places. He had gone to great lengths to cultivate influential officials in the Persian Gulf and elsewhere around the world. Bailing Bert Lance out of his financial jam was the first step in this new attempt to begin operating in the United States.

In November 1977, a month after his first meeting with Lance, Abedi introduced the Georgian to Ghaith Pharaon, a wealthy Saudi Arabian businessman who already had passed the tests of American regulators by acquiring substantial interests in banks in Detroit and Houston. Abedi explained to Lance that Pharaon was interested in buying Lance's bank stock and Abedi was serving as the Saudi's financial adviser. Lance thought it was a fine idea.

As world attention began to focus on rich Arabs and their international buying sprees, Pharaon was one of the figures destined to reach mythical proportions. A man of ample girth and substantial charm, he owned homes and mansions throughout the world and would one day buy automaker Henry Ford II's 1,800-acre plantation outside Savannah, Georgia. He traveled the world in private jets and, to his dismay, was often compared with the controversial Adnan Khashoggi, another Saudi who had grown wealthy trading on his ties to the royal family.

Pharaon was the son of Rashad Pharaon, a Syrian-born physician who had gone to Saudi Arabia in 1936 as the chief doctor for King Abdul Aziz, the kingdom's founder. At one point in the late 1930s, Pharaon had the only refrigerator in Saudi Arabia. He needed it to store chemicals to run his X-ray machine. Following the death of Abdul Aziz in 1953, Pharaon emerged as a leading political adviser to the sons who succeeded him, King Faisal and King Khalid.

Because of the physician's privileged status, his son Ghaith was educated in the United States. He attended the Colorado School of Mines and Stanford University and received an MBA from Harvard in 1965. His thesis at Harvard formed the outline for the creation of an engineering and construction firm in his native Saudi Arabia. However, it was his connections to the royal family that would propel young Ghaith to great fortune.

Returning to Saudi Arabia with a degree in petroleum engineering and an MBA, Pharaon was recruited to join the oil ministry by Sheik Ahmad Zaki Yamani, the minister of oil. He quickly discovered that the life of a bureaucrat was far too constricting for him. Pharaon was an entrepreneur at heart, and it was a perfect time to be one in Saudi Arabia.

"There were so many opportunities in those days for a young man going back to Saudi Arabia that I said, taking a risk for myself and working for myself would perhaps be more interesting," Pharaon once told a reporter.

So he dusted off his Harvard thesis and established the Saudi Research and Development Corporation, which became known as Redec. The kingdom's oil wealth was just beginning to grow and Saudi Arabia was trying desperately to modernize its cities. Redec received massive contracts, often in joint ventures with foreign firms, to build new sewer systems in Jedda and Dammam, a drainage system in Mecca, and a natural gas system in the country's eastern provinces. The government's Ministry of the Interior, headed by Pharaon's old friend Prince Fahad, provided Redec with ninety percent of its contracts in those days.

As the oil boom of the 1970s added more fuel to the rampaging Saudi economy, Pharaon began importing cement for the massive construction projects popping up throughout the country. (If this sounds like selling ice to the Eskimos, it is not quite so. Through an oddity of nature, the vast desert nation had to import cement because its own sand is too fine to be used to mix it.)

Diversifying into food storage, insurance, and hotels, Pharaon came into contact with a wide range of businessmen. He built the Hyatt Hotel in Riyadh (which would serve as headquarters for the U.S. military command and Western journalists during the Persian Gulf War in 1991) in partnership with Kamal Adham, the BCCI shareholder who was creator of the intelligence service in Saudi Arabia. It was the first of a string of Hyatt Hotels that Pharaon would build around the world. Just as important to his future, it was Adham who introduced Pharaon to the equally entrepreneurial Agha Abedi.

Since he first learned about American finance at Harvard, Pharaon had been interested in the idea of owning a bank or even several banks in the United States. As had the Rockefellers and the Carnegies before him, Pharaon recognized that banks can bring prestige and influence and be solid investments, as well.

"In America," he once explained, "a $400 million bank can be acquired for $20 million. Where else can you do that?"

Pharaon's earlier ventures in American banking had not been successful. In 1975, he had bought the Bank of the Commonwealth in Detroit using the law firm of former Texas governor John Connally as negotiator. Henry Ford II had helped smooth the way for the purchase by telephoning Jewish leaders to reassure them about the takeover of the state's sixth-largest bank by an Arab. Commonwealth was a troubled institution. It had gotten into trouble in the late 1960s when it was controlled by a local man named Donald Parsons, whose *modus operandi* bore a striking similarity to Abedi's own. Parsons had built a bank network cutting across several regulatory jurisdictions, held it together with amorphous committees of overlapping managers, and pushed it into hyper-growth through risky investments. The bank had been "rescued" by the Federal Deposit Insurance Corporation in 1972 in the agency's first big-bank bailout, but it never recovered. Pharaon sold his investment in 1976 for the same amount he paid for it.

Early in 1977, he had acquired twenty percent of Main Bank in Houston, where he had other investments in construction and engineering companies. This time, John Connally joined the deal himself as one of Main Bank's other major shareholders. That investment, too, was not profitable. Pharaon was in the process of selling his stock in Main in late 1977 when Abedi contacted him about the possibility of buying Lance's share of the National Bank of Georgia.

Agha Hasan Abedi already had served as Pharaon's financial adviser in another rather strange transaction that involved a series of delicate negotiations with government leaders in Pakistan, Abu Dhabi, and Saudi Arabia.

Until the middle 1970s, the exploration, refining, and marketing of oil in Pakistan had been done largely by Attock Oil Corporation. Attock was the operating arm of a small, privately owned, London-based firm called Attock Petroleum, which had been founded in 1913. Its near monopoly in Pakistan was threatened in early 1976 when a large field of oil was discovered in Pakistan's Dhodak province by a team under the supervision of a young government scientist, Shazad Sadiq.

Prime Minister Bhutto was gleeful. He saw the new oil as a means of improving the country's disastrous financial position and consolidating his own power as elections approached the following year. Backed by the promise of $110 million in financing from Canada, Britain, and the World Bank, Bhutto planned to create a public oil sector in the country by developing the rich new field and nationalizing Attock Oil, which had resisted his previous takeover efforts.

Attock's chief, T.A.T. Lodhi, wasted little time in taking preemptive action. He wanted to find someone of power and influence to acquire Attock and keep it out of the hands of the government. The man he chose to help him was Agha Abedi. From November of 1976, Lodhi had visited Abedi in London regularly. Near the end of the year, Abedi contacted Shazad Sadiq and asked whether BCCI funds might be required to assist in the oil industry development. Bhutto shrewdly grasped what was afoot and his response was to the point: "That arselicker Abedi is trying to buy Attock."

The game here was power and politics, two arenas in which Abedi had become an accomplished player. Later that year, a series of private meetings was held between Attock officials and the right-wing Pakistan National Alliance, Bhutto's opposition in the upcoming elections. A series of orchestrated newspaper attacks on the Bhutto-Sadiq oil plan began to appear. In February 1977, Pakistani newspapers reported that "unidentified Arab investors" were considering buying control of Attock.

The scheme was to create doubt about Bhutto's plan and soften him up for selling Attock to the group being formed by Abedi and Lodhi. Indeed, the two men had mobilized their considerable allies to stop the takeover. Among them was Sheik Zayed of Abu Dhabi, who was one of Bhutto's principal supporters in the Arab world. Abedi persuaded Bhutto to give up his plan to nationalize Attock in favor of a new role for some investors close to the sheik. Bhutto relented, and in March 1977, sixteen percent of Attock Petroleum, the parent of Attock Oil, was sold to the Kuwait International Finance Company, or KIFCO. The owners of KIFCO were Ghaith Pharaon, Kamal Adham, Faisal al-Fulaij, and Abdullah Darwaish, a financial adviser to Abu Dhabi's royal family. Abedi represented them in the deal.

A few months later, Bhutto did not matter anymore anyway. In July 1977, General Zia ul-Haq and his military allies seized power and arrested Bhutto. Zia rejected Bhutto's evolving socialism and opened the way for the Arab investors to acquire an even larger stake in Attock. That same month, Attock Petroleum sold fifty-one percent of Attock Oil, its operating arm, to KIFCO. Pharaon, Adham, and Fulaij were installed as the new directors of Attock Oil's London-based parent company and Lodhi remained as the chief executive officer. The notion of a publicly owned oil company that could develop the oil fields for the benefit of the country vanished. Interestingly, so did the promise of the Dhodak oil fields. In later years, operators of the wells there would say that they could not find enough oil for profitable operation. For the other oil-producing nations of the region, such as Abu Dhabi, Saudi Arabia, and Kuwait, this meant that there was one less competitor.

Losing the revenue from the oil fields was the least of Bhutto's worries. The new military regime began an investigation of his years in power. Almost immediately, the government's investigators claimed to have found evidence of massive corruption and vote rigging in the March 1977 election that had kept Bhutto in power.

A former secretary to Bhutto signed an affidavit in which he said that Agha Hasan Abedi had made several trips to Pakistan in the weeks before the March election. Each time, Abedi brought with him cash that he delivered to Bhutto. The former secretary said that the cash, which totaled $2 million to $3 million, was from a foreign head of state and was to be used to ensure Bhutto's reelection. The government White Paper containing the affidavit deleted the name of the foreign leader, but published reports at the time claimed it was Sheik Zayed of Abu Dhabi.

The White Paper may have been wrong in its speculation that the payments were intended to keep Bhutto in power. They coincided with the efforts of Abedi and his investors to stop the nationalization of Pakistan's oil fields and gain control over Attock Oil. In any event, Bhutto was hanged two years later on charges of corruption, and no one was ever accused of any wrongdoing in connection with the alleged payments to him or the Attock Oil venture.

The intriguing Attock Oil deal was only part of the relationship between Abedi and Pharaon. At Abedi's urging, it was Pharaon who had agreed to buy a portion of the BCCI stock that was being sold by the Bank of America. The stock price was never disclosed, but a BCCI executive, Nazir Chinoy, later said it was $34 million—not a bad return for Bank of America on its investment of $2.5 million. BCCI also was good to Pharaon. It had already made the first of a series of loans to him that would one day total almost $300 million.

So, despite having been unsuccessful twice before with investments in American banks, Pharaon was happy to buy control of the National Bank of Georgia at the suggestion of his good friend Agha Abedi. And the premium price he was willing to pay made Bert Lance a happy man, too.

Five days before Christmas, Lance announced publicly that he was selling his stock in National Bank of Georgia to Ghaith Pharaon. The total price was $2.4 million, or $20 a share. A few weeks before, the stock had been trading as low as $10 a share. Lance, however, has steadfastly denied that it was a bailout.

The proposal would give Pharaon control of sixty percent of the bank's stock, but the regulators approved it quickly. After all, Pharaon was a wealthy Saudi tycoon with a solid business background and some banking experience. Plus, there was no hint of BCCI in this transaction. Only later would regulators discover documents showing that BCCI had loaned Pharaon a portion of the money he used to buy NBG.

The deal was completed on January 5, 1978, the day after Bert Lance was relieved of yet another major financial problem. On January 4, the First National Bank of Chicago received an electronic money transfer from the BCCI in Luxembourg. The amount was $3.4 million and it cleared Lance's debt with the bank. Lance himself later described the favorable terms of the BCCI loan—no collateral, no schedule for repayment, and no set interest rate. (A BCCI spokesman later said that Lance repaid the loan in 1984.)

The timing suggests that a portion of the funds came from the sale of the National Bank of Georgia stock, yet the wire transfer came in the day before Pharaon turned over the money, and the amount was a full $1 million in excess of what Lance would receive from Pharaon. Later, it was disclosed that BCCI had recorded the $3.4 million as a loan on its books. But Lance and Pharaon both denied at the time and later that there was a connection between BCCI paying off Lance's loan and the acquisition of the National Bank of Georgia.

Clearly, Abedi played a role in the transaction by bringing together Lance and Pharaon. The deal and the BCCI loan bailed out Lance from serious money problems and put him in debt personally and financially to Abedi and BCCI. No one raised questions at the time about whether Pharaon had put up his own funds to buy the bank stock. Everyone knew he was one of those fabulously rich Arabs.

In the months after buying Lance's interest, Pharaon acquired the remainder of the outstanding stock of the National Bank of Georgia and installed his own management team. When it came to choosing a new bank president, Pharaon again relied on Abedi, who recommended Roy P. M. Carlson, Abedi's old champion with the Bank of America and Gokal's candidate for bank director at Chelsea National in New York.

After Carlson had left Bank of America in 1975, he had spent four years as managing director of a large group of companies in Iran. With the revolution, however, he fled the country. For a while he traveled around Europe with the expectation of returning to Iran once things settled down.

By the summer of 1979, Carlson had returned to the United States, where he was contacted by one of Abedi's subordinates at BCCI. The man said that Pharaon was looking for someone to run his bank and he invited Carlson to come to London. There, Abedi introduced him to Pharaon, and by November Carlson was installed at the Atlanta headquarters of the National Bank of Georgia.

But Abedi stayed in the background in his dealings with the Georgia bank. Not long before, the Pakistani banker had discovered what happened when American regulators found that BCCI was involved with one of their banks.

On the surface, it had appeared to be the banking industry's first hostile takeover, something that industry experts had long said was impossible because regulators would not allow an unfriendly acquisition of a bank. The story below the surface would remain hidden for years.

Even before the sale of his Georgia bank stock to Pharaon was completed, Lance had arranged for Abedi to meet with a group of investors in Financial General Bankshares, a medium-sized banking company with headquarters in Washington, D.C. It was late 1977 and the investors were looking for someone to buy the bank.

Financial General was an attractive prize. With assets of $2.2 billion, it was far from being the nation's largest bank, but it was one of a handful of bank holding companies that could own banks in more than one state through an exemption to a 1956 law known as a grandfather clause. So, from its headquarters building a block from the White House, the company controlled thirteen banks in the District of Columbia, New York, Virginia, Maryland, Georgia, and Tennessee.

Lance had known for some time that Financial General was on the block. It was Financial General that had sold Lance his controlling interest in the National Bank of Georgia in 1975. A year later, the company's chairman, George Olmsted, approached Lance about buying control of Financial General, but Jimmy Carter had just been elected president and Lance had other plans for getting to Washington.

It did not stop there, however, according to the U.S. Securities and Exchange Commission. The SEC said later that Lance and Olmsted had at least one conversation about acquiring the bank while Lance was Carter's budget director. The two men talked about a possible deal over lunch one day at the Metropolitan Club a few blocks from the White House. Also at the lunch was a former investment banker named William Middendorf II, who had been Secretary of the Navy under Presidents Richard Nixon and Gerald Ford.

Lance again declined, but Middendorf was interested. In April of 1977, he led an investor group that acquired control of Financial General. It proved to be no solution to the troubles at the institution. By June, the group had split, some said because Middendorf had rudely rebuffed salesmen for a data processing firm owned by a fellow investor. The investor was Jackson Stephens, and his faction started looking for a buyer to wrest control from Middendorf.

Stephens was a formidable opponent for Middendorf. He and his brother had made a fortune through their large financial firm, Stephens Inc. Based in Little Rock, Arkansas, it was considered the largest privately owned investment bank outside of Wall Street. *Business Week* magazine called the brothers "country slickers," and for years very little happened in Arkansas politics that they did not at least influence. Jack Stephens had met Lance in 1976 through their mutual friend Jimmy Carter, who had been a roommate of Stephens at the U.S. Naval Academy. Lance and Stephens had become close friends, sharing interests in Democratic politics, banking, and religion. Like Lance, Stephens was a Southern Baptist.

Another disgruntled shareholder was a Washington lawyer named Eugene Metzger. Through the summer and fall of 1977, he and Stephens had been shopping for a buyer. In October, Metzger suggested that he and Stephens might find a foreign bank interested in making an offer for Financial General shares. They were not opposed to a foreign buyer; Metzger had written a letter to a North Carolina bank that owned stock in Financial General suggesting that a foreign purchaser might pay a premium to insiders who controlled a quarter of Financial General's stock.

The discontent at Financial General coincided with Bert Lance's mission to find an American acquisition for Abedi and with the sale of his own bank.

In early November 1977, Abedi himself flew to Little Rock with his assistant, Abdus Sami, who had tried to help him swing the Chelsea National purchase. They came to talk with Lance and Jackson Stephens, who was serving as Lance's broker in the sale of his National Bank of Georgia stock to Ghaith Pharaon. Stephens, however, used the occasion to pitch the sale of Financial General. Abedi was interested.

The weekend after Thanksgiving, Abedi flew to Atlanta again and met with Lance and Stephens. Accompanying Abedi was Swaleh Naqvi, the number two man at BCCI, as well as Sami. At the meeting, the sale of National Bank of Georgia was wrapped up, and Lance announced it a week later. The session also provided an opportunity to push along the Financial General proposal. Abedi was so impressed with the prospects that he sent Naqvi back to London to set up a war chest of $1.35 million for the takeover.

Abedi had a busy itinerary in the United States, but he found time to call on Kamal Adham, the former Saudi intelligence chief and major BCCI shareholder, and line him up as an investor in the planned takeover of Financial General. On November 30, Abedi met Sami in Washington and they joined Eugene Metzger for an evening meeting at the Washington Hilton. With $1.35 million available, the BCCI bankers told Metzger to start bidding for the large blocks of stock that Stephens had said were for sale. They told Metzger he was acting for Adham's account. Two weeks later, Abdus Sami gave Stephens the go-ahead to also begin purchasing Financial General stock on the open market.

The game was afoot. The Abedi-backed group began to accumulate substantial shares of Financial General stock. U.S. securities law requires that investors file a statement with the Securities and Exchange Commission when they acquire more than 4.9 percent of the stock in a public company. Each time one of the BCCI purchases approached that figure, the stock purchases were switched to another account in an attempt to skirt the disclosure provisions.

On January 30, 1978, Sami sent a telex to brief Abedi on the purchases. He referred to BCCI's "intention to acquire control" of Financial General. He also told Abedi that he had hired Clark Clifford as chief counsel to handle any takeover litigation and filings with bank regulators. And Sami reminded Abedi of the need to keep each shareholder's stake below five percent and added a warning: "We must be careful that our name [BCCI] does not appear as financier to most of [the investors] for this acquisition."

Through this scheme, BCCI acquired more than twenty percent of the stock in Financial General. Lance had then tried to convince William Middendorf that a friendly takeover of the remaining stock should be executed quietly and without a fight, but Middendorf rejected the overture and vowed to retain control of the bank.

Aligned with Middendorf was B. Francis Saul, a prominent Washington real estate developer, who owned six percent of the Financial General stock. When rumors surfaced that Lance and others, fortified with Arab money, were intent on acquiring the company, Saul bought several more blocks of stock. In mid-January, he replaced Middendorf as chairman of Financial General.

Armand Hammer, then chairman of Occidental Petroleum Corporation and a Financial General board member, decided to play peacemaker. Hammer had a foot in both camps. In 1974, he had told a U.S. Senate subcommittee that a "prominent Arab," quickly identified as Ghaith Pharaon, had bought a million shares of Occidental Petroleum. On the other hand, Hammer had invested in Financial General as part of Middendorf's acquisition the previous April. Thus, he had good reason to want to calm the storm at the institution. Through one of his top executives in Washington, William McSweeny, Hammer had been receiving reports of friction between the Middendorf-Saul faction at the bank and the outside group led by Lance.

In late January, Hammer was in Washington to receive the Legion of Honor cross in a ceremony at the French embassy. Since the tycoon was flying back to California that night, McSweeny arranged for Hammer to meet Middendorf and Saul in a room at the embassy right after the ceremony. At the urging of the other two men, Hammer agreed to set up a meeting with Lance to try to iron out the problems.

The peace talks were scheduled for February 7, 1978, in Washington with Lance, Middendorf, Saul, and Hammer. On that day the city was in the midst of a severe snowstorm and the seventy-seven-year-old industrialist's private jet could not land. The meeting, however, went on without him.

Gathered in Occidental Petroleum's Washington office were Lance, his son David, Middendorf, Saul, and the Occidental executive, McSweeny. The group had lunch, exchanging social chitchat. Then Lance asked Saul to speak with him privately in another room. Away from the group, Lance announced the name of his client, the Bank of Credit and Commerce.

"We can do three things," Lance said in his affable drawl. "One, we can get together. Two, we can buy out. Or, three, we can take you over." When any of these happened, Lance made clear, he hoped to take a senior position with the bank.

Saul did not like what he heard, and he annoyed Lance in turn when he said that the bank would be hurt if it were involved publicly with the former budget director.

"But I'm well thought of around the country," Lance retorted.

The atmosphere did not improve when the two men returned to the dining room. Lance announced that his group had acquired about twenty percent of Financial General's stock and he left no doubt about the group's intentions, according to sworn statements given later by some of the other participants.

"If you bring together all members of our group, we've already acquired twenty percent of the bank's common stock and intend to take control," Lance said. "BCCI always wants control. They like to take complete control."

Middendorf asked if Lance's group intended to make a hostile offer, in which the group would proceed to try to buy enough shares for control without an okay from the bank's management.

"I cannot rule that out," Lance replied.

Later Saul said that when Lance had taken him aside at the lunch, the former budget director had said that he wanted either Saul's job as chairman of Financial General or Middendorf's as president. Lance later denied this statement, and many of the other statements attributed to him at the meeting by Saul, Middendorf, and McSweeny. Whatever was said, Lance had tipped his hand. Saul and Middendorf decided to counterattack.

Two days after the luncheon, Financial General issued a press release saying that purchases of its stock had been made by a "foreign bank which may be seeking to obtain control of the company." Lance was not named, but his remarks were clearly the basis for the release.

Lance, finally realizing that he may have made a tactical error in speaking so strongly, telephoned Saul and told him that the purchases of stock were not being made by BCCI. He said they were being made by a group of individual investors. However, as they say in Georgia, it doesn't do any good to shut the barn door once the horse is out.

The second step had already been taken. Right after the lunch, Saul and Middendorf had one of the bank's lawyers telephone the Securities and Exchange Commission to report Lance's remarks. They wanted to get the SEC and its attorneys on their side by reporting what appeared to be a violation of federal securities laws in the accumulation of stock by the Lance group. The lawyer found a willing audience. Since Lance had resigned from the White House, several attorneys in the agency's enforcement division had been scrutinizing every detail of the Georgia banker's finances.

On February 17, Financial General filed a civil lawsuit against Lance, BCCI, Abedi, Metzger, Stephens, and unnamed defendants, who would turn out to be Arab investors and BCCI clients. Later documents identified them as Kamal Adham; Faisal-al Fulaij, the prominent Kuwaiti businessman and associate of the Kuwaiti royal family; Sheik Sultan bin Zayed Sultan al-Nahayan, the crown prince of Abu Dhabi and Sheik Zayed's brother; and Abdullah Darwaish, the royal family's financial adviser, who was representing one of Sheik Zayed's sons, Mohammed al-Nahayan. The lawsuit claimed that the defendants were part of a group attempting to take over Financial General in violation of securities laws.

Lance and BCCI officials replied that there was no organized group. A BCCI official in London told a *New York Times* reporter that he had been in touch with Abedi about the matter. "None of us have any knowledge of this deal at all," said the official.

Despite the denials, the SEC attorneys were hot on the case, and it did not take them long to act. On March 18, the SEC filed a lawsuit in federal court in Washington against Lance, Abedi, Metzger, Stephens, and the Arab investors. All were charged with violating U.S. securities laws by failing to disclose that they had secretly bought about twenty percent of the shares in Financial General. As often happens in SEC civil matters, the defendants had negotiated a settlement of the lawsuit even before it was filed. Without admitting or denying their guilt, the defendants promised not to violate securities laws again.

Under the terms of the settlement, the members of what was termed "the Lance group" also pledged to make restitution to shareholders who had lost money as a result of the attempted takeover. Three of the Arab defendants—Adham, Fulaij, and Darwaish—agreed either to sell their holdings in Financial General or to purchase all outstanding shares of the company at an above-market price within a year. The entire group also promised that any change in control or ownership of Financial General would be approved by federal banking authorities.

Bert Lance's dream of a glorious return to Washington was dashed. Largely through his bragging, the secret takeover of Financial General had been discovered and exposed. On top of that defeat, Lance faced other, more serious problems. His banking practices before joining the White House had come under investigation by a federal grand jury in Atlanta.

So, too, was Agha Hasan Abedi's scheme for quietly gaining control of a major American banking company vanquished, but he believed that he could still buy Financial General. He would just have to find another route. Abedi remained determined to find a way into America. And, though he had blown the first run at Financial General, Lance had unwittingly provided the means for the second attempt.

Clark Clifford had defended Lance when the Senate was hounding him and he was representing him in the new federal investigation, too. During the Financial General case, it was Lance who had arranged for Clifford to be hired by BCCI. Along the way, he had introduced the influential lawyer to Abedi. As was true for almost everyone who met Clark Clifford, Abedi had been impressed by the tall, patrician lawyer. In the wake of his second defeat in trying to enter United States banking, Abedi apparently decided that perhaps Clark Clifford could be enlisted to help him gain control of Financial General. If Abedi had learned anything during his banking career, it was the value of influential friends.

CHAPTER SIX

Dancing Elephants

Not long after he became president of the United States in 1961, John F. Kennedy gave a speech at an exclusive club in Washington. In it, he joked that his friend and personal lawyer, Clark Clifford, did not want a spot in the new administration as a reward for his long years of helping Democrats.

"You can't do anything for me," Kennedy said Clifford had told him. "But if you insist, the only thing I would ask is to have the name of my law firm printed on the back of the one-dollar bill."

Kennedy's wit cut to the heart of the matter. Beginning his third decade at the center of power in Washington, Clark Clifford was the undisputed king of the city's permanent government, the one that runs on money, politics, and influence. He had come to Washington from St. Louis in 1945 as an idealistic young aide. He stayed on to become one of the city's best-known lawyers.

His deep baritone voice, theatrical gestures, and tall frame topped by a shock of white hair gave him the look and bearing of a diplomat. Because Washington's unique brand of self-importance transforms all of its fixers into statesmen, Clifford was regarded as one of the city's wise men. In truth, he had no need for the advertising on the dollar bill. Everyone knew Clark Clifford and the unseen power he wielded.

Certainly, there was much for which to honor Clark Clifford. When Harry Truman became president in 1945 upon the death of Franklin D. Roosevelt, Clifford had come to the White House with James Vardaman, his mentor from Clifford's hometown of St. Louis. In his later memoirs, Clifford would describe his first job at the White House as redesigning the Presidential seal, but he went on to become a speech writer and a trusted adviser to Truman. He was a tactician and strategist who helped shape Truman's agenda.

And he went on to become an intimate adviser and lawyer to a succession of Democratic presidents and party leaders, including Kennedy and President Lyndon Johnson. By and large, he shunned formal power, preferring to operate backstage. With great reluctance, he agreed to serve as Johnson's secretary of defense during the Vietnam War, emerging as a hero to a generation of Democrats and war opponents by persuading the president not to escalate the bombing of North Vietnam in 1968.

His years as a Truman aide and that brief stint as defense secretary were Clifford's only government service, a scant six years. What he had built his career on was navigating the shoals of government, and his seat of power was his prosperous law firm, Clifford & Warnke. His work required some expertise in law and government, particularly as Washington became more complex.

But what Clifford truly traded on was his good name and the access it brought. His word was accepted by presidents and bureaucrats alike, which made him a popular employee of corporate titans and foreign governments in search of favors in Washington. The firm's list of clients over the years read like the Fortune 500—AT&T, Firestone, RCA, Standard Oil, ABC, TWA, DuPont, Phillips Petroleum, Howard Hughes, and a host of others.

To each, when they were new clients, Clifford recited a speech that associates at his law firm could repeat from memory: "I look forward to our association. But before we proceed, there is one point I must make clear. I do not consider that this firm will have any influence of any kind here in Washington. I cannot, and I will not, represent any client before the president or before any of his staff. If you want influence, you should consider going elsewhere. What we can offer you is an extensive knowledge of how to deal with the government on your problems."

The speech was a wink at propriety, a convenient fiction. Years later, journalist Jonathan Alter would characterize it this way: "It is a distillation of everything that is phony about power in the capital in the second half of the twentieth century. The denial of 'any influence of any kind here in Washington' is Orwellian in its boldness."

One can assume that this speech was delivered to Agha Hasan Abedi when he hired Clifford to represent BCCI in the United States. In reality, it was Clifford's influence and reputation that would enable Abedi to achieve what he had failed to do with the assistance of Bert Lance.

Three Arab investors who were part of the original group seeking Financial General Bankshares had decided to proceed with a buyout. They had been joined by eleven other Arabs. All were BCCI clients and Abedi was their financial adviser on the transaction.

Abedi wanted Clifford to be their lead lawyer in the takeover effort. If they were successful, Abedi said, then the investors would want Clifford to become chairman of the banking company and assemble a management team that would be above reproach. The Arabs, said Abedi, were passive investors who would not interfere in the bank's operation. They were just looking for a safe haven for their money.

Although takeovers were not his specialty, Clifford could certainly represent the investors in their dealings with the federal banking regulators, who would have much to say about the outcome of the fight. A big firm that specialized in takeovers could be brought in for the specialized work and still leave a few million in legal fees on the table for Clifford & Warnke.

Clifford's reasons for accepting the management offer would be the subject of intense, and sometimes harsh, speculation in later years. He was over seventy years old and appeared to have all the money he needed. Back in the sixties, rumor had it he was the first lawyer to make a million dollars. He never denied making that much money, only that he was the first. He lived in a stately home in Washington, with a staff of servants, and people were honestly in awe of him when he entered a hearing room or a drawing room.

Later, Clifford would claim that money was of no concern. Rather, he was eager for the new challenge of turning Financial General into a major banking force in the nation's capital, a test of his skill at a time when his peers were in retirement or in the grave.

"I didn't want to retire," Clifford later told a congressional committee in his rich voice, dragging out each word and syllable. "I didn't want to just sit on the porch and rock and wait to die. I said, 'Here is the chance. What if I could take this obscure company and build it into something important and big and impressive?'"

Some of his former law firm associates, however, would offer a different reason. They would say that Clifford's sources of business were dropping off. Even if he was not interested in retiring, many of those who had sent him business were gone. The law firm not only could use the legal fees from the takeover battle, it also could use the legal fees that could be passed its way by Clifford in his position at the helm of Financial General. To these people, admittedly not big fans of his, Clark Clifford took on the job out of greed.

Then, too, there was a psychological appeal. Despite a prominence and power that had outlasted presidents and enmeshed him deeply and powerfully in the fabric of Washington, Clark Clifford was a career supplicant. He had always had to ask for favors on behalf of himself or his clients, whether he was talking to a cabinet secretary or a plain secretary. As chairman of what would become Washington's biggest bank, he would be in a different position. Let people come to Clark Clifford with their hats in their hands for a change.

The second takeover had the earmarks of an Abedi operation from the start. The fourteen Arab investors formed a new holding company, Credit and Commerce American Holdings, in the Netherlands Antilles, another of the fraternity of secrecy havens. Even the name of the new company had the ring of BCCI. Known as CCAH, it would serve as the primary entity to make the offer to buy Financial General.

Two other companies were also created as part of the ownership chain. Credit and Commerce American Investments, or CCAI, was registered in the Netherlands as a subsidiary of CCAH. And FGB Holding Corporation was established in the District of Columbia to serve as the actual operating entity once control was acquired. Critics would complain that the alphabet soup of corporate shells was a device to conceal true ownership and control; Clifford would defend the different companies as tax devices.

Bank holding companies, such as Financial General, are entities that own or control more than one bank. They are regulated in the United States by the Federal Reserve Board, an agency more often associated in the public's mind with setting interest rates and keeping an eye on inflation.

On October 19, 1978, CCAH filed an application with the Federal Reserve in Washington seeking approval to proceed with the acquisition of Financial General. Three men, Kamal Adham, Faisal Saud al-Fulaij, and Abdullah Darwaish, would each control twenty-four percent of the stock in the bank. Darwaish was acting as representative of one of Sheik Zayed's sons, who was a minor. The remainder of the stock would be split among the other eleven investors. The chief lawyers on the application were Clifford and his protégé, Robert Altman.

The application proved premature. The Arabs had not yet made peace with the Financial General executives, and the management opposed the acquisition. In battling the takeover, Financial General's lawyers had a legal advantage that not even Clifford could surmount. Financial General's Maryland subsidiary bank was among those units opposing the takeover. Maryland had a law that prohibited the hostile takeover of any Maryland bank. The Maryland banking commissioner said the deal would violate the law. On February 16, 1979, the Federal Reserve Board dismissed the application, citing the Maryland law.

Clifford and Altman challenged the board's decision, but they also worked behind the scenes negotiating with Frank Saul, William Middendorf, and other investors aligned against them. Before the appeal could be decided, the Arab investors reached an agreement with Financial General. In July of 1980, it was announced that the Arabs would buy the company for $130 million, about $15 million more than the earlier offer. The deal still needed federal approval, and in November CCAH made another application to the Federal Reserve.

Crafting the second application required special care. The lawyers and the investors did not want this one blowing up on them. Everyone, including the staff at the Fed, was aware of the Securities and Exchange Commission consent decree on the first attempted takeover of Financial General and the role of BCCI and Abedi in the incidents that led to it. Assurances would have to be made to the regulators that BCCI was in no way involved this time around. The regulators had to be convinced that this was different. Where Bert Lance had been Abedi's hired man the first time around, a far smoother team was now in place.

The new application specified that the Arab investors would be passive and take no part in the management or operation of Financial General. The management was to rest with a board of directors that would include Clifford as chairman, his long-time friend, former Missouri senator Stuart Symington, and retired Air Force General Elwood Quesada. In addition, an experienced banker would be chosen as president and chief executive of Financial General before final federal action on the application.

That was only the start. Clifford and company began a round of intense lobbying of the state and federal officials who would be involved in the decision. Abedi joined them for a meeting with John Heimann, who had moved up from New York bank superintendent to comptroller of the currency in Washington. Abedi stressed to him that this deal was not the same as the one that Heimann had rejected in New York. Clifford and Altman met with the banking commissioner in Maryland, providing assurances that this was a friendly transaction, well within state law. And the two lawyers met with Sidney Bailey, the Virginia commissioner of financial institutions, who was expressing objections to the sale of one of his state's banks to foreign investors.

Bailey had been a bank examiner with the U.S. comptroller of the currency for nearly twenty years before becoming the chief financial regulator in Virginia. He prided himself on running an extremely tight ship, keeping an examiner's close eye on the financial picture of all the banks in his domain.

Bailey did not like the fact that one of his state's largest banks was going to come under foreign control. Though his reasons would later be misinterpreted as a suspicion that BCCI was behind the takeover, in fact Bailey was opposed to the concept of any foreign investors owning a major bank in his domain. Indeed, at the time, Bailey made it known that he felt the fact that the owners of the bank would reside in foreign countries and be protected by a series of shell companies registered outside the United States was bad for all regulators. Clifford realized that Bailey had no legal grounds for blocking the sale, but he did not want the feisty regulator stirring things up with the Fed, so he and Altman went to see Bailey in his Richmond office.

"These are honest, honorable, upright people who would be nothing more than passive investors looking for a safe haven for their money," Clifford told Bailey. "They perceive the United States as being the best of all safe havens right now. Investing in a banking organization is the epitome of a safe haven. They have nothing more in mind than the well-being and improvement of this institution. They intend to do nothing detrimental to the institution or misuse it."

Clifford tried to ease Bailey's mind on his central objection, saying: "They will respond to any questions that any regulator might have. There is no cause for concern about these individuals, their purposes, or their relationships."

Bailey remained unpersuaded. In a voice nearly as deep as Clifford's, he summed up his objections: "You can't send the sheriff after them."

Virginia had no law against a foreign entity buying one of its banks, or any other institution for that matter. Bailey could complain all he liked, but Clark Clifford would no doubt prevail in a war of words up in Washington.

The Federal Reserve had its own concerns about the proposal. They centered on the independence of the investors from the Bank of Credit and Commerce. These concerns were obvious ones, in light of the role played by BCCI and Abedi in the earlier run at Financial General, which was stopped by the SEC. It would turn out, however, that there was little the regulators could do to discover the truth of the relationship between the bank and these customers and shareholders who claimed to be acting independently.

A key factor in the litmus test on independence was financing. Was BCCI bankrolling the purchase? The agency requested detailed information from the fourteen investors on their financial resources and the source of funds for buying the bank. The replies, most of which were certified by accountants, showed that the Arabs were people of considerable wealth and that the funds were coming from their personal resources.

That did not mean, of course, that the principals were required to come up with the $130 million in cash from their own pockets. Fifty million dollars of the money, in fact, was going to be a loan to CCAH from a small French bank, Banque Arabe et Internationale

Investissement. There was nothing unusual about the loan, which would be backed by the personal guarantees of the wealthiest investors. And there appeared to be no BCCI involvement.

What the regulators failed to discover was that the French bank and BCCI had interlocking boards of directors. In other words, a person who served on the BCCI board also served on the French bank's board. In this case, the common director was Yves Lamarche, who had once supervised the Bank of America investment in BCCI.

Lamarche had gotten to know Abedi during the years that the Bank of America and BCCI were partners. It was through his role at the California bank that Lamarche had first been appointed to a seat on the board of BCCI Holdings. But he had quit Bank of America in the mid-1970s and gone on to become the chairman and director of a new bank in Paris, Banque Arabe et Internationale Investissement. He had not, however, resigned his BCCI seat and he had retained close personal and professional ties to the bank and to Abedi. The two banks did a lot of business together.

Had the Federal Reserve uncovered the relationship between BCCI and the French bank, would it have made a difference in the outcome? Not by itself. There was nothing illegal about the relationship between the two banks. But had the interlocking boards and business dealings been disclosed, it would have suggested a possible link between BCCI and $50 million of the purchase money. That might have provided the necessary grounds for delving deeper into the exact source of the other funds. While the application to acquire Financial General did not disclose the relationship, it was no secret. The Fed staff could have uncovered the interlocking board with a little digging. They did not. Perhaps the failure to uncover the tie was an example of the faith that the staff put in the word of Clark Clifford that BCCI was not tied to the financing of the transaction.

What the regulators probably could not have discovered at the time was the secret deal between BCCI and the French bank, BAII, that was later alleged in a 1991 Federal Reserve proceeding against BCCI. The Federal Reserve contends that BAII was unwilling to make the $50 million loan solely on its own and had tried to assemble a syndicate of banks to share the risk. When that effort failed, BCCI stepped in and negotiated an agreement in which BCCI would guarantee the loan. BAII's attorneys rejected the idea, so another plan was needed.

The solution was a complicated one. According to the government, Adham would deposit $30 million of personal funds with BAII as collateral for the $50 million loan. In addition, he and Fulaij would sign personal notes guaranteeing repayment of the total amount in the event of a default. In fact, the entire $30 million for the deposit was loaned to Adham through BCCI's subsidiary bank in the Cayman Islands, International Credit and Investment Company Overseas. Adham allegedly received a written document from ICIC Overseas that said that he was not responsible for repaying the $30 million. In addition, he and Fulaij supposedly received written assurances that BCCI would be responsible for fulfilling their personal guarantees for the $50 million loan. In effect, BCCI had arranged for and financed the entire loan from the French bank. It had done so through a series of secret agreements kept from the regulators.

The loan arrangement was only part of the deception. Adham, Fulaij, and the other investors said in the application that they were using their own funds to purchase Financial General. Outside accountants would claim much later that, in a series of secret agreements, BCCI had loaned each of the investors the money used to buy the American banking company. In addition to the French loan, for example, Adham had agreed to put up $13 million of his own cash for his shares in Financial General. The accountants said that the money actually was a loan from BCCI, with the Financial General shares as collateral. Through similar arrangements with the others, BCCI had allegedly financed the entire acquisition and obtained the shares of the banking company as collateral. All of this, of course, was contingent upon the Federal Reserve not discovering the arrangements and approving Agha Hasan Abedi's clandestine move into the United States.

There was a curious omission in the background data collected on the Arabs, too. Checks were made with various federal agencies, such as the Federal Bureau of Investigation, the Central Intelligence Agency, and the Securities and Exchange Commission. Kamal Adham was the largest investor in CCAH, yet the CIA information on him did not disclose that he was the former head of Saudi Arabian intelligence. Federal Reserve staff members would say later that they were generally aware of Adham's past work in intelligence, but they said it was not grounds for objecting to him.

It is unclear how much the CIA knew about BCCI and its investors at this point. Later, the agency would acknowledge that it was moving money through accounts at the bank in the early 1980s. And a five-page report on BCCI written by CIA analysts in 1986 indicated that BCCI had obtained control over First American Bank, the successor to Financial General. In 1981, however, the agency did not have the total picture on BCCI. What the CIA did know for sure was that Kamal Adham had been chief of Saudi intelligence, for Adham had worked closely with the CIA and its agents in Saudi Arabia in earlier years. Eventually he had hired one of the agency's former station chiefs as a business consultant. Yet the CIA failed to report any of this to the Federal Reserve in 1981.

This was a high-profile case. There had been plenty of press about the aborted takeover effort, and there was heightened public concern over Arab investment in the United States in general. So, despite the sweeping denials in the application and in private meetings with Clifford and Altman, the Federal Reserve staff wanted a public record stating categorically that the Bank of Credit and Commerce was not involved in buying Financial General. It was unusual for the Fed to air a case in public, but this was an unusual case.

At nine-thirty on the morning of April 23, 1981, a public hearing was begun in Room B1215 of the Federal Reserve Building at Twentieth and Constitution in Washington. Present were six staff members of the Federal Reserve, led by deputy general counsel Robert Mannion, four of the Arab investors along with Clifford and Altman, and a host of other regulators from Maryland, Virginia, New York, and the comptroller of the currency.

The atmosphere was polite and friendly as Clifford shook hands with the regulators gathered in the large hearing room and introduced his Arab clients. Standing off to one side, apart from the others, was Sidney Bailey, the Virginia regulator. He had never changed his mind about the advisability of the transaction, and he was here to get his objections on the record. The more he had thought about this proposed deal, the more his opposition had solidified. There was a bit of xenophobia in his position: Bailey just did not want foreigners owning a string of banks that reached from New York through Washington and his own state. He was the only regulator to submit a list of written questions about the transaction before the hearing.

Bailey was the first speaker. As is his style, he was blunt. He ran through eight specific objections to the deal. The investors were outside the reach of U.S. laws in case of trouble. Loans and other transactions between Financial General's banks and foreign banks could not be monitored or controlled. And Bailey was concerned about the credibility of the financial statements provided by the investors, assertions he described as the "unsubstantiated claims with which the applications are replete." While Bailey had no way of knowing, among the omissions on the financial statements were the extensive lending relationships between BCCI and the prospective Financial General investors, such as Kamal Adham.

Based on what Bailey did know, the whole scheme did not seem to make sense from an investment standpoint. Why, asked Bailey, had these investors spent three years and millions of dollars to buy Financial General? Logically, the expenditure and effort seemed far beyond the financial value of the bank, particularly considering the hostility that greeted the initial bid.

"There can be little doubt that some incentive other than orthodox investment motives must have prompted this effort," said Bailey. "Virtually endless speculation on this question is possible. Why choose Financial General when numerous other investment choices with more attractive financial characteristics would have been available?"

Stone-faced and reading from his prepared text, Bailey answered his own question: "One obvious plausible answer to this riddle lies in the unique position of Financial General in the market. No other single financial institution is situated in both the financial and government hubs of the United States."

When Bailey finished, Mannion dismissed him with a curt thank-you. Regulators did not speak in innuendo or engage in speculation. They dealt in facts and the law. Mannion turned to the next speaker, Clark Clifford.

Here was a forum in which a man of Clifford's eloquence and stature could excel. He had made his reputation not through courtroom preeminence, rarely in fact setting foot in court. His was a mastery of the private meeting behind closed doors and the public presentation to awed government officials. These sessions are scripted and rehearsed as carefully as any courtroom drama. Clifford and Altman had spent much of the previous week crafting the opening statement that Clifford would deliver and the more detailed presentation by Altman.

A man who knows him once described Clifford's rich voice this way: "There's that soft, confidential, complimentary tone. All your defenses go down."

After expressing his thanks for the opportunity to describe the project "in which we believe so deeply," Clifford dismissed Bailey with a polite stiletto: he would respond to the Virginia regulator's questions in writing later.

Then he wrapped himself in the flag that many in Washington would believe Clifford himself had sewn. Thoughtful Americans, Clifford explained, knew it was in the country's interest to bring back as many of the dollars as possible that were being sent to Arab oil nations. Here was a chance to repatriate some of those dollars by allowing Arabs to invest in American banking. They would be, he assured his audience, passive investors. They would leave the banking to Clifford and the men who would join him on the board of directors of the new entity, outstanding Americans one and all.

For about twenty minutes, Clifford's oratory continued. Financial General, he felt, would grow as he and his friends brought in new business from their contacts with big American corporations. There was no down side to the deal, as Clifford saw it, only a very substantial chance to improve the bank and make it grow.

"Let me conclude on a personal note," he said, lowering his voice as he described his meetings over the past months with Kamal Adham, the leading investor. "I have come to have the deepest respect for his character, for his reputation, for his honor, and for his integrity. I'm proud to be an associate of his. I look forward with real anticipation to continuing to be an associate of his. He is the kind of man with whom I like to be associated."

Just as he had wrapped himself in the flag at the outset, Clifford was now lending his mantle to Adham and, by inference, the other investors. They were good enough for Clark Clifford, so they sure as hell must be good enough for the Federal Reserve Board.

Adham was gracious, even if he was not totally candid. He was, he said, educated in Britain and Egypt and spoke five languages. He described himself as a businessman, with holdings in construction and manufacturing. He neglected to mention that in 1977 he had retired as chief of intelligence in Saudi Arabia.

A contradiction arose when Adham described how he became interested in Financial General. He told the hearing that he had been contacted by a friend at the Saudi embassy in Washington who suggested the bank might be a good investment. Documents released earlier in the SEC case and the civil litigation brought by Financial General in 1978 indicated quite clearly that it was Agha Hasan Abedi who had first proposed buying the shares to Adham.

Mannion seemed to accept Adham's explanation that it was he who had asked BCCI to take a look at the prospects of Financial General, but he tried to pursue the international bank's role in assembling the investors in his questioning of Faisal Saud al-Fulaij, the Kuwaiti businessman. Fulaij said that he had been looking for investments in the United States when BCCI suggested Financial General. Though they were prominent customers of BCCI, both men said they did not know initially about the other's involvement. Indeed, they said they did not recall having spoken to each other for ten years. Their mutual involvement, said Adham, was mere coincidence.

"Such things happen in our part of the world where, if I have an interest in an investment, I usually tell my friends that we have an investment like this," said Adham.

Curiously, neither Adham nor Fulaij mentioned their joint interest in the Kuwait International Finance Company, even though KIFCO had promised to loan them part of the purchase price for Financial General the first time they tried to buy it.

At the hearing, Adham also dismissed the notion that he and the other investors were fronts for BCCI, saying, "I would like to assure you that each one on his own rights will not accept in any way to be a cover for somebody else."

Questions were asked, however, about the relationship with BCCI. It was Mannion who brought up the similarity of the names—Credit and Commerce American Holdings and Bank of Credit and Commerce International.

Coincidence, replied Clifford. Credit and commerce are terms used extensively in Persian Gulf financial affairs. Added Altman, "Other than similarity in certain respects, there is no connection between those entities and BCCI in terms of ownership or other relationship."

Lloyd Bostian, Jr., an official with the Federal Reserve's office in Richmond, pursued the relationship. He noted that BCCI had been an adviser early on in the deal and might be called upon later to provide similar help.

"What precisely is their function, if any, in this proposal at the present time?" asked Bostian.

"None," replied Clifford emphatically. "There is no function of any kind on the part of BCCI. I know of no present relationship. I know of no planned future relationship that exists, and other than that, I don't know what else there is to say, Mr. Bostian."

Reflecting on the day-long session several years later, Sid Bailey described his feelings in a straightforward and homespun manner: "I felt like a mouse in a room full of dancing elephants."

On August 25, 1981, the Federal Reserve Board unanimously approved the acquisition of Financial General Bankshares by Credit and Commerce American Holdings. The investigation had uncovered no overt links with BCCI. The investors appeared to be rich. A board of directors led by prominent Americans would be appointed to oversee the operations.

In the deal that wouldn't close, there was still a hitch. The transaction could not be final until the superintendent of banking in New York approved the group's application to take over two Financial General banks there, Bank of Commerce in New York City and Community State Bank in Albany. Political problems were stalling the okay in New York.

Manfred Ohrenstein, a state senator and leader of the Democratic Party in New York, claimed that the Arab investors were trying to "sneak in the back door" to acquire the two New York banks by buying

Financial General. Rather than the recycling-of-oil-money line peddled by Clifford, the New York politician saw a different motive.

"This is a sophisticated attempt to acquire a network of banks across the Eastern seaboard and put a stranglehold on the petrodollars coming into this country," charged Ohrenstein.

Clifford responded by hopping on an airplane and going to New York for a chat with Muriel Siebert, who had succeeded John Heimann as the state's banking superintendent. The white-haired lawyer assured Siebert that his clients were upstanding people interested only in returning American money to the economy and finding a safe place for their own wealth. Siebert had some qualms of her own about the deal, principally because American banks and investors did not have the same freedom to buy banks in Arab countries. In fact, in Kamal Adham's home of Saudi Arabia, foreigners were prohibited from owning any business or even land.

Clifford's clout did not reach outside the Beltway, at least this time. Chiefly through the efforts of Ohrenstein, the New York State Banking Board rejected the group's application to buy the two New York banks in November 1981. Eight votes had been needed to win and there had been only five in favor of the deal on the twelve-member board.

It was a setback, but one that could be remedied swiftly if the investors promised to sell the two New York banks once the deal was completed. That should have been simple enough, since neither bank was a large component of Financial General, but Abedi was intent on controlling banks in both New York, the financial capital of the United States, and in Washington, its government center. A compromise was proposed. The Arab investors agreed to sell their shares in the larger of the two New York banks, the Bank of Commerce. In exchange, they wanted permission for the Albany bank to open an office in New York City. There also was a threat: If the state regulators did not approve the new plan, both banks would be converted from state institutions to federal ones, essentially removing New York's jurisdiction entirely. Since federal regulators had already approved the acquisition, transferring the jurisdiction appeared to be little more than a formality.

On March 2, 1982, with this gun to its head, the New York banking board approved the new proposal by a vote of nine to two. In a letter to the Fed, the New York banking department said that "the information we received indicated that the investors were prestigious and reputable people."

Observed Muriel Siebert, "I've never seen so much political maneuvering in my life."

With the last obstacle removed, the takeover of this promising banking franchise in the nation's capital by a band of Arab investors was consummated on April 19, 1982. Three months later, the name of the institution was changed to First American. Clark Clifford was elected chairman of the board of the banking company. His young partner, Robert Altman, was named its president.

Before the boldly named bank could get the regulators out of its hair, however, there was another flap. Listed as one of the principals on the CCAH application to buy Financial General was Abdullah Darwaish, who was identified as the representative of one of Sheik Zayed's minor sons. Darwaish also was chairman of the Abu Dhabi Investment Authority and of the nation's Department of Private Affairs, or DPA. And, while the application was pending, he ran into trouble with the ruling family in that capacity.

As DPA head since 1975, Darwaish had been in charge of investing the billions of dollars in oil revenue flowing into the country. This was considered the sheik's money by one and all, since he was the absolute ruler. The investments were pretty conservative, with the bulk of the money invested in United States Treasury bonds.

At the end of 1981, Darwaish lost $96 million of the sheik's money investing in copper futures through an American broker living in Switzerland. The investments were registered in the name of Financiera Avenida, a Panamanian company. Sheik Zayed apparently thought his agents were buying gold. When he discovered they had plunged into the copper market and, worse yet, lost his money, he immediately placed Darwaish and his two senior assistants under arrest. Darwaish also was stripped of his positions with DPA and as representative of the sheik's son.

News of the arrests did not reach the United States until August 1982, well after the final application by the Arab investors and its approval by the Fed. In fact, the Fed learned of the incident when Jerry Knight of The Washington Post, who had been chronicling the long takeover saga, wrote a story raising questions about why the regulators had not been notified of Darwaish's arrest before it approved the Financial General takeover. The day after the article appeared, Michael Bradfield, the general counsel at the Fed, wrote a letter to Clark Clifford demanding to know what was going on with Darwaish.

In language that would one day become familiar, Clifford wrote back claiming that the Post story was "inaccurate, misleading, unwarranted, and irresponsible." Accordingly, he said, he had expressed his views to Benjamin Bradlee, the newspaper's executive editor. Further, said Clifford, Darwaish's activities as an investment adviser to the sheik were totally unrelated to his role as agent for the sheik's son. Nonetheless, the son had decided to fire Darwaish and would supervise his investment in Financial General personally.

There were some interesting footnotes to the incident. When officials in Abu Dhabi discovered that the $96 million had been lost, they began gathering up all the documents they could find about Financiera Avenida. The bulk of the information was discovered in file cabinets at the London headquarters of the Bank of Credit and Commerce International, where the Panamanian company had been given some office space.

The person who led the investigation for the government of Abu Dhabi, Ghanim Faris al-Mazrui, was the secretary general of the Abu Dhabi Investment Authority and a member of the board of BCCI Holdings. Also, during the time the losses occurred, one of Darwaish's advisers on the panel overseeing the sheik's investments was Agha Hasan Abedi. It seemed to be yet another example of the tangled relationships among BCCI, its customers, its shareholders, and the royal family of Abu Dhabi.

CHAPTER SEVEN

Noriega's Favorite Bank

The chartered Learjet out of Tampa described lazy circles in the crystal-blue sky above Omar Torrijos Airport in Panama City before receiving permission from the control tower to set down. With a thump and a squeal of rubber tires, the jet landed on the runway and taxied rapidly to a spot near the military portion of the field.

Armed guards in khaki uniforms watched distractedly as a handsome young man in a business suit stepped down the stairs of the private jet and walked toward a waiting limousine. He was carrying a large suitcase and a leather attaché case, but no attempt was made to search his luggage or examine his passport.

Steven Kalish, who was lugging the two bags, had a problem. He had too much money, literally. His lakeside home in Tampa, Florida, had a swimming pool, a Jacuzzi, a carport for his Ferrari and BMW, and several rooms filled with cash.

On September 22, 1983, the day his private jet landed in Panama, the high school dropout was sitting on $35 million in profits from recent marijuana smuggling operations. The money machines used to count the dollars had been shut off. They could not keep up with the volume, so the counters had switched to weighing the money. A single U.S. currency note weighs one gram, about 450 bills to the pound.

For several weeks, Kalish had been searching for a new way to move his cash out of the United States and into the banking system of some foreign country. The dilemma had taken on an air of urgency because he had just bought one million pounds of high-grade marijuana in Colombia. He expected to earn $300 million when it was brought to the United States and sold. His organization had been doing some of its illegal banking in the Cayman Islands, but Kalish did not think that the banks there could handle the volume of cash he was about to generate.

So he decided to try Panama. It had a reputation as a place where bankers did not ask too many questions about large cash deposits. Through two intermediaries, Kalish had arranged a trial run. Bring at least $2 million, he was told, as a sign that he was a serious person.

The suitcase that Kalish shoved into the trunk of the waiting limousine weighed about forty-four pounds. It contained $2 million, all in one-hundred-dollar bills. The briefcase, which Kalish kept by his side, contained $300,000, also in hundreds. This smaller amount represented the token gift he had been instructed to bring for an important person, General Manuel Antonio Noriega, who had just become military commander of Panama.

After the short drive from the airport, the limousine pulled up in front of the Bank of Boston building in downtown Panama City. Kalish got out with his bags, but he bypassed the American bank branch. Instead he took an elevator to a private club atop the building. There, he met Cesar Rodriguez.

A one-time drug pilot whose friendship and business deals with Noriega were making him rich, Rodriguez liked to flaunt his wealth and his connection to Noriega. He had bought a $1.2 million house next to one of Noriega's homes and operated a fleet of limousines and jets. Often both the planes and the cars were used for drug trafficking. He owned the Tower Club, where he was meeting the young drug smuggler.

When Kalish explained his cash flow problem, the Panamanian was eager to help. He offered an entire package of banking and investment services, right down to an armored car that would pick up the cash at Torrijos Airport and transport it to a bank downtown—naturally, all without the formality of customs checks and under the watchful eye of the military. And naturally, all for an up-front payment and a percentage of each shipment.

As for a bank, Panama City was a very cosmopolitan city and a small town. Rodriguez said he knew all the important bankers. Many of them belonged to the private club where they were sitting.

With the help of Rodriguez and local lawyers, Kalish that day set up a dummy corporation and deposited the $2 million in an account at a bank in Panama that afternoon. The following afternoon, he was taken to meet Noriega at one of the general's homes. They had a brief conversation. As Kalish was leaving, Noriega mentioned that he had forgotten his attaché case.

"Oh, it's for you," said Kalish as he walked out the door, leaving that famous pockmarked face smiling behind him.

Less than a month later, Kalish was back for more. Again, he brought $2.5 million in cash. Again, his jet taxied to the military portion of Torrijos Airport and Kalish was picked up by a limousine. When he arrived downtown, Rodriguez treated Kalish like an old and honored friend. The first deposit and the forgotten briefcase had clearly worked. He was a serious person.

"The general wants to see that you get the best service, so I will help you open an account with General Noriega's favorite bank," said Rodriguez. "It is called the Bank of Credit and Commerce International."

BCCI's man in Panama was Amjad Awan. Since his arrival two years earlier in his post as country manager, Awan had presided over a sharp rise in deposits, the ultimate measure of success at BCCI anywhere in the world.

Not only had he made BCCI the favorite bank of Noriega, Awan himself was Noriega's favorite banker, thanks to an array of professional and personal services that he had lavished on the general. In return, Noriega often referred customers to BCCI and helped fuel its growth in the country.

Though chilling stories would one day be told about his violence, perversity, and venality, Noriega could be a charming associate. In part because of his own background, Awan got along well with the general.

Amjad Awan was born in Kashmir on July 30, 1947, two weeks before the creation of Pakistan. His father, Ayub Awan, had joined the government of the new nation as a top police official. Eventually, he became chief of Pakistan's domestic intelligence service, a post that Noriega once held in Panama. Awan's father-in-law, Mohammad Asghar Khan, was Pakistan's first air force chief of staff and later chairman of Pakistan International Airlines.

After his graduation in 1968 from a leading Pakistani university with a degree in economics, Awan had pursued a career in banking, rather than government service. He spent three years with United Bank in Karachi, where he brushed shoulders with its president, Agha Hasan Abedi.

Unlike Abedi, however, Awan stayed on at United Bank for two years after it was nationalized. Much of Awan's career had been spent in United's London office. That is where he was working when, in 1976, he joined a subsidiary of the Bank of Montreal as a vice president of marketing. Part of Awan's territory was Dubai, the small Persian Gulf nation next to Abu Dhabi.

Late in 1978, Awan received a telephone call from his countryman and former United Bank colleague. Similar calls had been placed to Pakistani bankers around the world in recent years as BCCI sought to staff its swelling network of branches.

"I need you to come work for me," said Abedi.

Awan was young and full of energy, and he was well aware of BCCI and its growth. Many friends from his days at United already had joined the bank. Awan was not inclined to resist the overtures to patriotism and membership in the family of BCCI profferred so persuasively by Abedi. By early December, he had signed on and was marketing manager of BCCI's main branch in London.

BCCI's major customer base was still the immigrant community in Britain, particularly the Pakistanis whose savings and transfers of money home had formed its original base. Many Third World customers came to BCCI because they felt they were treated shabbily at Britain's staid institutions, such as Barclays and Lloyds. Shortly after Awan arrived at BCCI there was an influx of Ugandans who told him that they found BCCI a far more comfortable place for their banking than the other London banks. The bank did a booming business in North London, where it catered to hundreds of small Asian-owned businesses. At the same time, BCCI was still wooing the rising number of free-spending Arabs who had discovered gambling and other pleasures of life away from the parched desert shiekdoms.

The Bank of England's concerns about BCCI remained, although its regulatory actions were limited. When Britain passed a new banking law in 1978, the regulators were able to divide banks into two classes. A "recognized" bank was a full-service institution deemed to have met the highest standards. A "licensed deposit taker" was a lower class of bank that was prohibited from doing some forms of banking business. BCCI was denied the higher status, but there was no indication that the action affected its growth or its management.

Indeed, although still registered legally in Luxembourg and the Cayman Islands, the bank's headquarters were in London. And it was from those offices that its headlong expansion was being guided. Espousing its radical Third World political rhetoric and exploiting its association with an organization called the Third World Foundation, BCCI was making inroads with developing nations throughout Africa, Asia, the Middle East, and Latin America. Often it did so by cultivating local leaders and by aligning itself with various self-help projects designed to polish its image.

In this milieu, who you know can be more useful than what you know, and Amjad Awan was a welcome addition to those who were cultivating this part of the world on behalf of BCCI. The prominence of his family and that of his wife's opened many doors, including those of the diplomatic circles. His own intelligence and polish made him instantly likable.

"He can talk about international banking or any number of other

79

subjects with knowledge and humor," one of his later associates said in describing Awan. "He is just a charming fellow to be around. A real gentleman."

In his rounds of the various diplomatic emissaries in London, one of the men Awan met soon after he arrived at BCCI was Guillermo Vega, the Panamanian ambassador to London. Vega was already a friend of Awan's boss, a Pakistani named Allaudin Shaik, and he took an immediate liking to Awan, adding him in his social and business circles.

When Panamanian President Arístides Royo came to London in 1979, Awan and Shaik were among those invited to a dinner at Vega's residence. There, Awan met Royo and an entourage of ministers and military leaders. Royo's party included General Omar Torrijos, the military dictator of Panama since 1968 and the man who had picked Royo as the puppet president. Another member of the group was a lieutenant colonel named Manuel Antonio Noriega.

Noriega was chief of G-2, the Panamanian intelligence service, and a man of increasing power in Panama. Torrijos, who had negotiated the Panama Canal Treaty the year before, was beginning a gradual retreat from the day-to-day running of the country.

For years, Noriega had been selling information to the American and Cuban intelligence services. During the Panama Canal Treaty negotiations, he had even supplied the Central Intelligence Agency with information about his own country's positions and strategy. At the same time, he plotted with other military men and flunky politicians within Panama. As Torrijo's interest in ruling Panama waned, Noriega's waxed.

BCCI was trying to open a branch in Panama, so Shaik, who was head of central marketing for the bank, had instructed Awan to be as helpful as possible to the visiting Panamanians. In a pattern that he would repeat often in the coming years, Awan arranged dinners for the Panamanians at fancy restaurants and escorted them around the city. Noriega loved traveling and staying in lavish hotels, and he was in London often. Over the course of his many visits, he was escorted frequently by Awan.

This type of coddling paid off. In 1980, the government of Panama granted the Bank of Credit and Commerce International a license to open for business. Abedi flew over to Panama from London for the opening festivities. President Royo dedicated the office, and Colonel Noriega attended as the personal representative of General Torrijos. Abedi gave a speech announcing that Panama would be his bridge to Latin America. The ceremony was followed by a lavish reception in the Portobello Room of the Panama Hilton. It was the most extravagant bank opening the town had seen. And why not, for BCCI had just received the key to a golden kingdom of green money and white powder.

Bank competition in Panama was intense, with virtually every major international bank in the world operating there. Barclays was in Panama, as were Citibank, Chase Manhattan, Bank of Boston, Union Bank of Switzerland, and dozens of others. Part of the lure was the trade that moved through the Panama Canal and the Colón Free Trade Zone, which served as a jumping-off point for much of the world's exports to South America. But there was a greater appeal, at least to some of the bankers.

During the late 1970s and early 1980s, illegal dollars began to enter Panama in vast quantities via private planes, baggage on commercial flights, and as air freight. The corruption in the Panamanian military made it all easy and risk-free; soldiers supervised the off-loading of cash into armored cars that hauled the money directly to the banks. Once the money was tucked away in a bank account, anonymity was guaranteed by tight bank secrecy laws and a coterie of lawyers willing to serve as front men.

By the end of the administration of President Jimmy Carter, U.S. intelligence had recognized Panama's increasing importance as a center for laundering drug money, particularly for the cocaine kingpins of neighboring Colombia. Not long after that, a Panamanian justice minister, Jorge Riba, summed up his country's attitude when he said: "There is no such thing as good or bad money. To me, money is neutral."

Late in 1981, Awan asked for a transfer out of London. After three years in London with BCCI and two with Bank of Montreal, he was eager for a new country. He was offered Zambia or Panama. He chose Panama.

Outside influences also were at work. The first manager of the Panama City branch was not working out to Noriega's satisfaction. He was too cool to Noriega's business partners, too cautious to play the drug-money game. Noriega showed his displeasure without much subtlety. When the manager's brother flew in for a visit, airport immigration officials kept him sitting for eighteen hours while they checked to see if his visa was genuine. When the manager complained about the incident to London, the bank's higher-ups decided that his services were no longer needed in Panama. Another BCCI official was dispatched to tell Noriega that a new, more flexible manager would soon arrive.

When Awan arrived with his wife Sheereen and two preteen children, they were met at the airport by a local BCCI employee and Noriega's secretary, Marcela Tason. The secretary ushered Awan and his family to the diplomatic lounge while Panamanian officials rushed his baggage through customs.

"It's curious," said Awan. "As an executive of this bank, I've had the opportunity to travel a lot, but this is the first time I've been received in the diplomatic lounge." He would soon get a taste of what real power could do.

At the time, BCCI's operation in Panama was prospering but not prosperous. The bank served businessmen on the periphery of the large international trading community built around the Colón Free Trade Zone. Mostly they were Palestinian and Lebanese merchants living in Panama. Accounts averaged from $50,000 to $200,000. Few inroads had been made into the world of international finance and corrupt cash, where the real money was to be made.

One of the keys to changing that was Noriega. In July of 1981, Torrijos had been killed in an airplane crash. After the death of Torrijos, Noriega had been vying with three other generals to grab control of the country. He was clearly a man on the rise, and an account with him would send a signal to others that BCCI was a player in Panama.

Renewing his relationship and cultivating Noriega became Awan's top priority. It took several weeks and a series of expensive dinners and long conversations, but Noriega finally agreed to open an account at BCCI.

"This will be a secret account, a secret service account," explained Noriega, who was still intelligence chief. "You must keep it highly confidential. None of the staff at the bank must know about the account, particularly the Panamanian employees. I am the only one who will control this account. You will act only on verbal or written instructions from me and nobody else."

The account was opened in the name of the Panamanian Defense Forces with a deposit of around $200,000 in cash. Soon, it swelled to several million dollars. Eventually, the balance would exceed $20 million.

As instructed, Awan handled the account personally. Credit cards were issued to Noriega, his wife, and his three daughters. The bills were sent directly to Awan at BCCI and paid out of the account. As Noriega's confidence in him grew, Awan began handling even more sensitive matters.

Noriega became military commander of Panama in August 1983 after promising to support the presidential candidacy of another general, Ruben Dario Paredes. Secretly, however, Noriega moved quickly to prepare for the elections scheduled for the following May. Acting behind the scenes, he used other politicians to denounce and neutralize Paredes. Within weeks, Paredes was finished as a politician. The way was open for Noriega's candidate for president, Nicolas Barletta.

Up to that point, the secret BCCI account had been used to finance trips and lavish spending by Noriega and his family. With the campaign, the general found another use for it.

He began to telephone Awan at the bank. Someone will be coming by with a note signed by me, Noriega would say. Give him the amount of cash on the note. When the visitor arrived at BCCI's head office in a complex attached to the Panama City Hilton, Awan would draw the cash from Noriega's account and hand it over to the man bearing the note. Many of the faces he recognized. They were prominent Panamanian politicians.

On election day, Panamanian soldiers fired on demonstrators and the military slowed the vote count to a crawl, afraid that Barletta was going to lose. In the end, more cash payoffs were made so that Noriega's candidate could win by a narrow margin.

Noriega's inner circle also was doing business with Awan and BCCI. One of the general's closest friends and business partners, Enrique Pretelt, opened an account for his chain of exclusive jewelry stores. Pretelt in turn brought in Cesar Rodriguez, who opened accounts at the bank for some of his many enterprises. He often referred customers to BCCI, too.

Among those recommended by Rodriguez was Ricardo Bilonick, an American-educated Panamanian pilot and sometime-diplomat who owned an airfreight company that specialized in flying cocaine for Colombia's Medellín cartel. For each load, Bilonick paid a fee of several hundred thousand dollars to Noriega on behalf of the cartel.

One day in 1983, Bilonick walked into the main BCCI branch in downtown Panama City and told Awan that he wanted to open an account with a $1 million line of credit for his cargo business. No, he said, he did not intend to put up any security for the account. When Awan politely told him that he would need security for such an account, Bilonick left.

A few days later, he returned and opened an account through one of Awan's assistants. He deposited a large amount of cash into the account and immediately took out a loan against it. The amount of the loan was almost the same as the account, minus a one percent fee charged by the bank. Bilonick never returned and the bank simply took his cash deposit in payment on the loan.

This was not an unusual transaction for BCCI or other banks in Panama. BCCI even had a name for it—"a cash-collateralized advance." Fancy name aside, it was a simple but effective form of money laundering. The bank accepts drug cash as a deposit and makes a loan of almost an equal amount to the money launderer. To curious law enforcement or tax authorities, the loan looks like a normal business transaction, except no one involved expects it to be repaid.

Questioned later about the Bilonick transaction, Awan would deny any knowledge of illegal motives or suspicions about the origins of the cash deposit. "I can only conjecture to what his motives were," said Awan. "But it can be a business-related transaction which is normal over there."

Such services also were normal in BCCI's London offices, where Awan had first joined the bank. In those cases, the cash involved was not necessarily tainted. Usually, the intent was to assist businessmen in evading Britain's heavy taxes, such as its Value Added Tax or VAT. All the person needed to conceal business income from the tax collector was a relative or friend abroad.

"The businessmen would deposit 'black money' that did not go in their VAT records with the bank in the name of one of their relatives abroad," a former BCCI executive in London explained. "In return, the bank would extend to them a loan of the same sum, charging one percent of the amount as its fee. Because nonresidents do not pay UK tax, the system also enabled them to get out of paying composite rate tax."

The former executive said it was easy to spot these transactions on the bank's books. The loans were always matched against the deposits, but first one had to be able to see the books, of course.

This simple technique for hiding money had been around far longer than BCCI. Meyer Lansky perfected it in the 1950s for the American Mafia. He used Swiss banks and a plainer name. It was called a "loan back."

BCCI also did a brisk business in cash at its branch at the free-trade zone in Colón, the Atlantic port that was Panama's second-largest city after the capital of Panama City. In the free-trade zone, contraband of any nationality could be bought and sold. Many of the buyers were smugglers running the American economic embargo on Cuba. For instance, one of the bank's best customers in Colón maintained a substantial business selling hotel equipment made in the United States to Cuba. Other merchants dealt in high-tech items and arms. For all, the preferred method of payment was cash.

Steven Kalish had returned to Panama on October 11, 1983, carrying another $2.5 million in drug profits. As promised, Cesar Rodriguez was going to see that the marijuana smuggler got the preferred-customer treatment at General Noriega's favorite bank.

The next morning, Rodriguez and Enrique Pretelt took Kalish to the main office of the Bank of Credit and Commerce International. There, they introduced him to Amjad Awan. With the banker's assistance, Kalish opened an account at BCCI and deposited $2 million of the cash. He received a top-secret manager's ledger account, M/L18. A month later, he withdrew half a million dollars as down payment on a Boeing 727 jet he was buying for Noriega. The remainder of the currency was used to buy Kalish a twenty-five percent interest in a Panamanian corporation. His partners were Rodriguez, Pretelt, and Manuel Noriega.

BCCI was not the only bank laundering money in Panama, as U.S. drug investigators would soon discover. The practices used by Amjad

Awan were employed at many neighboring bank offices. The National Bank of Panama made substantial amounts of money by charging banks a one percent fee for the cash they transferred to the central bank. And many of the big American banks operating in Panama made use of variations of the loan-back scheme. The most popular variation was to take in cash in Panama as a certificate of deposit and loan it out in New York or elsewhere as a legitimate loan.

In his testimony before the U.S. Senate Subcommittee on Terrorism, Narcotics, and International Operations in early 1988, Ramon Milian-Rodriguez, a Cuban-born accountant who spent years as a top money launderer in Miami and Panama for the Medellín cartel, explained the eagerness of the big banks for such deposits in the early eighties.

When he flew to New York to arrange such transactions, said Rodriguez, the banks would have a limousine meet him at the airport. Though he said he no longer remembered their names, Rodriguez claimed to have met with top officials at major banks in the nation's financial capital for transactions that he said both sides knew were charades.

"We were breaking laws in a very big manner and you always have to have plausible deniability," said Rodriguez. "And the New York banks are no fools."

Neither was the Bank of Credit and Commerce International. And, among all the financial institutions operating in Panama, only BCCI could boast that it was General Manuel Antonio Noriega's favorite bank. Unfortunately, the relationship was not enough to keep Awan in Panama after he made a mistake of the worst kind, one that cost the bank money.

Criminals learn the advantage of keeping a distance from some aspects of their schemes. Often, they use lawyers to maintain that distance. One of the reasons Panama had turned into such a booming money-laundering haven was that its laws allowed a lawyer to set up a shell corporation and never have to reveal to anyone the identity of the real owner. The principal occupation of Panama City's thousands of lawyers is creating and administering these shell companies on behalf of offshore owners. As a convenience to clients, many lawyers set up the corporations and kept them "on the shelf," complete with corporate papers and ready directors.

One day in the fall of 1984 one of these lawyers came into Awan's office at BCCI in Panama City. He wanted to open an account in the name of one of these dummy corporations. He said a substantial amount of money would be transferred into the account soon in the form of U.S. Treasury checks.

"We never know who the beneficial owners of the corporation are,"

Awan said years later, in explaining what happened. "We base our account opening on the reputation of the attorneys."

A risky business in any country, let alone Panama, as Awan discovered in this case.

Not long after the account was opened, $3.7 million worth of Treasury checks did indeed come into the account. BCCI sent them to The Bank of New York in Manhattan and they were cleared, which means they were deemed legitimate. The day they cleared, the bank paid out money from the account on the basis of the checks in the name of the dummy corporation.

Later that same day, a couple of U.S. Treasury Department investigators paid a call on Awan at the BCCI office. The checks, they explained, had been forged. They were the work of a sophisticated gang operating out of Hong Kong and Taiwan. The credit on the checks was being reversed and BCCI would have to eat the loss of almost $3.7 million. Family or not, this was fiscal humiliation. The BCCI brass in London reacted the way bankers everywhere respond to embarrassment and loss of money. Since Awan had accepted the bogus checks and the bank needed a scapegoat, it was decided that he would be transferred out of Panama, even though his three-year tour was not up. And he would be going to work in the bank's representative office in Washington. The office was not a banking operation; rather, its primary job was to serve as liaison with the World Bank. BCCI was working with the World Bank in its capacity as banker to many Third World nations, which received development loans from the World Bank. The BCCI representative office was in the headquarters building of First American Bank, the new name of Financial General.

When Awan told Noriega that he was being transferred, the general was adamant that his favorite banker not leave Panama. Noriega telephoned Abedi in London and demanded that Awan remain where he was. Abedi said that Awan had to go, but he offered Noriega a compromise: Even though he was in Washington, Awan could still serve as the general's personal banker. He would retain sole control over the secret account and could travel to Panama regularly to discuss that and other business. Noriega accepted the plan, and at the end of 1984, Awan was off to Washington.

CHAPTER EIGHT

Feeling the Force

The Bank of Credit and Commerce International turned out to be popular with many dictators and wealthy lawbreakers as it grew at an unprecedented pace in the late seventies and into the eighties. To some it seemed there were few clients who were turned away. From its offices around the world, BCCI was becoming a cash conduit for drug traffickers, terrorists, despots, arms merchants, and other scam artists and lawbreakers.

Under the euphemism of EMP, cash was being bounced electronically around the world, from BCCI branch to BCCI branch. With each transaction, the origins of the money were obscured further. And all of this growth was taking place with no effective meddling by banking regulators. BCCI was a stealth bank, the institution that did not show up on the radar screen long enough for any regulator to get a fix on its position.

This secrecy went hand in hand with other cultlike qualities at BCCI. From the start, Agha Hasan Abedi was a charismatic leader who defined his mission in terms that were more philosophical than businesslike. He dreamed of forging the world's largest bank out of the ruins of Pakistan's nationalized banking industry, of creating an Islamic financial institution to rival and eventually surpass the banks of the Western world. And his employees were inspired to follow him in this grand and exciting scheme. Converts to the vision, they worshiped Abedi and carried out his orders without question. And if they got rich along the way, all the better.

In a business, people resign and go off to other jobs. In a cult, people defect and they are hounded and pursued.

One of BCCI's London managers became a chronic gambler at the Playboy casino there. After losing all of his own funds, he dipped into some Iranian accounts at the bank. To protect the bank's secrecy, the manager was given a $600,000 "redundancy" payment to restore the embezzled funds. The bank could not risk the publicity involved in firing the man or, far worse, reporting the crime to the police. Cults cannot tolerate bad publicity.

BCCI demanded total loyalty from its employees on all issues, as one long-time employee, Masood Asghar, discovered. Asghar became disenchanted with BCCI and quit the bank in 1978. When he left, he claimed that he had a contract worth $3 million. Abedi offered a buyout— $250,000 and a new Mercedes. But Asghar threatened to sue the bank and write a book exposing its inner workings. Since he had spent a good deal of his time in the Caymans, this was a potentially dangerous vow.

Ignoring advice from his friends, Asghar returned to Pakistan and planned to bring out his family, but one morning while inside his house in Karachi, Asghar answered a knock on his door to find a group of soldiers on his front step. They rushed into the house and beat and raped him. Asghar subsequently decided that his days at BCCI were better left unchronicled.

A Pakistani named Aziz Rehman did not have any success when he tried to blow the whistle on BCCI either, although he was never beaten. In the early 1980s, Rehman was working as a chauffeur and jack-of-all-trades at the bank's office in Miami. His chief job was driving important customers around the city in one of the bank's cars, either the Lincoln Continental Town Car or the Cadillac Seville. When the customer wanted to do some shopping or stop to eat, Rehman was always there to pick up the tab.

Sometimes his job entailed driving to a customer's business or a freight office at the airport to pick up a cash deposit for his bank. Once he thought he had hurt his back lugging a bag containing $700,000 in small bills. Pickups were generally twice a week, and over one three-month period he deposited $3 million in the bank. Some of the deposits, he said, were recorded at a phantom branch the bank claimed to maintain in the Bahamas. It was a way to invoke Bahamian bank secrecy laws before BCCI had an office there.

The flow of drug cash into Miami was matched only by the savagery of the gun battles that were occurring on the city's streets. Rehman grew afraid. He worried that someone would kill him to steal the huge sums of cash he was transporting. "My life is in danger," he complained to his supervisors. "I don't want to do these deposits anymore. I will do anything else. Somebody will kill me. This is not my job. You send somebody else."

Rehman's bosses were unmoved. "This is part of our job," he was told by the office manager. "We do this same thing, you know."

But Rehman was adamant that he would no longer perform what he deemed a dangerous chore. It was decided by the bosses that they could no longer trust Rehman, and they fired him. Rehman responded by going to the IRS, taking with him reams of bank records to support his tale of extensive money laundering at the Miami branch.

In April 1984, shortly after he was fired, Rehman was interviewed by several agents in the IRS criminal division in Miami. Based on his tip and evidence, the IRS opened an investigation of BCCI in Miami. Near the middle of 1985, the head of the criminal division in Miami recommended that the IRS open an undercover operation targeting BCCI in Miami. The request was approved within the Miami office but rejected at the next level within the agency.

The agent pushing the investigation was told only that she was fighting a losing battle. Few within the IRS were pushing undercover operations at the time anyway, and BCCI in Miami was a small operation, just an agency office that was supposed to serve foreign nationals. But no one gave the Miami agent a reason for refusing to start the inquiry. So, for reasons that remain a mystery, the U.S. government lost an early opportunity to get behind the scenes at BCCI, and the bank managed to escape scrutiny that could have started its collapse far earlier.

There were other reasons for maintaining strict secrecy at the Bank of Credit and Commerce, such as the account maintained at the bank's marble-and-glass branch office on Sloane Street, in the heart of London's Knightsbridge shopping district.

This branch was the BCCI office frequented most often by the royal families of the Middle East when they were in London. One morning in 1980, the manager of the branch summoned one of his senior assistants, Ghassan Qassem, to his office. Qassem was told that an important client was coming to the bank to open a large account. The client was a representative of the government of Iraq, and his account was to be handled efficiently and with the utmost discretion. The manager also instructed Qassem to make sure the branch looked active and that the staff were hard at work when the client arrived.

About an hour later, a man arrived at the branch and was escorted immediately to the manager's office. When the manager emerged, he told Qassem that the client wanted to transfer a substantial amount of money to BCCI from a branch of Midland Bank near Marble Arch. The manager provided Qassem with the documents authorizing the transfer and Qassem carried them himself to Midland Bank and arranged the transfer of $50 million to BCCI.

Within months, the mysterious account was being used to finance arms transactions. The first two transactions totaled $32 million and

BCCI collected about $100,000 in fees on the deals. In addition, the client had agreed that his account would not pay interest, which provided BCCI with a no-cost source of funds.

The Iraqi representative traveled often in Europe and the Middle East. When he was in London, he often used the Sloane Street branch as a personal office. He sometimes spent the entire day in one of the offices, making telephone calls around the world and sending telexes over the bank's machine. Providing special services for a big client was nothing new at BCCI. However, Qassem noticed something strange about the client's telexes: they were coded. Few of BCCI's customers were as security conscious as this one, whose name Qassem eventually learned was Samir Najmadeen.

Too, some of the transactions arranged by Najmadeen were unusual, even for someone who was dealing in arms. At one point, he used BCCI to provide the financing for six Mercedes-Benz sedans. A letter of credit was provided to the manufacturer, listing the destination of the vehicles as Iraq, and instructions were sent along for some unusual options. The sedans were to be equipped with launchers for grenades and small rockets, concealed at the front corners of each car. However, when the Mercedeses arrived in Iraq they were deemed unacceptable by Najmadeen's contacts there: the weapons were too visible. The bank refused to provide the payment to the manufacturer and the vehicles were returned.

Qassem was born in Syria in the middle fifties, but he was raised in Jordan. He had come to Britain in 1969 to attend university and joined BCCI in 1973. He was a trusted employee, so when Najmadeen told the bank that an extremely important contact was arriving at Gatwick Airport outside London one day in 1981, Qassem was dispatched in one of the bank cars to pick up the contact at the airport.

The contact carried an Iraqi passport in the name of Shakar Farhan. He said little to Qassem, identifying himself only as a businessman based in Kuwait who sold electronics and photocopying equipment. He seemed to speak little English, but he spoke so little at all that Qassem was never sure about his fluency. Qassem drove him to his hotel that first day and, in a pattern that continued for several years, often escorted Farhan on shopping trips around London. One time, they went to a tailor's on Oxford Street so the customer could buy some suits. Another time, it was a cigar store on Jermyn Street just behind Piccadilly Circus. Farhan's favorite store seemed to be Selfridges, the large department store where he was able to stock up on all sorts of items.

The balance in the account at Sloane Street always hovered around $50 million. Money would be paid out for arms transactions and it would flow in from commissions on those deals and from other sources. Among the other sources were governments of various Middle Eastern states, which Qassem found provided regular monthly deposits to the account.

The focus of Farhan's business with BCCI, like that of Najmadeen, was arms transactions. Over the years, BCCI provided letters of credit and other forms of financing for transactions that sent weapons of all sorts to various destinations in Europe and the Middle East. In 1985, BCCI provided financing for the shipment of riot guns and ammunition intended for Syria. When British authorities refused to approve a license to export the sensitive equipment to Syria, the bank arranged for an African diplomat to be paid to sign documents claiming that the material was destined for his country. In fact, records showed that the shipment was diverted to East Germany, where it was divided between East German state police and the Palestinian terrorist Abu Nidal.

The organization run by Abu Nidal, the nom de guerre for Sabri al-Banna, was one of the most violent and ruthless in the world. By 1985, its agents were blamed for the deaths of more than 200 people in dozens of attacks on Western locations as well as spots in moderate Middle Eastern companies. In the early 1980s, the organization was based in Baghdad and protected by the Iraqi government. By 1985, Abu Nidal had worn out his welcome there and moved his headquarters to Syria.

Qassem believed that the man he knew as Farhan was a representative of the Iraqi government when he first started doing business at the bank. The earliest arms deals supported that view. At the time, Iraq was mired in its long war with Iran. Qassem said that he had been told by his superiors that assisting Farhan and Najmadeen was part of the bank's efforts to show its wealthy Middle Eastern backers that it was a staunchly pro-Arab institution. "During the Iran-Iraq War, the bank wanted to show to the Arab world that we supported Iraq," explained Qassem later.

There was more at play, however, as the banker would find out later when he discovered that Shakar Farhan was actually Abu Nidal himself.

By 1982, when Abu Nidal's organization was beginning to use BCCI extensively, the bank was well-suited for someone who needed to shift money around the globe quickly and quietly. The bank had fifty-nine offices in Europe, ninety-three in the Middle East, fifty-eight in Africa, thirty-four in the Far East and Southeast Asia, and fifteen in North America and the Caribbean.

There was a long-standing banking operation in Hong Kong and another in Switzerland. There were branches in South Korea and Indonesia, and a major unit in Manila. Two branches had recently been opened in Colombia, two were operating in Panama, and a new one had opened in Jamaica. BCCI owned forty percent of a bank in Nigeria and had a profitable operation in Zimbabwe. In Swaziland, on a vital border of South Africa, BCCI had become so powerful that it was functioning as the central bank. The nation's king was a shareholder in the local affiliate.

In the United States, despite its rejection by the Federal Reserve, the bank had received permission from state authorities to open limited-service offices in New York in 1978, and Miami and Los Angeles in 1982. These offices could not take deposits from American citizens and the money they took in from foreigners was not insured. However, the offices were permitted to provide trade financing and other business loans to corporate clients. In its pitch to California regulators, BCCI had stressed its connections to the home countries of new immigrants to the state.

"New Californians wishing to establish businesses in California may have difficulty in making financing contacts because they have no credit history here," the bank said in its application. "BCCI would have the advantage of either knowing them from their home countries or having the capability of establishing their worth and reputation in their country of origin."

Because they were not full-service branches and would not be federally insured or take deposits, banking regulators in all three states did not conduct major inquiries into the bank's finances, practices, or background.

In public statements, the bank was attributing its growth to trade financing and retail banking, which means consumer deposits. It did not make public the fact that one of its most important source of consumer deposits was flight capital.

Most Third World countries have strict currency controls designed to keep capital at home, where it can contribute to economic development. Rich people do not like such restrictions, often because they fear that they could lose their fortunes in these politically and economically unstable nations.

What BCCI became particularly adept at doing was taking deposits from these rich individuals in their own countries and moving them to BCCI branches in more hospitable countries, such as Switzerland or Britain. This was a highly profitable line of business because most Third World depositors are so pleased to have a foreign cash hoard that they are not concerned if the nest egg does not yield much interest. Among the countries where large amounts of flight capital originated were India, Pakistan, and many African nations.

BCCI was far from the only bank in the world accepting flight capital. Many international banks are eager to accept deposits from these customers when they smuggle money abroad. Not often, however, are the banks themselves accused of violating currency-exchange laws. Usually it is an individual within the bank who takes the fall and is quietly dismissed. The fact that BCCI got caught and punished in public as an institution, however, was an indication of how widespread the practice was within the organization.

In the eighties, BCCI was accused of breaking exchange laws at least half a dozen times. The countries where laws were violated included Mauritius, Sudan, India, Kenya, Colombia, and Brazil. The bank was found guilty in India, Mauritius, Kenya, and Colombia. In Kenya, a BCCI branch manager and two senior officers were arrested on charges that they had failed to report $34 million in foreign exchange earnings from coffee exports; the bank was fined $30 million. In Brazil, the president of the BCCI subsidiary was stopped by police at São Paulo airport and accused of trying to smuggle $150,000 in traveler's checks to Paraguay. Those charges were later dropped.

In Colombia, the bank was found to be running a secret flight capital operation on the second-floor of its main office in Bogotá. The bank was helping rich Colombians move money out of the country through its affiliate in the Bahamas. When the operation was discovered, Colombian authorities found that BCCI's Nassau branch had $44.6 million in illegal deposits from Colombia. BCCI was fined $11,000 and two of its top administrators were ordered out of the country.

The punishment might have been more severe, except that BCCI had strong ties to the Colombian government and banking community. Colombia had strict laws about ownership of its banks by foreign entities. However, BCCI had acquired a medium-sized Colombia bank, Banco Mercantil, in 1984 after receiving the first waiver of the regulations granted by then-President Belisario Betancur. The acquisition, which took nearly two years to complete, was arranged with the assistance of Rodrigo Llorente, a prominent leader of Betancur's Conservative Party and a former finance minister and ex-president of Colombia's central bank.

Nonetheless, for a bank that crowed about its dedication to serving the needs of Third World nations and did seventy-five percent of its business in those countries, moving money out of poor nations was a particularly cynical practice. Capital flight can prove disastrous for developing countries. It undermines prospects for long-term development, robs the government of the ability to build the infrastructure vital to economic prosperity, and can make paying a country's foreign debt harder. In the end, capital flight steals the opportunity for the poor to improve their standard of living and enriches only the wealthy.

It was not only in the Third World that BCCI was running into legal and regulatory trouble. When BCCI's branches reached forty-five in Britain in 1978, the Bank of England asked the bank to freeze its growth. Saying they had no clear picture of the bank's finances, the regulators also refused it permission to engage in some forms of currency-exchange trading.

Despite its limited public presence in the United States, BCCI also ran into trouble there. Agents from the Internal Revenue Service and Drug Enforcement Administration stormed a BCCI representative office in Chicago and arrested an officer on charges of conspiracy, fraud, and failure to report cash deposits over $10,000. The arrests climaxed an eighteen-month investigation that also implicated an officer of the Bank of Pakistan.

The BCCI representative office in Chicago was not supposed to conduct banking business. It was supposed to restrict its operations to marketing the bank's services outside America. U.S. regulators had never granted BCCI a license to take deposits from domestic customers. State regulators in New York, Florida, and California had granted the bank limited licenses for what are called agency offices. These offices, which were located in New York City, Miami, and Los Angeles, were permitted to transact business with foreign customers but could not take domestic deposits. In addition to the one in Chicago, by the mid-1980s the bank had representative offices in Boca Raton, Houston, San Francisco, Tampa, and Washington.

BCCI also had a growing secret empire. Despite attempts by U.S. regulators to ensure that BCCI had no domestic banking presence in the United States, it operated its restricted agency and representative offices in direct cooperation with First American Bank in Washington and the National Bank of Georgia in Atlanta.

The links between the operations were demonstrated on April 24, 1985, when representatives of the American operations met in New York for the first strategy session of a new group created on orders from Abedi. It was called the Americas Coordinating Committee and its task was to coordinate all of the bank's operations in North and South America.

"BCC has been a success in the Third World and now we are embarked on establishing an equally successful business in the most competitive country in the world," said Aijaz Afridi, the First American Bank of New York executive vice president who opened the meeting. "We must work together to overwhelm the U.S. market and act in a unified manner and be supportive to each other."

Afridi had served as BCCI's general manager in Luxembourg and Geneva before joining First American Bank of New York in July 1983. He took the First American job at the request of Abedi, and phone records showed that he was in contact with BCCI's London headquarters almost daily.

The others present also had long-standing ties to BCCI. Among them were Amjad Awan, who was now assigned to BCCI's Washington representative office; Raja Allahad from BCCI in Canada; Dilip Munshi from the Los Angeles agency office; and Tariq Jamil, an executive at the National Bank of Georgia and a former BCCI officer.

According to the later Federal Reserve charges, by this point BCCI had maintained a controlling interest in First American for several years as a result of its loan agreements with the original investors. On January 1, 1985, the Fed said, BCCI had obtained similar control over the National Bank of Georgia through a loan to Ghaith Pharaon that granted BCCI control over his shares at any point BCCI sought to exercise it.

The two-hour session was brought to a close by Khusro Karamat Elley, a senior vice president of First American Bank of New York. Elley had been head of BCCI's New York agency office in 1983 when he moved to First American. He had been hired after Swaleh Naqvi suggested that he would be a good man for the job to Robert Altman, the lawyer, protégé of Clark Clifford, and president of First American's parent company. (Clifford and Altman later defended the consultations with BCCI officials by saying that it was their belief BCCI was acting as the financial adviser to First American's Arab shareholders; the two American lawyers denied that BCCI exerted any control over the management decisions at First American.) While working at First American, Elley's pay was allegedly supplemented by BCCI.

This was a familiar pattern for First American executives. Bruno Richter, the first president of First American in New York after the acquisition in 1982, was suggested for the job by Abedi. When he recruited another American for a post at the bank, the applicant was interviewed by Elley and Altman and then flown to London for interviews with Abedi and Naqvi.

So it was natural that, in his concluding address to the strategy session, Elley should refer to the banks as one big family. "In America, we are sitting on seven billion dollars in assets and this is just the beginning," said Elley.

At the time, BCCI's assets in the United States, through its agency offices, were less than $1 billion. However, the combined assets of First American Bankshares, National Bank of Georgia, and those BCCI offices did total about $7 billion.

Many of the same faces were on hand later in 1985 when Agha Hasan Abedi showed up to address what was billed as the "Bank of Credit and Commerce International Conference of the Americas." It was held at the Grand Bay Hotel in Miami, where Abedi was staying in a $600-a-night suite. The highlight of the conference occurred on Sunday, November 3, in one of the ballrooms at the hotel. It was the chance to listen to Agha

Sahib exhort the bank managers to work together as a single dynamic force to grow and prosper. The speech was a sparkling example of Abedi-speak.

"Management is providing a purpose and a direction to the dynamics of an organization, to the dynamics of an energy system," said Abedi. "I have to reach to you the meaning of this. What is the meaning of dynamics in the literal sense? What are the components and ingredients of the dynamics, the productions, the elements that have to be there and that have to be built in the meaning of dynamics? What is the quality of energy, flow movement, power?

"You live, you exist, for your dynamics is part of the order of dynamics of existence," continued Abedi. "It is the dynamics of cosmos, during which that dynamics of our universe that is known to us."

For those who may have been confused, Abedi offered another definition of dynamics: "Technically this is an organization. This is the universe. This is the organization of the universe. This is dynamics. Don't call it organization. Now call it dynamics. And the function of the manager is to put a purpose and a direction into that dynamics. Whether it is your branch, it is a dynamics. Your branch is nothing. Call it from today by the name of dynamics. BCC is a dynamics."

At various points in the three hours of remarks, Abedi interrupted his monologue to address individual members of the audience. Someone near him was smoking and Abedi told him it was all right. Abedi enjoyed the man's smoking. He benefited from it because he could see how much the man relished it. A few minutes later, when Abedi was talking about a dynamic force that was driving BCCI to open more and more branches, he singled out Amjad Awan.

"Mr. Awan," said Abedi, "may I ask you, do you feel the force within, which within you drives you? How many times do you feel? And what does it make you feel? What do you become when you feel that? How many times do you feel it? For what do you feel? And where is that driving force located in you? What does it taste like? What does it feel like?"

"Sir, I certainly feel the force," replied Awan. "Off and on, not all the time."

"How often do you feel and then what is that feeling?" asked Abedi, refusing to let Awan escape without a full testimonial.

"It's a feeling of living within, something much greater, which you try to relate to," said Awan.

Sometimes the force failed. In fact, not long after Abedi's Miami speech, Masihur Rahman was back in London wondering how the bank was going to survive.

BCCI's management organization was loose, to put it kindly. Abedi and his top aide, Swaleh Naqvi, stressed repeatedly to those around them that the officers in the field were the ones who produced results, who fueled the all-powerful growth and profits. When Rahman, as the bank's chief financial officer, challenged the assumption that upper management had no oversight role to play, his advice was rejected.

"What can you do, sitting in London?" Abedi asked once. "So leave them alone."

So when a new division was created within BCCI in 1983 to handle the bank's growing trading in the world's stock and commodities markets, there was no centralized control at the London headquarters. The division was called the treasury department and its head was a Pakistani banker in his early forties named Syed Ziauddin Ali Akbar. While Akbar would execute the trades out of London, they were to be entered on the bank's books in the Cayman Islands.

American banks are prohibited from participating in stock and commodities trading. The prohibition stems from the collapse of the nation's banking industry in 1932. At the time, many blamed the collapse on the stock market crash of 1929. So in 1933, Congress passed the Glass-Steagall Act forbidding banks from playing the market or underwriting stocks, although they have been trying to beat down that wall ever since.

European banks were under no such restrictions and so, in its quest to join the big international banks, BCCI had opened its treasury department. The idea was to pool surplus deposits within the bank and invest them in conservative assets, such as U.S. Treasury bonds, British government bonds, and blue-chip stocks. This would enable the bank to earn a higher rate of interest than they were paying to the depositors, a traditional means of making a profit in banking. No more than ten percent was to be used for riskier trading in commodities and the foreign currency exchange markets.

But, as sometimes happened at BCCI, that restriction was ignored almost from the outset. Akbar and an assistant, under the supervision of Naqvi, soon began taking large positions in commodities transactions, including the highly volatile options markets, where an entire investment can be wiped out in a few ticks of the stock. The result was that they began to lose substantial amounts of money that belonged to the bank's depositors. With each loss, they resorted to the gambler's solution and bet more on the markets in hopes of recouping the previous losses. By the middle of 1985, the traders were taking exposures equal to $1 billion or more.

At the time, the bank was being audited by two big accounting firms. Price Waterhouse did the books in the Cayman Islands and Ernst &

Whinney was responsible for audits of operations out of Luxembourg. Between them, the two firms were collecting fees of $4 million or so a year from BCCI.

In January of 1986, accountants from Price Waterhouse came to Masihur Rahman with startling news. In auditing the books of the treasury department for 1985, the accountants said, they had come across a series of irregular transactions. As a result, they went on, the bank had lost somewhere between $300 million and $500 million in commodities trades. That was equivalent to the entire cash capital of the bank. There was no way BCCI could survive such a devastating loss.

Rahman was angered both by the losses and impending disaster and by the failure of Price Waterhouse to pick up the transactions earlier.

"Look," he said, "the department has ten people. It has maybe a hundred files. And they were all sitting in one small section of one floor and you did not find them until now."

There was no satisfactory explanation. In the coming days, the magnitude of the losses became clear. A total of $430 million had vanished in bad trades. Most of it had been lost when interest rates went up at a time the bank had bet they were going down and bought U.S. Treasury bond options that were wiped out.

After Rahman broke the news to Abedi, the bank's founder got on the first plane to Abu Dhabi for a meeting with Sheik Zayed and his financial advisers. When he returned, he told Rahman that he had secured $150 million in new cash. It was enough to keep the bank afloat for at least the time being. When Rahman asked Abedi the source of the funds, he got no clear answer. When he asked the accountants from Price Waterhouse, who would have to verify the money in order to sign off on the bank's audit report, he was told that it had come from the staff benefit fund, ICIC Holdings. Confronting Abedi with the information about the raid on the employee assets, he was told not to worry.

"Yes, we have done it," said Abedi. "But do not worry. More is coming from other shareholders and you soon will see a complete revival and we will have more capital and more shareholders. Very heavyweight."

Indeed, soon after that, one of the most powerful and wealthy nonroyal families of Saudi Arabia acquired a big chunk of stock in the Bank of Credit and Commerce. The bailout came from the Bin Mahfouz family, which was led by Khalid Salem bin Mahfouz and his brothers. Their holdings included The National Commercial Bank, the largest bank in Saudi Arabia. In exchange for injecting $150 million in new capital into the bank, five nominee companies controlled by the Mahfouz brothers acquired twenty percent of the stock in BCCI. Most of the stock was purchased from Ghaith Pharaon. The Mahfouz brothers also acquired shares in First American at the same time. During this period, the Mahfouz family obtained $141 million in loans from BCCI. The loans were made, outside auditors would later say, without loan agreements, promissory notes, or security documentation for collateral.

The huge treasury losses were kept secret within the bank. Only the top four or five executives were aware of what had happened. There was some fallout outside the bank, however. Ernst & Whinney, angered that the treasury losses had jeopardized the entire banking company, withdrew as auditors of BCCI's Luxembourg operations. Responsibility for auditing the entire operation fell to Price Waterhouse.

The Bank of Credit and Commerce slipped through 1986 with the outside cash infusion, but the bank never recovered fully and the impact of the treasury loss was felt throughout its network. The $150 million was not enough to cover the loss. Not by a long shot. So new pressure was applied to the people in the field to gather more deposits, open more branches, bring in money any way possible. It was vital to keeping the scheme alive.

PART TWO

Busting the
Bank

It's the dumb people that get caught.

—Ricardo Argudo,
former BCCI employee

CHAPTER NINE

The Legacy of Al Capone

Al Capone unwittingly provided the impetus for a financial trade destined to encompass a range of sophisticated techniques that the notorious Chicago mob boss could never have imagined. The trade would become known as money laundering, and it would be more useful than a tommy gun to a big-time criminal.

Capone was convicted of tax evasion and sent to prison in 1931. The Internal Revenue Service got him because he had not concealed the profits from his rackets. When that happened, the kingpins of American organized crime recognized that they needed to develop ways to hide those illicit gains.

This recognition came at an important juncture for the mob. Salvatore "Lucky" Luciano, a visionary hoodlum if ever there was one, had just directed a violent coup against the old-line Mafia leadership. He consolidated the mob's far-flung operations under its first unified leadership and simultaneously broke the taboo against heroin trafficking. It was this entry into the lucrative drug trade that created the mob's demand for sophisticated ways to launder the new wealth.

Enter Meyer Lansky. A business partner of Luciano's, Lansky was the first to come up with the idea of moving the mob's money overseas. In 1932, he opened an account at a Swiss bank for Louisiana Governor Huey Long, who had allowed the mob to open gambling houses in New Orleans. Lansky spent the next four decades perfecting techniques for getting money out of the United States and into nice, clean bank accounts.

Most of the banks he used were in Switzerland, and the route of choice was from mob-run banks in Miami to Swiss banks directly or through branch offices in the Bahamas. In the 1960s, one of Lansky's favorite partners was the Geneva-based International Credit Bank.

ICB, as it was called, was itself an innovator of sorts. Its main legitimate activity was collecting funds for Israel from Jewish communities in Europe. There was a subterranean side to that relationship, however. The bank also financed the purchase and shipment of weapons to Israel and was rumored to serve as the European paymaster for Mossad, the Israeli secret service. It also was banker to the agents of Bernie Cornfeld, whose giant Investors' Overseas Services was siphoning hundreds of millions of dollars out of developing countries in violation of currency-exchange restrictions.

For Lansky, ICB served as a convenient depository for the profits rolling in from mob criminal enterprises—profits from the sale of narcotics, skim from the casinos in Las Vegas, proceeds from extortion rackets. Millions of dollars were moved to Switzerland through wire transfers over telephone and telegraph lines from other banks or by cash-carrying courier. And millions came back to the mobsters through legitimate-looking loans and other covers that disguised the origins of the funds.

By the late 1970s, a sophisticated international network of banks and money launderers was in place, moving billions of dollars of dirty money around the globe in the blink of a computer screen. The international network relied on reputable financial institutions and a host of shadowy offshore banks. Its evolution coincided with the rise of a new breed of multinational crime organizations—the Colombian drug cartels.

The permissive attitude toward drugs in the United States during the late 1960s and the 1970s had mushroomed into a veritable blizzard of cocaine by the end of the seventies. In the beginning, cocaine was a fashionable drug, replacing marijuana at jet-set parties and among entertainment stars, but as greater amounts poured into the United States, the drug infiltrated the youth culture and the inner cities. As a result, demand soared.

With rising cocaine sales came a tidal wave of cash. Cocaine trafficking became the richest criminal enterprise in history, its money accumulating by the ton, dwarfing the profits collected by the Mafia. Drug dealers found themselves with suitcases so filled with cash that the handles broke off, money-counting operations so vast that people had to wear protective masks against the high lead content of currency they handled.

And the sheer volume of the money presented a logistical problem, too, because the primary beneficiaries of the trade were not home-grown criminals. They were Colombian drug lords, whose empire was centered in a triangle formed by the three Andean cities of Bogotá, Cali, and

Medellín, with the latter city dominating. These suppliers banded together in cartels.

In Senate testimony in 1989, David Wilson, a Drug Enforcement Administration expert on financial intelligence, described the fully evolved operation of these organizations:

"The Colombian cartels provide drugs to their wholesale distributors which in turn supply the retail distribution network. The money flows from the neighborhoods where drugs are sold back to central collection points, generally in large cities. The cartels employ specialized money couriers or collectors who are outside the drug distribution network. These individuals collect, sort, count, and package the money for shipment."

A decade earlier, in the beginning of the cocaine bonanza, the chief means of moving money simply involved walking into a bank carrying a suitcase or a grocery bag full of cash. Sometimes the money would be neatly counted and banded; at other times it would be stuffed in, willy-nilly. A friendly banker would accept the deposit and transfer the funds to a bank account in Colombia or some other country outside the reach of prying law enforcement authorities and bank regulators, all for a fee, of course.

Miami was the chief American link in this mushrooming drug operation, a city that became synonymous with cocaine and money laundering. Astronomical amounts of tainted cash, deposited in Miami's banks, stoked the city's economy. In 1979, the Federal Reserve Bank of Miami reported a cash surplus of $5.5 billion, greater than the combined surpluses of every other Federal Reserve Bank branch in the country.

The government's response to the epidemic of drugs, crime, and money was a pioneering attack on the laundering of drug proceeds. It was called Operation Greenback, a joint investigation by the U.S. Customs Service and the Internal Revenue Service that started in early 1980 with volunteer agents from around the country. Naturally, the starting point was Miami.

The challenge and excitement of this new war was captured in the emblem created for the investigators. Against a bright green background was a cloudburst and beneath the cloud, in small letters, were the words "In the beginning." Circling the edge of the emblem was: GOD CREATED GREENBACK.

In some ways, the pickings were easy. Since the money launderers had been operating with near impunity, they had not bothered to hide much. The probe's initial success came that first year. A young Colombian woman was arrested at Miami International Airport trying to smuggle $1.5 million out of the United States in six Monopoly boxes. Three months later, police at a small Florida airport seized $1.6 million from a private plane bound for Colombia.

Investigators soon began to concentrate on South Florida's banks. The Bank Secrecy Act of 1970 required financial institutions to file a currency transaction report, or CTR, for every deposit or withdrawal of $10,000 or more in cash. However, many bankers simply looked the other way when traffickers brought in suitcases, cardboard boxes, and duffel bags filled with cash. In 1981, Customs investigators estimated that banks in South Florida had failed to report $3.2 billion in cash.

Early in 1981, Greenback agents searched a branch of Landmark Bank in Plantation, a bedroom community near Fort Lauderdale. They discovered that Hernan Botero Moreno, a soccer team owner from Medellín, had laundered $56 million through the bank. Less than a month later, Greenback scored another goal: Raids on two Miami banks resulted in charges that Isaac Kattan Kassin of Cali had laundered $71 million through one of the banks.

Another Greenback target was a convicted marijuana smuggler named Robert Walker, who owned a fleet of six airplanes, a yacht, his own island, and a so-called brass-plate bank in the Turks and Caicos Islands off the southernmost end of the Bahamas. His background in drug trafficking and his apparent lack of legitimate income earned Walker the distinction of becoming the object of Greenback's first undercover operation.

Until Greenback, the few money-laundering arrests were spin-offs from drug cases and other so-called underlying crimes. This operation turned a spotlight on the money men and the banks, to the extent it could. Equally important for the future of such investigations, however, was the use of the undercover strategy against money launderers. Long after Greenback, federal agents would concede that they could rarely make the big money-laundering cases without the help of an informant inside the ring or an undercover operation of their own. This would prove to be a vital lesson in the war against the people who handle the dirty dollars for the world's drug trade.

In the case of Robert Walker, the undercover operation was a last resort. Dennis Fagan, one of the Customs agents involved in Greenback, had been nosing around Walker's empire for months, but his best informant was getting cold feet. His quarry was well guarded. A private investigator screened Walker's employees, presumably looking for law enforcement connections. His planes could outrun the good guys' aircraft. A sophisticated radio room monitored traffic on the frequencies used by the DEA and FBI. And Walker was developing friendships with some politicians in the Caicos that would provide an extra layer of security.

Watching Walker operate, Fagan had determined that one of the suspect's weaknesses was women. "He was a sucker for women," said the agent. Up until this point, few women had played major roles in undercover operations. They were involved occasionally, but only posing as girlfriends or secretaries. Perhaps, Fagan figured, this was a way to get through Walker's vaunted defenses.

Near the middle of 1981, an informant in Puerto Rico agreed to introduce two undercover Customs agents to Robert Walker. They told Walker they represented a Chicago organization with Mafia ties that needed help laundering money. Walker agreed to a second meeting at a hotel in Atlanta where he would meet the organization's head. Arriving at the hotel, Walker met a short blond woman. Her real name was Bonni Tischler, but Walker would not find that out until too late. She had become the lead undercover agent in Greenback's biggest case.

"He was just an unattractive old guy, but he liked me," Tischler said later in describing Walker. "He just took the whole bait, hook, line, and sinker. I mean, it wasn't the hardest thing I ever had to do in my life."

Indeed, Walker responded by trying hard to impress the young woman. He described in great detail how he had created a blind trust in his offshore bank and named as trustee his lawyer in the Bahamas, yet another jurisdiction profiting from its strict bank secrecy laws.

"So what you have," he told her, "is, you have an attorney's confidentiality there, plus the secrecy of the banking act. Most everything that we have is buried in that trust. If somebody ever came and looked at the corporate structure, they're going to find that all of the stock ends back, is in that trust, locked up in a safety deposit box in Nassau."

Walker said that he was moving money through the Nassau branches of two big Canadian banks, the Bank of Montreal and the Bank of Nova Scotia, but he sang the praises of Panama and its ruler at the time, General Omar Torrijos.

"One thing about Panama is that you can get to the general and he'll cut a deal," said Walker.

His bragging was providing Greenback agents with more than the secret of Robert Walker's operation. They were getting a blueprint for state-of-the-art money-laundering techniques. The only part of the financial seminar that had an unwelcome, even chilling note for Tischler and the agents monitoring the Atlanta meeting from the next hotel room was a story that Walker told about security at the private airfield he maintained outside Tampa.

"The only time that I've ever known of a problem is I got a phone call from a guy, and he said, 'I'm not gonna tell you who this is but I make a hobby of listening to the Feds.' He says, 'I've got every conceivable thing to listen to them with and I figured I better call you up and tell you your airport's staked out.' "

The bust of Robert Walker was scheduled for a steamy morning in July of 1981. Tischler and an agent posing as her Mafia boss borrowed a suitcase of cash from the Federal Reserve Bank of Miami and traveled down two miles of dirt road, through stands of scrub pine, and arrived at the private airstrip. The agents had figured that Walker was planning to fly them in one of his Cessna 414's to Nassau to launder the money. Tischler handed Walker $25,000 in cash as his fee and he walked into a nearby office.

Once the money was passed, her undercover partner, a Customs supervisor named William "Blue" Logan, stepped away, saying he had to make a last-minute call. With that telephone call, he was supposed to alert a raiding party waiting nearby in helicopters to swoop in and make the arrests. Somehow, and no one ever found out what happened, the phone message never got through. The raiding party was left sitting in their helicopters just a few minutes away from the airfield.

Wondering where the hell help was, Tischler and Logan were put into separate Cessnas for the flight to Nassau with Walker and two of his pilots. As the planes started to taxi down the runway to take off, Blue Logan took matters into his own hands. He was in the first plane and he pulled his service revolver and shouted, "Police." Pointing the gun at the control panel, he told the pilot, "I'm putting a bullet through the control panel if you don't stop the plane."

The Cessna stopped on the runway and so did the second plane. Logan ordered the pilot in his plane out. In their confusion, Walker, Tischler, and the pilot of the second plane got out, too. Just then the helicopters swooped in over the trees and landed, and armed agents jumped out. Dennis Fagan had gotten worried waiting for the message that never came and decided to break up the party anyway.

Within minutes the airport was under the control of the federal agents. They were slapping handcuffs on everyone in sight, including the much-relieved Bonni Tischler. Now her only worry was what had happened to the $25,000, which also had been borrowed from the Federal Reserve. It was not until the following day that agents discovered it inside Walker's safe at the airport.

Tischler had learned a great deal in a short, intense period. Undercover work was exciting and scary. Some agents were natural actors, able to slip easily into their new roles. Tischler, however, had remained nervous and tense for weeks. She also learned that physical danger was secondary. The biggest danger was psychological.

"You start thinking these people aren't so bad," she said. "It becomes difficult to bring a case down sometimes, if you get too close to them. Denny Fagan calls it the 'Bambi syndrome.' You just can't shoot Bambi in the end." That was one reason, she decided, that it was a good idea to have a case agent overseeing an undercover operation, providing some distance and some objective judgment. For Bonni Tischler, the fear and psychological impact of working undercover would be something that she would never forget, and something that, years later, would alter the way she would handle an even more important undercover operation.

As for Walker, the case brought good luck and bad luck. Twenty-two people were indicted as part of the drug-and-money ring, and eighteen of them went to jail. Walker managed to get the charges against him dismissed on a technicality and then he disappeared. A month later, his corpse was discovered alongside a stream just north of his Tampa airfield. The cause of death, the county coroner said at an inquest, was "a fourteen-inch cord around a fifteen-inch neck."

The Greenback crew learned later that Walker had planned to use some of their money as payment for a load of cocaine that had already been delivered to him. The Colombians apparently had decided to set an example for others who might try to avoid paying for their drugs on delivery.

The Walker case was Operation Greenback's biggest success, for it had given them a glimpse at the rising level of sophistication available to clean the dirty dollars of the drug trade. Among those who learned those lessons were Bonni Tischler and the agent who supervised the Walker undercover operation for the IRS. His name was Robert Mazur.

Despite such victories, Greenback was riddled with frustration. There was rivalry between the Customs and IRS agents, and there was a rivalry between Greenback agents and the Drug Enforcement Administration. Customs and the IRS shared the limited jurisdiction over financial crimes involved in drug dealing; the DEA was supposed to handle the drug cases themselves. This led to inevitable conflicts because the DEA agents thought there was never a case until drugs were on the table, whereas the Customs and IRS agents viewed the DEA personnel as unsophisticated.

But the biggest problem was that the federal agents lacked the legal muscle to do much about the laundering by financial institutions. They could bust a dozen Colombian money launderers a day, and there would be a dozen more the next day to take their place. The same was true with street dealers and couriers and pilots. Bodies were not the vulnerable point. Banks were.

"It is a money business, and if you intercept the flow of money, you've seriously damaged the business," says Senator Donald Riegle, the Michigan Democrat who heads the Senate Banking Committee.

Yet there was no federal law against money laundering when Greenback started. The only weapon that the agents had to use against the banks was violation of the CTR law, which required banks to report cash transactions of $10,000 or more. Bankers often escaped prosecution by filing CTR reports but claiming they had no idea the money was from drugs. Other money launderers caught in Operation Greenback were charged only with violating the reporting requirements.

"Sometimes it was a misdemeanor to do a $10 million deal," Roger Markley, who prosecuted some of the first Greenback cases, complained later.

The money launderers also got wise to the limitations of the law. They began to structure transactions to avoid the $10,000 cash-reporting requirement. Called "smurfing," the practice involved having individuals make numerous cash deposits just under the reporting limit. Some smurfs would travel to a dozen or more banks in a day, depositing $9,800 or so in cash. This relieved the banks of the responsibility for filing a CTR and made it even tougher to prosecute financial institutions that were funneling drug cash into the world's money system.

Smurfing, however, was time-consuming for the launderers, especially the big guys dealing in multimillion-dollar payoffs. For them, it was far easier to find an accommodating banker in the United States or even to physically transport the cash to an offshore location, such as Panama or the Bahamas.

If investigations such as Operation Greenback were to really have an impact on the drug trade, there had to be a way to stop the money before it entered the banking system, for once there, criminal money looks the same as all other kinds of money. With the push of a computer button and the speed of light, funds can be spirited out of reach of U.S. authorities and regulators.

"I can hide money in the twinkling of an eye from all of the bloodhounds that could be put on the case, and I would be so far ahead of them that there would never be a hope of unraveling the trail," William Mulholland, chief executive officer of the Bank of Montreal, explained to a committee of the Canadian Senate examining the adequacy of bank regulations.

The proof of Mulholland's warning can be found in the heart of the American financial capital. It is a place where billions of dollars move with the speed of light and with unsurpassed secrecy, a place that sophisticated money launderers could not have designed better had they created it themselves. This place is not the creation of the criminal world, but of the banking world.

Behind a series of unmarked steel doors in a nondescript office building in midtown Manhattan sits a large room where the temperature is always seventy-two degrees Fahrenheit. Within that room, banks of computers and a handful of technicians control the flow of American dollars around the world. As much as $1 trillion a day changes hands inside the memory banks of a computer network that stretches around the world.

The place is called the New York Clearing House Interbank Payment System, or CHIPS. Its existence is virtually unknown outside the international financial community. Yet ninety-five percent of the world's U.S. dollar transactions between banks flow through its Unisys A-15 mainframe computers.

Since going electronic in 1970, CHIPS has made the world's payment system far more efficient. So dependent has the global financial system become on CHIPS that a complete duplicate center, including mainframe computers and waiting desks, has been set up across the Hudson River in New Jersey. A visitor to the New York City location can walk over to a window and, with proper guidance, pick out the small office building across the river where the clone stands ready in case some calamity shuts down the New York system.

The room in Manhattan that contains the Unisys computers is hospital white and about half the size of a football field. The temperature is kept constant and humidity is carefully controlled to provide the best possible working environment for the computers.

On a typical day, a white-coated technician sitting at a computer terminal punched in a command: SHOW VOL. Onto the screen popped the figure $815,880,067,480, the volume of dollars that had been transferred through CHIPS that day. Twenty seconds later, the technician typed in the command again. The new figure was a staggering billion dollars higher.

Here is how CHIPS works: A bank in Spain is instructed by a customer to transfer $1 million to an account at a bank in Panama. The Spanish bank transmits electronic instructions to its correspondent bank in New York, where a computer operator enters the transaction into the CHIPS computer through a secure link over private telephone lines. The CHIPS computer authenticates the transaction codes and automatically deducts the $1 million from the Spanish bank's account and adds it to the account of the bank in Panama. It also sends a message notifying the Panamanian bank of the transaction. At the end of the day, the transaction is included in summary reports of all the day's transactions, showing which banks owe money and which have money due.

This happens in a matter of seconds 150,000 times each business day at CHIPS and involves banks in almost every country of the world. In processing a transaction, the CHIPS computer knows and records only four scant pieces of information: the account number of the sender, the identity of the sending bank, the identity of the receiving bank, and the number of the receiving account. Often there are no names for the account holders. When one or both of the banks involved is situated in a country with strict bank secrecy laws, anonymity is guaranteed.

The importance of CHIPS in money laundering schemes was demonstrated in 1987. Drug Enforcement Administration agents involved in a major undercover operation deposited $500,000 in cocaine proceeds in the bank account for the traffickers. The agents then watched as the money was moved out of Los Angeles through CHIPS to a bank account in an Asian country. The Asian account was held in the name of a phony company.

In a second wire transfer, the money was sent to Miami, where it was disguised as a loan to a phony business there. The business then used most of the $500,000 to buy three tractor-trailer trucks that were used for hauling cocaine and cash around the country.

Do big-time drug suppliers use CHIPS? Consider the case of Jose Gonzalo Rodriguez-Gacha, a top member of the Medellín cartel who was killed in late 1989 by police in Colombia. Before he was shot, authorities raided Rodriguez-Gacha's ranch and discovered twenty-two rooms containing seven computers and lots of other high-tech equipment and records. Using the seized data, the DEA traced and obtained court-ordered freezes on some $61.5 million in drug proceeds in banks around the world.

Before all the accounts could be frozen, however, the drug lord's financial advisers were able to transfer $23 million of the money out of accounts in such places as the British Virgin Islands, Hong Kong, and the Cayman Islands. The system used for the transfers was CHIPS, and the safe haven for the funds was a bank in Panama.

John Lee, a pleasant, gray-haired man whose business card bears neither a phone number nor an address, is the president of the New York Clearing House Association. Its members are the eleven largest banks in New York. Together, they operate CHIPS as a nonprofit service for the world's 132 largest banks. Thousands of smaller banks worldwide have access to CHIPS through correspondent banking affiliations with the larger institutions.

Lee estimates that ninety-nine percent of the transactions passing through CHIPS are legitimate, but it is only an estimate, based on extrapolations that are themselves educated guesses. Lee arrives at his figure by dividing the estimated total profit from drug trafficking into the total volume of dollars going through CHIPS. The total for CHIPS is precise; the drug money is not.

No one knows how much money is laundered around the world. A 1989 report by the U.S. State Department estimated that drug profits in the United States were $110 billion a year. Others have put the figure as low as $10 billion. A report in 1990 by the seven leading industrial nations said drug dealers in the United States and Europe earn $232,115 a minute. Some of the smartest minds in law enforcement, people such as Treasury Department financial crimes expert Brian Bruh, believe there is no way to come up with an accurate measure of the underground money market. Yet it is known that untold billions of that money move through CHIPS, quickly and anonymously.

"There is no way to deter illegal money transfers," says Lee, with the resignation of one who has worked long and hard at the problem. "It's like putting a drop of ketchup in a gallon of milk—it may turn pink for a minute, but then it will disappear."

The trick, according to Lee and others who know, is to stop the funds before they get into the system, before they pass the teller's window and become a drop of ketchup in an ocean of milk.

The U.S. government's crackdown on banks involved in laundering money went big-time in 1985. Instead of an obscure bank in Florida, the scandal centered on the Bank of Boston, at the time the nation's sixteenth-largest bank. It also had the third-largest overseas network among American banks.

Loan sharks and racketeers, it seems, had been bringing shopping bags filled with cash to the bank for deposit. In what the institution said were unrelated transactions, more than $1.2 billion in cash was transferred through Swiss banks and returned to the United States. All went unreported to the authorities. In addition, the bank acknowledged that it had failed to report $110 million in transfers between its Miami branch and the Caribbean.

In the wake of the scandal, dozens of major U.S. banks, hoping to avoid charges, admitted that they had neglected to file some of the required CTRs. Among them were such pillars of the New York financial community as The Chase Manhattan Bank, Chemical Bank, Irving Trust, and Manufacturers Hanover Trust Company. On the West Coast, Crocker Bank paid a fine of $2 million for failing to report $4 billion in cash transactions between itself and six Hong Kong banks as well as similar transactions with its branches on the Mexican border. And Bank of America, which had provided such a timely lift to Agha Hasan Abedi, negotiated a fine of $4.75 million for its failure to disclose cash transfers of more than $12 billion.

The American Bankers Association, the banking community's professional organization, was reported to be negotiating with the U.S. Treasury Department on behalf of forty-five banks, and dozens more were under investigation.

The Reagan administration's Treasury Department had gotten the message across to America's bankers: Report cash transactions, beware of suspicious deposits, or face substantial fines and big embarrassment. Congress got into the act, too. Hearings were held on the growing problem of money laundering. Among the witnesses were veterans of Operation Greenback, including Bonni Tischler. Responding finally to the pleas of law enforcement authorities, Congress approved a series of changes in the laws that culminated in 1986 in a much stronger statute that made money laundering a federal crime.

Among the provisions of the Money Laundering Control Act of 1986 was a requirement that bankers report transactions deemed "suspicious." No longer would they be able to turn a blind eye to drug deposits and escape punishment. For the first time, money laundering itself became a crime with the creation of two new federal offenses. One was a financial "transactions" offense, which covered such activities as "smurfing" and other means of evading reporting restrictions. The other was a "monetary transportation" offense, which covered the international movement of funds. Another section of the law made it a crime to knowingly engage in financial transactions of more than $10,000 involving money derived from criminal activity. Violations of the law could bring up to twenty years in prison.

Finally, Congress had supplied law enforcement with a broad weapon for attacking banks and bankers involved in money laundering as well as the money launderers themselves. It also tossed gasoline on the smoldering rivalry between agencies.

The Treasury Department, which includes the Customs Service and the IRS, argued that it had developed the expertise to handle the new breed of money-laundering cases. Fearing the loss of some of its turf, the Justice Department replied that its agencies, principally the DEA and FBI, controlled investigations of most underlying crimes that would produce money-laundering prosecutions, so the primary jurisdiction should rest with it. The dispute grew so heated that Justice and Treasury were forced to sign a memorandum of understanding concerning investigative jurisdiction under the act.

The formal truce in Washington did not stop the turf battles on the front lines of the war. A race was on in the field to show who could best wield the new weapon in the war against drugs and dirty bankers.

CHAPTER TEN

Abreu and Mazur

Miami is cosmopolitan and full of intrigue, a contemporary Casablanca on the Atlantic Ocean, where cocaine cowboys trade gunfire from fast-moving Ferraris. But Tampa, sitting on Florida's west coast next to the warm waters of the Gulf of Mexico, wears a patina of age and tradition.

Flying into Tampa, over meadows with a water table so high that ponds sprout anywhere nature or real estate developers gouge the surface, one circles a beautiful natural harbor. Waves of algae bloom across the blue expanse of water. The city hangs between two broad inlets. To the east, the channels fork around the modern development of Harbour Island. One leads to the Hillsborough River, another to the docks of Ybor City, the nineteenth-century settlement of Cuban cigar makers. To the west, long causeways cross the shallows of Old Tampa Bay, providing access to handsome beaches and mammoth traffic jams. A sheltering peninsula, with St. Petersburg at its tip, protects the broader expanse of Tampa Bay to the south. The hot, humid breath of the Gulf creates an oppressive atmosphere that prickles the flesh for much of the year.

In the late eighteenth century, these natural features drew pirates like flies. Where other civic cultures celebrate explorers and pioneers, Tampa glories in its buccaneers. The major local festival each year honors the memory of Gasparilla, a renegade Spanish naval officer with a nasty temper who covered his crimes with a veneer of gentility. According to legend, when Gasparilla's pirates captured a ship, they killed the men and older women and kept the younger women for pleasure and ransom. Those fortunate enough to have wealthy families who could pay to get them back were placed in a stockade on what is now Captiva Island, south of Tampa.

Gasparilla thrived for three decades. His end came in 1821 when the

United States annexed Florida and his ship was sunk by the USS *Enterprise* on its maiden voyage. But the Spanish pirate's memory lives on in Tampa's version of Mardi Gras.

Twentieth-century Tampa retains that buccaneering spirit through its criminal element, too. Until his death in 1987, Santos Trafficante, the Mafia boss in Tampa, enjoyed much greater prestige and power within organized crime than any of the more famous New York dons. And he multiplied that influence by working in tandem with his mob neighbors to the west along the Gulf, the Carlos Marcello family in New Orleans. Together, they had plied the drug trade and used the money-laundering services of Meyer Lansky and his associates in south Florida and Las Vegas, where Lansky had helped the mob develop methods for hiding the money they skimmed from profits at the casinos they controlled.

It was in this hot, humid area, where crime had germinated and prospered over two centuries, that the seeds of a new money-laundering investigation were planted in 1986. At the time, no one knew that this organism would spawn a financial scandal destined to reverberate around the world.

Whenever more than three federal agents cooperate on a criminal investigation, they have to give it a name. Some of these names have become legendary—Operation Greenback in Miami, Operation Greylord in the corrupt courts of Chicago, Operation Exodus at the nation's ports. The monickers are catchy and motivational, imbuing a sense of team spirit and camaraderie in the agents, particularly if they happen to have been brought together from different agencies.

The Tampa money-laundering investigation was known as Operation C-Chase. As often happens, the brass in Washington and a good many reporters would get the name wrong.

Because Operation C-Chase centered on money laundering, outsiders immediately thought that the "C" stood for C-note, slang for a hundred-dollar bill. The Customs brass in Washington would decide they liked that explanation, too. In fact, the origin of the name was much less inventive. The apartment complex near the Tampa airport where the investigators set up their first undercover residence was called Calibre Chase. "I'm going out to C-Chase," an agent would say in the Customs enforcement office near the airport, and so the investigation came to be called Operation C-Chase.

As is usually true of these investigations, it started with a small fish. Gonzalo Mora, Jr., ran a modest import-export business in his native Medellín, a mountain metropolis of more than one million people situated in a river valley in north-central Colombia, but he was really a money-laundering wanna-be.

All around him, Mora saw the riches of big-time cocaine trafficking transforming peasants into feudal lords. The Ochoas, hard-working restaurant owners a decade earlier, were rich and respected. Pablo Escobar, a petty criminal and sometime enforcer, was one of the world's wealthiest men. They lived on vast ranches, surrounded by their own armies. They swept into Medellín in their fancy cars and flew around the globe in their own jets.

Like Escobar, Gonzalo Mora, Jr., was plump and short, about 180 pounds and five feet, six inches tall. Unlike Escobar, he was still trying to strike it rich. For two years, Mora had been running a small-time money-laundering operation under the cover of his import-export business. He or some associates would pick up cash generated by drug sales in Detroit, Miami, Los Angeles, and New York. Mora would deposit the money in amounts of less than $10,000 into his U.S. bank accounts. Then he would write checks on those accounts and sell them to money brokers on the black market in Colombia. The brokers would pay him in "cleaned" pesos, after subtracting their own fee. Mora would then pass along the pesos to the drug suppliers, minus his own commission of six to seven percent.

Using the money brokers as intermediaries, while cumbersome and somewhat crude, provided an additional layer of protection for both Mora and the suppliers. Mora also laundered cash this way for some of his import-export customers who wanted to evade taxes or escape Colombian currency restrictions.

Most of the cash that Mora laundered belonged to a mysterious member of the Medellín cartel known as Don Chepe. Not as flamboyant as Escobar or Carlos Lehder, Don Chepe was nonetheless a power within the cocaine trade. Drug authorities in the United States would one day determine that he was one of the silent leaders of the Medellín cartel, although it would take them months to uncover his identity. The amount of business Don Chepe was passing through Mora's ring was peanuts. Rarely did the pickups amount to more than $10,000 or $15,000 at a time.

Ambitious and greedy, Mora was eager to get a bigger piece of the action. He was confident that he could get more business from the drug suppliers, particularly Don Chepe, but first he had to develop a bigger network to handle the cash.

In July of 1986, Mora contacted another Medellín resident, Alvaro Uribe, and asked for his help in expanding Mora's little laundering operation. Mora knew that Uribe had done some drug business in Florida before. He wanted Uribe to return there and open several bank accounts that Mora could use to launder more drug money. What Mora did not suspect was that Alvaro Uribe was a paid informant for American law enforcement authorities.

Police have always used informants and there have always been criminals willing to provide information on their partners in crime in exchange for money, vengeance, or their own freedom. The escalation of the war on drugs brought with it the necessity of penetrating the Colombian cartels. This was difficult, since the cartels tended to distrust anyone who was not Colombian and dealt with traitors and suspected traitors in a very violent and public fashion.

As a result, at a time when the role of informants had been elevated to a new level of importance, so had the risks. Those willing to chance the wrath of the Colombians were well compensated for their troubles. Alvaro Uribe had been paid thousands of dollars in the past by Customs agents. For his initial tip and assistance in setting up C-Chase, he would eventually receive a $250,000 payoff from the U.S. government.

As soon as Uribe arrived in Florida with his orders from the expansion-minded Mora, he contacted agents in the Customs Service in Tampa and described Mora's plan. The agents immediately recognized an opportunity to get inside a Colombian money-laundering ring, but it was a small one. It might not lead anywhere. The trick was figuring out how to see where this trail would lead as fast as possible. There was plenty of work chasing money launderers and no one wanted to waste a lot of time on a dead-end investigation.

The plan was hatched one night just a few days after Uribe's initial contact. A small group of agents sat in the Customs Service's enforcement office in a small office complex near Tampa International Airport and examined their options. They were led by Paul O'Brien, the assistant special agent in charge of the Tampa region and head of enforcement. With him were several veteran agents, among them David Burris, an IRS agent who had worked with Customs since Operation Greenback, Emir Abreu, a Spanish-speaking Customs agent, and Robert Mazur, who had switched to Customs from the IRS in 1983.

It was Mazur who pointed out the potential value of Mora. Sure, he wasn't the most sophisticated or senior money launderer in Medellín. His use of smurfs with cash deposits under $10,000 and presigned checks was dangerous and outmoded. But Mora's ambitions made him vulnerable. A properly structured undercover sting could appeal to him by pretending to offer something he desperately needed—an efficient, safe means of moving drug money into the banking system. With this asset, Mora could hustle new business in Medellín and perhaps push his way to the top of the financial heap there. The U.S. Customs Service would make it all possible and be around to bring it all down.

The logic appealed to O'Brien and the others. The first step would be for Uribe to introduce Abreu to Mora as an experienced launderer who could set up additional bank accounts and help expand Mora's smurfing business. Once Mora was comfortable with his new associate, Abreu and Uribe would nudge the Colombian toward bigger pickups and more sophisticated laundering techniques. As the business expanded, so would the penetration of the Colombian drug and money networks set up in the United States. "We would ask Uribe to plant a seed in Mora's ear that this smurfing was crazy," explained Bob Moore, a Customs supervisor on the case. "It's the old-fashioned way to launder money. It's labor intensive and it's dangerous because too many people know about your business."

Bob Mazur, who had by that time spent thirteen years with Customs and the IRS, was assigned to be the case agent. His chief responsibility would be maintaining contact with Abreu while he was undercover and keeping the supervisors informed, too. What Mazur really wanted, though, was a chance to go undercover himself.

At the age of sixteen, Emir Abreu had left the small village in Puerto Rico where he was born for San Juan. He joined the Customs Service as a uniformed patrol officer there in his early twenties and specialized in drug interceptions along the Puerto Rican coast.

After thirteen years, Abreu had joined the service's elite corps of special agents and moved to the mainland. It was similar to moving up from beat cop to homicide detective, although the crime in which Abreu would specialize was narcotics trafficking. It was a brotherhood apart, and one in which Abreu's Spanish made him a sought-after agent for undercover operations. By his own guess, the tough, wiry agent with a wacky sense of humor had played more than fifty undercover roles. Some had lasted an hour or less. Others had gone on for weeks. None had consumed as much of his life as would his new role as Emilio Dominguez.

Alvaro Uribe had telephoned Gonzalo Mora in Medellín and described his new friend to the businessman. Mora had sniffed the bait and arranged for his brother, Jimmy, to take a firsthand look at things.

The meeting occurred on July 14, 1986, in a room at the Sheraton River House Hotel in Miami. The Sheraton's location on an exit from Miami International Airport made it a favorite rendezvous for businessmen eager to get in and out of town in a hurry. When Jimmy Mora arrived, Uribe introduced him to Emilio Dominguez and explained that Dominguez could help with his brother's money-laundering operation.

Jimmy Mora, whose given name was Gabriel Jaime, was exhausted and on edge. He had driven cross-country from his home in Los Angeles and had planned to pick up ten kilos of cocaine in Miami to take back with him. However, someone had reported a break-in at the house in nearby Kendall where the cocaine was stashed, and when police arrived to investigate, they stumbled upon a van containing 450 kilograms of the white powder. The loss was the responsibility of the cocaine's suppliers, but it meant that Mora would return to Los Angeles empty-handed. In order to salvage something from the trip, he was eager to set up the deal with Uribe and Abreu.

The two men explained to Mora that Uribe would open up accounts in Tampa at banks with Miami branches. Abreu had an organization in place that could pick up cash from drug sales in cities across the United States. All Gonzalo Mora had to do was provide instructions on where the drops would take place. The cash would then be deposited in Uribe's bank accounts in Tampa and Miami in amounts of less than $10,000. Uribe would provide Gonzalo Mora with presigned checks that Mora could complete in Colombia and sell to the money brokers. The amount of the checks would correspond to the amount of drug money deposited in bank accounts, minus a three to four percent fee for Uribe and Abreu. That money would remain in the Florida bank accounts.

The scenario sounded fine to Jimmy Mora. He said he would telephone his brother with his recommendation to go ahead with the scheme. The following day, July 15, Uribe telephoned Gonzalo Mora in Medellín and was instructed to open two accounts at Tampa banks. The scheme was under way.

Nine days later, Abreu and Bob Mazur took Uribe to an office of Barnett Bank in Tampa. There, they met with a bank officer named Nancy Goetz, who helped them open a checking account in Uribe's name. The following day, the three men went to a branch of Florida National Bank in St. Petersburg, just across the causeway from Tampa. An assistant vice president named Rita Rozansky helped them open a second checking account for Uribe.

Barnett Bank and Florida National Bank were among seven large banks in seven cities that either had already agreed or would subsequently agree to cooperate with Operation C-Chase. Goetz and Rozansky, along with key employees at each of the other banks, knew only that the accounts were part of a law enforcement investigation. They did not know any of the details.

The cooperation of these banks was a key element in the undercover operation. Each institution had agreed to accept any amount of cash that the agents brought in for deposit. This meant that the government had solved the most difficult aspect of any money-laundering scheme— getting the money into the banking system. The drug trafficker's cash could be converted readily into a variety of financial instruments and sent anywhere in the world.

On August 1, Uribe and Abreu returned to Miami and met again with Jimmy Mora. This time the meeting was at a popular restaurant on

Southwest Eighth Street and the Colombian brought along his father, Gonzalo Mora, Sr. Uribe handed over several blank, presigned checks from the accounts he had opened at Florida National Bank and Barnett Bank. Uribe also handed Jimmy Mora something else. It was an engraved white business card. On it were the names Financial Consulting Inc. and Robert L. Musella.

"That guy's big," Abreu told the Moras. "I work with Musella and he is hooked up with a big money-laundering business. He'd be interested in meeting you."

The following month, Gonazalo Mora, Jr., telephoned Uribe from Medellín with a coded message. His father had sixteen dozen flowers for his shop and Uribe should pick them up. This meant that the elder Mora had $16,000 at his apartment in Miami that was to be picked up and deposited in the accounts.

A few days later, on a Friday, Abreu flew to Miami to pick up the money, but the old man was not home. His wife searched the apartment for the cash and finally discovered $12,000 in boxes in the back of a closet. Abreu took the money back to Tampa with him. Over the weekend, Mora, Sr., showed up in Tampa with the additional cash. He apologized for the mix-up.

Mora had another request. He knew that Abreu was setting up the laundering operation's headquarters in a small apartment near the Tampa airport. Mora would like to stay the night there before returning to Miami.

The apartment at Calibre Chase, a new complex of apartments and swimming pools tucked behind a grove of trees dripping Spanish moss, had a bedroom, living room, and kitchen, and it was filled with tape recorders and video cameras. Lacking the vast technical resources of the much larger FBI, the Customs agents had planned to install the devices over the next few days to monitor later meetings. Right now, the stuff was strewn throughout the apartment.

Abreu was in a jam. The future of the whole operation could be hanging in the balance. If he turned Mora down, it might make the old guy suspicious. It was too early in the relationship to take that risk. So he said sure and offered to drive Mora there. Before they left, Abreu slipped away and telephoned Bob Mazur.

"Get over to the apartment right away and clean it out," he said urgently. "I gotta take old man Mora over there."

When Abreu and Mora turned into the complex off Hillsborough Avenue about an hour later, the undercover agent silently prayed that the apartment would be cleaned. What he saw made his heart sink. Mazur's car was still in the parking lot outside the apartment. Slowly, Abreu got out of the car and walked to the apartment with Mora. He rattled the door hard as he inserted the key and began to open it.

Mazur heard the noise. Grabbing the last piece of video equipment, he jumped into the living room closet and pulled the door shut behind him. Hunched in the bottom of the closet, clutching a video camera and unable to stretch out his legs, Mazur listened as Abreu and Mora talked and talked in Spanish. They talked for four hours. At one point, Abreu tried to persuade his guest to go out for a bite to eat. No, Mora said, he was too tired. Finally, Mora said good night to Abreu and got ready for bed.

Trapped in the closet, Mazur listened carefully as Mora's rhythmic breathing turned to rasping snores. After several more minutes, he opened the door a fraction, peered out, and then crawled from the closet. His legs were stiff and cramped, but he managed to get across the living room to a window and slip out, taking the camera with him. It was four o'clock in the morning.

Over the next several months, Abreu picked up over $100,000 in cash in Miami on orders that Mora, Jr., passed along through Uribe. The system worked smoothly and efficiently. The Moras became more comfortable with Abreu, although they resisted his delicate efforts to extract the identity of the drug supplier who was their principal client. The money-laundering operation itself was still small-time. The Customs agents were anxious to speed things up, to move into the big time.

In November, Mazur and Abreu told Uribe to bring up the name Robert Musella again. In a telephone call with Mora, Jr., he suggested that the Colombian come to Tampa to meet this financial consultant named Musella. The guy had a lot of connections and maybe he could help them expand their business. Anyway, said Uribe, Musella is loaded and he'll pay for your trip up.

When Mora agreed to the meeting, it touched off a frenzy of activity among the Customs agents. They had been constructing a false identity for Musella slowly, not knowing when the new character would enter the drama. Now they knew, and it was soon. Musella would have to be too good to pass up, someone who could offer Mora and his Colombian drug connections all the right avenues for laundering large amounts of cash.

The man who would play the part of Musella was Bob Mazur, the case agent. With his financial background from IRS and his long experience on money-laundering investigations, he was the natural choice. Undercover assignments are all volunteer in federal agencies. Mazur volunteered for the job because he loved the rush of undercover work and honestly believed his efforts helped in the battle against drugs. This was one gig where Mazur would not be sitting backstage, tucked away in an office monitoring the work of agents on the street. They could find a new case agent. He was going under. This was why he had joined the Customs Service in the first place.

Robert Mazur was the sort of person some people would describe as "brilliant" and others would label "arrogant." Reactions to him were usually strong, and few people were left sitting on the fence when asked their opinion of him. Not surprisingly, he often inspired admiration and dislike in equal portions.

"Bob Mazur is one of the smartest agents I've ever seen," says John Hume, who spent fifteen years as a federal prosecutor before going into private practice, ultimately representing one of the defendants in Operation C-Chase. "He is also among the most arrogant."

To Hume and his colleagues at the defense table at the climax of C-Chase, Mazur would come to seem the embodiment of the bullying, enticing, deceitful undercover agent whose charm and intelligence tempt honest people to cross the line.

Fellow agents admire some of those same qualities in Mazur, though they will argue vehemently that no one was entrapped in C-Chase. But when asked what makes Mazur a successful undercover operative, they would invariably list two chief attributes—his brains and his relentless determination.

"He is the best agent I have ever worked with in my life," says a top law enforcement official who was involved in the C-Chase case. "He will do what it takes to get the job done. That is a quality that is not common in federal law enforcement. The guy really takes his job seriously."

An undercover agent's mind is whirring all the time, worrying about staying in the role, avoiding a potentially fatal misstep, balancing between getting the right conversations and words on tape and not going too far and breaking the law by entrapping the quarry, all the while drawing the bad guys along without slipping in too deep himself. As for nerves, they are most vital when something unplanned occurs, when simple chance or innate stupidity undo the careful planning, leaving the agent on his own.

"Undercover could be an hour or a day or a couple weeks or months and months," said Steve Cook, a veteran Customs official who became the C-Chase case agent near its conclusion. "Personally, I don't get paid enough to do that. But Mazur, he is a real dedicated guy. He had to keep these people cool and worry about touching all the bases for the prosecution to work. It creates a lot of pressure, a tremendous burden on him. All the rest of us are just supporting cast."

In his college days at little Wagner College in New York City, Mazur played on the varsity football team although he is under five feet, ten inches tall. He once described his college football days by saying, "It was a lot of fun, but that's about as far as I could go at my size. And even then, there were giants all around me."

It was a revealing statement for a very private man, a man who said so little about himself that some of his colleagues did not even know he was married. The struggles that a smaller man goes through playing football against bigger opponents are not unlike the challenges confronted by an undercover agent. Both must survive by agility and intelligence, not brute strength. Part of what others interpreted as Mazur's aloofness was actually his inner security, a sense that he could depend on himself.

Even as he approached his late thirties, Mazur retained an athletic build from his college days, making him look imposing despite his medium height.

Mazur grew up in the middle-class New York borough of Staten Island. At Wagner, he majored in business administration and finance, with three years of course work in accounting. Recruited upon graduation by the IRS in 1972, he spent three years on a variety of investigations and then began to concentrate on money-laundering cases when he transferred to the Tampa field office in 1975.

As with any trade, undercover work involves both an apprenticeship and natural instincts. Everyone always said that Mazur was a natural, that his self-control and intelligence made him impossible to rattle, impossible to jolt out of his role, but he also served a long apprenticeship, picking up tricks and learning skills over the years. These he accumulated in many ways. Routine investigations, tracking money through banks and front businesses, taught him how to make his way through the financial mazes built by money launderers. Supervising and planning undercover operations showed the value of strategy and caution. And the actual undercover work, venturing onto the street posing as one of the bad guys, both fascinated and inspired him.

With this thirst, each undercover stint yielded lessons or contacts that made the next more effective. Each time Mazur went into the field, whether for a few hours or a few days, he was laying the groundwork for a more ambitious project down the road. He accumulated false identities and business contacts, storing them for future use. One day, he knew, it would all be required for the role of a lifetime.

When Operation Greenback was formed in early 1980 in Miami, other regions picked up the new idea. The original Greenback crew in Miami, who called themselves the Wild Bunch and developed a close-knit camaraderie that lasted throughout their careers, sometimes looked down on their new rivals. Relations between the original Greenbackers and the regional imitators later became suprisingly touchy. Nonetheless,

Mazur pushed and cajoled his IRS supervisors into setting up the Tampa version of Greenback.

Often, Mazur had bristled at the lack of imagination and daring involved in undercover investigations. With Greenback in Tampa, he saw a chance to go all the way for a change. Since it was a joint operation with Customs, he also would get a chance to see how the other agency operated, for Customs had a reputation as a wilder group than the agents of the Internal Revenue Service. He was not disappointed.

One of Mazur's first Greenback cases taught him the value of friendly banks. In August 1981, officers of a small bank in St. Petersburg became suspicious about a new account. A Colombian businessman with an English name was bringing in large amounts of cash, but he never deposited more than $10,000 at a time. It appeared to be a classic case of smurfing, and the bank president telephoned the IRS. David Burris, an IRS agent working with Greenback, came up with the idea of placing Mazur inside the bank, where he would pose as an employee. It was the first time that the IRS had tried this particular tactic in Florida.

His first day on the job, Mazur met the Colombian, Vincent Graham Taylor, and accepted a bribe to divide a large cash deposit into a series of transactions, all under the $10,000 reporting limit. Rather than make a quick arrest, Mazur struck up a relationship with Taylor, a gregarious man who had attended the U.S. Naval Academy in the 1950s and had once been expected to become secretary of the navy in Colombia.

Over the next three months, Mazur learned that Taylor was at the top of an extensive smurfing ring that laundered money for several drug rings in the Tampa–St. Petersburg area. Dozens of couriers were depositing $150,000 a day in as many as fifty different banks. Taylor, well aware of the opportunities presented by a friend inside a bank, introduced Mazur to four prominent money launderers in Miami. One of them, in turn, put Mazur in touch with an independent drug ring in Arizona that needed to launder money.

After three months, Greenback teams fanned out to Tampa, Miami, and Phoenix and made simultaneous arrests to smash the entire operation. Taylor was caught with a suitcase full of cash and eventually was sentenced to ten years in prison, a stiff term for a money launderer back then.

The bankers who alerted the IRS were given commissioner's awards, the highest commendation available from the IRS. More important for Mazur, he had seen the fruits of being patient and following a trail. And he had made some new friends in a financial institution who would be there when he needed them in the future.

Mazur picked up a little more knowledge a year later, in 1982, when he posed as a member of a drug distribution network looking for a way to launder its profits. The targets were a middle-aged financial consultant named Charles Broun and a mystical marijuana smuggler named Bruce Perlowin.

Broun's basic laundering technique was deceptively simple. After collecting cash from Perlowin, he carried it to the Cayman Islands in flight bags. There, he deposited the money in accounts of corporations registered in Luxembourg and the Netherlands Antilles. The money would then be transferred back to U.S. accounts in the names of these shell corporations and blended in as profits in a series of seemingly legitimate businesses. Among the businesses was a chain of motels in which Perlowin owned a substantial hidden interest.

As part of the undercover operation, Mazur perfected his acting skills. One of his chief tasks was getting close to Perlowin, whose marijuana ring was bringing multi-ton shiploads of Colombian marijuana to San Francisco on a weekly basis. Perlowin had survived for years because he was extremely suspicious of newcomers. However, the first time he met Mazur, he told him: "I'm a very intuitive person. If you were the heat, I'd know it." A few months later, both Broun and Perlowin were arrested and their operation was smashed.

Bob Mazur was getting hooked on the rush of undercover work, but he found the IRS too cramped for his style. The agency seemed unimaginative in its approach to these investigations, and the IRS often had difficulty obtaining cooperation from the offshore tax havens that were being utilized more and more by big-time launderers. The narrow outlook and restrictive mandate bothered Mazur. In addition, he had gotten to know and like the people and style of Customs. So in 1983, he quit the IRS for the rival agency. The move, he believed, would give him a crack at bigger cases, with more overseas contacts. And he didn't even have to switch desks: he kept the same one in the Greenback office in Tampa. With his undercover skills refined, Mazur was ready for a total confrontation. And Gonzalo Mora, Jr., was the ticket to the show.

CHAPTER ELEVEN

Setting the Hook

On December 2, 1986, Gonzalo Mora, Jr., flew to Tampa from Colombia. Uribe picked him up at the airport and took him to the Calibre Chase apartment. There, Uribe introduced Mora to Emilio Dominguez and Bob Musella, the undercover names for Emir Abreu and Robert Mazur. A week of seduction and deceit was under way.

With Abreu translating, Mazur welcomed Mora to Florida and said that he would like Mora to relax for a few days so they could get to know each other and talk a little business.

"I've been led to believe that it would be in your interest to expand our business relationship because up until now the types of transactions we have been conducting have been of a smaller nature," said Mazur.

He described himself as a businessman with a lot of different financial interests in the United States and abroad. He confided that some of his clients, although not all, were involved in illegal activities. Mazur, however, never touched drugs. Just money.

Abreu, he explained, worked for him, supervising the cash collections from drug dealers around the country and sometimes making pickups himself. Even his legal clients, Mazur said, sometimes used his money-laundering services to move funds out of the country and evade taxes.

Part of the beauty of his operation, Mazur explained, was that he operated a string of legitimate businesses that generated cash and helped conceal the drug proceeds by mingling dirty money and clean. Among his holdings were stakes in a financial services company, a mortgage broker, an air charter service, and a stock brokerage. It was the bank accounts of these businesses, which conducted lots of legitimate cash transactions, that were used for the ring's deposits in cities across the country.

For his part, Mora seemed eager to expand the volume of cash flowing into his money-laundering operation. He said that he knew a number of Colombian cocaine suppliers whose businesses generated large amounts of cash in a number of American cities. He just needed the right setup to draw more from them. As far as the increased volume of checks used to clean the money in Colombia, Mora said it was no problem. He knew an attorney who was involved with the Colombian stock exchange and would buy huge numbers of checks on the black market.

Mora said that he, too, had clients with both legal and illegal funds and that part of his service involved hiding funds for legitimate businessmen. Some of these clients in both categories had bank accounts in Panama because the exchange rate was better there than in Colombia. The two men agreed that there should be a code to distinguish between the sources of cash coming into the operation. This would help determine the level of secrecy required. Clients whose money came from cocaine dealing, they decided, would be referred to as "VIPs."

As the partnership progressed, conversations with the Moras and others would be peppered with a homemade code and jargon from the Colombian drug culture. For instance, Jimmy Mora had a plain-looking sedan in Los Angeles with an unusual feature—a hidden compartment installed for cocaine. The car was called a *caletas*, Spanish slang for thieves who steal through holes. Cocaine was referred to as *merca*, from *mercancia*, or merchandise. Sometimes the money to be moved to Colombia was described as "lentils," since Mora was using his cover as an importer of beans. A *communista* was not a communist, but a money broker who worked on commission. *Matones* were hired killers.

From that first night Mora had proven as hungry as Mazur had predicted. Far from showing the caution that the undercover agents had anticipated, Mora was eager to iron out an agreement right away. He proposed a fifty-fifty split on commissions and seemed ready to start immediately. But Mazur did not want to rush things. He injected some caution, telling Mora that he had several days of activities planned to show him his mini-empire.

Mazur's experience had taught him that this was a time for patience. He wanted to make certain the hook was in deep before playing out the line to see where this fish led them.

The following day, Mazur and Abreu took Mora to Sunbird Airlines near St. Petersburg. Mazur handed the Colombian a brochure that Customs had had made up. It listed Mazur as Sunbird's director of international finance and described him as someone who raised capital for the business. Mazur himself explained that Sunbird was a charter service for passengers, mail, and cargo between Florida and the Bahamas. But, he told Mora confidentially, Sunbird really was a front business owned and operated by one of Mazur's clients, a drug dealer.

As had happened with the banks, an executive of the air charter company had agreed to allow Mazur to work his fraud on Mora. Similar activities were planned for the following day, when the men were to fly to New York and Mora would get a glimpse of Mazur's big-time connections there. Similarly, the location of Financial Consulting, Inc., which Mazur had set up in New Port Richey, a few miles northwest of Tampa on the Gulf coast, was in reality the offices of a legitimate company owned by another of Mazur's acquaintances. When Mazur was expecting visitors, a plastic sign with the Financial Consulting logo was placed over the other firm's sign.

Before they could leave Sunbird, a man drove up to the office and walked in carrying a large bag. He handed the bag to Mazur and left. As he opened it nonchalantly, Mazur made sure that Mora got a peek at the stacks of cash inside. "Two hundred K," said Mazur. It was another bit of Customs' stage management.

On the way to lunch, the men stopped by Florida National Bank in St. Petersburg. Asking Mora to wait in the car, Mazur and Abreu deposited the $200,000 in one of their accounts. The message was clear to Mora. There had been no need to divide the cash into packages of less than $10,000 for smurfing. Clearly, Mazur routinely dealt in large amounts of cash. To Mora, who relied on relatively unsophisticated techniques, here was a doorway through which unrestricted amounts of illegal money could be put into the American banking system.

That afternoon, Mazur and Abreu took Mora for a ride on a big Hatteras fishing boat that supposedly belonged to Mazur. Mora had no clue that he was being entertained aboard a Customs Service boat designed to spot and intercept drug shipments. The radar and other sophisticated equipment were locked away in cabinets for the excursion.

Customs had put up Mora at a beachfront condominium that was supposedly Mazur's home. On the morning of December 4, Abreu and Mazur picked up their guest and drove to the airport. They caught a flight to Newark, New Jersey, and made the short drive into Manhattan. They checked into the Vista International Hotel, an expensive but convenient spot favored by business executives with appointments at the World Trade Center next door or on nearby Wall Street.

Later that day, Mora was introduced to a broker at Merrill Lynch's huge corporate headquarters on lower Broadway. The broker was an acquaintance of Mazur's who had agreed to go along with the scheme. Next, the men visited a discount brokerage firm nearby. Mazur said the place was run by his cousin, actually another accommodating friend from an earlier case.

Leaving the brokerage, the group headed for the heart of Wall Street.

Mazur's "cousin" gave them a tour of the tumult and excitement on the floor of the New York Stock Exchange. All around them, an army of people shouted and waved their hands in the air. To Mora, it must have seemed completely incomprehensible and incomparably thrilling. Here was the heart of capitalism, with millions of dollars being made and lost on every tick of the clock. And beside him was his ticket to a piece of the pie. The rush of the floor visit was followed by the calm of a real investment seminar put on by the "cousin" for Mora and legitimate investors in one of the rooms at the stock exchange's dinner club.

The point of this elaborate charade was to demonstrate Mazur's extensive connections with the financial community, connections that showed him to be a man of substance, a man with many avenues for cleaning cash. Executing a successful sting demanded constructing a net that reached far beyond minnows like the Moras. The cash delivery at the charter service, the dip into the frenzy of the stock exchange floor, these were stories that Mora would boast about among his associates in Medellín, bait that Customs hoped would attract the sharks and barracudas of the drug world.

That day, as they visited the financial hotspots of Manhattan, Mazur carried a thin leather briefcase. Inside were the usual papers and notebooks. But concealed within the case was a tiny microcassette tape recorder; barely larger than a package of cigarettes, it was model SME-700, manufactured by Sal Mineroff Electronics, and was connected to two microphones concealed on the outside of the briefcase.

After breakfast on December 5, 1986, the three men returned to a room at the Vista International to pound out the details of their arrangement over the course of about two and a half hours. Groundwork for a critical element of the trap had to be laid here.

A provision of the money-laundering statute called for the forfeiture of assets obtained through criminal enterprise or used as part of it. Often in dealing with Colombians, however, these assets were tucked away in foreign bank accounts or Colombia itself, out of reach of U.S. authorities. Mazur and his associates had devised a scheme to try to avoid losing at least some of the proceeds. It also would help them gather evidence about Mora's clients. Customs intelligence agents were still drawing blanks in efforts to learn the identity of Don Chepe.

"It's important for us to develop some investment relationships with your clients in Colombia," Mazur explained to Mora in the hotel room. "That way, if we're, ah, challenged by law enforcement here in the United States, we can hold ourselves out as true investment counselors. Having some legitimate activities is a cover for our other stuff."

He proposed that Mora persuade some of his drug suppliers to leave a portion of the illegal proceeds in the United States. Mazur could invest the money in certificates of deposit or pieces of property. He and Mora, added Mazur, would add to their own profits by splitting the investment fees in these transactions.

The response from Mora was more sophisticated than Mazur might have imagined. The Colombian said that his clients were reluctant to invest in the United States. They were worried about losing their property through U.S. forfeiture laws.

In a risky strategy, Mazur also tried to push Mora to move things along. He said that he could handle more volume and he insisted that the Colombian start bringing in larger amounts of cash within forty-five days or look for a new partner.

Mora proved as willing to escalate as Mazur had predicted. He responded to the demand with new details on his money-laundering operation. He listed several cities in which he anticipated bringing in more business as a result of the new joint system.

In some of those cities, Mazur said, he already had people in place. In others, Abreu or someone else would have to fly out to pick up the cash. Pressing his advantage and trying to enhance his credibility, Mazur said that Mora would have to agree to share the expenses involved in picking up cash in some places. This was hardly the normal strategy of an undercover agent trying to lure someone into a trap, but Mora went for it, too, agreeing to split the pickup costs fifty-fifty.

Shortly after Mora returned to Colombia, Bob Mazur went to the Florida National Bank branch in St. Petersburg where Rita Rozansky helped open a new account in the name of Financial Consulting, Inc., the first of four that Mazur would open at Florida National in this phase of the undercover operation. When he received his printed checks a few days later, he presigned a batch and shipped them via Express Mail to Mora in Medellín. As in the previous scheme, Mora would fill in the amounts and the payee once the money started to flow into the Financial Consulting account.

The wait was short. On January 2, 1987, Gonzalo Mora, Jr., telephoned Abreu in Tampa. He had $200,000 in cash that was going to be picked up from a jewelry store owner in Los Angeles. This was big time, the most money that the undercover agents had handled so far in C-Chase. Clearly they were moving up in the world of drug trafficking and money laundering.

In retrospect, many people had difficulty believing Bob Mazur's explanation of how Operation C-Chase crossed paths with the Bank of

Credit and Commerce International. The element of chance loomed too large for skeptics, but Mazur has stuck to his story and no one has produced anything more than supposition to dispute it.

"Bob Mazur is the most careful person I've ever met," said John Hume, one of the defense attorneys in the later case against BCCI. "He wouldn't go to the bathroom without preplanning it, right down to the time and place. The idea that he just wandered into BCCI is completely implausible."

However, Hume acknowledges that neither he nor anyone else has any evidence that BCCI was brought into C-Chase in any way except the one described by Mazur.

The events that Mazur said led to the involvement of the bank were touched off in December. Gonzalo Mora, Jr., had mentioned that some of his Colombian clients liked to use bank accounts in Panama for laundering money. Mazur wanted to be ready, so he decided to make contact with a bank that had a branch in Panama. For convenience, he wanted a bank with a Tampa office.

This task was a pressing one as Mazur drove across the Hillsborough River into Tampa's high-rise financial district one day that winter. Sitting near the bridge in his car during a long red light, he saw a large gold sign with a hexagonal emblem on the street level of an office building. Two words caught his eye: *Bank* and *International*. Maybe this was a place that could handle the transfers he needed to make. The full name on the emblem was the Bank of Credit and Commerce International.

A few days later, on February 11, 1987, Mazur found his way back to that office in the Riverside Plaza Building. Inside, he found that the operation was a representative office, which could not take deposits or perform any routine banking functions. It served solely as a marketing office or contact point for the bank with potential clients. Any business would be referred to an overseas branch or to BCCI's agency office in Miami. The agency office could accept international deposits and perform other limited banking transactions.

Unlike his prearranged relationships with Florida National and Barnett Bank, there would be no wink and nod this time. Mazur's intention was to use BCCI for limited purposes, certainly not as a deposit point for drug cash. So when Mazur walked into BCCI, he introduced himself as Robert Musella to Ricardo Argudo, the young bank officer. Describing himself as a financial consultant with South American clients who had accounts in Panama, Mazur said he was looking for an international bank's services to transfer and receive funds on behalf of these clients.

Of course, Argudo said, BCCI was just the place. He handed Mazur a

BCCI promotional brochure: "A local bank, internationally. A bridge between the developing and the developed countries of the world. Branches and offices in 72 countries."

For convenience, Argudo said, Mazur could open an account with BCCI in Panama through the Tampa office. Funds deposited in the account could be transferred to BCCI's Miami office within twenty-four hours and then made available to Mazur.

Argudo was extremely helpful. Asking if Mazur thought he would need to move funds in "the opposite direction," Argudo assured him that the bank had many clients who transfer money confidentially out of the United States to foreign accounts.

In the past, he said, BCCI clients with such a need made deposits directly to a Grand Cayman branch of BCCI, but Argudo was no longer recommending that route because the Cayman Islands had signed a treaty that enabled U.S. law enforcement authorities to obtain bank records there. Most of those clients were now using BCCI in Panama City, he said. Further, suggested Argudo, if any of Mazur's clients needed to transfer their own funds in a secure manner, they should consider opening accounts at one of BCCI's Panama branches.

At Argudo's request, Mazur provided copies of the corporate records of Financial Consulting Inc. and signed a form allowing Florida National Bank to provide BCCI with background information on the new client. He also wrote a check for $10,000 to open his new BCCI account.

The information release was mailed to Florida National Bank. On February 19, Rita Rozansky responded with a letter that said Financial Consulting maintained a good account relationship with the bank and "Robert L. Musella is a very reputable businessman."

Over the course of several conversations and meetings in March and early April of 1987, Mazur learned more about BCCI from Argudo. The hungry spirit of BCCI was certainly alive in this young banker. When Mazur mentioned that he might like Argudo to meet one of his Colombian clients, Argudo said BCCI had about twenty offices in Colombia. Many Tampa residents did direct banking with the South American country through BCCI's Tampa office. In fact, said Argudo, he could open accounts at any BCCI branch around the world. The records of the account opening then could be forwarded to the foreign branch and thus made inaccessible to U.S. authorities.

When Mazur told Argudo that his Colombian client was in the currency exchange business and some of his clients accumulated cash in the United States, Argudo said this was commonly called the "black market" and it was not unusual for it to be used for transferring funds to Panama. The banker cautioned Mazur, however, that cash was an increasingly difficult commodity to move into the banking system. Deposits of $10,000 or more are reported to the IRS, he said, but there were ways around the system.

"It's the dumb people that get caught," Argudo assured Mazur.

Customs agents say the bank was not a target at this point in the investigation, and that the practices described by Argudo (who was never charged with a crime) were common at many banks. Mazur has claimed never to have heard of the bank before, despite a handful of reports in the U.S. press that had raised questions about BCCI and rumors in some law enforcement circles that BCCI was a dirty bank.

The most astute of the American articles was a piece in *Forbes* magazine in 1986 by Allan Dodds Frank which described the flow of dirty dollars through the international banking system. The article mentioned Panama, Miami, and the Bank of Credit and Commerce International. The British press, led by the *Financial Times* and *New Statesman*, had written extensively about BCCI's tactics and growth, but these were publications that Mazur and the Customs agents were unlikely to have seen. And no one in the press or law enforcement yet understood what the bank was all about.

However, the Bank of Credit and Commerce was not a stranger to everyone in law enforcement. On September 30, 1986, the Central Intelligence Agency had prepared a brief report on BCCI that said in sketchy terms that the bank was involved in money laundering and other illegal acts worldwide. The CIA report also said that the Pakistani-run bank had obtained secret control of Financial General, the predecessor to First American Bankshares.

The five-page September 1986 document was one of several reports that the agency had prepared on the bank since it first began monitoring BCCI activities in the early 1980s. At the same time, the CIA was paying operatives of its own through the bank, using front companies and other concealment devices to hide its activities from the bank.

While the 1986 CIA report was a classified document, such reports are often circulated to the intelligence and enforcement arms of other agencies in Washington. Under normal procedure, copies of the report would have gone to the Federal Reserve Board, the State Department, and the Treasury Department, which oversaw Customs and the IRS, but the routing of the September report remains a mystery. Federal Reserve officials later would deny seeing a copy and the other agencies refused to disclose any information about such intelligence matters.

In 1987, the bank that the CIA was using and watching was expanding into every corner of the world. Since its inception, the bank had put growth ahead of all other considerations, but in this period, the demand for new deposits was driven by a desperate need to help cover the massive losses by the bank's treasury department and keep the bank alive. This demand for deposits may have been one of the reasons for what happened to Ghassan Qassem when he discovered the true identity of the biggest customer at BCCI's Sloane Street branch.

By 1987, Qassem had been promoted to manager of the branch and was still pampering his best customer, Shakar Farhan. Then one day, someone showed him a copy of the French newsmagazine *L'Express*. In it was a photograph of Farhan, only he was identified as Abu Nidal, the most-wanted terrorist in the world. Shocked and frightened, Qassem took the magazine and hurried to the bank's headquarters on Leadenhall Street in the financial district, where he showed the photograph to a manager.

"Look at this," urged Qassem.

"Take this back," said the manager. "Destroy it immediately, and go back to your branch and don't you ever mention it to anyone because the general manager has got enough problems without having to add anymore."

Qassem was shocked once more. He had long been aware of the account's connection with Iraq and later Syria; he could accept that as part of the bank's business and its support of Arab causes. What troubled him deeply was that the bank's favor had been extended to someone as notorious and violent as Abu Nidal.

The banker returned to his branch and, as instructed, destroyed the magazine and did not discuss its contents with any of his colleagues. However, with a friend's assistance, Qassem arranged to meet with agents from MI5, one of Britain's intelligence services. The meeting took place at a large hotel in London's posh Mayfair neighborhood. After explaining that Abu Nidal maintained an account at his branch, Qassem answered dozens of detailed questions about the account and the transactions involving it. In the end, he agreed to pass on information to MI5 about the account activities; he even promised to copy documents related to the account and other suspect customers and provide them to the intelligence agents.

Within weeks, information provided secretly by Qassem bore fruit. British intelligence was able to link Syria to an attempted terrorist bombing in 1986 involving an Israeli El Al jetliner at London's Heathrow Airport. Payments from the BCCI account of a Syrian intelligence officer were traced to an Abu Nidal agent who had used his unsuspecting, pregnant girlfriend in an unsuccessful attempt to smuggle a bomb aboard the airliner.

The British also shared data from their new source with the CIA. Documents provided by Qassem demonstrated that Abu Nidal's network drew millions of dollars from many sources. Moderate Arab governments made regular payments into the BCCI account, buying peace from terrorist attacks on their diplomats abroad and on potential targets within their borders. The documents also showed that Abu Nidal ran a thriving business selling arms and other goods to the Mideast through a company based in Warsaw, Poland. Shortly after Qassem turned banker-spy, the United States government pressured the Polish government and the company, SAS International Trading and Investments, was shut down.

The reaction when Qassem had raised the alarm at BCCI's headquarters illustrated the basic philosophy of the bank—deposits were accepted from all comers, no questions asked. But the senior manager's reference to "problems" also reflected the struggle in which the bank was engaged at that time to increase its deposits to cover for the massive trading losses discovered the year before.

Another example of this desperation involved the central bank of Peru. In 1986 and 1987, Agha Abedi and Swaleh Naqvi authorized BCCI officials in Peru to pay $3 million in bribes and kickbacks to two officials with the South American country's central bank, according to a later criminal indictment. At the time, Peru's new president, Alan Garcia, had said the country would stop making most payments on its debt, which was held by the world's largest banks. The Garcia administration was worried that the international banks would try to freeze the country's limited supply of hard currency in an attempt to force repayment of the staggering debts. So the Peruvian central bankers were looking for a place to hide the money.

BCCI was the perfect solution. Desperate for cash for its own reasons, the bank also had the ability to move millions of dollars through its branches worldwide as part of Abedi's EMP program. A deal was allegedly struck in March 1986. BCCI would accept the deposits at its Panama branch and guarantee to keep them secret from the creditor banks. According to the later criminal indictment against the bank, Abedi, and Naqvi, BCCI promised in exchange to pay bribes to two top central bank officials based on a percentage of the country's money that was deposited at BCCI.

At first glance, it would seem that Peru would be happy just to find a safe haven for its cash, so why pay bribes? The truth lies in the details of the arrangement, for it was tilted heavily in BCCI's favor. In return for its deposits, the central bank of Peru received a much smaller line of credit; it was only $60 million at first against a deposit of $100 million. The central bank used the credit to set up an import-export fund to help finance its foreign trade.

But BCCI did not keep the upper hand for long. News of its deteriorating financial condition began to reach Lima, and mid-level bureaucrats began to get nervous. On July 13, 1987, the chief of the investigations department wrote an internal memo pointing to the sharp decline in BCCI's earnings and warning that the central bank should move out its deposits as quickly as possible. Two weeks after the memo was written, a London-based bank rater, IBCA Bank Analysis, sent a telex to clients warning that BCCI had sustained substantial losses in the options market, that the bank's unusual organization made it impossible to get accurate numbers on its financial condition, and that the bank had no lender of last resort ready to step in on behalf of customers should the bank fail. But the warnings did not prevent one last deal. The head of BCCI's Panama office flew to Lima and offered to increase Peru's line of credit to keep the account. By mid-August, BCCI was granting a draw of $160 million against central bank deposits of $250 million.

Similar pushes at other BCCI branches around the world helped make the bank a perfect partner for Robert Mazur and Operation C-Chase.

When Bob Mazur first mentioned his BCCI connection to Gonzalo Mora, Jr., he drew a much grander portrait designed to inflate his importance in the eyes of Mora. Mazur boasted that he wanted the Colombian to meet a "very good friend" of his at an international bank that had opened accounts for him around the world. Mora's response was intriguing. He claimed to have conducted his own transactions through BCCI offices in Panama and Colombia in the range of millions of dollars.

The money launderer was still getting the royal treatment from the undercover operatives when he came to Tampa on April 7, 1987, for meetings with Mazur, Abreu, and the BCCI banker. On the morning of April 8, for instance, the two agents took Mora to Mazur's air charter service and gave him an air tour of Tampa. After landing at Tampa International Airport, they got into a waiting car and drove to BCCI downtown. They picked up Rick Argudo and returned to the airport for lunch at a restaurant on top of the Marriott Hotel at the airport.

Argudo and Mora hit it off right away because Argudo spoke Spanish. And, as the lunch went on, the banker proved full of ingratiating suggestions as he described the various services available from BCCI. He proposed that Mora and Mazur create a system of double invoicing business expenses through a Panamanian shell corporation to avoid U.S. taxes. He also suggested that they consider depositing funds at a foreign BCCI branch and allowing Argudo to arrange a loan of an equal amount at another branch in the United States or Colombia. That way, he explained, the money would appear to be a nontaxable loan.

It was what Amjad Awan called a "cash collateralized advance" and Meyer Lansky had known as a "loan back." Using cash as collateral for a loan is not illegal per se; it is a common banking practice. The trouble comes when such transactions are used to conceal income or when the funds involved are derived from criminal enterprises.

It was clear that Mora believed they could get more laundering business with an account in Panama, and Argudo seemed to offer the way. Indeed, the following day Mora told Mazur that he had a "VIP client" who was interested in throwing business their way once they got a Panama account.

But Mazur wanted another piece in place first, so soon after the lunch, he contacted a Panama City lawyer, Miguel Sanchez, and set up a Panamanian company, IDC International. Coupled with the new relationship with BCCI, the company would put him in a position to move funds offshore directly.

On April 14, Mazur and Abreu flew to Los Angeles. Mora had gone on ahead of them and they were planning to meet up with the Colombian and his brother, Jimmy. Panama and BCCI were still hot topics. Because it was the center for so much legitimate foreign trade and its currency was U.S. dollars, Panama offered the money launderers a better cover for the increasing quantity of checks. With Panamanian accounts, Mora told Mazur and Abreu, they could increase their business even more. Further, the brokers who bought Mora's checks were willing to pay more for checks drawn on Panamanian banks than on U.S. banks because of the extra security provided by Panama's banking laws.

Why not just use the Financial Consulting account now open in Panama? asked Mora. Mazur's checks already had such a good reputation on the black market that they commanded a premium. But Mazur said he did not want any FCI checks coming back to the United States bearing the imprint of a Panama account. His operations were too delicate to risk making American authorities suspicious. Instead, he said, he had begun a safer process.

"First, though, I have to see if I can trust the people I know at the Bank of Credit and Commerce," Mazur said to Mora. Then, he would "grease the skids" and open an account in Panama in the name of IDC International, a Panamanian company he claimed to have "had for a while."

Once everything was in place, Mazur spelled out how it would work. Cash pickups deposited into the accounts of his front businesses would be transferred to the Financial Consulting account at Florida National. From there, the funds would go through the FCI account at BCCI to the new IDC International account in Panama. There, checks would be provided to Mora and he could sell them to the brokers.

However, that was not why Mazur and Abreu had come to Los Angeles. They had traveled west because, finally, they were going to meet the man behind the recent increase in their money-laundering business. It was a critical move up the ladder and the agents were excited.

In the drug world, they knew him as "the Jeweler," and indeed he did own a small jewelry store in Los Angeles. He later claimed that he got into the drug business at the urging of Colombians who patronized his shop.

The Jeweler was a Chilean who had come to the United States in the 1960s. He had spent much of the past two decades working with Colombian drug suppliers. At the age of forty-nine, he had worked so long with the men from Medellín and Cali that he spoke Spanish with a Colombian accent.

Here was a man who enjoyed the good life. He and his wife, Gloria, owned a $2 million 4,300-square-foot mansion a few blocks from the Rose Bowl in Pasadena, an enclave for the old money of Los Angeles. Neighbors caught glimpses of his two Rolls-Royces, a pair of Mercedes-Benz sports cars, and a $100,000 Porsche 928 parked in the drive or pulling out of the electronically controlled gates. Had they been invited inside, the neighbors would have marveled at the tasteful furnishings, which were worth close to $2 million—a painting by Marc Chagall, an etching by Joan Miró, jade carvings large and small.

But neighbors were not invited in. And he was a mysterious figure on Putney Road in staid Pasadena. Some residents gossiped that he might be a drug dealer, rumors fed by the constant comings and goings of swarthy men at all hours of the day and night.

Several times in the first weeks of the new partnership with Mazur and Abreu, Gonzalo Mora, Jr., had boasted about the Jeweler. The Jeweler once laundered $24 million in two months. The Jeweler handled cash collections for the Medellín cartel in New York, Detroit, Chicago, Philadelphia, and Los Angeles. With each story, Mazur and Abreu grew more anxious to meet the Jeweler, to put a face and a name to this major player. Other than the Jeweler, the only name they knew him by was Roberto.

But the Jeweler had grown rich and lasted long in a dangerous trade by being careful. Even at the urging of Mora, Jr., he had resisted meeting the Colombian's new partners. He would not even allow his money to be handed over directly to the new boys. Instead, the cash that his organization was channeling through Mazur and Mora was picked up by Mora's flunkies or by the Moras themselves. They would then hand it over to Abreu or his people.

The first major cash from the Jeweler's organization was $160,000, not the $200,000 that had been promised in early January 1987. On February 17, the Jeweler himself had taken the money to a store on West Seventh Street, near downtown Los Angeles. It was called Casa Musical Sonora and it was owned by the Mora family. He handed the money over to Gonzalo Mora, Sr. Not until the man left did Mora, Sr., notify Abreu that the drop had been made. Then Abreu telephoned the Customs office in Los Angeles and two Spanish-speaking undercover men were sent out to get the cash from the elder Mora.

When the Customs agents returned with the money, it was put in front of a dog trained to sniff out the cocaine residue often found on money used in drug payoffs. The dog "alerted," as they say, to the presence of cocaine residue on the money. The money was then counted and deposited in a bank and transferred to Mazur's account at Florida National Bank.

A week later, the process was repeated: the two undercover agents picked up the cash at Casa Musical. The pattern continued for a month and a half, with all of the pickups running between $90,000 and $200,000. The Jeweler was doing what any smart businessman does with a new system. He was testing it, with more than $2 million in drug proceeds in the first two months. Were the men running it honest with him? Did the system get the cash where it promised and on time? Were there any signs of cops? The Moras had done the same thing a few months earlier, although their tests had been conducted with far less cash.

For their part, the Moras were anxious to land a bigger share of the Jeweler's business. So far, the pickups had been restricted to Los Angeles, but the Jeweler's confidence had risen with each deal. Moreover, he wanted to move some of his laundering business out of Los Angeles. So when the Moras proposed that he meet their partners in the middle of April to discuss expanding their business relationship, the Jeweler agreed.

On the afternoon of April 15, Jimmy Mora and Gonzalo Mora, Jr., drove Mazur and Abreu to the Westin Bonaventure Hotel, an ungainly collection of silo-like glass towers in downtown Los Angeles. There, they were introduced to the Jeweler, a smiling man who spoke good English. His name was Roberto Baez Alcaino. He would turn out to be one of the main cash collectors used by the Medellín cartel in the United States.

That day, Alcaino listened thoughtfully as Mazur and Abreu described the network they had established to handle the cash the Jeweler was collecting. The pattern being used in Los Angeles could be repeated in other cities. Abreu would telephone his contacts and send them for the money, or he would fly to the city himself and pick up the money. Then it would be deposited in one of the operation's bank accounts in the United States and come out clean on the other end when Mora wrote a check in Colombia to the drug suppliers. Along the way, Mora, Mazur, and Alcaino would all get their cuts.

In cities where Customs had Spanish-speaking agents, Abreu would simply do as he had done in Los Angeles: Call the local office and arrange for a couple of undercovers to get the money. For other places, Operation C-Chase had its own jet, a swift and comfortable twin-engine Citation. From Mora's boasts and their brief conversation, it was clear the Jeweler was a man with serious money. So, along with the drug pickups, Mazur made his pitch for a whole line of investment advice. He described the front businesses that he ran, suggesting they could help invest funds in the United States in ways that would conceal the money's ownership and source. Here, too, they found a receptive audience in the once-shy Alcaino. He said that he was planning to build an apartment building in Los Angeles. The catch was he wanted to finance it with drug cash.

No problem, Mazur assured him. They could launder the money for Alcaino and come up with a clean-looking mortgage out of the proceeds. The Jeweler could even deduct the interest payments from his tax returns.

The scheme appealed to Alcaino so strongly that he would later ask Mazur to structure a transaction that would create a $500,000 home improvement loan. He wanted an elevated tennis court, underground parking, and a 4,200-square-foot addition for his house in Pasadena.

Such opportunities were a potential bonanza for C-Chase. They would know where to go when it came time to freeze Alcaino's assets. And, with the apartment loan in the near future, they could test the cash-collateralized loan scheme that Rick Argudo had described at the Bank of Credit and Commerce International.

Three weeks later, Operation C-Chase collided with another government sting, Operation Pisces.

On May 6, 1987, U.S. Attorney General Edwin Meese held a press conference in Los Angeles to announce the conclusion of a mammoth undercover investigation called Operation Pisces. Over the course of three years, it had led to the arrests of more than 400 drug traffickers and the seizure of nine tons of cocaine and $47 million in cash. Drug

Enforcement Administration officials at his side described Pisces as "nothing less than the largest and most successful undercover investigation in federal drug law enforcement history."

Also standing alongside Meese at the press conference was Carlos Villalaz, the attorney general of Panama. Meese praised the Panamanians for their assistance in freezing seventy-seven accounts at eighteen Panamanian banks. The loss of funds was inconsequential to the drug traffickers but what it signified was not: The Panamanian government would not stay bought.

Since 1982 at least, the leaders of the Medellín cartel and other traffickers had been paying large sums of cash to General Manuel Noriega. In return, Noriega had turned his country into a way station for the white powder trade. He allowed the traffickers to ship American-bound cocaine through Panamanian ports and airstrips, protected their drug-processing laboratories, provided safe haven for the kingpins, and helped launder narco dollars.

Along the way, Noriega collected millions of dollars in bribes. Much of the bribe money found its way into Noriega's secret account at the Bank of Credit and Commerce International, as did some of the drug funds. Indeed, when the DEA persuaded the Panamanians to freeze suspected drug accounts at eighteen banks as part of Pisces, fully one third of the accounts were at the Bank of Credit and Commerce International in Panama.

In exchange for Noriega's help, DEA administrator John Lawn sent him a letter that praised the general for his personal assistance and said, "Drug traffickers around the world are now on notice that the proceeds and profits of their illegal ventures are not welcome in Panama."

The disclosure of Panama's cooperation touched off deep concern among the drug dealers and the banks doing business there, including BCCI. It also troubled Bob Mazur and his cohorts in C-Chase.

Their first concern was strategic. Would Panama really be shut down for money laundering? If so, they would have lost months of planning with the Moras and the entree with BCCI. New tactics might have to be adopted, new countries scouted for laundering.

The second worry was more immediate. Mazur knew from his contacts that the DEA undercover operation was very similar to his. DEA agents and local police had posed as money launderers, picking up cash from the collectors and passing it through friendly bank accounts. Cocaine suppliers had been alerted to the possibility of long-term, large-scale undercover penetration. Worse, Operation Pisces had focused on Miami and Los Angeles and one of those named, but not charged, in the indictment was Jimmy Mora. According to the indictment, Mora and another man had been seen delivering a large amount of cash.

This was the more immediate problem, and the C-Chase agents mulled it over in countless discussions in and out of their Tampa office. Mazur, who slipped over to the Customs office during the undercover operation when he thought it was safe, liked to go jogging with the desk-bound deputy special agent in charge of the office, Paul O'Brien. As O'Brien huffed and puffed beside him one day, Mazur tried to convince O'Brien that his scenario was the best one. Put the Colombians on the defensive. Don't wait for them to raise questions or doubts about Mazur and Abreu. When the brainstorming sessions ended, the other agents had agreed to Mazur's plan.

So on May 20, when Jimmy Mora came to Tampa to meet with Mazur, it was Mora who was on the receiving end of hostile questions. Mazur, his voice menacing, complained about the lack of security on Mora's end of the operation. Then he pulled out copies of the Pisces indictments. He said he had had his lawyer get them so he could check out the names. As he read the names aloud, he asked Mora if he recognized any of them. Shaking his head, Mora replied, "No," to each one. Until Mazur came to Gabriel Jaime Mora.

Mora was obviously disturbed. He was hearing his own name in connection with Pisces for the first time. Mora then explained that he had been stopped two years before at Los Angeles International Airport, but, Mora protested, his operation was secure.

"The best thing for us to do is just stop and take a look and do a damage assessment," Mazur said. "It wouldn't be wise for us to go forward."

The C-Chase agents had calculated this move carefully. They figured that the Colombians would expect a government undercover operation to want to hurry business, not slow it down. "It seemed to us that that would be something that would throw them off balance," Mazur later explained.

The slowdown also reflected a basic Customs Service principle. The Service simply didn't want to move too much drug money. It suspected that some launderers would deal through a government sting even after they "made" it because the risk of the eventual bust was more than balanced by the efficiency and security that the undercover operation provided while it ran. Mazur and his colleagues were aiming for the maximum penetration they could achieve while moving the smallest practical volume of dirty money. They succeeded at both counts, largely thanks to Mazur's psychological manipulation.

When Mora said he was returning to Los Angeles to assess the damage to his organization, Mazur cautioned him to go to another city first, such as San Francisco. From there, he could call and check out the damage before flying on to Los Angeles.

Mazur wanted to appear extremely cautious. He knew that Operation C-Chase was going to be buffeted by another storm in a month. The FBI had been running an undercover sting called Operation Cashweb Expressway since 1984, which was going to be brought down with a series of arrests and seizures in thirty days.

In Expressway, FBI agent Robert Paquette had done almost exactly the same thing as Mazur in C-Chase. Paquette had set up a financial services company in Greenwich, Connecticut. It was near an exit on the Connecticut Turnpike, hence the code name Expressway. Through his company, Paquette had been moving money for drug rings in New York and New Jersey. A total of $200 million had been tracked, $14 million of it to Panama.

Expressway would reach high into the Medellín cartel, targeting two of Pablo Escobar's closest associates and top money launderers. It also would reach close to Gonzalo Mora, Jr. Later, Mora would tell Mazur that FBI agents had lured one of his close friends to Aruba, the Caribbean island, along with two other money washers, and then kidnapped him on the high seas and taken him to Puerto Rico to be arrested.

Even before this second jolt, Gonzalo Mora, Jr., sent word from Colombia. He needed a letter from Mazur listing his business contacts and the fronts used in moving Mora's money. People were suspicious. With those suspicions, the money pickups slowed down. Small amounts were picked up a couple of times in June and July, but the pace was not nearly what it had been before Pisces went down.

When Mora next met Mazur face to face at the end of August of 1987, he was apologetic. His clients were indeed highly suspicious and the letter had been necessary to try to calm their fears. Mazur said he understood, adding that the Panamanian account of IDC International was "operational" and had been in use for a month and a half for other business.

"I have had the complete assurance of the people with the Bank of Credit and Commerce here that they will do everything to help me as long as I will be careful not to do anything to jeopardize them," Mazur explained.

Here clearly was an appeal to Mora's greed. Someone had been persuaded that the Americans could be trusted after all. By the fall of 1987, C-Chase was picking up more cash than ever. The Jeweler was using the ring for pickups in New York and Philadelphia as well as Los Angeles. And Gonzalo Mora, Jr., was handling a considerable amount of business in southern Michigan from the mysterious Don Chepe. Abreu had now added Detroit to his list of cities as he flew around the country picking up cash.

Every time Emir Abreu flew in the twin-engine Citation jet, he liked to remember how the operation had come to own it.

Budgets of undercover operations are not bottomless, so agents often use confiscated automobiles and other goods as part of their cover. The green Mercedes-Benz 300E that Bob Mazur drove as his personal car during the undercover operation had been seized from a drug dealer. The Citation jet, too, was seized from a drug smuggler and the C-Chase agents immediately wanted to use it for their operation, but Mazur was a stickler for security. The fewer people who knew what was going on, the better, even those at other government agencies. For this reason, the agents did not want to register the jet with the Federal Aviation Administration as a government aircraft and risk disclosure.

"The likelihood of betrayal is almost nil," said Steve Cook, who took over as one of two C-Chase case agents after Mazur went undercover. "But the key is, and Bob is an expert at this, that you don't make any disclosures that aren't a hundred percent necessary. So in a case like this, you do as much as you can for yourself."

By now, the agents were adept at concealment. They simply took a page out of the crooks' book and used a front. The plane was going to be sold at auction, with the proceeds going to the Customs Service. A major Miami law firm was hired through Financial Consulting Inc. to bid on the plane. The firm was instructed to go as high as necessary at the auction.

The sales price wound up a cool $1 million, and the plane was registered clean in the name of FCI. The lawyers never knew who had really hired them. Had they, the little hitch might never have occurred.

FCI never paid the Florida state sales tax due on the $1 million purchase price. It never paid the purchase price either. The transaction was simply a transfer of assets on the books of the Customs Service, which would have gotten the money anyway. They could use the plane and sell it later.

But the State of Florida had no idea what was going on, so it sent the law firm a letter demanding payment of $50,000 in sales tax from its clients. Mazur told the lawyers that the plane would not be kept in Florida, and the law firm helped negotiate a release from the sales tax, all without the lawyers ever learning the true identity of their client.

As the ring flourished, the private jet carried Abreu to cities across the United States, where he picked up suitcases filled with cash from dangerous, sometimes nervous strangers. Just like legitimate money couriers, Abreu often arrived with nothing more than the number of a telephone beeper. Beepers were the communication instrument of choice for drug dealers because they could be registered in fake names and disposed of easily and cheaply.

The pickups were fraught with risks to Abreu's safety and to the security of the operation itself. Abreu always arranged for backup from local Customs agents, but if things went wrong and they had to show themselves it could blow Operation C-Chase to hell. Or they could be too late in responding and find Emir Abreu blown to hell.

Sometimes the connections were not only dangerous, they were bizarre. In one instance, as Abreu waited to pick up cash outside a supermarket in New York City, a van wheeled around the corner and two kids hopped out. Right in the middle of the street they unloaded four heavy boxes that Abreu had to hurry over and haul away. It took a team of ten agents several hours to count the contents of the boxes—$2 million in cash.

A credit card was the source of a close call. Because Detroit did not have a Spanish-speaking Customs agent, Abreu and the case agent, Steve Cook, flew up there regularly for pickups once drug money started flowing their way from Mora's new clients.

One snowy night they picked up four suitcases of cash and brought them back to the airplane, which was sitting at a small commercial airport outside the city. They had an attendant fuel the plane and deice the wings. The attendant then came over with a bill for $1,100. Abreu gave the young man a credit card, but the guy handed it back and said, "I'm sorry, sir. Your card has expired."

Without batting an eye, the agent stepped back into the plane. The attendant, fearing that he was about to see $1,100 fly away, stuck his head into the plane and looked around. What he saw was Abreu opening a suitcase filled with cash and pulling out a stack of hundred-dollar bills. Abreu counted out the money and handed it over. The attendant smiled and waved good-bye.

A few days after they returned to Tampa, the agents telephoned Customs in Detroit. No, there had been no report of suspicious activity at the airport. On the next trip to Detroit, the C-Chase agents used the same airport. This time they got the red carpet treatment literally. The attendant ran out to the plane and, unrolling a strip of carpet, greeted them enthusiastically and politely. It was another telltale sign of what the agents knew all too well—everyone likes cash and too few people ask questions about it.

Usually, Abreu would bring the cash back to Tampa. Customs agents would count the money and deposit it in the FCI account at Florida National Bank. From the start, the agents could not get their cash counts to match the Colombians. The agents usually found themselves coming up short of the tally provided by Mora's people, which could create trust problems in the long run. They hit upon the idea of selling money-counting machines to the Colombians, just like the ones used in banks and more sophisticated drug operations.

During a demonstration for a skeptical Colombian housewife in a Chicago hotel room, an agent was trying to explain the machine's operation as he fed bills into the whirling cylinder. When he leaned over the machine, his dangling tie fell into the counter and the cylinder snatched it and dragged the red-faced agent to his knees. As the agent struggled to shut off the machine, the woman shouted gleefully: "Eat you tie. Eat you tie."

The incident, recorded on the hidden videocamera, became popular viewing at the Customs offices in Tampa. One of the agents defended the incident, claiming: "It broke the ice. We sold them two machines."

CHAPTER TWELVE

A Full Service Bank

On November 24, 1987, Bob Mazur walked into the offices of Financial Consulting in New Port Richey, Florida, and found a message waiting to call a Mr. Hussain at BCCI in Panama City. It was a telephone call that would change the course of Operation C-Chase in stunning fashion, moving it from the minors to the major leagues, although ironically Mazur didn't bother to tape the conversation when he returned the call.

Syed Aftab Hussain, a junior officer at BCCI in Panama City, informed him that someone had come to the bank to cash a check drawn on Mazur's IDC International account. However, there was a discrepancy. The amount on the check in numbers was $110,300, but the amount in writing was an even $110,000. Hussain wanted to know which amount to honor.

Mazur was flustered. He knew the check was from a presigned batch that he had sent Mora after a recent deposit from a pickup of drug cash in Detroit. Since he had no way of knowing which amount was right, he said he would have to talk to someone else and get back to Hussain.

Before hanging up, Hussain suggested politely that Mazur contact him in the future before checks of this type were to be cashed. Mazur could provide Hussain with the amount of the check and the name of the payee in advance to avoid any confusion.

As Mazur discussed the conversation with his fellow agents, it began to worry him. It was unusual that a banker would call from Panama about a discrepancy. Why not just reject the check and leave it up to the person holding the paper to get a new one? With Operation Pisces fresh in everyone's mind, Mazur feared he was about to get the boot at the

148

Bank of Credit and Commerce International. Or had they stumbled onto something else here?

By late November, the operation had laundered a total of roughly $6 million in drug cash. Most of the transactions had been handled through about 200 checks issued on the account at Florida National Bank, but the last $2.2 million had gone through the IDC International account at the Bank of Credit and Commerce International in Panama. The new system seemed promising although it had taken a while to get started.

Back in the summer of 1987, Rick Argudo had quit BCCI to take a job with another bank in Tampa. His replacement, Dayne Miller, seemed as cooperative as Argudo when Mazur opened the IDC account. When Miller had asked for bank references for the company, Mazur replied that IDC was a recently purchased shell corporation. The banker said that he understood. Mazur filled out the account forms. Miller assured him the forms would be kept in Panama. As an added precaution, Miller said, Mazur should allow BCCI Panama to mail his statements to Miller so that no one would be aware of the Panama account.

Mazur said he was also interested in BCCI accounts in Liechtenstein and Puerto Rico. Since BCCI did not have offices in those countries, Miller suggested that Mazur supplement the Panama account with accounts at either BCCI in Luxembourg or Banque de Commerce et de Placements, an affiliate of BCCI in Switzerland known within the bank as BCP.

Within a couple of weeks, Miller had delivered the IDC checks. Because of the slowdown caused by fallout from Operation Pisces, Mazur did not turn over any presigned checks on the new account to Mora until September. And drug money was not moved through BCCI for nearly two months after that, more than a year since the start of Operation C-Chase.

Laundering drug money through BCCI was complicated, but from his years of working on cases of money launderers, Mazur had broken the process down into several steps.

The first step was picking up the cash. On November 9, 1987, Emir Abreu and another agent went to Detroit and picked up $609,045. The money was counted and deposited by government agents in an account set up with the knowledge of bank officials at the National Bank of Detroit. Step two: The next day, the $609,045 was wire-transferred to Mazur's Financial Consulting account at Florida National Bank. Step three: On November 12, $590,775 was wired to the Bank of Credit and Commerce in Panama City and credited to Mazur's new IDC account; the amount was less than the original $609,045 because Mazur had kept his commission. Step four: Gonzalo Mora, Jr., filled out the presigned checks in the names of the drug suppliers or their brokers and passed them out over several days. It was the discrepancy in amounts on one of these checks that had caught the attention of Syed Hussain in Panama.

After his initial conversation with Hussain on November 24, Mazur telephoned Gonzalo Mora, Jr., in Colombia to find out the right amount for the check. Then he called Hussain again that same day. Mazur said that the check should have been written for $110,300. A new one would be issued in that amount and Hussain should cash it when it was presented at the bank later. By the way, Mazur added, another $899,080 would be deposited in the account by the following day.

Again, Hussain was eager to be of service. Although still a trainee, he had been instilled with the drive to bring in new deposits. Hussain said he would be in Miami in early December. Perhaps they should get together. Before hanging up, Hussain told the American: "BCCI is a full service bank."

It was a Saturday morning, but undercover was a seven-day-a-week job. Bob Mazur was nervous as he drove toward his ten o'clock appointment with Syed Hussain on December 5, 1987. He got lost for ten minutes even though he was looking for one of the best-known corners in Miami—Brickell Avenue and Eighth Street, which was known locally as Calle Ocho and represented the main street of the city's thriving Cuban district. At the point where Calle Ocho met Brickell, it was all high-rise office and residential towers fronting the blue waters of Biscayne Bay.

Finally, Mazur found the address and turned into the Brickell Key Condominiums, a tall building situated on a wedge-shaped island where the Miami River emptied into the bay. It was on this spot that Seminole Indians conducted their first trade with the settlers of the New World. It had not turned out to be such a good deal for the Seminoles.

Waiting in the lobby was a man who was large and round, soft-spoken and shy. Syed Hussain, known to his friends by his middle name of Aftab, had just turned thirty. He had only a two-year degree in economics and had tried several jobs without success, including selling Oriental rugs. An uncle who worked for BCCI finally got him a job with the bank and he had been shipped off to Panama as a $20,000-a-year trainee early in 1987.

BCCI was Hussain's best job, but he still was not making enough to support his wife and new baby, and to pay for medical care required by his retarded son, so he had kept his eyes open and watched for an opportunity to move up fast.

Though many of BCCI's customers in Latin America were merchants of Arab and Jewish descent, the bank's principal marketing target was the "high net worth" individual, a person with the means to make deposits of millions of dollars at a time. One of the intriguing things Hussain had spotted soon after arriving at BCCI in Panama was that senior officers accepted these large cash deposits without asking questions. Much of that money, he learned, went to the "manager's ledger," where specially numbered accounts, code-named M/L, were kept segregated and confidential.

It was luck that had brought Hussain into the flap over the check, and it would turn out to be the worst luck of his life. There had been a commotion in the branch when a teller refused to cash the check, and Hussain, who had gone over to calm the excited Colombian courier trying to cash it, had wound up calling Mazur after examining the brief history of the IDC International account.

Hussain had seen immediately that the American's method of moving money through the bank was amateurish. Guessing what Mazur had been up to was not hard, even though the IDC account had been open only a short time. Big deposits were flowing into the account, and money brokers were drawing out large amounts with checks that bore Mazur's signature but not his handwriting in the other spaces. Hussain had even sensed the customer's discomfort when asked which amount was right on the $110,300 check. The guy didn't know what the right figure was because he hadn't written the check. Hussain had a better idea. And the novice banker was about to see how far his better idea and that bit of initial luck would carry him.

As he guided Mazur to a small alcove off the lobby, Hussain explained in poor English that he was in Miami because his son required specialized medical care. The two men sat in low chairs, talking in whispers. Mazur placed his briefcase on the coffee table in front of them. Inside, the hidden tape recorder was spinning silently.

"What type of service do you want from us and what do you expect from us?" asked Hussain in the conversation picked up by the recorder.

"Okay. As of, well, thus far, I've had most of my dealings with either the Tampa agency of BCCI or your branch of BCCI," replied Mazur, who decided this was not a brush-off but a pitch. "I anticipate that I will be expanding my contacts with BCCI branches to include some of them in Luxembourg and others in Europe, too. I have a definite need to aid clients of mine who at times are looking to place funds in investments and to transfer funds. But the thing that is of utmost desire for me is to maintain the confidentiality of the client's transactions with you people."

"We are totally, all the confidentiality, all the secrecy," Hussain said, the words tumbling out. "Even sometimes our own staff doesn't know what is happening."

Here was the opening. Hussain took it. Clients who wanted privacy, he said, should not use checks. "I would definitely advise you, my personal advice is don't use a check," said the young banker. "Don't write the check. Don't give anybody checks."

Was he referring to the recent government crackdown in Panama? asked Mazur. Yes, Operation Pisces, said Hussain. The only people who got caught were ones who used checks, he explained. Clients who used another popular method had not been caught.

Hussain proposed his alternative. Instead of turning over checks to the money brokers, Mazur should open an account for $2 million at the BCCI branch in Luxembourg, one of the more secure banking havens in Europe. The funds could be placed in an interest-bearing certificate of deposit. Then Mazur could take a loan for an equal amount at the Panama branch, minus the bank's fee, which would be negotiable. When the $2 million CD matured, it would be used by the bank to retire the loan.

For Mazur, this was a new wrinkle on the cash-collateralized advance scheme: In case some nosy third party made inquiries, Mazur could designate a parcel of property as security. But that was just a cover. "Definitely, we are not going to give you a loan against the property," explained Hussain. "We'll give you a loan against the dollar deposit."

Mazur wondered how extensive this practice was at BCCI. Argudo had described the same basic transaction to him. Was it in the bank's training manual? How many millions of dollars were being washed through BCCI in this manner?

Misjudging the contemplation for hesitation, Hussain said he understood that selling the idea to clients might be tough for Mazur. "I know that they are very rigid in their ways," he said. "They are very fidgety, very devious or rigid. They are very tough to handle."

To ease Mazur's concern for secrecy, Hussain said that such loans were handled by what he called "an inner team." He offered to introduce Mazur to some members of that team who worked in the Miami office. "They are all professional and top high-level people," he said. "They know how to talk and when to talk. They don't talk loose."

Hussain was eager to close a deal. Could Mazur possibly have a deposit by the end of December? The implication was that it would seal the bargain for special service for Mazur.

"It's good for the bank and then the bank can help the clients," he said, fumbling for a business card as the two men started to part. He had left the cards upstairs, so he hurried to get one. By the time he came down and the men exchanged farewells, it was twenty minutes past noon. Mazur promised to get back in touch with Hussain as soon as possible about a new transaction. He said he was not sure of the timing.

As he walked away, Mazur turned the clasp on his briefcase, switching off the recorder.

In slightly more than two hours, the previous year's work had become just a prelude. Operation C-Chase was getting its first look at a new, far more important quarry.

Driving back to the airport, Mazur could not believe what had occurred. Here was a junior bank officer laying out a scheme that seemed to be routine within this huge international bank. When he replayed the tape for other C-Chase agents, they were equally surprised —and exultant.

"Here was this guy laying the whole thing out," exclaimed Steve Cook, who was sharing the supervisory duties of case agent with another senior Customs agent, Laura Sherman.

The agents wanted to strike fast—secure the deal with Hussain and follow the new trail—but they needed a big chunk of money to launder. That was out of their control. That was why Mazur had been indefinite about when he would do the new deal. They would have to wait, hoping that Hussain did not return to Panama before they came up with the cash.

When Alvaro Uribe first came through the door with his tip about Gonzalo Mora, Jr., a year and a half earlier, an assistant U.S. attorney in Tampa named Mark Jackowski had been assigned to supervise the investigation. A veteran drug prosecutor, Jackowski had paid scant attention to C-Chase since then. He figured the best the agents would do was round up some money launderers and maybe a minor drug supplier. It just did not appear too promising. In addition, he had a number of other cases under way that seemed far more significant, among them the Tampa investigation of General Manuel Noriega's connection to drug dealers.

But when Laura Sherman told him what happened with Hussain on December 5, Jackowski was suddenly very interested. C-Chase might snare a bank in its net and that would be a big case. So the prosecutor began taking a more active role in what would prove to be a dangerous dance to keep the investigation on track, fighting off incursions from the DEA and even other offices of the Customs Service itself.

On December 8, word came that a million dollars in cash was ready for pickup in Detroit from Don Chepe's people. Speed was vital. Abreu flew to Detroit that day to get the money and, rather than take the time to return to Tampa, he had the money counted in Detroit and deposited in a friendly account at the National Bank of Detroit. The following day, $1.18 million was wired to Mazur's account at Florida National Bank.

That was all Mazur needed. Shortly before nine o'clock on the morning of December 9, he telephoned Hussain in Miami. Mazur said that he had received a large amount of money and wanted to do a deal. They agreed to meet late that afternoon at the bank's offices in Miami.

The Bank of Credit and Commerce International's offices were at 1200 Brickell Avenue, one of the gleaming towers in the heart of Miami's financial and legal communities, both of which had prospered enormously in recent years by catering to the drug trade. Miami defense lawyers who used to specialize in white-collar cases had even been tagged with a new name: the white powder bar.

BCCI's operations were spread over three floors of the building; the bank's fast-growing Latin American and Caribbean business on fifteen, day-to-day operations on seventeen, and special transactions on nineteen. Mazur took the elevator to nineteen.

Sipping coffee in a conference room overlooking Biscayne Bay, Mazur explained to Hussain that he wanted to try the scheme outlined on Saturday. He would deposit $1.18 million in a certificate of deposit and be issued a loan for a corresponding amount. He listened as Hussain went over the details of the agreement. The money would be transferred directly to Panama without Mazur's name or account number showing up. In Panama, the money would be deposited in a special account on the "manager's ledger." Only a handful of people would be aware of the account's existence and it would identified by number, not name. The number would be preceded by the letters M/L, for manager's ledger. The loan proceeds would be recorded as a credit to the IDC International account in Panama.

Three times during the meeting, Hussain had telephoned someone and spoken in Urdu, the language of the Mohajir Muslim refugees in Pakistan. Then he stepped out of the room and returned with documents for Mazur to sign. The papers opened the new account, which would be number $M/L306$. Hussain also proposed a code name, John Hussain, to be used when Mazur contacted the bank.

Then came the delicate part of Mazur's job. Jackowski had stressed before the meeting that conviction under the money-laundering statute would require that the banker be aware of the source of the funds involved in the transaction. That meant Mazur had to let Hussain know clearly that his clients were traffickers. If Hussain balked or threw Mazur out, BCCI and the banker would be in the clear. If not, well, that would be another story. Luck provided a dramatic vehicle for the disclosure.

"One of the reasons for my initial inability to plot a course here with you, as of last week, is that there was the untimely demise of one of my client's associates," Mazur said matter-of-factly. "And I see it's in the paper. And it's just something that we ought . . . when it comes to money, they don't have a whole lot of patience."

With a chuckle, he handed Hussain a clipping from the *St. Petersburg Times* dated December 6, 1987. The clipping recounted the bloody death of a notorious Medellín cartel figure, Rafael Cardona Salazar. He and a young secretary were inside his classic car dealership outside Medellín when they were cut down by a barrage of automatic weapon fire from a gang of men. At the time, the article said, Salazar was the subject of an extradition request from the U.S. government. A few hours before Salazar was slain, six young men had been killed at a house in Medellín. The article said police believed the killings were linked to rivalries among narcotics traffickers in Medellín.

"You know this, this man?" asked Hussain incredulously.

"Mr. Salazar. Not directly, but indirectly."

"How, how was he killed?"

"He was gunned down. Machine-gunned."

"Huh."

Mazur stared intently at the young banker and explained: "The fact of the matter is that I will discuss only with you, but never with anyone else ever again, is that obviously this money comes from some of the largest drug dealers in South America and that is something that needs to be kept between us. I need to have complete confidence in you as an individual."

Hussain did not back out of the deal, and he would later claim it was because he was too scared by Mazur's chilling nonchalance over the murders. Instead, he negotiated the bank's fee for the transaction. It would be one and a half percent of the deposit, $17,700. And it would be handled discreetly. The interest rate on the loan would be greater than the interest earned on the CD. The bank would pocket the difference as its share of the deal, up front of course.

"This drug-related money," said Hussain, "they put their money in CDs?"

Yes, sometimes they do, Mazur said. And he was working on them to do it more often.

The next day, Mazur picked up Hussain at the Brickell Key condos and they drove to the bank to finish the deal. With Hussain whispering instructions to him, Mazur told a woman at Florida National Bank to wire $1.18 million to Panama for him. The money would be transferred to a correspondent bank in New York, which would then notify BCCI to credit account M/L306 in Panama. The transfer would take place through CHIPS, the computerized electronic transfer system for moving dollars around the world swiftly and anonymously. Once the money arrived in M/L306, the "loan" proceeds would be transferred to the IDC account, minus the interest differential. In their haste to make the transaction, they had decided to forgo the added cover of a European account.

Hussain wondered how much of this sort of business he might expect from his new customer. About $5 million a month, Mazur replied. Hussain said he would like a large deposit by the end of the year. It would help make the young banker and his office look good when the bank examined and ranked each of its branches worldwide.

Later in December, undercover agents collected about $1.5 million in pickups in Detroit and New York, but rather than simply passing it through Hussain, the money was to be used as leverage. It would lead them higher up at BCCI. It was apparent that Hussain was a low-level employee. Someone had taught him this scheme. At the first meeting, Hussain had mentioned higher-ranking people who "didn't talk loose." On December 9, he had made three telephone calls and obviously received instructions. It was simple. Dangle the money at BCCI and see who came running this time.

On December 22, Mazur telephoned Hussain, who had returned to Panama. He said he wanted to set up another loan back, this time for $1.5 million. But Mazur still had not received all the documents from the first deal, so he told Hussain that he wanted a contact in the bank's Miami office, someone closer.

"Is there someone who can really be trusted?" asked the agent.

"Amjad Awan is on the team," replied Hussain. He would arrange a meeting for Mazur.

Amjad Awan had been rehabilitated. He had been transferred out of Panama in mild disgrace over the loss of $3.7 million in the fake Treasury bond scam in the middle of 1984, but he had retained the Noriega account, which played a major role in his comeback.

Since moving to BCCI's representative office in Washington, D.C., Awan's principal duty had remained taking care of the Panamanian dictator and his expensive tastes. Noriega's account at BCCI was used to pay for trips around the world for Noriega, his wife, and his three daughters. Usually, they would be accompanied by an entourage of security men and associates. Their bills, too, were paid from the all-purpose, bottomless slush fund.

Awan provided personal service, BCCI style. He arranged for hotels and booked airplane reservations, hired limousines and paid for Dom Pérignon champagne and the flowers that filled Noriega's hotel suites. Most of this he put on his own American Express card. When the bills came in, he simply paid them out of Noriega's account. Often, he would be on hand to greet the general and assist him when he traveled to the United States.

One such occasion was particularly memorable for Awan. Noriega had flown to New York on June 8, 1986. He wanted to spend a few days in the city before going on to Washington, where he would present an award. He flew on a Boeing 727 specially outfitted for him and assigned to the Panamanian military. Marijuana smuggler Steven Kalish had bought the plane for Noriega for $2.2 million as a favor back in 1983.

In New York, Awan had booked an $850-a-night suite for the general and his wife at the Helmsley Palace on Madison Avenue, their favorite hotel. He also had arranged for limousines to whisk Noriega to his meetings and his wife, Felicidad, to Bloomingdale's and her other favorite shopping spots. Awan himself had gone to New York and rented a room in the same hotel to oversee the arrangements.

On June 12, Noriega flew to Andrews Air Force Base, the installation outside Washington, D.C., used by U.S. government planes and aircraft belonging to VIPs. Later that day, he was to present a Panamanian medal to the head of the Inter-American Defense Board, U.S. Lieutenant General Robert Schweitzer. Noriega's presence in Washington and the award presentation were clear signals to the world of his alliance with the Reagan administration. But before the plane bought for him with drug money even landed, Manuel Noriega had become the victim of a carefully planned, bitterly ironic trick played by the editors of *The New York Times*.

When Noriega stepped off the jet at Andrews that morning, he was fuming. On the trip down, he had seen the morning's *Times*. Atop the front page was the headline "Panama Strongman Said to Trade in Drugs, Arms and Illicit Money." Below was an explosive story by Seymour M. Hersh, a Pulitzer Prize–winning investigative reporter. Timed by the paper's editors to coincide with the visit to Washington, it accused Noriega of horrendous crimes—his links to the torture and beheading of one of his political rivals, Hugo Spadafora, his participation in money laundering and drug trafficking.

By the time Awan spoke with him later that day, Noriega was still furious about the Hersh article. He denounced it as a pack of lies to the banker. Awan nodded in agreement and kept silent. It was not his job to ask Noriega about such allegations.

Awan might have drawn his own conclusions, even without the steady flow of cash and checks into Noriega's account. In March of 1986, the corpse of Cesar Rodriguez, Noriega's long-time confidant and business partner, had been found by police in Medellín. With him was Ruben Paredes, one of the sons of Noriega's predecessor as military chief. The newspapers were awash with stories that they had been killed during a drug deal. There had been other rumors, too—that Noriega was paid off by the drug traffickers to protect them, that the CIA and the Pentagon's Defense Intelligence Agency paid him for information.

Evidence of this activity was plentiful in the transactions connected with Noriega's secret account at the Bank of Credit and Commerce International. Despite monthly expenses running into tens of thousands of dollars for Noriega's personal excesses, the account balance was always healthy, usually hovering around $20 million or so. Funds to replenish it came from a variety of sources. Although Noriega made use of many of Panama's 140 banks, a portion of the protection money he was paid by the Medellín cartel found its way into Noriega's account at BCCI, often dropped off by one of Noriega's close military aides, such as Colonel Luis del Cid. And some of the money that made its way into the account was from the Central Intelligence Agency. The agency, which had had Noriega on its payroll since the early 1970s, later would acknowledge paying him about $200,000. The general would claim he received far more.

It was the ultimate manager's ledger account at BCCI, and Amjad Awan maintained strict personal responsibility for it. He alone had seen the pattern of transactions for years. The notion that this was an intelligence account set up by Noriega for the Panamanian Defense Forces was ludicrous. Awan was too smart not to draw some chilling conclusions about where his patron got his funds, but his job, as he and BCCI defined it, was not to ask questions.

Through the eighties, the general's personal fortune grew substantially and his accounts with BCCI were consolidated in London. Awan played a key role in setting up this more sophisticated financial network for Noriega. Awan had arranged for Noriega to buy a chateau in France, a favorite hideaway for Noriega's assets. And $500,000 worth of checks from Noriega's BCCI accounts were passed through First American Bank in Washington, where Awan used office space assigned to the BCCI representative office.

Monthly, and more often if the need arose, Awan would fly to Panama. He would go over the monthly charges on the account, ticking off the credit card bills from the shopping trips taken by Noriega's wife, Felicidad, and their three daughters, listing the hotel and limousine services.

In January 1987, Noriega, his wife, and several associates ran up a bill of $4,764 to Elegant Limousine Service in Los Angeles. Later that same month, the Noriegas and their friends spent $10,359 at the Helmsley Palace in New York and $2,623 on stretch limousines from Manhattan Limousine Ltd. A month later, they were back and the hotel bill was $9,788 and the limos cost $1,279.

In May 1987, there was $30,000 worth of tickets for the Noriegas and associates for a trip that began in San Francisco and wound through Taiwan, Tokyo, and Honolulu before winding up in Los Angeles. On May 22, Awan submitted a handwritten voucher to Noriega listing $149,010.53 in expenses for the year so far.

Amjad Awan and BCCI were always ready to help a customer. Late in 1986, Awan received a telephone call at his house from Eric Arturo Delvalle, the president of Panama. Noriega had given him the banker's name. The government was trying to sell a tropical island called Contadora. Delvalle wondered whether Awan might have any customers or investors who would be interested.

Contadora was rich in modern history. It had been developed as a private resort, with the government of Panama providing most of the financing under General Omar Torrijos. It had been the site of the negotiations over the Panama Canal Treaty in 1979. At one stage in his gilded, short-lived exile, the Shah of Iran had stayed there. In return for providing a haven for the Shah, the U.S. State Department had quashed a gun-running indictment in Miami against a Panamanian crony of Noriega's. Yet Noriega hated the island because of the connection to Torrijos and the fact that its owner, businessman Gabriel Lewis, was one of Noriega's chief political opponents.

When the resort failed in 1984, Noriega took control of the facilities and installed Cesar Rodriguez as its manager. Despite Rodriguez's lavish efforts, which included flying in entertainers from the United States, the resort failed. For a time, while it was under Rodriguez's control, its airstrip had been used for drug smuggling. Then Lewis announced that the island was being sold to a Japanese businessman who would develop it and sell shares in the development company to island residents. Noriega was determined to undermine the sale by bringing in his own buyer.

After Delvalle's call, Awan consulted colleagues in London about potential buyers. The name that came up was Ghaith Pharaon, the wealthy Saudi Arabian who had acquired the National Bank of Georgia from Bert Lance nearly a decade before.

Pharaon had sold his stock in BCCI earlier in 1986, but it went to his brother, Wabel, and Pharaon retained close ties to the bank and its founder, Agha Hasan Abedi. Just the year before, he had bought another American bank, Independence Bank, in a deal spotted by BCCI bankers and arranged and financed by Abedi.

Independence Bank was a medium-sized bank in Encino, California, a community near Los Angeles in the San Fernando Valley. In November 1984, a team of BCCI employees who had traveled to California learned that the bank was for sale. They wrote a letter to Abedi that said "acquiring Independence Bank will give us much required 'freedom' for our future growth and progress in this part of the world."

On April 30, 1985, Pharaon bought it for $23 million. His application to the Federal Reserve Board said he was putting up $8.5 million of his own money and borrowing the remaining $14.5 million.

By 1985, however, the building boom had stopped in Saudi Arabia and Pharaon's own finances were deteriorating. His primary company, Interdec, was restructuring loans with its bankers around the world. When he had trouble getting the $14.5 million loan, he turned to BCCI. The lender, Bank of Boston, accepted a letter of credit guaranteeing a portion of the money. The letter of credit came from Banque Arabe et Internationale d'Investissement in Paris, which was run by Abedi crony Yves Lamarche, one of several Bank of America executives who had remained associated with BCCI after the American bank pulled out of its partnership in the late 1970s. BAII was the same institution that had loaned $50 million to the Arabs who bought First American Bank in 1982. That transaction, too, had been orchestrated by Abedi and his top associates at BCCI.

Not until much later would federal banking regulators contend that the $8.5 million down payment was a loan to Pharaon from BCCI and that BCCI had arranged the letter of credit and guaranteed the Paris bank that it would be reimbursed for any losses.

Once Pharaon acquired control, a former BCCI executive, Kemal Shoaib, was installed as president of Independence Bank, and the institution embarked on an ambitious growth program that would triple its assets to $600 million and put the bank on the road to financial problems.

So it was logical that Awan would be directed to Pharaon when BCCI needed a potential investor to help out a major client. The Saudi entered into some preliminary talks with the Panamanian government. He said he planned to turn the island into another Club Med location, the resort chain in which Pharaon held a substantial amount of stock.

For his part, Noriega used the talks with Pharaon to ruin the proposed sale to the Japanese businessman by Lewis. He announced that he had arranged for an Arab investor to acquire Contadora. Not long after that, Pharaon pulled out of the deal. Noriega proceeded with the sale to the Japanese company, but he cut Gabriel Lewis out of the deal.

Hitching his star to Noriega had put Amjad Awan's career back on track at BCCI. Near the middle of 1987, the bank was ready to reward him. They decided to transfer him to an executive slot in the New York office. Promotion or not, Awan had spent enough time in New York to know that he did not want to live there. He felt it was no place for his family. He tried to convince Abdur Razzak Sakhia, who would be his boss in New York, to cancel the transfer. However, Sakhia felt that Awan was simply trying to avoid coming under his strict leadership.

"Awan was a very free-spirited person, a very independent person," recalled Sakhia. "I was known as a conservative, tough administrator, so he wouldn't go to work under that discipline."

After failing to persuade Sakhia not to move him, Awan went to Agha Sahib, telephoning Abedi in London.

"Sir, I'm not the fellow for this position," he said to the bank president.

"Where do you want to go?" Abedi asked.

"I'd take Zimbabwe. I'd take Zambia. But not New York," said Awan.

"Well, how's Miami?" asked Abedi.

"Perfect. I can handle it."

So Awan was appointed head of marketing for the bank's hottest growth area, which was called the Latin American and Caribbean Region Office. Known within the bank as LACRO, it was based in Miami and covered BCCI's operations from Tampa to Argentina. The office did not handle regular banking transactions. It was billed as an administrative and marketing operation for the region. Its main function, however, was implementing BCCI's signature EMP program—moving cash deposits out of developing countries and into more hospitable tax and political environments.

Awan packed up his wife and their two children, left their home in Bethesda, Maryland, a nice suburb of Washington, and bought a new house in one of Miami's most exclusive neighborhoods, the Cocoplum section of Coral Gables. His experience in Panama would very soon come in handy.

CHAPTER THIRTEEN

The American Secret

The Miami office that Amjad Awan joined in August of 1987 was one of the spokes in the growing, hidden empire that Agha Sahib and the Bank of Credit and Commerce was building in the United States. Within the bank, the United States was viewed as the "second leg" of the growing institution, with the first planted firmly in Europe. Despite being outlawed by American regulators, the bank had acquired control over banks with assets in excess of $10 billion in the country. And even bigger plans were afoot. The lure of the world's richest banking market was too much to resist for a man devoted to creating the world's biggest bank.

Abedi made his plans clear a few weeks after Awan's transfer to Miami. It was September 30, 1987, and the occasion was a gathering of executives from BCCI and First American at the bank's office on Park Avenue in New York City. As usual, Abedi's language was florid, but there was no mistaking the meaning, the conviction, the sense that nothing would stand in their way.

"It will be a new creature," Abedi said of the BCCI empire in the United States. "What will be the volume and size of this creature? I am placing you into a situation where you will be creating assets of $10 billion and profit of $200 million for the group, though this may not be reflected in your books. You will not be sitting in this building. You will have a building with twenty-five floors. You will become an executive in the real sense of the word. You have to have a clear direction and vision to become that.

"How many people will you have? What capability will they have? How will you develop their qualities? Quality is there. It will take time to bring it out. There should be clarity about the goals and directions."

Little had interfered with Abedi's mission. When Pakistan had

162

nationalized his United Bank, he had created another and structured it to be free of the control of any single government or regulator. When American regulators had blocked his expansion efforts in the seventies, he had gone underground. When the Bank of England tried to limit his growth there, he had directed his efforts to Asia and Africa. When severe losses from the bank's runaway trading operation had threatened to demolish all that he had built, he had overseen a giant financial fraud that propped up the bank with money entrusted to it by hundreds of thousands of depositors. So when Agha Hasan Abedi told his key executives that they would build a new creature in the United States, what was there to stop him?

The plan was ambitious. Abedi wanted to make another run at gaining the approval from U.S. regulators to open a full-service banking operation in the United States. All that he operated legally in the United States were agency offices, second-class banks that could not take domestic deposits. With $20 billion in assets on the books elsewhere, branches in seventy-three countries, and the best lawyers money could buy, Abedi was confident that he could win approval for a full-fledged bank. He would start slowly, receiving approval to acquire a small bank in New York, Florida, Texas, or California. The bank would be an iceberg; beneath the tip would be the immense secret network of banks and branches already under the control of BCCI in the United States.

Portions of the strategy were spelled out in a memo to Abedi dated October 22, 1987, less than a month after his New York speech. The memo, signed by Abdur Sakhia, the bank's North American manager, stated the case for owning a U.S. bank outright and discussed a series of options for doing so. The plan itself contained nothing illegal. Rather, it provided a public strategy that would build on what Abedi and his frontmen had already accomplished in secret. Indeed, Sakhia was either unaware of the earlier rejections of the bank's efforts to acquire U.S. institutions through legal means or chose to ignore them.

"The home of BCC is in U.S. dollars," wrote Sakhia. "The flag of BCC is U.S. dollars. It is therefore quite surprising that BCC does not have a 'real' presence in the home of the dollar—the United States of America. It would make immense sense to have a direct access to U.S. dollar deposits in the largest economy in the world, which is expressed in U.S. dollars. Having a branch/bank will open our doors to a deposit base of 3 trillion dollars in the United States."

Already, the bank had invested heavily in offices and employees in the country. Converting to a full service bank would cost little more. In addition, he said, the bank had a corps of American officers working abroad who could provide executive staff immediately for any institution that BCCI acquired.

"United States is the land of immigrants," wrote Sakhia. "Our own experience since the beginning of our operations here confirms that U.S. customers will do business with us if we can meet their standards of service and quality, notwithstanding that we are a foreign bank. We believe that, after the third-world countries where BCC achieved its major successes, the U.S. is the first industrialized country where we will find a high degree of acceptability."

A month later, Sakhia wrote to Abedi about the possibility of implementing the plan with the purchase of The Hibernia Bank in San Francisco. Its Indonesian owners, operating through a series of Hong Kong entities, had recently put the bank up for sale. With assets of $1.6 billion and forty branches in the San Francisco area, the bank offered a strong entry point for BCCI, said Sakhia. Not long after the memo, however, Hibernia was bought by Security Pacific National Bank, at the time the second-largest bank in California behind the Bank of America.

In early December 1987, Sakhia flew to London for a BCCI meeting. While there, he discussed the planned American expansion with Abedi. Soon after returning to New York, Sakhia had good news for Abedi. "In reference to our discussion in London on the subject, we have come across a small bank in San Francisco which is believed to be clean," Sakhia wrote in a letter addressed to "Agha Sahib."

The letter did not identify the bank, but described it as a five-year-old institution with assets of $39.9 million. "Since the bank is so small," wrote Sakhia, "it can be effectively assessed and can be assimilated into our corporate culture."

This deal, too, fell through, but the corporate culture at BCCI made anything seem possible. Indeed, it was that culture, and the friendships it nourished, that had ushered the bank into dozens of other countries around the world. As with everything at the bank, it was something that flowed from the top down.

Over the span of two decades, Abedi had cultivated political leaders and others of influence around the world, persuading them to lend or sell their names and prestige to the Bank of Credit and Commerce. It was not so much that these dignitaries performed favors—some did nothing more than appear at gatherings with Abedi and other BCCI officials, but the association was enough, and on that foundation, Abedi had expanded his bank.

Sheik Zayed of Abu Dhabi and Clark Clifford of Washington had only been the start. Lord Callaghan, a former prime minister of Britain, was a paid economic adviser to BCCI. While she was prime minister of India, Indira Gandhi presented a $10 million Third World prize established by BCCI. President Zia of Pakistan and countless Arab leaders were supporters of Abedi and his bank. Javier Perez de Cuellar used the bank's customized Boeing 727 on business as secretary-general of the United Nations.

The biggest of these catches was a former president of the United States. As he had promised at their first meeting in 1977, Bert Lance had introduced Abedi to Jimmy Carter, but it was not until 1981, after Carter was defeated in his reelection bid by Ronald Reagan. Without Air Force One but still with a worldwide agenda, Carter had responded happily to Abedi's offer of BCCI's 727 jetliner as a sometime transport. Abedi also donated $500,000 early on to help establish Carter's presidential library and the Carter Center, a public policy institute at Emory University in Atlanta.

But former presidents are not so easily bought. What cemented the relationship was the apparent shared concern of the two men over the plight of people living in the Third World. There is no doubt that Carter was sincere, for one of the most positive legacies of his presidency had been his commitment to humanitarian goals worldwide. Indeed, while Carter was discredited as a politician in the United States, he remained a respected and influential figure in the developing world. In Abedi, Carter told associates, he believed he had found someone who shared his plans for improving health care and living conditions in the world's poorest countries. Carter's mission did correspond neatly with Abedi's image of BCCI as a Third World bank. It would be a long time before anyone recognized the yawning chasm between rhetoric and reality when it came to Abedi and BCCI. By then, Jimmy Carter had provided Abedi with his most powerful calling cards in places where he wanted to do business.

The primary vehicle for this relationship was Global 2000, an ambitious effort started by Carter in the mid-1980s to bring modern medicine and health care to beleaguered portions of Africa, Asia, and China. The project was bankrolled by Abedi and Ryoichi Sasakawa, an aging Japanese billionaire and one-time war criminal who earned his fortune as a master of gambling on motorboat races.

Abedi donated at least $2.5 million to Global 2000 as a start-up contribution. Over three years, BCCI and various related entities donated between $6 million and $8 million to Global 2000. In fact, Abedi and Sasakawa were the only two donors to Global 2000, together contributing more than $19 million between 1986 and 1990. In exchange, Abedi became aligned with Carter and his wife, Rosalynn, in numerous countries.

For instance, in late June 1987 the Carters flew to China for a week-long visit as guests of the Chinese government. The former president was well regarded in China. While he was president, the

United States and China had reestablished full diplomatic relations. The purpose of the 1987 trip was to examine avenues of cooperation between Global 2000 and various organizations in China. The stay included a dinner hosted by key members of the Chinese National People's Congress in Tibet and meetings and elaborate dinners with Chinese leaders in Beijing.

At Carter's side during each of these functions, soaking up the reflected glory, was Agha Hasan Abedi. The banker had been courting Chinese officials for years, trying to expand the small representative office that he had been allowed to open in late 1982 in Beijing and another office in the Shenzhen trade zone opened in 1986. Although Abedi was no stranger to top Chinese officials, Carter offered him a higher level of exposure. At a banquet in Beijing on June 29, Chinese Foreign Minister Wu Xueqian praised Carter for his contribution to Sino-American relations and expressed his thanks to Abedi and his wife for their interest in China's economic undertakings.

For his part, the night before the state banquet, the banker had hosted a dinner for the Carters and Chinese officials in Beijing. In Tibet he used the government-sponsored dinner to announce that BCCI was donating $50,000 a year to help build the University of Tibet and would offer scholarships for two outstanding students each year to study in the United States and Britain.

The climax of the visit was a ceremony with Chinese Premier Zhao Ziyang at which Carter and Abedi signed a letter of intent for cooperation between the China Welfare Fund for the Handicapped, Global 2000, and BCCI. The joint project involved technical and financial assistance to help China educate the handicapped and build a factory to produce artificial limbs.

Jimmy Carter maintained an equally high profile in other parts of the world. A similar artificial limbs factory was to be built in Kenya by Global 2000 and BCCI. In Bangladesh, Carter and Prime Minister Mizanur Rahman Chowdhury launched a project in which Global 2000 and the government would try to improve health and agricultural programs in the impoverished country. At Carter's side was Abedi. Indeed, the two men and Rosalynn Carter flew into Bangladesh from the United Arab Emirates aboard BCCI's 727 jet. And when they left together, it was for Pakistan.

Accompanying the Carters and Abedi on the trip to Bangladesh in 1986 was Andrew Young, then mayor of Atlanta and a former United States representative to the United Nations. Like his friend Carter, Young had formed a close business and personal relationship with Abedi during the 1980s.

During his two terms as Atlanta mayor, he was on a $50,000 annual retainer from BCCI that was to be paid into his small trading company through a line of credit that the company opened with Ghaith Pharaon's National Bank of Georgia in 1982, the year that Young became mayor. The loan rose to $175,000 and was transferred to BCCI in about 1985. Eventually, BCCI forgave the loan after Young's business partner informed that bank that he and Young had done enough consulting work to equal the amount of the loan.

Over the years, Andy Young had introduced Abedi to various Third World leaders Young had met while in the UN, serving as a sort of ambassador for BCCI and Abedi in much the same way that Jimmy Carter did.

"I saw them as a Third World bank," Young said later. "They were very free-market oriented, but non-European. Consequently, they had the trust of a lot of people who saw themselves as socialists or as victims of neocolonialist exploitation. Every good idea that Carter and I had, Abedi was willing to finance." He also said that he entered into his relationship with BCCI thinking that he was helping the people it was serving, not necessarily the bank.

After BCCI's troubles surfaced, Carter defended his relationship with Abedi through aides and written statements. The former president said that he had actively sought "international funds to address international problems." Aides said the money was donated with no strings attached.

"We don't have any reason to be embarrassed because we didn't do anything wrong," James Brasher, Carter's fund-raiser, told an *Atlanta Constitution* reporter in the spring of 1991. "He's not out there as a for-hire commercial influence peddler."

In fact, the value to Abedi of the former president of the United States and others willing to lend their names and prestige to BCCI endeavors was intangible and invaluable. The ambitious banker knew that people are judged by the company they keep.

The former president also had business dealings with Ghaith Pharaon and the National Bank of Georgia, which the Saudi Arabian had bought from Bert Lance in 1978. At one point, the bank was the single largest lender to Carter's family business, peanut farms and warehouses.

Carter and his wife also socialized with Pharaon, who made Georgia his base of operations in the United States after acquiring the bank and buying automaker Henry Ford's former plantation, Richmond Hill, outside Savannah in 1981. The mansion, which was built in 1938, is a reminder of the days when Henry Ford seemed to own the surrounding town of Richmond Hill. Its new owner had similar pretensions when he acquired the estate. He wined and dined numerous blue-chip guests at the colonial-style mansion with its gold-plated fixtures. In 1983, the

Carters were among Pharaon's guests at a special screening of the film *La Traviata* at Savannah's Johnny Mercer Theater. The film was produced by a company owned by Pharaon and the showing was to benefit Savannah cultural organizations.

With his mansion, his bank, an insurance company, a plastics factory, and a fleet of Mercedes-Benzes and corporate jets, Pharaon cut a wide swath through Georgia society. Even after he suffered his financial setbacks in 1985, the news was slow to reach the American South. In the spring of 1987, the *Atlanta Business Chronicle* wrote a lengthy cover article about Pharaon under the headline "The Richest Man in Georgia." The occasion was Pharaon's pending sale of the National Bank of Georgia to First American Bankshares of Washington, D.C.

Back in June 1986, First American told the Federal Reserve Board that it wanted to buy the Georgia bank. The problem was a state law that prohibited out-of-state financial institutions from buying Georgia banks unless Georgia banks had the right to buy institutions in the home state of the acquirer. In this case, First American was based in Washington, which did not allow outside financial institutions to buy its banks.

So the National Bank of Georgia launched an aggressive lobbying campaign in the Georgia legislature that resulted in a change in the law. The law was changed in the space of a single session of the part-time legislature, a remarkable accomplishment. The effort had another, quieter partner: Agha Abedi and BCCI paid some of the bills for wining and dining Georgia's legislators.

In reality, Abedi had been involved in the negotiations for the sale from the outset. The chief negotiators for First American were its top executives, Clark Clifford and Robert Altman. They also had remained the top lawyers for Abedi and BCCI in the United States, bringing millions of dollars in legal fees into their law firm in Washington. National Bank of Georgia's side was led by Roy Carlson, the bank president recommended by Abedi to Pharaon nearly a decade earlier. And Abedi sat in on the most critical talks himself.

Other banks had been interested in the National Bank of Georgia, which had quadrupled in size to $1.7 billion in assets since being taken over by Pharaon. Among them was NCNB, the powerhouse regional bank from Charlotte, North Carolina. NCNB was anxious to expand in the rich Atlanta area. However, it was unwilling to offer more than $200 million, and some of the money would come from NCNB stock.

First American made an all-cash offer valued at $220 million. In the *Atlanta Business Chronicle* article, Pharaon explained that First American's offer was better than that of NCNB. He also said that he was more comfortable with the investors in First American's holding company, Credit and Commerce American Holdings. Among them were two of his longtime business partners, Kamal Adham and Faisal al-Fulaij. They had been partners in various enterprises, explained Pharaon, such as BCCI and Attock Oil. But he defended the price as fair, claiming: "I'm dealing with people with whom I have other dealings and I can't afford to pass on to them something that they wouldn't be totally happy with."

In explaining the other side's motivation for the transaction to a reporter for the American Banker, a trade publication, Clark Clifford said: "Our investors encouraged us to consider the purchase. They had known of the ownership being in the hands of Pharaon. They encouraged us to do it."

The Federal Reserve Board in Washington later provided yet another version of the transaction: First American was actually buying the Georgia bank from itself. Through the loans and side agreements with the Arab investors in First American's parent company, Abedi and BCCI held a controlling interest in the Washington banking company. In similar arrangements with Pharaon, the Fed said, BCCI controlled the National Bank of Georgia, too.

Evidence of BCCI's control was demonstrated through its role in hiring top officers at National Bank of Georgia, which was the same as its role with First American. For instance, Abedi had recommended Carlson for the top spot at NBG in 1979. Two years later, Swaleh Naqvi recommended that a BCCI executive named Tariq Jamil be hired at NBG as a senior vice president. Ostensibly, Jamil was to handle international matters, but the bank was a consumer-oriented institution that did little overseas business. Two other former BCCI employees, Mehdi Reza and Asif Mujtaba, also were hired by NBG during the 1980s. Mujtaba was the office manager in Panama who had so annoyed Colonel Noriega.

Under the Fed's scenario, the hidden control over the Georgia bank dated at least to 1981, when BCCI controlled fifty percent of the shares of the company set up by Pharaon as owner of National Bank of Georgia. When Pharaon's empire teetered on the edge of collapse in 1985, BCCI was afraid that his creditors would seize the Georgia bank and BCCI would lose its hidden investment. So in December 1985, Pharaon arranged to sell his remaining fifty percent of the bank's holding company to an entity controlled by BCCI. According to the Fed, the complicated set of secret transactions left the banned bank with total ownership control over the Georgia bank.

Even the timing of the sale to First American appeared to have been motivated by BCCI's internal demands. In 1987, Price Waterhouse raised concerns about the bank's extensive loans to Pharaon. At the time, the loans totaled nearly $300 million. Selling NBG offered a way to pay down those loans and get the accountants off the back of BCCI. As a result, when First American bought the National Bank of Georgia for $220 million, Pharaon collected only a small amount of the money, $14.3 million, according to the Fed's figures. The rest allegedly went to BCCI, which used the money to pay down Pharaon's loans and improve its own balance sheet.

Along with the glowing profile of Pharaon, the *Atlanta Business Chronicle* article had contained an intriguing report from an anonymous source, most likely the press-savvy Pharaon himself. It said that the Saudi investor was considering investing in one of Florida's largest savings and loans.

The Great American Savings and Loan Disaster was just beginning at this time. One of its early victims was very nearly a high-flying Miami institution called CenTrust Savings Bank. But Pharaon and BCCI rode to the rescue and kept the institution alive long enough to add a few hundred million dollars to the eventual rescue cost paid by the American taxpayers.

In August 1987, four months after the *Atlanta Business Chronicle* article appeared and days after the completion of the National Bank of Georgia sale, CenTrust announced that Ghaith Pharaon had acquired nearly seventeen percent of the institution's stock. The disclosure said it was a friendly investment and Pharaon had expressed no intention to take over the institution. By early 1988, Pharaon had upped his stake to 24.9 percent and brought his total investment to $22 million.

Here again were the familiar fingerprints of BCCI. Pharaon had borrowed the $22 million from the bank and used his shares of CenTrust as collateral for the loan.

At the time, CenTrust had the outward appearance of a healthy, even robust institution. Its chairman, entrepreneur David Paul, maintained opulent offices in one of the most glittering new buildings on the Miami skyline, with a $3 million marble staircase and a gold-plated bathroom sink. In his home, he maintained a collection of paintings by old masters, bought with funds from the savings and loan. A liberal Democrat, Paul donated heavily to politicians and entertained them lavishly. Pharaon, too, was a high liver who entertained politicians and others who could be useful to him. So it was natural that he and Paul became fast friends, taking vacations together on their yachts in the Caribbean and Mediterranean and flying around on each other's private jets.

The situation was not so pleasant at CenTrust. By the spring of 1988, regulators were pressuring Paul to raise more capital for his institution, which was suffering heavy losses. The regulators even threatened to shut down CenTrust unless more cash was pumped in. Paul and Pharaon both met with federal regulators in Washington, who eventually agreed to relax the stiff rules being applied to CenTrust and allow the institution to raise new capital and stay open. To raise the money, Paul turned to the New York securities firm of Drexel Burnham Lambert, then still the home of the infamous junk bond king Michael Milken. Drexel agreed to underwrite an issue of new bonds aimed at raising $150 million from the public to inject into CenTrust. Unfortunately for Paul, nobody was too high on S&L investments by 1988 and the bonds went begging. None sold.

In May, Ghaith Pharaon arranged for BCCI to buy $25 million of the bonds. The deal was done through a brokerage firm owned by Pharaon. A Drexel subsidiary bought another $10 million worth about the same time. The two purchases soothed the savage market, allowing Paul and Drexel Burnham to sell the remaining bonds and fend off the regulators for the time being. Two months later, on July 27, 1988, CenTrust repurchased the bonds from BCCI at the exact price the bank had paid for them.

The secret deal would not be uncovered until an auditor's examination of CenTrust a year later. By that time, the institution had been declared insolvent and taken over by the regulators. Its failure was expected to cost the American taxpayers more than $2 billion, one of the biggest bills of any thrift failure. Shortly after the takeover, the federal Office of Thrift Supervision described the CenTrust-BCCI deal this way: "It is highly likely that this transaction was consummated only to preserve investor perception of CenTrust's ability to sell the entire $150 million issue."

BCCI's Miami offices took up three floors of a skyscraper just a few blocks from the CenTrust silver skyscraper. By the time of the unusual junk bond transaction, Customs undercover agent Bob Mazur was a familiar figure in those BCCI offices. It was a relationship, however, that started out in the men's room.

CHAPTER FOURTEEN

A Clear Relationship

Twin microphones concealed in Bob Mazur's briefcase picked up the sound of his zipper. He was in the restroom on the fifteenth floor of the Bank of Credit and Commerce International offices in Miami. He had run into Aftab Hussain there before they were to meet with two senior bank officials. Hussain had taken the opportunity to prep Mazur for the upcoming meeting.

"They'll ask you who is your bankers," explained Hussain. "They'll begin the questioning."

"Have you had an opportunity to tell them why it needs some very careful handling?" asked Mazur.

"Yes, I have told them," replied Hussain. "You also mention it. Tell them it should be very carefully handled and it should be exclusively handled by Mr. Hussain."

It was 10:37 on the morning of January 11, 1988, when they left the restroom and walked into an L-shaped conference room at BCCI. Hussain said he had various presents for his new customer. He presented Mazur with a large desk calendar and a small pocket calendar, both emblazoned with the BCCI logo. As they settled onto two comfortable couches in a corner, Mazur placed his briefcase on the glass-topped coffee table. Suddenly there was a burst of laughter as the door to the conference room opened and two men walked in.

"Mr. Bilgrami," Hussain said, introducing Mazur to the first man in the door, a handsome Pakistani who spoke excellent English and had gone to college in California. Now in his mid-thirties, he was the bank's top producer in LACRO, bringing in deposits all across South America. It was Bilgrami who had engineered the acquisition of the Banco Mercantil in Colombia.

172

To Mazur's trained eye, Akbar Bilgrami was polished and smooth, a banker who was clearly several notches above Aftab Hussain.

"And that's Mr. Awan," said Bilgrami, gesturing to the trim, well-tailored man who had followed him through the door. Awan was more restrained than the outgoing Bilgrami and the overeager Hussain. As the meeting progressed, Mazur began to think of him as the central figure in this part of the C-Chase drama.

The dance began. Mazur described himself as a financial counselor who was affiliated with a New York securities firm. Previously, he had done business with Florida National Bank in St. Petersburg and Crédit Suisse. But he said he was very satisfied with the service he was getting from Hussain in Panama.

A few minutes into the meeting, a secretary stuck her head in the door and said, "Mr. Mora is here for Bob."

"Oh no," stammered Mazur, for once surprised.

He had planned to meet Gonzalo Mora, Jr., later. He had told Mora that he had a meeting first with his bankers at BCCI, but Mazur had never imagined that his sleaziest client would track him down at this sensitive business meeting. Mora and the bankers represented two opposite ends of the investigation, two poles that Mazur only wanted joined through drug cash. Perhaps Mora had his own motives. Perhaps he wanted to check up on Mazur, make sure he really did have connections with these BCCI bankers.

It was Awan who urbanely eased Mazur out of this awkward situation. "Why don't you invite him in here?" he said. "And we'll come back. Okay?"

As they left the conference room, the Pakistani bankers brushed past Mora and another man with Mora without speaking. Scarcely looking around, Mora demanded the checks, which Mazur fished out of his briefcase. With the second man translating, Mora proceeded to give the horrified Mazur instructions for the next cash pickup in New York and mentioned that he would soon be meeting with one of Roberto Alcaino's associates.

For well over a year, Mazur had arranged his life in leakproof compartments; keeping the phases of the undercover operation separate was the most secure way to avoid unwanted revelations. The investigation depended on it. So might Mazur's life. Yet here was Mora stumbling into a critical session, a session on which the most important phase of C-Chase depended. Mazur did little to disguise his impatience as he tried to hustle the two intruders out the door. As Mora and his associate were leaving, the associate observed to Mora: "*Mala gente*"—mean man.

When the bankers returned, Mazur had regained his composure. He apologized for the interruption and said he would insulate them from his clients in the future.

"In other words, we'll be dealing directly with you?" asked Awan. "I'm much more comfortable with that."

"There might be exceptions," explained Mazur. He might want some of his established clients, educated men, to meet the bankers. "But in ninety percent or better of the instances, I think it would be safer for everyone if I just dealt with the client."

"Fair enough," said Awan.

In a sense, the interruption had broken the ice. Formalities could be dispensed with. The four men, particularly Awan and Mazur, talked and laughed like old friends as they went through the business of learning about each other.

Mazur explained that he had dealt with some of his clients for a long time, gradually educating them in more sophisticated ways of dealing with their money. The next lesson, he said, was shifting some of their funds to Luxembourg or Switzerland. He was leaning toward Geneva and Zurich, where he understood that BCCI had an affiliate. Some of his clients also might be interested in purchasing property that could be held as collateral for loans from the bank. He said he thought he would be investing $5 million a month through BCCI.

"I'm sure things will develop to the point where we'll all feel very, very comfortable," said Mazur. "I feel extremely comfortable with Hussain and, ah, and you gentlemen as well. The key to my dealings here is a necessity for the confidentiality and I feel very comfortable with that. My clients are not exactly the greatest fans of the tax system here."

Awan laughed and said, "We can't really blame them for that, can we?"

Both Awan and Bilgrami said they understood the need for confidentiality. And certainly BCCI had the global reach that Mazur required. Awan explained that the bank operated in seventy-two countries, with particularly strong operations in Latin and South America. Awan spent a long time describing the global reach of BCCI and its backing from wealthy Arab families. He explained how he had been recruited to the bank by its founder in 1978, the same time as Bilgrami. Together, they had arranged the acquisition of a bank in Spain for BCCI and later had worked together in Colombia before both were posted to Miami.

After a time, Bilgrami excused himself and then Awan left for another meeting. As he moved toward the door, Awan asked if Mazur came through Miami often.

"I have a fiancée who lives in Key Biscayne," he said, referring to the wealthy island-enclave in the bay linked to Miami by a short causeway.

Richard Nixon lived there when he was president, but his oceanfront house had since been sold to a pilot for the Medellín cartel, who had expanded it dramatically.

"Quite frequently," said Awan.

"Quite frequently," echoed Mazur.

Another agent might have been bolder, but Bob Mazur had learned patience, learned to go with the flow in these sensitive meetings. Awan and Bilgrami were a couple of sophisticated characters. Mazur had seen no reason to mention the source of his investment funds, and they had not asked. The discussion had been harmless, a get-acquainted session. The only reference to any criminality, Mazur's mention of his clients' dislike of the tax system, had been passed off as a joke. Aftab Hussain had been more direct because he was less experienced.

After Awan and Bilgrami left, Mazur and Hussain spoke in a more direct fashion about various investments. Mazur wanted to know about sending large amounts of cash to the bank in Panama via courier. Since Operation Pisces, however, banking authorities in Panama had taken a dim view of large cash deposits at the country's banks. Hussain explained that regulations were strict, but he offered an alternative. Mazur could bring cash, $4 million if he wanted, in twenties, fifties, and hundreds. It would be placed in a safe deposit box at the bank. "A big box." And it could be fed gradually into the money flow, over several days. The young banker wanted to cover all the angles.

At the end of January, Hussain's efforts to cultivate Mazur had earned him a certificate from BCCI honoring him as "performer of the month," although to his sorrow there was no raise. However, for Mazur, Hussain was already a secondary blip on the screen. The agent's radar had zeroed in on Awan. There would be plenty of time to make sure that Amjad Awan knew the origins of the money he was handling. In terms of importance, Awan added up to more, far more, than Hussain—or even Gonzalo Mora, Jr.

The reference to a fiancée in Key Biscayne was more than idle chatter. The Customs Service had decided to invent a girlfriend for Mazur. It wasn't that he was lonely. It was a safety precaution.

The Colombians had seen a number of undercover operations launched at them, and as the undercover tactics became more sophisticated, so did efforts to detect them. As part of their defenses, the Colombians often used two straightforward tests. The strangers would be offered drugs and women. Suspicions would focus immediately on those who refused either one.

Drugs had proved to be the easier test to pass. Undercover agents typically responded that they did not use drugs out of personal choice. They did not object to those who did; it was good business. But using them yourself, that was bad business. Mazur had made a point from the start with the Moras that he did not use drugs.

The logic was harder to apply to women. In the early days, a typical undercover operation involved a meeting or two, an hour or two. Undercover cases were becoming more prolonged and intimate in the eighties. Agents spent days and even weeks with their targets, wooing them with lavish spending and high living. Sexual encounters, either by chance or for pay, were inevitable. Refusing to participate could raise all sorts of alarms.

Mazur himself had learned the dangers in 1982 when he was investigating the money-laundering and marijuana-smuggling operations of Charles Broun and Bruce Perlowin. On one of his trips to Las Vegas to change small bills into large ones, there had been a knock on his hotel room door in the middle of the night. Looking through the peephole, he saw an attractive young woman. His new associates, he concluded, were either being sociable or setting him up to see how he responded to the sexual enticement. Mazur's solution was simple. He went back to bed, pretending not to hear the knock. The next time Mazur went to Las Vegas, he took along a female agent.

Early in the C-Chase investigation, Gonzalo Mora, Jr., had suggested to Mazur and Emir Abreu that all three of them hire some hookers for a night. The two undercover agents had bowed out gracefully, but now Mazur determined that he needed some protection.

The solution was Kathy Ertz, a tall Customs agent in her middle thirties. Ertz was a fraud investigator in the Miami office and happened to be available when C-Chase needed a volunteer. Using the name Kathleen Erickson, she would be introduced to the targets as Mazur's girlfriend. Along with providing an out if Mora or someone else showed up with a pair of hookers on his arms, Ertz offered strategic values, too. With two pairs of eyes and ears, the agents could watch each other's backs. Too, a woman could develop leads and confidences through avenues not open to a man. Before C-Chase was over, Kathy Ertz would play a critical role in calming the suspicions of a powerful and dangerous Colombian.

Mazur's role as Robert Musella, financial consultant and money launderer, was a total immersion in the character. He had created a separate life for himself, shuttling between Tampa, Miami, his phony office in New Port Richey, and a dozen other cities. In a life where every fact is partly an illusion and the illusion continues for months and months, the risks are personal as well as professional.

Occasionally Mazur strayed from the path, returning to his old life. There were regular meetings with other Customs agents to discuss strategy and other matters, runs along the shore with Paul O'Brien, the veteran supervisor in the enforcement division and the man on whom Mazur depended most. Once every couple of weeks, he would take the ultimate chance and meet his wife somewhere or even spend a night at his home with her. But each time he stepped out of character, Bob Mazur increased the deadly risk that someone would make the connection between his two lives. The consequences could be fatal.

Pulling top BCCI officials into the operation would require big bucks. That meant that Mazur had to persuade Gonzalo Mora, Jr., to abandon the original laundering scheme in favor of the loan-back arrangement.

Although Mora was quite satisfied with the check-cashing arrangement, he listened as Mazur explained the risks. The biggest problem was that they lost control once the checks were moved into the black market by the money brokers with whom Mora dealt. The checks could wind up being renegotiated back in the United States, Mazur said, which could create suspicions among any U.S. authorities who might examine Mazur's financial affairs.

A foolproof alternative had been provided by BCCI, said Mazur. He then explained the loan-back arrangement to Mora in some detail. This way, he said, Mora could pay the drug suppliers directly with checks drawn on the Panama accounts because the money there was already clean.

Mora accepted the new scheme, even agreeing to split the one and a half percent fee that BCCI was charging. Since he had hooked up with Mazur, Mora's business had expanded so sharply and profitably that he was willing to follow almost any advice from his American partner.

In fact, on the day in January when Mazur described the arrangement to him, Mora had some news of his own. Don Chepe was so pleased with the way things were working that he wanted to add some other cities to their money-laundering route. While Don Chepe's identity remained secret, Mora said that the new business had been sent their way by one of the big man's associates, Javier Ospina.

A Colombian with an unpleasant tendency to drink too much, Ospina was one of a handful of men who helped organize the collection of money from the cartel's drug distributors in the United States. Once they had collected a sufficient amount, they turned it over to Mora and the Mazur ring for laundering.

Mora was anxious for Mazur to meet Ospina, for the Colombian held the key to even more business. He told the American that he was trying to arrange a get-together in a few weeks, but Ospina was reluctant to come to the United States. It might have to be somewhere else.

With Mora's okay and the expectation of collecting more drug money, Mazur was free to move ahead at the bank. He wanted to test the extent of corruption within this globe-girdling institution.

On January 25, 1988, Mazur returned to the BCCI offices in Miami and met with Awan and Bilgrami. He gave them documents permitting him to transact business in the name of a new shell corporation, Lamont Maxwell. He had purchased the corporation from the same Panama lawyer who set up IDC International.

Forms were executed to open accounts for Lamont Maxwell at BCCI in Panama and the Banque de Commerce et de Placements, the bank affiliate in Switzerland known as BCP. Mazur told the bankers that he had had two transfers for the Swiss account, one for $1.2 million and one for $476,000. The money would be held in ninety-day certificates of deposit and counterbalancing loan proceeds would be deposited in the IDC account in Panama.

While waiting in Awan's office that day, Mazur learned something new about BCCI. At the time, it did not seem to be of major significance. Later, however, this knowledge and Awan's eventual elaborations on it would emerge as the most explosive information uncovered during Operation C-Chase.

The first piece of this puzzle, however, was transmitted innocuously enough. Awan telephoned the First American Bank affiliate in New York to arrange the transfer of the funds to Switzerland. As he waited for someone to answer at First American, he explained to Mazur: "First American is a bank which is unofficially owned by us. Uh, we don't disclose this fact. It's sort of bought by people who are shareholders in our bank. And we haven't—"

At that point, the telephone was answered in New York and the subject of First American was dropped. But Mazur had picked up the reference on the tape recorder concealed in his ever-present briefcase, and it was a matter that would come up again. Over the telephone, Awan issued the instructions for the transfer in Urdu to the person on the other end. He ended the conversation with the traditional Muslim phrase— "llah Akbar."

Awan mentioned something else to Mazur that meant nothing to C-Chase, then or later, but it turned out to be intensely interesting to another group of investigators. Awan had returned just the day before from a flying trip to Peru and Panama. He brought back with him Akbar Mehdi Bilgrami, the manager of the Panama branch. A. M. Bilgrami, an older man who had worked at the Bank of America before joining BCCI, was not to be confused with Akbar A. Bilgrami, Awan's young sidekick, and Awan brought them together in the room so Mazur could see the difference. (Awan chuckled to Mazur about an example of young Akbar's chutzpah: he had once circulated a memo to all the BCCI branches declaring that he was to be called "Akbar A." and the other Bilgrami was to be known as "A. M.") They were all gathered in Miami, Awan told Mazur, for a high-level meeting that afternoon. Mazur never asked what it was about, but years later a commission of Peruvian senators wondered at the coincidence. They were tracking the Peruvian central bank reserves that former President Alan Garcia had deposited with BCCI in Panama. A. M. Bilgrami was the account officer. In early 1988, the money moved to Europe and was dispersed through a network of friendly banks. Was Awan's trip part of this money trail? Had he fit Mazur into a busy day devoted to a far more important client? Garcia's Peruvian enemies wanted to know, but the C-Chase team never realized there was a question.

Foremost in Mazur's mind that day was making clear to Awan the source of the money moving through the bank, a critical element in any eventual prosecution for money laundering. Late in the meeting, when they were alone, Mazur decided the atmosphere was right to sound out the banker. He opened by explaining how important it was to him that the funds from the loan arrangements be available quickly and that the transactions appear to be routine loans guaranteed by property.

"We'll never discuss this again," Mazur said, lowering his voice, "but the people with whom I'm dealing are the most powerful and the largest drug dealers in Colombia. And I don't care to overstate my abilities. I don't care to create any unnecessary concern. We deal on tremendous faith and trust because we've known each other for many, many years. And being able to rely on those two issues of the appearance of the funds coming from the property loans and, secondly, the turnaround time is all that I ask."

"I want to be very clear and possibly blunt with you," said Awan.

"Huh," grunted Mazur.

"I'm not concerned . . . it's not my business about who your customers are," Awan continued.

"Right."

"Or whatever. I deal with you. As long as we have a relationship and we have a straightforward, clear relationship, the funds are strictly legit and clear and everything."

"Right," said Mazur.

"I'm not concerned further than that because, you know, I'm not really responsible for the morals of your customers. I deal with you. As long as you and I have a clear, straightforward, legitimate business, we will provide you all the security, all sorts of security and anonymity. Further than that, I don't want to know."

With this pledge of straightforward dealings, the men agreed to seal their new understanding with dinner that night at an Italian restaurant in the trendy Coconut Grove section of Miami.

Bob Mazur had gotten what he wanted, recorded conversations with Aftab Hussain and Amjad Awan that prosecutors could use to indict and convict the two bankers of money laundering. They were crucial in establishing the new path for Operation C-Chase. However, world events were about to intervene and send the investigation spinning in a new direction.

Amjad Awan was becoming Americanized. On January 31, 1988, he held a party at his house to watch the National Football League's Super Bowl on television. Of the guests, only Akbar Ali Bilgrami was rooting for the Denver Broncos. As a former Washington resident, Awan was a fervent Redskins fan, so he won some money from Bilgrami when the Redskins beat the Broncos with a stunning second-half comeback.

"This morning he says it was a lousy game. Really bad," Awan said to Bob Mazur the next day as he joked about Bilgrami's reaction.

The two men were meeting on February 1 at the BCCI offices to clear up a minor problem with the power of attorney Mazur had provided for Lamont Maxwell, his latest shell corporation. Not long into the meeting they were interrupted when Awan took a telephone call.

"Hello. Hello. Yes. Friday's okay?" Awan asked the person on the other end of the line. "Yeah, I know. Well, what is it? What'd he say? No, that's not the point. The point is that under the circumstances, and I told him this last Friday, that it will be best if we have the least possible contact because who knows who is listening on the telephone."

After another minute or two in which Awan discussed plans for a trip somewhere later in the week, he hung up and, turning to Mazur, said, "My friend is in deep trouble these days."

"Who is that?" asked Mazur.

"General Noriega," Awan replied with a laugh.

"Oh, yes," said Mazur. "I think I'll hold off on my trip there. I'm rather concerned about it."

"No," Awan assured him, "things will work out. You know, it's rather like the Kurt Waldheim situation. They'll indict him. They won't let him come to this country."

"Uh-huh," said Mazur with a nod.

"And that sort of thing, he's going to harden his stand against the U.S. because he isn't getting out. The only way he'll get out is by the bullet."

Stories in newspapers and on network television newscasts in the last two days indicated that the U.S. Department of Justice was on the verge of indicting General Manuel Noriega on drug charges. The Reagan administration's disaffection with its one-time ally in Panama had deepened to animosity in recent months. Many would trace the slide to Seymour Hersh's article nearly two years earlier in The New York Times. But many events no longer allowed the administration to promote the fiction that Noriega was a hero of the drug war as he had been portrayed in Operation Pisces.

There was the matter of the ouster of the elected civilian president of Panama, Nicholas Barletta, in early 1986, although for a time some in Washington were willing to let it go because Noriega had stolen the election on Barletta's behalf in the first place. A more serious crisis erupted in June of 1987 when a former military commander in Panama, Colonel Roberto Diaz, openly accused Noriega of complicity in the brutal 1985 torture-murder of Hugo Spadafora, a leftist who had made too many accusations that Noriega was involved in drug running. The charges by Diaz were not new, but they had incited public protests that were suppressed only with force. To Noriega and Awan, the anticipated drug indictment was just another round in the struggle to do business.

Noriega, aware through his lawyers in Miami of his likely indictment, had been in touch several times with Amjad Awan. Now, he wanted BCCI to assist him in transferring his fortune out of Panama and into secret accounts before the U.S. government tried to freeze the funds.

The atmosphere was tense when Mazur returned to BCCI the following day. Awan apparently had spoken with Noriega on the telephone the night before. He and Bilgrami were worried about what was going to happen to banking in Panama when the inevitable occurred and the general was indicted. Both had seen the crackdown in the wake of Operation Pisces. This could be worse. Noriega's corruption had protected his favorites, but who knew what would happen if he were charged? Now was the time for damage control. Bilgrami and Awan wanted to isolate themselves from Panama.

Bilgrami advised Mazur to limit his conversations with Hussain and anyone else in the BCCI office in Panama to matters concerning his Panama accounts only. His dealings with the bank elsewhere in the world should be kept secret.

"The reason we have is that the least people who know about the contact with the bank . . . because we don't want anyone, you know, in Panama, if there's an investigation, you know, the situation in Panama is not legal," said Bilgrami. "If any of our officers there is subpoenaed to come in there and give evidence about any account, this is a situation we are trying to avoid over here."

Awan did not want Mazur to be too alarmed. "This is just a precaution," he said.

And Bilgrami said that contact with Hussain was okay because he was "very much part of the team."

One day earlier, on February 1, 1988, two teams of federal prosecutors from Miami and Tampa had gone to the main headquarters of the Justice Department in Washington. They secured final approval for simultaneous indictments of Manuel Antonio Noriega on drug and conspiracy charges.

The explosive indictments were announced on February 4 at a joint press conference held in Miami by Leon Kellner, the U.S. attorney in Miami, and Robert Merkle, the U.S. attorney in Tampa. There were headlines around the world. In Panama, Noriega thumbed his nose at the charges, accusing the United States of trying to intimidate Latin leaders who dared to criticize the Americans.

Charged along with Noriega were leaders of the Medellín cartel and other assorted drug traffickers. One of the defendants was Roberto Steiner, the man who had bought Richard Nixon's house on Key Biscayne. Many of those indicted with Noriega were unfamiliar to the public, just more Latin-sounding names in another drug enterprise.

But some of them rang bells with Amjad Awan. Among them were Noriega's longtime associate Enrique Pretelt and another former BCCI customer, pilot Ricardo Bilonick. And newspaper stories said that the Tampa charges against Noriega and Pretelt were based on the testimony of Steven Kalish, the marijuana smuggler who had been referred to BCCI in Panama by Noriega's late friend Cesar Rodriguez.

At this point, the agents in Operation C-Chase were unaware of the extent to which Awan and BCCI had served as bankers to Noriega. Awan's mention of Noriega following the phone call on February 1 had piqued the interest of the agents, to be sure, but they had nothing else to go on.

Although C-Chase and one of the Noriega investigations were run out of Tampa, the details of both were kept secret. Only those with a need to know were aware of either investigation. In fact, the most extensive security surrounded C-Chase because a leak would have endangered Mazur and Abreu.

"It was an undercover operation dealing with a lot of Colombians," said one federal law enforcement official involved in the case. "That meant there was always a possibility of somebody disappearing forever if word leaked. People in the office knew some sort of money-laundering investigation was under way, but nobody knew the specifics of it. It was kept that way intentionally."

But one man knew the details of both investigations. And what he knew made him believe fervently that it was vital to penetrate the Bank of Credit and Commerce as deeply and successfully as possible.

Mark Jackowski was regarded as one of hardest-working, most tenacious federal prosecutors in Tampa. When U.S. Attorney Bob Merkle, whose own personality had earned him the nickname "Mad Dog Merkle," had a tough case or a big case, he assigned it to Jackowski. And in Florida in the 1980s, that meant drug cases.

At the start of C-Chase, Jackowski had paid little attention. He was devoting far more time to Noriega and a half dozen upcoming drug trials, including one of a doper named Leigh Ritch, who had been Steven Kalish's partner.

There was little expectation among prosecutors that Noriega would be brought to trial in the United States, at least not any time soon, so Jackowski was able to devote more time to plotting strategy in C-Chase. His deeper involvement could not have come at a better time.

The biggest worry for the Customs agents at the time was a bungle by their own colleagues. By then, Customs agents in Los Angeles, Chicago, New York, Detroit, Philadelphia, and Houston had helped with the cash pickups and other aspects of C-Chase. In addition, agents from the DEA had been used from time to time to assist in keeping pickup sites and other aspects of the undercover work under surveillance.

There were factions within Customs and DEA that regarded money-laundering cases as nickel-and-dime stuff. Unless there were drugs on the table, it was a pissant case. The extended family of C-Chase was not a happy one.

As Mazur and Abreu escalated the size of the cash pickups, federal agents across the country were getting glimpses of bigger and bigger players in the drug world. In particular, the appearance of Roberto Alcaino in Los Angeles marked the first time that a major launderer and drug trafficker had been lured to the surface. Customs agents in Los Angeles were anxious to nail Alcaino, and their fervor created tension with the C-Chase agents.

Drugs and money are almost always kept separate at the stage in trafficking where Mazur and his team were operating. Money from street sales or bulk sales was collected at a central spot, away from the drugs, to minimize risks from the cops. Then the money was delivered to Mazur's pickup teams.

However, agents in Los Angeles and the other cities were tracking the

C-Chase money launderers back to the drug distribution networks that employed them. Sometimes they ran across drugs in the process. The result was an understandable but highly dangerous urge—at least to Mazur and Abreu—to seize the drugs, particularly since DEA policy said that undercover operations are not supposed to allow large quantities of drugs to hit the streets. And sometimes drugs and money did get mixed up in the same deal.

In one instance, in late January 1988, a tractor-trailer truck had been spotted near one of Abreu's cash pickups. DEA agents in Detroit had had the truck under surveillance on its trip north from Texas and believed that it contained a huge load of cocaine. They desperately wanted to stop the truck, arrest the occupants, and seize the dope. The risk was that Don Chepe and his associates would connect the bust with the money laundering, thus exposing Operation C-Chase.

This was a problem inherent to long-term undercover operations. Events occur through the life of the investigation that have the potential to destroy the undercover operation. At the same time, dedicated agents in the war on drugs cannot be expected to ignore multi-ton shipments of cocaine. Yet when a load of cocaine is seized and people are arrested, it touches off legal proceedings and publicity that have the potential to reveal details of the underlying investigation.

Sometimes, subterfuge can be used. When Customs agents were using wiretaps to monitor the operations of a Colombian money-laundering ring in Los Angeles in 1988, they picked up word that a 1,000-pound load of cocaine would be leaving Los Angeles for the Midwest. They alerted authorities along the route and the truck carrying the cocaine was stopped supposedly for a routine traffic violation near St. Louis, Missouri. But more often, there is neither time nor ability to put so much distance between the undercover agents and the arrests.

Had C-Chase been under the control of the FBI or DEA, the tensions might not have run so high. Those two agencies are run along military lines, with the special agents in charge of the field offices under the direct control of officials in Washington. In Customs, there is no central authority for enforcement efforts, or in any event, it is traditionally a weaker one. These weaknesses were eventually identified in a report issued in 1991 by a blue-ribbon task force that criticized the service for mismanagement and cronyism. Among the systemic problems listed in the analysis were inadequate training for supervisors and agents alike, inattention to allegations of corruption and mismanagement, and the lack of central control.

Indeed, regional Customs commissioners have far more power and independence than their FBI or DEA counterparts. The result is a bunch of fiefdoms that one federal prosecutor compared to feudal England. This creates problems on many levels for people trying to run a national or international investigation that requires close communication and cooperation between regions.

Mark Jackowski learned about this threat to the longevity of Operation C-Chase in the week after the Noriega indictments. He sat down with Laura Sherman and Steve Cook, who had been sharing the supervisory duties as case agents, and was briefed on the status of the investigation and the competing interests.

It was clear immediately to Jackowski that the investigation had to be kept alive. He wanted to see how many people at BCCI were ready, willing, and able to help launder drug money. So he decided to bring together as many of the agents and prosecutors as possible in Tampa to clear the air. He wanted to make sure the authorities in the other cities realized what was at stake. He wanted to make sure they knew who was in control of this investigation. And he wanted to slam home the point by doing it on his turf.

There was little trouble persuading the agents and prosecutors to come to Florida in February, at least not the ones from the Northeast and Midwest. In the second week of the month, about fifty or sixty federal law enforcement officers gathered for a series of meetings at the Sheraton Hotel in nearby Clearwater. Jackowski had purposely selected a location away from the federal building in Tampa to maintain security.

To say that the parochialism evaporated in the Florida sun would be nice, but it did not happen that way. In his discussions with the other prosecutors, Jackowski tried to make his case for protecting the underlying investigation. In talks with their counterparts, Sherman and Cook stressed the need to safeguard their undercover operatives. Their warnings were particularly strong when directed at their colleagues from Los Angeles. Customs in Tampa felt that the LA agents had been sloppy in some of their surveillance and made some busts that jeopardized C-Chase. The LA agents were equally forceful in defending their right to operate as they saw fit.

When it became clear that there was strong reluctance to lay off the drug seizures, talk turned to methods that could be used to minimize the impact on the undercover sting. The agents and prosecutors discussed using highway stops and other means of making the arrests seem to be cold hits. They also discussed ways to add new layers of information to the C-Chase intelligence, so that it could be protected from discovery by defense lawyers.

The results were disappointing to the Tampa crew. One of them summed it up this way: "There was no acquiescence that Tampa would run things. The agreement was that they would try to work with us as best they could."

To some of the Tampa agents, C-Chase's days appeared to be numbered. It was only a matter of time before someone grabbed a load of drugs and Colombians and brought down the undercover operation, too. They expected the end to be written by the cowboys from Los Angeles. Until then, the pace of C-Chase would accelerate.

CHAPTER FIFTEEN

Precious Friends

The BCCI connection spawned new friends and great expectations in all directions. Amjad Awan and his associates at the bank were shoveling money into the bank's deposit system, which made them popular with their superiors. Don Chepe and his gang of traffickers were pleased with the smooth efficiency and apparent security of the operation, so they were funneling more cash into it. And Mazur and the other federal agents were fairly licking their lips over the prospects of uncovering dirty bankers in every corner of BCCI's worldwide operations.

By February 1988, about a year and a half after C-Chase started by laundering $16,000 for the Moras, here is what a typical transaction looked like:

On February 8, Emir Abreu picked up $803,890 in cash in Detroit from two of Don Chepe's gofers. The money was counted by government agents and deposited in an account at the National Bank of Detroit. From there, it was wired to Mazur's account at Florida National Bank. The following day, Abreu was in Houston, where he picked up $490,110 of Don Chepe's money from another man. The agent took this money back to Tampa and it was deposited in the Florida National account on February 10.

These two deposits were combined and, after subtracting Mazur's commission, a total of $1.26 million was transferred from Florida National through First American Bank in New York to Banque de Commerce et de Placements in Geneva, where it was placed in a ninety-day CD on February 12. Eleven days later, $1.2 million, minus the bank's fee, was wire-transferred from BCP-Geneva to the Lamont Maxwell account at BCCI in Panama as a loan credit. The same amount was then moved into the IDC International account at BCCI on February 23.

The funds were then disbursed through IDC checks that Mora provided to the representatives of the drug suppliers. For instance, one of them cashed a check for $23,918, another cashed a check for $500,000, and a third cashed one for $400,000.

A week later, the whole business started over. This time it involved $725,749 in drug money.

With each transaction, Mazur would telephone Aftab Hussain and, speaking in code, let him know that a "shipment" was coming. He would then provide an invoice number that would correspond to the amount of cash being transferred.

Mazur also was spending a good deal of time at the BCCI offices in Miami, working to insinuate himself deeper into the confidence of Awan and Bilgrami and searching for new avenues of pursuit. He was getting along fine with Awan, but the relationship with Bilgrami was more difficult. The younger banker seemed to want to keep his distance from the American businessman. There was nothing rude or even impolite about his manner, but Mazur sensed that Bilgrami harbored some doubts about him.

In February, Awan spent two weeks traveling on business to Europe and elsewhere in the United States, so Mazur spent more time alone with Bilgrami. Mazur still had not told Bilgrami that the money he was moving through the bank was derived from drugs. Without doubt, Mazur thought, Awan and Hussain had informed him, but that would not stand up in court. So one day near the middle of the month, Mazur and Bilgrami sat in the BCCI office discussing Mazur's recent transfer of funds through BCP-Geneva and Mazur steered the conversation to their business relationship. First, he tried to reassure Bilgrami.

"The most important thing to me, um, the two most important things that I would never do anything to jeopardize," he said. "One is my client's funds and two is those precious friends who are involved in helping me with those things."

Next was to come a discourse on the need for that confidentiality. No doubt it would have been along the lines of the disclosure to Awan earlier. Mazur seemed to follow scripts for certain situations, with phrases recurring often. But Bilgrami did not appear to be receptive to any further disclosures at this point. Mazur sensed this was not the time to bring up the drug connection, so he decided to wait before drawing Akbar Bilgrami fully into his trap.

The Bank of Credit and Commerce International was one of several banks mentioned in newspaper stories that month about the Noriega indictment. Among the others were Bank of America, Citibank, and Chase Manhattan. All apparently had been used in one fashion or another to move some of Noriega's funds around the world. No undue attention was focused on BCCI and there was no indication of illegality on the part of any of the banks.

Nonetheless, BCCI executives had raised the issue with Awan when he was at the bank's headquarters in London. He had assured them that there was nothing to worry about. He joked that they should be happy to have been named along with the major American banks. It was a serious matter, however, as Awan learned when some of the questions directed at him came from Agha Hasan Abedi, the founder of BCCI.

When Awan returned to the United States, he stopped in New York and gave officials there a complete rundown on the bank's transactions with Noriega. At the time, questions also were asked about the size of the loans to Bob Mazur. Since BCCI did very little commercial lending for banks of its size, no branch was permitted to lend more than $3 million to a single customer without approval from the managing board in London. This was true whether or not the loans were collateralized with cash.

Upon his return to Miami, Awan described some of these concerns to Mazur in a meeting on February 24. He said that he and Bilgrami had discussed them, too. The unusual attention stemming from the unstable situation in Panama and concerns at headquarters, they had decided, might necessitate a change in the way business was being done with Mazur.

"As far as we're concerned, this is a legitimate transaction," he said to Mazur. "And we should carry on this way. But we thought, or at least Mr. Bilgrami thought, that we might slow down for the next couple of months. Let the dust die down a little bit."

Was Bilgrami getting cold feet? Mazur told Awan that he had tried to explain to Bilgrami that handling his clients' funds responsibly and the assistance of trusted friends were his top priorities.

"Both of those are the most precious things that I deal with," he said.

"I understand that," said Awan. "This is, you know, the banking business is based solely on trust and confidence. If that isn't there, what else is in it for the bank to offer the customer?"

If the situation worsened in Panama, Awan said he foresaw the possibility that he or another BCCI executive might wind up being hauled before Congress or a grand jury to explain the bank's operations in the Latin American country. In fact, Awan disclosed, the bank had recently been served with an unrelated subpoena issued by a federal grand jury in Washington investigating the Iran-Contra arms smuggling scandal.

The subpoena demanded bank records involving the transfer of $10 million made by Adnan Khashoggi through his account at BCCI in Monte Carlo. Once described as the wealthiest man in the world, Khashoggi had made a fortune brokering arms deals and other transactions for Westerners in the Arab world. Along the way, he had worked closely and become friends with Kamal Adham, the fellow Saudi Arabian who was one of BCCI's largest stockholders and founder of the Saudi intelligence service. The BCCI transaction under scrutiny by the grand jury involved a murky deal between Khashoggi and Manucher Ghorbanifar, who served as the Iranian middleman when the Reagan administration was trying to trade arms for hostages.

Awan explained that a portion of the transaction, about $100,000, had passed through the BCCI office in New York and that was the subject of the subpoena, but he downplayed the problem and said that Khashoggi was someone the bank had tried to avoid because of his notoriety. (Eventually, Lawrence Walsh, the special prosecutor investigating the Iran-Contra affair, said that BCCI had done nothing illegal in that scandal.)

Notoriety in Panama was to be avoided, too. Perhaps, suggested Awan, the solution was to find an alternative route for Mazur's funds. He said that the European Economic Community and some other nations were negotiating a treaty that would require the disclosure of bank data to law enforcement and regulatory authorities. Switzerland and Britain were among those Awan expected to sign the eventual agreement. However, he said neither Luxembourg nor France was expected to participate.

Mazur said that he was planning a trip to Europe on other business at the end of March and might check out some new countries. He mentioned that one of his lawyers had suggested opening accounts in Liechtenstein or Andorra, two tiny duchies famous as secrecy havens.

Awan said that he would not recommend either of those places, and he said that he and the bank had no contacts in either country.

"For the moment what we feel is that, you know, the good places to do business from our concern are France and Luxembourg," said Awan, offering to provide Mazur with a list of BCCI contacts for his upcoming trip to Europe.

Shifting funds from one country to another had been standard policy within BCCI almost from its inception. The practice fell under Agha Hasan Abedi's concept of EMP, or external market program. Often, these transfers involved flight capital from depositors anxious to avoid an unstable economy, but political conditions also played a role in EMP.

When the U.S. Department of Justice and the DEA disclosed Operation Pisces in May 1987, BCCI had been one of eighteen banks in

Panama ordered to freeze certain accounts. In a meeting of the Panama operation's marketing committee the week after the announcement, bank officials expressed fears over what they termed "a mini deposit run" as frightened customers pulled cash out of BCCI and other Panamanian banks.

The strategy adopted by the bank to retain the deposits was a perfect implementation of Abedi's EMP plan, which utilized BCCI's worldwide branches to move and conceal money. Customers were persuaded to shift their funds to other BCCI branches in countries where bank secrecy was still certain. The countries suggested by the bankers were Luxembourg and France. Within a matter of months, millions of dollars in deposits had been moved from Panama to those two countries. By the start of 1988, the Panama branches had opened 116 accounts at foreign BCCI branches compared with sixteen before Operation Pisces.

So shifting funds out of Panama, as suggested by Awan, was a common practice within the bank in response to concerns over security and stability there. It also offered Mazur a grand opportunity. Taking advantage of Awan's proposal, he could work himself deeper into the BCCI organization. France and Luxembourg would wind up being just fine.

Mazur was not the only undercover agent trying to move money out of Panama in the aftermath of the Noriega indictment. Drug Enforcement Administration agents engaged in a similar long-running investigation out of Atlanta were probing their targets for corrupt banks in other countries.

The exodus of money had been precipitated by a freeze on assets in Panamanian banks the previous March. After Noriega's indictment, his political opponents fought to have his government declared illegal. Exiles in the United States persuaded a federal judge to order a freeze on Panama's assets in the United States. It effectively blocked American banks from serving as clearinghouses for financial transactions involving Panama. In response, Noriega had been forced to close Panama's banks on March 3 and freeze all transfers of foreign funds.

Later in March, Noriega survived an attempted coup d'état by some of his own officers. The coup attempt followed widespread street demonstrations and a series of general strikes by workers that started when the banks were closed.

Among the funds frozen in early March was $725,000 in drug money that Mazur had transferred to his IDC International account at BCCI. Since then, Awan and Aftab Hussain had been trying desperately to get Mazur's funds freed for him. Countless sums of drug money were sitting in Panama's banks under the same circumstances. Colombia's drug kingpins now felt it was a necessity to find alternate routes for their money.

The DEA agents were trying to find new routes, too. And they were getting some advice from Eduardo Martinez-Romero, a drug financier in Medellín who was one of the ringleaders of a Colombian money-laundering operation that handled more than $1 billion.

At a series of meetings with an undercover DEA agent in early March 1988 on the West Indian island of Aruba, Martinez suggested that the agent try to open an account with a bank that had operations in Uruguay as an alternative to Panama. He said it could be done without even going to Uruguay. By way of example, Martinez said that he had once opened an account at the Bank of Credit and Commerce International in Panama City simply by going to the bank's office in Miami.

The same investigation had earlier uncovered evidence that another major Colombian money launderer, Juan Francisco Perez-Piedrahita, had an account at BCCI in Panama. The account number was M/L187—a special manager's ledger account.

Martinez and Perez popped up in a DEA investigation known as Operation Polarcap. It was destined to uncover one of the largest money-laundering operations in history, a ring that relied on jewelry stores in New York and Los Angeles as fronts for cleaning $1.2 billion in just eighteen months. The system for moving money out of the United States was so successful that its participants dubbed it "La Mina," the gold mine.

One of the drug suppliers who used La Mina to move his cash was Jose Gonzalo Rodriguez-Gacha, one of the top leaders of the Medellín cartel. After his death in a shootout with Colombian police, a raid on one of Rodriguez-Gacha's ranches uncovered a huge cache of documents outlining how his organization had stashed more than $100 million in banks around the world. Among the documents were the records of four accounts at the Bank of Credit and Commerce International in Luxembourg. Six Pakistani employees of BCCI's Colombian bank were listed in Rodriguez-Gacha's records as administrators of his accounts at the bank's Luxembourg branch.

BCCI popped up elsewhere in La Mina, too. Investigators discovered evidence that the laundering operation had used 800 accounts at 215 banks around the world. BCCI was one of them. Other names that were part of Operation C-Chase surfaced in La Mina. For instance, in the summer of 1988, two DEA agents interviewed a confidential informant who told them that one of the big players in La Mina was a Colombian supplier known as Don Chepe. The informant said that Don Chepe owned an entire city block in downtown Medellín and operated his own airline for shipping drugs to the United States.

These were the sort of crisscrossing investigations that, if mishandled, could bring down C-Chase or Polarcap, or both for that matter. It was a different dilemma than the one prosecutor Mark Jackowski had warned about back in February at the Clearwater meeting, but it was dangerous, nonetheless.

The C-Chase team was generally aware that the DEA was running a long-term investigation called Polarcap. Within the Tampa offices, it was known as "Polarcrap." Similarly, the DEA agents and prosecutors working with them knew something was being run out of Tampa, but security considerations, gilded by interagency rivalries, kept the two sets of agents operating independently. And that translated into greater risks to the men and women who were undercover.

BCCI's connection to Jose Rodriguez-Gacha was only part of its growing business in Latin America, a business that seemed geared toward serving the heavy-dollar demands of the drug cartels and other criminals.

For instance, among the bank's thirty branches in Colombia, the fifth-richest was in Envigado, a city of only 90,000 that happened to be the hometown of drug lord Pablo Escobar. In a 1990 book, La Coca Nostra, Colombian journalist Fabio Castillo said that government investigators found that money used to pay for the January 1988 assassination of a crusading official, Carlos Mauro-Hoyos, came from the BCCI branch in Envigado.

During the same period, the bank was financing such activities as an elaborate coffee-smuggling and arms-selling business allegedly operated by a Jordanian businessman named Munther Bilbeisi. His brother happened to be manager of the bank's branch in Amman, Jordan, but the scheme was run out of a BCCI office set up in Boca Raton, Florida, apparently for the almost exclusive use of Bilbeisi.

Dozens of letters of credit from BCCI were used to finance what authorities charged later in a criminal indictment were illegal shipments of millions of dollars worth of Central American coffee into the United States in violation of international quotas. The coffee involved was sold on the black market to major coffee companies in the United States, and Bilbeisi reaped huge profits, according to the charges.

Bilbeisi was a full-service merchant. While shipping coffee to the United States, he also was said to be shipping helicopters from the Mideast to Guatemala. He reportedly brokered the $5.1 million sale of three American-made helicopters to Guatemala from Jordan in a transaction financed by BCCI. Bilbeisi's day-to-day transactions with the bank were overseen by Hassan Parvez, the stepson of Swaleh Naqvi, the bank's number two officer.

Another letter of credit provided by the bank was related to an arms transaction of a far greater magnitude. In 1987, a Pakistani-born Canadian named Arshad Pervez tried to buy twenty-five tons of superstrong steel from an American manufacturer and a small amount of a material called beryllium from another U.S. company. Both the steel and beryllium are restricted exports because they are used to make nuclear weapons.

The transaction was to be financed with a letter of credit from BCCI arranged by a retired Pakistani general, Inam ul-Haq, who was identified in U.S. intelligence reports as a buyer for Pakistan's nuclear weapons program. But before either material could be shipped to Pakistan, Pervez was arrested in Philadelphia. Pervez was convicted and sent to prison in December 1987, but Pakistani officials said that ul-Haq had disappeared.

That was not BCCI's only connection to Pakistan's long-secret efforts to build what some called the "Islamic bomb." From the middle to the late 1980s, the bank donated $10 million to finance a secret science and technology center in Pakistan run by A. Qadir Khan, the scientist regarded as the leader of Pakistan's efforts to develop nuclear weapons. The money came from a tax-free foundation established in Pakistan by BCCI and headed by the country's former finance minister and future president, Ghulam Ishaq Khan. While finance minister, Ishaq Khan had played a key role in allocating government funds for Qadir Khan's nuclear project. Both men maintained the development was for peaceful purposes, an assertion disputed by numerous international organizations and the U.S. government.

All of this is not to say that BCCI engaged only in nefarious dealings. On the contrary, the bulk of its business was devoted to gathering deposits from honest customers and financing legitimate international trade, but it was the widespread willingness of the bank to ignore all sorts of laws in its quest for more and more business that propelled it and its employees into almost any transaction where there was a dollar to be made. BCCI was the bank that asked no questions.

Awan's house was in Coral Gables, a suburb of Miami a few minutes south of downtown. The 5,500-square-foot home was on an acre of land in the exclusive Cocoplum neighborhood, where Awan's neighbors included Miami's wealthiest businessmen and lawyers as well as some celebrities, such as baseball superstar Jose Canseco of the Oakland A's. Awan and his wife Sheereen had seen the house back in the summer of 1987 when they were moving to Miami from Washington. It was still under construction at the time. There were five bedrooms, five bathrooms, a separate guest suite, an indoor sauna, and a heated pool in the backyard. There was also a tennis court, which Awan had gotten at a bargain price.

When he and his wife first saw the house, the tennis court was half finished. Since he didn't play the game, Awan had persuaded the builder to complete the court for $10,000 less than it would have cost otherwise. Awan figured he would have a good resale point when it came time to transfer again. The Awans had paid $725,000 for the new house, a substantial stretch for an $80,000-a-year banker. They had moved in in the middle of August 1987. Since then, their son and daughter had begun to play tennis and the court was a welcome addition to the comfortable home.

One night in early March 1988, after eating dinner at Awan's house with his family, Mazur and the banker had resumed their discussions on an alternative to Panama. Awan feared that if Noriega was toppled or brought to the United States to stand trial, the United States would install a new leader who would abandon the bank secrecy laws. Of the hundred and forty banks in Panama, he predicted that a hundred of them would leave the country, including BCCI. Awan did not advise shutting down Mazur's business in Panama yet, but planning was in order.

"So, the intelligent thing would be to consider alternatives," said Awan. "Now it all depends on what will be more suitable for you and manageable for you."

Mazur said some of his Colombian clients were finding Panama too hot for their money. They were considering other South American countries as alternate spots, such as Uruguay and Paraguay. They had even suggested flying money to Colombia, with some of it going on to Bolivia to pay for new cocaine processing laboratories under construction to replace those the cartel expected to lose in Panama.

"Tell me something," said Awan. "Where is the cash?"

"The cash is here in the States," said Mazur.

"In the U.S.? Okay."

"Detroit, Houston, New York."

"Can it be transported?" asked Awan.

"That's part of what I offer," replied Mazur, reminding the banker that one of his businesses was an air charter service.

"What I was just contemplating was that if cash be delivered, say, to Uruguay, then you have the ultimate disposal of it in other locations," said Awan.

Mazur said he would like to make some decisions soon. He had a meeting with four of his major clients from Medellín coming up soon in San José, Costa Rica. Awan was reassuring. Something could be worked out—either in Europe or elsewhere in Latin America.

Two days later, the men met for a drink in the two-story lobby of the ornate Grand Bay Hotel in Coconut Grove. They were surrounded by large potted palm trees and ficuses. Mazur said his trip to Europe had been delayed until the middle of April. In the meantime, he had to go to Los Angeles and San José, Costa Rica, to meet with clients. As a matter of fact, he said, his client in Los Angeles might be able to use some help from BCCI.

"We're constructing a small apartment complex in Los Angeles, a twelve-unit complex," he explained. "And what I'd like to do is just structure that through you folks."

"We could work that out," said Awan. "We have a branch in Los Angeles. And, you know, we could structure something pretty good on that."

"Because we could easily put the funds on deposit and then just use the project as collateral," said Mazur.

"Uh-huh. Right."

A few days later, Awan telephoned Mazur and said it would be okay to talk openly about the apartment transaction with Iqbal Ashraf, manager of the bank's office in downtown Los Angeles.

Arriving in Los Angeles, the first person Mazur met with was Roberto Alcaino. It was the Jeweler who was building the apartment complex. He wanted to take Mazur up on the proposal he had made months earlier to launder some of his drug cash through the project. Alcaino said that he was paying $12,000 a week in cash to the contractor's payroll and had spent $62,000 in cash on the land. He was worried because he did not report enough income to the IRS to cover the money he was putting into the project.

Alcaino said he expected to put a total of $825,000 into the complex and then sell it. The proceeds from the sale would be clean money. Until then, the Jeweler said he wanted to create dummy loans that would appear to be the source of the funds.

Mazur said he could come up with documents that would indicate a foreign investor had bought the project from Alcaino and backdate them to January 1988. The ownership would appear to belong to a Delaware corporation that is owned by a Hong Kong corporation. The transaction would pass through one of Mazur's companies, Dynamic Mortgage Corporation, and BCCI. Alcaino would be shown as the project manager. Nothing more. On the side, Mazur would draw up correspondence covering Alcaino's true ownership.

Before his plane left for Tampa on March 21, Mazur had a brief meeting at Los Angeles International Airport with Iqbal Ashraf. The young Pakistani banker, trim and handsome like Awan, was polite and quiet as Mazur described his desire to finance an apartment complex in Los Angeles owned by one of his clients through a cash deposit and counterbalancing loan at BCCI.

Four days later, Mazur and Abreu flew to San José, Costa Rica, where they met with Mora and Javier Ospina, Don Chepe's lieutenant. Ospina said that his organization had $12 million to $20 million a month available for delivery to the laundering operation in seven American cities. He was agreeable when Mazur suggested alternatives to Panama, such as Europe.

Mazur was pushing to get more business from the drug suppliers connected with Ospina. He urged the Colombian to introduce him to someone who could make decisions on where big chunks of money were placed. Ospina responded that he would do just that. He promised to arrange for Mazur to meet with Rudolf Armbrecht, who would turn out to be a major step up the drug ladder.

Amjad Awan had always been ambitious. Just how high his sights were set became clear to the undercover agents near the end of March 1988. Or maybe he was only trying to impress an attractive woman.

Kathy Ertz, the Customs agent from Miami who was posing as Mazur's girlfriend Kathy Erickson, had been introduced to Awan and some of the other targets a few weeks earlier. She had attended a few social functions with Mazur as a way of slowly acclimating the young woman to her first major undercover role.

Ertz had one advantage that her supervisor did not know about when he plucked her from a routine job in the Customs fraud division in Miami for this undercover assignment. As a child, she had traveled widely with her father, a government employee who worked in U.S. embassies around the world for an unspecified agency. She spent time in India and Pakistan, and her knowledge of their culture delighted the BCCI officers. Her new colleagues in C-Chase were impressed, too, by her wide range of interests. "She reads books," one of the agents marveled.

On March 28, Ertz had arranged to fly from Miami to Tampa with Awan. In Tampa, they would hook up with Mazur and they were scheduled to fly to New York City, where Mazur was going to give Awan a tour of the securities firm with which he was affiliated.

En route to Tampa, Awan told Ertz how he had been recruited to come to the bank nearly a decade earlier by its founder, Agha Hasan Abedi. A month ago, he said, Abedi had suffered a severe heart attack at his home in London. At first, there had been fears that he would not live. In the first hours after the initial attack, Abedi's aides had reached out for help to his good friend Jimmy Carter.

The former president had personally telephoned Dr. Norman Shumway, a cardiologist at Stanford University in Palo Alto, California, and asked him to fly to London to examine a personal friend of Carter's who had suffered a massive heart attack. Carter had to telephone Shumway twice because the surgeon does not like to fly.

At the same time, Dr. Charles Rackley, chief of cardiology at Georgetown University Hospital in Washington, received a telephone call from Dr. Walter Somerville, a well-known London heart specialist. "I'd like for you to come to London tonight and examine a patient of mine, and bring along your top neurologist," said Somerville. When Rackley asked the name of the patient requiring such immediate attention, Somerville refused to identify the patient, revealing only: "It is an individual of some economic influence whose illness, if widely publicized, might have an impact on the world banking system."

That evening, one of the three limousines owned by BCCI's representative office in Washington picked up Rackley and a neurologist and took them to Dulles International Airport outside Washington. From there, they flew first-class to Heathrow Airport in London, where they were met by another BCCI limousine and whisked to Cromwell Hospital in London.

Cromwell, the largest private hospital in Britain, was owned at the time by the royal family of Abu Dhabi and a foundation financed by BCCI. Within medical circles and the bank, the facility was known as "BCCI's hospital." Signs at the modern 360-bed facility are printed in English and Arabic, and the bank maintained a small branch inside the hospital's main lobby.

When Rackley entered the room to examine the mystery patient, he was surprised to find ten or twelve other specialists assembled to evaluate him. Among them was his friend Norman Shumway, and Rackley discovered that Shumway, too, was in the dark about the patient's identity.

The physicians gathered in the room quickly reached the conclusion that the patient had sustained massive cardiac and neurological damage. They determined that the heart was too damaged for bypass surgery and recommended an immediate transplant. Several of the doctors went to a nearby room and outlined the recommendations to an attractive young woman introduced to them as the patient's wife.

The prospect of a heart transplant created a religious problem for Abedi, a Muslim. Organ transplants are viewed with uncertainty under Islamic law, which tells followers that all details of their lives must have a rule. "An issue like that, something you take into your body, is going to give rise to questions for the very religious Muslims," Frank Vogel, an Islamic law expert at Harvard University, explained later. In this case, however, doctors found that Islamic scholars had issued rules approving organ transplants. Within twenty-four hours, Abedi had a new heart.

The transplant surgery was performed by Dr. Magdi Yacoub, an Egyptian-born surgeon regarded as one of Britain's leading transplant specialists. Because of the dangers involved in moving the critically ill patient, the surgery was performed at Cromwell Hospital, even though the facility was not one of Britain's five designated transplant centers.

At the time of the surgery, there was a waiting list for heart transplants under Britain's National Health Service program. However, as a private, paying patient, Abedi was able to undergo surgery immediately.

While the operation was under way, Rackley and his neurologist companion were taken back to Heathrow for a flight home. Not until nearly a year later would the Washington surgeon discover the identity of the patient: at Christmas of 1988, Rackley received a card, signed by Agha Hasan Abedi, thanking him for the care he had provided when Abedi was ill.

The heart transplant in February 1988, which signaled Abedi's removal from virtually all bank operations, was a stunning blow to the 14,000 employees, many of whom regarded Abedi as a godlike figure and the head of their family. As in any organization built around the cult of a single person, the vacuum created by Abedi's absence ignited a gigantic power struggle for succession. The obvious pick was Swaleh Naqvi, and he quickly assumed Abedi's duties on an acting basis, but Naqvi's grasp on power was tenuous and cliques and cabals were forming throughout the vast bank. Even Amjad Awan saw potential personal gain in the demise of Agha Sahib.

"I think that I have a better than average chance of attaining the position of president within the next two to five years," he boasted to Ertz after telling her of the president's heart attack.

Mazur was waiting with a limousine when the pair arrived. On the drive to the offices of Financial Consulting, Awan said that new pressures were being applied to the bank as a result of its extensive operations in Panama. BCCI and five other banks were being scrutinized by a U.S. Senate subcommittee headed by Senator John Kerry because of their involvement with Manuel Noriega, he explained. Awan said he expected Kerry's inquiry to cover some of his activities in Panama because he was the manager of the main branch when an American marijuana smuggler opened an account there. Awan said he did not remember the customer, who had been identified as Steven Kalish.

In testimony in January 1988 before the U.S. Senate Permanent

Subcommittee on Investigations, Kalish had indeed described how he moved millions of dollars in suitcases and boxes through Panama. When he landed at Omar Torrijos Airport, he would taxi his custom Learjet to the Panamanian air force terminal and armored cars would help transport the cash to banks in Panama City. One of the banks was BCCI, and Kalish showed the senators a debit slip for half a million dollars drawn on his personal account there, M/L18, another manager's ledger account.

At the time, Kalish's story had attracted little attention in the press, but it had been recirculated the following month as part of the coverage of Noriega's drug indictment.

Just four days after the indictment, two other witnesses had mentioned BCCI in testimony before another panel, Kerry's Senate Foreign Relations Subcommittee on Terrorism, Narcotics, and International Operations. Leigh Ritch, who was Kalish's smuggling partner, said that they had laundered money through BCCI. And Jose Blandon, a former Panamanian diplomat and Noriega confidant who had turned against the general, also mentioned the bank. Blandon, however, had reversed the letters, referring to it as ICCB.

Kerry, a freshman Democrat from Massachusetts, had been engaged in a series of hearings on the effects of drugs and money laundering on U.S. foreign policy. Of particular interest to him was the government's relationship with Manuel Noriega. A former prosecutor, Kerry was accustomed to pursuing clues or pushing his investigators to do so. As a result, when the BCCI-Noriega connection popped up at his hearing and before the investigations subcommittee, he instructed his staff to dig into the bank's dealings in Panama. A subpoena was approved in March 1988 by the Senate for BCCI records. But it had not yet been served.

In a conversation in late March with Mazur, Awan said the bank had learned about the investigation from some "friends" close to the Senate committee overseeing the probe. BCCI, he said, had lots of friends in Washington because it had bought and controlled the First American Bank in Washington as well as the National Bank of Georgia in Atlanta. The bank itself was prohibited by law from owning and running the institutions, said Awan, so Clark Clifford was one of the people working on behalf of BCCI to gain control of the banks.

This was the second time that Awan had mentioned BCCI's secret control over First American, but at this juncture in Operation C-Chase, nobody on the team cared about what seemed to be a civil banking violation at worst. Nor did they care that power broker Clark Clifford may have helped the bank in its scheme. Aside from some of Mazur's laundered funds being transferred through First American in New York en route to Geneva and Luxembourg, there appeared to be no connection with the C-Chase investigation. These allegations by Awan sounded like civil banking matters, no more than technical transgressions.

However, the matter did not go unreported. Prosecutors in the Tampa office wrote a memo describing details of the two tape recordings in which Awan had mentioned the bank's connection to First American. The memo, dated March 30, 1988, was addressed to William Weld, the assistant attorney general in charge of the criminal division. It arrived in Washington the very day that Weld announced his resignation from the Justice Department, accusing Attorney General Edwin Meese of playing politics with the agency. The Weld resignation threw the criminal division into chaos, and there is no record that the memo was ever acted on. It was not passed on to the Federal Reserve, and it did not touch off a flurry of new investigations within the Justice Department.

Awan's disclosure also came in the midst of a delicate transition in C-Chase itself. Paul O'Brien, the assistant agent in charge of enforcement and a veteran on whom Mazur and the others relied, was leaving. He had gotten a plum transfer to a Customs post in Ireland. The way was clear for Customs Commissioner William von Raab to realize one of his main administrative ambitions. He could appoint the first female special agent in charge of enforcement.

His candidate was the Operation Greenback veteran Bonni Tischler, who had spent the last five years in Washington learning how to deal with the bureaucracy at headquarters and with Congress. During that time, she had developed into one of the commissioner's favorites. Von Raab had already offered to send his protégé to the Los Angeles office, but she had refused in the hopes of returning to her native Florida. So she jumped at the chance to take over the Tampa office.

Tischler was no political innocent. She had once worked as a secretary for the Republican National Committee in Washington, and she possessed the bureaucratic instinct not to go looking for political trouble. Stick to the facts and ignore the politicians. So she, too, showed no interest in pursuing allegations about Clark Clifford, one of the most powerful men in Washington, regardless of political party.

In fact, Tischler was already kicking around the idea of closing down Operation C-Chase. Soon after she arrived in Tampa in February 1988, Tischler had had discussions with Mazur, case agent Steve Cook, and others about making plans to roll up the operation in the fall. Later there would be speculation that Tischler was timing the shutdown to coincide with the November 1988 presidential election. It would look good for George Bush and her mentor, William von Raab, to have a major drug bust close to the election. But no date was set and the talk would continue for weeks.

Of more immediate concern to Mazur and other Customs agents in late March was the investigation by a Senate subcommittee. The last thing that the undercover operation needed was bumbling congressional investigators poking around BCCI and scaring people. Soon, however, the Customs Service and the prosecutors would get the chance to put a lid on the Senate inquiry, at least for a time.

CHAPTER SIXTEEN

Lee Iacocca with a Twist

The focus of Operation C-Chase had gradually but radically shifted by May of 1988. BCCI was all-important. The federal agents were determined to reach as deep into the bank as possible. Bringing down a corrupt bank and its officers would score a first for Customs. The first trip to Europe that month would be the critical opening gambit of this phase of the operation. It was a risky one, too.

In Tampa and Miami, Bob Mazur had been able to bring the bankers along slowly over a period of weeks and months. If the time did not seem right, he was free to skip revealing the incriminating details crucial to winning the case in court. He still had not talked about drugs directly with Akbar Ali Bilgrami. If there was no pickup of drug cash, he could wait patiently for a call from Gonzalo Mora, Jr., before pumping more money into the laundering system.

Such luxuries would not be possible in Europe. Too much advance planning and expense were required to set up undercover meetings in foreign countries. Mazur and Emir Abreu would have to move fast. There would be no chance to schmooze for days or weeks with BCCI executives. They needed to blind the bankers by offering a huge deposit, then make it clear that the money was coming from drugs.

As for the money, Mazur needed a lot. It would be the equivalent of "flash money" in a drug-buying operation. Agents flash a suitcase filled with cash to show that they have the goods before the dealers reveal the location of the cocaine. In a rare move, $5 million in taxpayer funds had been wired into Mazur's account at Florida National Bank and he was prepared to deposit it with BCCI in Paris to demonstrate that he was a major player, worthy of special attention.

It had taken weeks to get approvals from authorities in Switzerland,

France, and Britain to use hidden recorders to monitor undercover meetings in those countries. Because they wanted to be as mobile as possible, the recording would be done by Mazur with his James Bond briefcase, but U.S. authorities still needed to get foreign approval to avoid possible later objections from defense attorneys about the admissibility of the taped evidence. A Swiss magistrate had heard the request in a secret session and finally approved it late in April. Britain had been slightly easier, since a court visit was not required. In France, the Customs attaché at the U.S. Embassy in Paris had discussed using wiretaps with French customs officials and was given a quick green light.

Another layer of complexity involved the Colombians. Since the trip to Costa Rica, Gonzalo Mora, Jr., had decided that he would go to Europe, too. Rudolf Armbrecht, one of Don Chepe's lieutenants, was leery of establishing the new laundering network, so Mora was bringing him along. He could meet Bob Mazur and Mazur could persuade him to buy into the system. By the way, Mora had added, he would be bringing his wife. He planned to make a holiday out of the trip by going on to Madrid and Rome.

Bright and early on the morning of May 12, Mazur drove into the parking garage at 1200 Brickell Avenue in Miami and took the elevator to Awan's office on the fifteenth floor. In a few days, he was leaving for Europe. He wanted to go over the last details of the itinerary that Awan and Bilgrami had planned for him.

The first stop would be BCP in Geneva, where Mazur would meet with Franz Maissen, a bank official whom he had met briefly once before in Miami. BCCI owned a majority interest in BCP, but a Swiss bank held the remaining stock and Maissen answered to the Swiss. A few days earlier, Maissen had telephoned Bilgrami and asked questions about the nature of Mazur's business, since he had been moving large amounts of money through the bank.

"I would suggest you don't tell them anything of it at all," advised Awan. Bilgrami added that Mazur should simply tell BCP that his businesses in the United States included a securities brokerage, a mortgage company, and a real estate firm and that Awan and Bilgrami handled the account.

Less trouble was envisioned at the next stop, Paris. There, Mazur was to meet with Nazir Chinoy, BCCI's chief for Europe, and perhaps some other officials. "Paris is quite happy to do whatever you want," said Awan. "They would handle everything, no questions asked."

The prospect of Mazur depositing $5 million in BCCI tantalized the bankers. They questioned him repeatedly about the timing of the deposit, with Bilgrami urging him to place the money by June 30. That was the close of the bank's half year and it would make them look good if they could take credit for a major deposit on the books then.

Mazur and Abreu flew by commercial airline from New York to Geneva, Switzerland, arriving on the morning of May 18. From outward appearances, it seemed to be a romantic vacation, for they were accompanied by undercover Customs agents Kathy Ertz and Linda Kane. Since Mora had said he was bringing his wife, it was decided that the agents should be accompanied by the women who had been introduced to the Colombian previously as their companions. It also would provide another layer of cover if they were invited to social functions during the trip.

The next morning, Mazur and Abreu went to the BCP offices in Geneva's financial district and met with Franz Maissen and his general manager, Azizullah Chaudhry. Maissen was a button-down Swiss banker and, as expected, the meeting was formal and cool. Mazur described his business enterprises and said he hoped to increase his transactions with the bank. Near the end of the brief meeting, Abreu rented a safe deposit box and paid a year's fee in advance. Then they departed, with neither side any wiser about the other.

Paris was different. Arriving at the Bank of Credit and Commerce International's offices on the wide Champs Elysées on the afternoon of May 20, Mazur and Abreu were greeted warmly by Nazir Chinoy. The bank's general manager for Europe provided the service that had made BCCI famous in many parts of the world. He fussed over his customers, inquiring about their hotel and promising to send a car there the following evening to bring the four Americans to his apartment for drinks with his family.

The business discussion was different, too. The agent and the banker talked openly and with seeming candor. This was the time to flash the big dollars and pull Chinoy into the net.

Mazur said that he hoped to deposit $1 million in the Paris branch within the next few days on behalf of a client. He added that he intended to transfer $4 million to BCCI Paris soon on behalf of himself and Abreu. These two deposits would remain for six months and Mazur said he did not intend to borrow against them. Gravy for the bank. And protection for Mazur's money. For the agent had no intention of paying out $4 million from these accounts to Gonzalo Mora, Jr., or his friends. This was Uncle Sam's money, the $5 million arranged by Customs headquarters in Washington. He would be leaving it in the bank as bait.

After tossing out the big numbers, Mazur launched into his patented pitch about the need for strict confidentiality for his clients, many of whom he explained were South American. The $1 million deposit, he explained, was money that belonged to a client named Rudolf Armbrecht.

The banker assured the American that he would be able to trust him and two of the branch's senior officers, Ian Howard, the country manager in Paris, and Sibte Hassan, Chinoy's chief assistant. Chinoy introduced Mazur briefly to Hassan and said that he would meet the Englishman Howard later.

No doubt to reassure him that the bank could keep a secret, Chinoy told Mazur a story. An army general had died, leaving 60,000 British pounds in illegal funds in an account at another bank. The man had been a friend of Chinoy's and his distraught widow approached the banker for help. The other bank was demanding probate records to release the funds to her, but that would show the general was a crook. With Chinoy's help, the widow got the funds without disclosure of the general's unnamed illegal activities. Chinoy told Mazur he was surprised that someone would risk his reputation for 60,000 pounds. Sixty million pounds, now that, he said, he could understand.

"If some of your clients have a problem, we will try our best to hide it from [the authorities]," Chinoy assured Mazur. "We'll give you as much cover as we can."

Mazur explained that he had recently witnessed a demonstration of the bank's loyalty. He described a telephone call he had overheard in Awan's office. An associate of General Manuel Noriega had called the banker. It was after the February indictment. Awan agreed when the associate asked him to help Noriega conceal his funds by moving them through the BCCI system. Mazur said he was impressed by Awan's loyalty to Noriega.

"Today, it's him [Noriega]. God forbid tomorrow it might be us," interjected Chinoy.

Unfortunately, the American continued, one of his own clients had been less loyal to the general, despite a history of profitable dealings between the men. After Panama's banks froze all cash in March, the client had sent Noriega a coffin containing a note: If the client lost any of the money he had in Panamanian banks, Noriega would need the coffin. Mazur observed that he had been much more impressed by the way Awan had aided a customer in trouble.

"It's worth it," replied Chinoy. "It's an amazing position of power. We had benefited and we'd made money. When the tide changes, we cannot change. Because we owe him. There's a certain amount of gratitude."

"I think if you, eventually if you meet some of my friends, I think if they were in a room with Lee Iacocca, they could easily be mingling with corporate executives," said Mazur. "Iacocca sells cars and they sell coke. And that's the way they deal in their business. Everything is professional, professional, professional."

"That is how it should be with every major client 'cause it's a close personal relationship," agreed Chinoy.

Withdrawing some papers from his briefcase, Mazur said that he wanted to open an account in the name of Nicesea Shipping Ltd. Mazur said he wanted to obtain a power of attorney over the account for Armbrecht. Mazur also said he wanted to open an account in the name of Saintsea Shipping for Emir Abreu and another under the name of Barkeville Ltd. for himself. Kathy Erickson also would have power of attorney for Barkeville. Chinoy summoned Sibte Hassan, who helped fill out the proper forms.

When Chinoy and Mazur were alone again, the agent told the banker in confidential tones that he wanted Amjad Awan to remain his lead account executive. "I don't have to talk of this, you know, drug dealers in Colombia are the types of people that—"

Chinoy interrupted, saying: "Yeah, I've understood it. I didn't ask, okay, but I followed the deal."

At Chinoy's apartment the following evening, Mazur moved the banker to one side of the living room and spoke privately with him. Several important clients would be visiting him from Colombia. It would help his negotiations if Chinoy met them. Chinoy was happy to accommodate him, even suggesting that he could assign a BCCI account executive to the customers. It would be convenient since the executive already traveled to Colombia regularly to consult with other clients there.

The Hotel de la Tremoille is a small, elegant hotel on the street of the same name in what is known as the *haute couture* district of Paris. It was around the corner from the glitzier Plaza Athénée, about half a mile from the Arc de Triomphe and the Champs Elysées. Mazur and Abreu, with their companions, had arranged for separate suites at the hotel.

It was in Abreu's suite, Room 110, that they met with Gonzalo Mora, Jr., and Javier Ospina on the afternoon of May 22, 1988. The two Colombians had just arrived from Caracas, Venezuela. They were tired and hungover from too much drinking on the long flight. Nonetheless, the first thing Ospina wanted when he got to the room was a Scotch.

"Let's get to the point," he said once he got a drink in his hand.

Ospina explained that Rudolf Armbrecht was in Paris, too, along with a Colombian lawyer, Santiago Uribe. Indeed, they had come over on the same flight. Armbrecht, whom he described as a former commercial airline pilot of German and Colombian descent, planned to launder $5 million this trip, $4 million of it going to a bank in Germany where Armbrecht's uncle worked and the remainder with Mazur in Paris.

This $5 million was not important, said Ospina. What mattered was that Mazur would have to convince Armbrecht that his organization had the capacity and security to handle large volumes of money. Mora explained that money previously laundered through Panama was now looking for a new home. The Colombians no longer wanted to deal with an unstable government and distrusted Noriega, fearing he might sell them out to the Americans in a deal to erase his indictment. Thus, he said, it was important for Mazur to win Armbrecht's confidence so they could land a big portion of the rerouted money. To help, he suggested that Mazur introduce Armbrecht to "the heavy bankers."

Armbrecht was hosting a dinner that evening for all of them and their companions. Mazur objected, saying he had a previous engagement with a top BCCI banker, but Ospina insisted, arguing that Armbrecht was too important to risk offending. Mora, who was far more reasonable than the slightly drunken Ospina, explained that a meeting that night was especially important.

A potential competitor was coming to Paris the next day. His name was Eduardo, and he was trying to back up his operations in Panama with new contacts in Europe. Panama is finished, said Mora. Later, Customs agents were able to identify the competitor as Eduardo Martinez-Romero, the big Colombian money launderer targeted by Operation Polarcap.

Had Mazur been less compulsive about planning, or if he had found Ospina less intolerable, he might have given in and changed his plans, but he held fast, insisting that he would meet with Armbrecht the next day. He told Ospina to arrange it.

On May 23, in the lobby of the Georges V, one of the finest and most expensive hotels in Paris, Mazur finally met the pilot-turned-drug-financier. Recalling the way Gonzalo Mora and his cousin had burst into his meeting with Awan and Bilgrami five months earlier in Miami, Mazur had worried about the impression that Armbrecht might make when he introduced him to the BCCI bankers in Paris. There seemed no reason for such concerns now.

Armbrecht was far more impressive than the drunken Ospina or rotund Mora. He was about five feet, six inches tall, compactly built, and balding. He was poised and quiet, and spoke excellent English as a result of extensive stays in the United States. Much of that time was spent supervising money laundering for Don Chepe, but there was still time for buying and flying airplanes.

The Colombian expressed no hard feelings over the missed dinner.

Instead, he seemed anxious to learn more about Mazur's American network. Mazur responded with a rundown on his operation and its security, the CD-loan scheme and the BCCI connection. Armbrecht, he said, should consider investing some of his cash in property through one of Mazur's businesses. But Armbrecht resisted, saying: "We are not very interested in investing the money in property. We are cash oriented." A bit later, Armbrecht explained. "I'm in all these money matters because basically I'm very trusting."

The two men left the Georges V and walked toward the Hotel de la Tremoille, where they were to meet with the others for additional discussions. On the way, Armbrecht cautioned Mazur not to reveal too many details of his system to Ospina because he was weak and could be pressured. Armbrecht had been disgusted by Ospina's behavior at dinner the night before. He drank too much and talked too loud. Mazur, whose initial distaste for Ospina in Costa Rica had only been strengthened in Paris, was happy to agree. He said that he would arrange for a private meeting between his banker and Armbrecht the next day to go over details.

Armbrecht was indeed very trusting. In Mazur's suite, he explained in great detail what he was looking for as a mechanism to launder funds for his employer, Don Chepe. Looking over the power of attorney and other forms that Mazur had had created for him at BCCI a few days earlier, he said: "This is a mil. No big deal, okay. So we don't like to put all these eggs in one basket unless it's a very, very good basket. And even then we are not going to do it. But the basket could eventually grow and be a very sizable kind of thing."

After the long meeting, the men were joined by Lucy Mora, Kathy Ertz, and Linda Kane for dinner and a trip to La Scala, a trendy Paris disco. Shortly after midnight, Armbrecht took Mazur aside in the disco and told him that Javier Ospina was being sent back to Colombia on the pretext that he was needed there. A few minutes later, Abreu spoke in Spanish with Uribe and Armbrecht. He later told Mazur that Uribe had asked him to kill Ospina if it became necessary.

The C-Chase agents never saw Ospina again after that night. They heard various rumors. That he had been killed in a gunfight. That he had been murdered for making sexual advances toward Armbrecht on the flight to Paris. That he was alive and still operating in Colombia on behalf of Don Chepe.

Customs intelligence agents had been scouring their files and probing other agencies and informants. Don Chepe, the mastermind of the cocaine ring supplying the cash for the operation, remained unidentified.

Several names had come up. A major figure in the Cali cartel, one of the rivals to the Medellín cartel, used the nickname. So did a couple of minor figures in the Medellín organization. The Cali one did not wash at all. Everything pointed to Medellín.

One of the recurring names was Gerardo Moncado, a member of the Medellín cartel's upper echelon but one who kept a low profile and maintained his riches in the shadows. As time had passed, the C-Chase team came to believe that Moncado was their man. So, when Gonzalo Mora, Jr., arrived at Abreu's room at the Tremoille on May 24, 1988, Mazur asked him if Moncado was among the Colombians arriving in Paris that day.

Yes, said Mora. Armbrecht might be able to arrange for Mazur to meet Moncado. But Mora was reluctant to say much about Moncado, except that he and Armbrecht were on the same team.

The prospect of meeting with the suspected Don Chepe raised the hopes of Mazur and Abreu. Here was the chance for a double victory. Nazir Chinoy was the highest-ranking BCCI official yet caught up in C-Chase. ·Maybe Gerardo Moncado would move them up the ladder within the Medellín cartel, too.

Shortly after three o'clock on the afternoon of May 24, Mazur escorted Armbrecht and Uribe to the BCCI offices on the Champs Elysées to meet Ian Howard and Nazir Chinoy.

As on the previous day, Armbrecht was full of detailed questions about bank secrecy rules, the fees BCCI planned to charge, the bank's general philosophy. He was particularly concerned about the potential for a bank failure, since there was no chance his organization would recover any funds lost in such a disaster. For the agent of a drug lord, he talked like a bank examiner. Armbrecht knew that BCCI did extensive business in Third World countries, including some through its branches in Colombia. Did BCCI lend to Third World countries? Could the failure of any single company topple the bank?

Chinoy was reassuring. The bank saw itself as a bridge to the Third World and dealt with many of those countries on trade finance matters, but, he said, its loans were minimal. As far as fees, Chinoy said the bank was flexible with its customers and interested in long-term relationships. One percent was the usual fee on a certificate of deposit. But it was negotiable, especially when large sums were involved.

"I am having a very good impression of the bank, and of yourselves," Armbrecht told the BCCI bankers.

Two brief meetings were held between the undercover agents and Ian Howard the following day. Mazur rented a safe deposit box for documents from the accounts he had set up earlier in the week and told

Howard that he would be transferring $1.8 million into his Barkeville account and $1.2 million in Armbrecht's Nicesea account. It seemed the bankers had made a good impression on the cautious Colombian. Howard and Mazur agreed to set up a code for telephone communications concerning the accounts.

Later that day, Abreu took Gonzalo Mora, Jr., to BCCI and introduced him to Sibte Hassan, saying that he wanted to show Mora what a strong relationship he and Mazur had with the bank.

"These people handle a lot of money from proceeds from narcotics, especially cocaine," Abreu explained in English to Hassan. Gesturing to Mora, he said, "He understands the needs and he understands how to help and how to assist."

"Any friend of yours is a friend of mine," replied Hassan.

That night it was time to assess the Paris trip. Armbrecht and his entourage, which now included the Moras, were leaving the next morning for Rome and the C-Chase crew was headed for London.

From the operational viewpoint, Paris was a rousing success. Chinoy, Howard, and Hassan were added to the list of BCCI trophies. Armbrecht was a big step up the Medellín ladder. Pleased with the BCCI arrangement and confident of Mazur's operation, he had agreed to begin sending $5 million to $10 million a month through the system.

There had been a couple of disappointments. They never met Gerardo Moncado, and were not even sure he ever came to Paris. And Kathy Ertz had gotten terribly sick the second day in Paris. Food poisoning in the world's food capital. She had spent much of the trip in bed.

London was an anticlimax. The reception was nowhere near as cool as in Geneva, but not nearly so warm and productive as in Paris.

The agents checked into the Portman Hotel, a large, fairly expensive place on Portman Square in central London on May 26. Amjad Awan had arranged for Mazur to meet with Asif Baakza, the manager of BCCI's corporate unit at its Leadenhall Street headquarters. Mazur expected to meet Baakza for lunch on May 27, but the banker canceled. Instead, they met in Mazur's hotel room at six o'clock that evening.

"What we need to accomplish has to do with the placement and transfer of funds in a very, very confidential and secure fashion," Mazur said.

The banker was somewhat cautious. He explained that BCCI London offered a manager's ledger account to customers seeking total privacy. He compared it to a numbered account in Switzerland. Only he and one other individual in the bank would have access to Mazur's records. But, he added: "I don't want to know anything that I don't need to know. It's as simple as that."

211

Undeterred, Mazur said that his clients were mostly respectable Colombians. By way of comparison, he trotted out the analogy he had used with Chinoy.

"Really, I think that if they were in the same room with Lee Iacocca, they probably would be confused as being corporate executives with Chrysler," he said. "It's just that they aren't in that business and, you know, these people are very, very feared people. That's why I made sure I researched everything to the nth degree before I actually moved here."

"Uh-huh," grunted the banker, not knowing exactly how to keep this American from telling him more than he wanted to know.

"When you're dealing with the most powerful men in Colombia, who are involved in drug dealing, you need to make sure you know what you're doing."

"That's right. That's right," agreed Baakza.

"Iacocca sells cars and they sell coke. And that's the only difference. But they're executives about the whole thing."

It was Mazur's only meeting with Baakza. Indeed, the ultimate goal of the trip to London had been to meet with Swaleh Naqvi, who was running the bank as a result of Agha Hasan Abedi's heart surgery and continuing health problems. For weeks, Mazur had tried to persuade Awan to set up a session with Naqvi, but it did not happen, nor was Mazur able to arrange meetings with any other BCCI officials in London. So he and his crew packed up and headed home to some unexpected trouble.

Akbar Ali Bilgrami slipped into the net on June 6, 1988. The time was shortly after nine in the morning. Mazur went to BCCI's offices in Miami to report on his trip to Europe. Awan was out of town, so he met only with Bilgrami.

The trip had been a resounding success in Paris, said the American. Already he had deposited $4 million in accounts there. Franz Maissen had proven to be cool and conservative, and the relationship with Baakza and London was just beginning. Sensing some anxiety on Bilgrami's part, Mazur added that he intended to deposit another $2 million in his Lamont Maxwell account through Miami in a matter of days.

A short way into the conversation, Bilgrami took a telephone call. The conversation was conducted in Urdu, but Mazur picked up the words "U.S. Customs Service." He questioned Bilgrami when he hung up the phone.

"I heard you mention my client's adversary there," said Mazur. "You, you do business with the U.S. government?"

Bilgrami shook his head no, explaining that BCCI was providing a financial guarantee to the Customs Service on behalf of a client, Eastern Airlines. Under its controversial new zero-tolerance program, the Customs Service was seizing property any time it found even a small amount of drugs. In this case, Bilgrami explained, the authorities had seized one of Eastern's jetliners after discovering a kilo of cocaine aboard. BCCI's guarantee would allow Eastern to essentially bail out the plane and continue using it.

Mazur nodded and said, "If you were to meet my clients—"

"No, no," interrupted Bilgrami, waving his hands. "I'm not interested in meeting your clients."

He didn't want the banker to meet his clients, Mazur said reassuringly. He only wanted to explain that they were professional, people who would mix well with, say, Lee Iacocca.

"He sells cars and they sell cocaine and that's the end of it," said Mazur. "Never to be brought up again."

Bilgrami, who had been far more cautious than Aftab Hussain, Awan, or Chinoy, was flustered and slightly angered.

"I don't want to know what they sell," he stammered. "I won't tell you, I, I'm not interested in what they do, what kind of business, in dealing with you. We know your business. And, ah, ah, we keep all client relations confidential."

With that, Bilgrami turned the conversation back to a more suitable subject. They resumed their discussion of Mazur's money transfers within BCCI.

Later that morning, Mazur met Rudolf Armbrecht at Miami International Airport and they took the 12:30 Eastern Airlines flight to Tampa. On the way, Armbrecht announced that he was going to Nashville, Tennessee, to pick up a used Rockwell Commander 1000 airplane that he was having refurbished. Among the additions, he said, was a $150,000 computerized navigational system. Once that was done, Armbrecht would fly the plane to his associates in Colombia.

Touring Mazur's offices in New Port Richey, Armbrecht provided as succinct a definition of money laundering as one would ever hear anywhere.

"The system is like a merry-go-round," he said. "We get the money over here. We reroute it. We clean it. We do everything with it. Okay. Then we have it in legally and totally nice accounts with everything over there."

He repeated his promise to Mazur that far larger volumes of cash would soon begin to flow through the American's network. However, he cautioned Mazur that he liked to keep an eye on a new associate. "Sometimes there are fishy things to watch," he said.

As they prepared to go to Mazur's beachfront condominium and meet

Kathy Ertz for dinner, Armbrecht asked Mazur if he would be interested in a little import business. Not cocaine, but marble desks. He said there was a good market for them in the United States, and a big markup.

Like many pilots, Rudy Armbrecht fancied himself a ladies' man, and Kathy Ertz was a lady who sparked his interest. After dinner, the two of them left Mazur behind and walked along the Gulf of Mexico beach for more than an hour. When they returned, they played chess until two in the morning.

If timing is everything, what happened at the end of June 1988 in Detroit could scarcely have been worse for C-Chase. The blame could have been laid on Don Chepe's organization for mixing drugs and money, but the real culprits were federal agents. And there was not much they could have done to avoid it.

Don Chepe's drug distribution in Detroit was carried out predominantly by a group of Chaldeans. These are Christian Arabs, usually from Iraq, and they had been attracted to Detroit's large Middle Eastern community. Unfortunately for C-Chase, they were a bit sloppy and mixed drugs and money.

In the Detroit operation, the same large truck used to carry cocaine north from Florida or Louisiana was used to haul money back south for laundering. Since Emir Abreu had started making the cash pickups, the money was no longer going south, but they were still using the truck to deliver the cash to him.

DEA agents investigating the Chaldeans had spotted the suspicious truck back in January and reluctantly done nothing about what they figured was a load of drugs after Customs agents assured them the truck contained money. But the DEA agents warned their Customs counterparts in Detroit that they would not let the truck pass if they thought it contained a shipment of cocaine.

"They're not using that truck for money," said a DEA agent in a phone call to a Customs agent in January. "We don't think they're bringing money north to you. If this truck comes back up, we have every reason to believe it's cocaine. If it comes up again, we're going to arrest it."

On June 28, as undercover Customs agents prepared to make another cash pickup in Detroit, they discovered that there were two trucks at the site. One was the white tractor-trailer that the DEA was watching. The drivers were unloading boxes marked DOLE'S BANANAS and stacking them on a small blue Chevy pickup. The banana boxes weren't full of cash; they contained kilo bricks of cocaine. The Customs agents had to act or lose control of the situation. They busted everyone in sight, arresting nine people and seizing a hundred kilos of cocaine.

It was the biggest cocaine bust in Detroit history. There were headlines in the papers and hard feelings in the law enforcement community. The DEA felt betrayed. They had passed up what they believed was a solid seizure six months earlier only to have Customs come in and hog the show now. As the lead agency in the fight against drugs, DEA was supposed to make all the big busts.

A DEA agent began accusing Customs of having let an earlier cocaine shipment of equal size be distributed. The Customs SAC called him on the telephone and they traded obscenities. A short time later, the two men ran into each other in a bar and nearly got into a fistfight.

Word of the fracas quickly reached Washington. In early August, the *Washington Times* ran a big story by one of their top reporters, Michael Hedges. The headline was "Customs Fumbled on Big Drug Cargo, DEA Says." It went on to accuse the Customs service of allowing one hundred kilos of coke to slip onto Detroit's streets in January. DEA agents were quoted, but not named, accusing Customs of trying to grab the glamour and glory of the war on drugs.

"They got all these new boys on the block, and they think they know what they are doing, but they've got a lot of lessons to learn," said one DEA agent.

It was not a total loss. Neither the *Washington Times* story nor any other account mentioned the undercover operation, but this major drug seizure was precisely the type of mistake that Mark Jackowski and the investigators had feared would happen back in February. Avoiding it had been the reason for the Clearwater meeting. They had expected Customs in Los Angeles to mess up the delicate balance. It had been Detroit. It didn't make any difference. Jackowski and the others on the C-Chase team had known that it was inevitable.

Since the arrests stemmed directly from information gathered during the C-Chase investigation, the existence of the investigation itself would have to be disclosed to defense attorneys once the Detroit case got started in the judicial system. While the names of the undercover agents involved, Mazur and Abreu, could be deleted from the court papers, their mission would be compromised nonetheless. Mark Jackowski and the Customs agents in Tampa succeeded in persuading prosecutors in Detroit to hold off on filing the papers as long as possible. But there was no way that C-Chase could remain secret for much longer.

This problem illustrated a central management deficiency within the Customs Service. Because the agency was broken down into distinct, largely autonomous regions, there was no central command in Washington that could have stopped the Detroit arrests and kept the cover on C-Chase longer.

The clock had started to tick. Operation C-Chase was going to have to be rolled up. Indictments would be returned soon on the people arrested in Detroit. That meant the legal process would get under way. Defense attorneys would file motions for discovery of information related to the government's case. The cocaine deal had been under surveillance because of information obtained during C-Chase. That would have to be disclosed, and probably fairly early in the process. The question was how long they could hang on.

"We weren't burned per se, but we were toasted," said one of the federal officials involved in the sensitive discussions about how to react to Detroit.

Jackowski's biggest fear was that the Colombians would somehow connect the bust to the money laundering and bolt. He wanted bodies to prosecute. He did not want a repeat of the Noriega case, with all but two minor players free in Colombia and Panama.

The Detroit fiasco pushed the C-Chase crew to move faster at the Bank of Credit and Commerce International. The investigators still hoped to climb the ladder within the bank, and Mazur had been trying to set up a meeting in London with Swaleh Naqvi and other high-ranking officials.

Ian Howard solidified his place in the ultimate case when he telephoned Mazur in June with a new proposal. If Mazur could deliver cash in bulk to BCCI Miami, it could be mailed to BCCI in London and deposited in accounts there. When Mazur described the proposal to Awan, the Pakistani banker was leery. He said that cash transactions were watched too carefully in the United States. As an alternative, he suggested that Mazur transport the cash to London. If he could do that, Awan was sure the bank could handle up to $10 million a month.

On June 30, 1988, Awan and Bilgrami told Mazur that they would be leaving BCCI by the end of the year. They planned to form an office in Miami associated with a business based in London called Capcom Financial Services Ltd. They assured Mazur that his relationship with the bank would remain unchanged and his accounts would be handled by someone of equal sensitivity and skill. But they also offered something else.

Capcom was run by a former colleague at BCCI, Syed Ziauddin Ali Akbar. The former head of BCCI's treasury department, the man blamed within the bank for the massive trading losses that took BCCI to the brink of collapse, he had gone to work at Capcom when he left BCCI in 1986. He was handling trading and investments for wealthy individuals. Capcom also had a Chicago subsidiary, Capcom Futures, which traded futures on the Chicago Board Options Exchange. Awan and Bilgrami intended to take their list of wealthy Latin American clients with them to the new job.

"Maybe there'll be some things we can do through the new company," said Mazur.

"Yes, that's what we're thinking," responded Awan, who added that he had been considering ways that they could dispose of cash for Mazur.

The night of June 30, Mazur and Kathy Ertz had invited Amjad and Sheereen Awan and Akbar Bilgrami and his Colombian wife, Gloria, to their house in Miami for drinks. They planned dinner afterward at a nearby restaurant. The agents knew the Awans and Bilgrami, but this would be the first time that they would meet Bilgrami's wife, who supposedly came from a wealthy Colombian family.

It was a pleasant social evening. Close to midnight, they wound up at Regine's, a fancy, private supper club and disco on the penthouse floor of the Grand Bay Hotel in Coconut Grove. As they sat around a table in the club, Mazur and Ertz said they had big news. They were getting married. The date was not set yet, but it would be soon and probably in Tampa. They hoped that the Awans and the Bilgramis and their other friends from BCCI would be their guests for the celebration.

No one would remember who came up with the idea of a wedding. There was a late-night brain-storming session the day after the Detroit bust. Steve Cook, Bob Moore, and Laura Sherman had been there. So had Bonni Tischler. Also attending was David Burris, the crack IRS agent attached to the investigation. All of them were searching for a way to draw as many of the targets together as possible for a mass arrest.

Plenty of tricks had been tried in bringing down other stings. A typical ploy was some sort of free cruise or big party. Operation Cashweb the year before had arrested three of its suspects by luring them aboard a boat and sailing into international waters, where they could be nabbed legally.

"Why not have a wedding?" said someone. "It's something that has never been tried."

It sounded logical. A chorus of voices supported the novel plan. Mazur had insinuated himself into the social as well as the business lives of some of his clients. Many of them knew Kathy Ertz, too. It was natural that they would invite them to the wedding. This would be a perfect opportunity to get them all together and make sure that Mark Jackowski did not wind up with a hollow case.

That night the scene was set for the showy takedown of Operation C-Chase. It would be in Tampa, where it could be planned and pulled off with the most security. The trick was to keep things up and running until they could set a date and make the arrangements for the final episode.

CHAPTER SEVENTEEN

Closing Down C-Chase

In Medellín, there was considerable uneasiness about Mazur's operation. Separate incidents in Houston and New York raised the suspicions of the Colombian drug lords. Finally, they dispatched Rudy Armbrecht to Miami to get answers to some very serious questions.

On June 27, 1988, Emir Abreu had flown in the Citation jet to Houston to pick up $1 million of Don Chepe's money. The drop was set for a hotel parking lot. Abreu was waiting inside the hotel when he saw the designated car drive up. When he went out to meet the couriers, he found himself dealing with a nervous woman named Nellie and her twelve-year-old son, Roberto.

Inside were a duffel bag and a shoe box containing $1 million. As Abreu helped drag the bag from the back seat, he noticed an Uzi machine gun stuck under the driver's seat. Nellie was nervous, almost paranoid, as if she were being watched. She and Roberto hurried through the drop off and drove off as fast as they could.

Lugging the duffel bag behind him and cradling the box under one arm, Abreu headed back toward the hotel and watched as Nellie drove away. Behind her were the backups from the Houston office, following so closely it appeared to Abreu to be a caravan.

Two days later, Gonzalo Mora, Jr., telephoned from Colombia to ask how the woman and the boy had behaved.

"The lady was nervous," Abreu replied. "The kid, he was pretty good. But the lady was nervous."

"Look," said Mora, "I just got a call from Don Chepe's office, from one of his secretaries, that Nellie told him that there was some suspicious activity during the time that she gave you the money."

Abreu laughed it off. "Oh, you know, they get nervous. Every time they turn around, it seems like the police are following."

A single incident of botched surveillance might have been overlooked by those in Medellín, but it was followed by another incident two weeks later in New York City.

On July 13, a woman known as Marta delivered $448,000 to Abreu in Manhattan. Marta, too, thought she noticed some suspicious activity as she was leaving the drop site. When she and her husband relayed her anxiety to Medellín four days later, the reaction was swift.

Gonzalo Mora, Jr., was summoned to a meeting with Don Chepe himself. The drug suppliers already were suspicious of Mora because of his incessant boasting. They still viewed him as a small-timer, and they thought he talked too much, a dangerous character trait in his business. Tough questions were fired at him about the security of the American operation. Mora tried to be reassuring. He knew he could fall out of favor in a heartbeat, and that it might be his last if he did. He promised to contact the Americans and find out what was going on.

The following day, he telephoned Abreu and relayed the complaints that had been fired at him. Don Chepe's people were suspicious, he warned. First, it had been Houston. Then something had happened at the drop in New York. He urged Abreu to talk to Mazur and straighten out the situation. Otherwise everything was in danger.

Abreu was dispatched to New York the next day. Calm the Colombians there and get them to smooth it out in Medellín, he was told. When he confronted Marta and her husband, they feigned surprise.

"We don't have any problems," said Marta. "Everything is fine with us. We don't know what the problem is."

There had been close calls before. Everything that could be planned was planned carefully in C-Chase, but some elements cannot be controlled. Coincidence is a factor that often gets less credit than it deserves, as Bob Mazur had found out a few weeks earlier on a trip to New York.

Mazur was meeting Roberto Alcaino, "the Jeweler," in New York's ornate Helmsley Palace Hotel. As they stood in one of the rooms of the elegant mansion that had been converted into the hotel lobby, Mazur heard a familiar voice, chillingly familiar.

"Buon giorno, mi amici," it was saying. "Good day, my friend." He turned and saw the white hair and smiling face of Charles Broun, the Florida investment banker–turned–money-launderer whom he had sent to jail a decade earlier. Broun knew immediately that Mazur was undercover. His clothes were too expensive for a Customs Service employee, and he had grown a beard. For a moment, Mazur's life was in his hands.

But Broun had changed. In jail he had seen close up what drugs were doing to people, and he had found religion. He was genuinely grateful that Mazur had saved him from what he now called a satanic trap. After putting Mazur on the spot, he helped him wriggle free. Instead of calling him by name, he asked for Mazur's business card and played along with his new identity. As Alcaino listened to another confirmation of Mazur's fictious identity, the two banker-launderers discussed the ins and outs of laundering money through hotel chains.

But Mazur wanted to make sure that Broun stayed on his side. So he arranged a private meeting for later that afternoon, and they talked shop of a different kind.

"Do you have any advice?" Mazur asked.

"Before I was arrested," Broun said, "I thought that you looked, acted, and smelled just like the heat. If you hadn't come to me so well recommended, I wouldn't have had anything to do with you."

"What were the signals I was giving?" Mazur asked, growing alarmed.

"You were too attentive to the money," Broun replied. "The people who deal with transferring money in that bulk look at it as merchandise. They don't think of it as valuable. You were so solicitous of the money, it attracted my attention."

"I was following Customs regulations," Mazur protested, but he took Broun's advice to heart. As C-Chase drew to a climax, Mazur was going to need all the help he could get.

The blown surveillances in Houston and New York had presented another major risk for C-Chase. Mazur was about to need another bit of luck and all of his guile.

Rudy Armbrecht arrived in Miami on August 4 and immediately summoned Mazur to his room at the La Quinta motel at 2:42 A.M. It was a crucial moment; only Mazur's ability to convince Armbrecht that he was running an untainted operation would keep things intact until the big bust.

Armbrecht had remained distant with Mazur. He told the American that he found him to be intelligent and a quick learner, but what he had never needed to say was that it was Kathy Ertz, the American's fiancée, he really liked. A mildly flirtatious relationship had formed between them. Ertz slipped into the role as a means of allaying Armbrecht's suspicions.

Portraying herself as someone who had been taken care of all her life by men, Ertz had told Armbrecht that she wanted a measure of independence. They discussed Armbrecht's idea of importing marble desks together. The C-Chase agents thought that Ertz was fulfilling an important, if not necessarily pleasant, part of an undercover agent's job. However, Customs enforcement chief Bonni Tischler, who had not liked the theatrics of undercover during her days as a street agent, complained that Ertz was flaunting herself.

How much the attentions of an attractive woman did to keep Rudy Armbrecht in the picture was impossible to measure, but any little bit of residual goodwill was vital as Bob Mazur sat in that motel room in Miami with him in the wee hours of August 4.

There was a philosophical streak to Armbrecht. Often he discussed politics and he enjoyed playing chess. This night, however, he wasted little time in getting down to business. His voice was flat. There appeared to be no emotion here. Strictly business. A dangerous business.

His employers in Colombia were very alarmed over recent developments within Mazur's organization. They were reluctant to engage in any further business with the American.

"Little things are adding up," said Armbrecht.

For one thing, the Colombians were more comfortable doing business with their own people, even in the United States, because they had leverage over them. Armbrecht called it "a chain." With Mazur, they had no such leverage. That meant the American could cut a deal with the government if he got squeezed, giving up his associates to save himself.

Mazur allowed that the world was not a big enough place for someone who crossed such friends. Quick to agree, Armbrecht said, "And there, there isn't a hole that's deep enough."

It was not the prospect of losing money that had alarmed his associates in Colombia, the pilot assured the agent. It was that someone outside their control, someone living in the United States, was learning more about their organization than they felt was healthy. Gonzalo Mora, Jr., had talked too much, revealed too much. This made the Colombians paranoid.

"My associates are not worried about losing money because that is no big deal," explained Armbrecht. "It is how much of a knowledge somebody develops of the inside of the mechanism, as to how things work."

There was little doubt about what Armbrecht meant. Mora had made a dangerous mistake in Paris mentioning Gerardo Moncado's name to Mazur and then asking Armbrecht to arrange a meeting between the two men.

Several times in the tense conversation, Armbrecht took pains to reassure Mazur that his honesty was not in doubt. It was just, well, if Mazur got caught, who would he give up? And that was where the recent incidents in Houston and New York came into play. They appeared to the Colombians to be security lapses that put the network at risk. Hence, they were at risk, too, since Mazur knew so much about them.

Mazur tried to assure Armbrecht that his associates were

221

overreacting. When Abreu had confronted Marta in New York, she had claimed there were no problems with the pickup there.

A good sign, said Armbrecht. The Colombians had invested too much time in establishing the relationship with Mazur to break it off completely.

"Not cut it off, but slow it down and cool it off a lot," he said.

Armbrecht said he was trying to be a teacher to Mazur because he liked him and was certain of his personal honesty. Indeed, he had some good news, too.

"I will give you an encouraging notice," he said. "We have started dealing with those guys over there."

"You mean the BCCI branches in Colombia?" asked Mazur.

"On my suggestion, we started to probe and to analyze and to touch and to get a little bit more information of what was happening over there," explained Armbrecht. "And then we opened some accounts. Some big accounts. And that kind of thing. And the people that are working over there are very cooperative. They even offered to give us credits on deposits that we had on the BCCI anywhere in the world. So that was a good thing. Because it makes and gives a positive attitude toward this. And toward this bank."

The two BCCI officers in Miami with whom he worked supervised the operations in South America, said Mazur. He offered to introduce Armbrecht to them. But Mazur had been having some difficulties with BCCI, too—in particular with Akbar Ali Bilgrami, who had always been the suspicious one.

In late July, when the more trusting Awan was in the midst of a six-week business trip and could not protect the agent, Bilgrami had confronted Mazur with an unnerving accusation, and one that may have been Bilgrami's way of camouflaging concerns that were really his own.

According to Bilgrami's story, a colleague had told him that he had reviewed Mazur's accounts and had determined that Mazur was structuring transactions to evade taxes. Bilgrami and the colleague then discussed the transactions in a general way with someone at another bank. The other banker warned the BCCI men that the account holder could be the DEA. The banker cautioned them that the DEA had recently laundered $300 million through three American banks and that each bank had been fined $5 million. Bilgrami said he was nervous. Mazur tried to reassure him by using what had proven to be the most effective technique—discussing his plans to move more money through the bank.

Nonetheless, it was yet another indication that Operation C-Chase was running out of time. By late July, plans had been completed for the wedding of Robert Musella and Kathleen Erickson. It would be on October 9 at the Innisbrook resort outside Tampa. The invitations would be going out soon, but Mazur already had secured promises from Amjad Awan and Akbar Bilgrami that they would attend. Mazur was pushing for more of his associates to come to the wedding. And he was pushing to involve additional BCCI bankers in the scheme.

Awan had his own troubles, too, and his six-week trip was anything but restful. At Senator Kerry's hearing in February 1988, Jose Blandon had mentioned that General Manuel Noriega had used BCCI to hide his money. One of the general's greatest fears was that the U.S. authorities would use his indictment to seize the millions of dollars he had hidden in bank accounts around the world. The public mention of BCCI had led him to raise with Awan the issue of removing the money from the bank.

When Noriega first brought up the possibility of moving his money, Awan had gone immediately to London and met with Swaleh Naqvi and Dildar Rizvi, the Pakistani who was then head treasurer of BCCI. At the time, Noriega had $23 million sitting in three accounts in one of BCCI's London branches. According to the later indictment of Naqui, Rizvi, and others, the men decided to transfer the $23 million to a single account at BCCI in Luxembourg. Awan tried to reassure Noriega that this added layer of secrecy was sufficient to protect his money.

Awan was already planning his departure from the bank, and he wanted to take his major clients with him. A month earlier, he had talked to Mazur about the financial services firm he hoped to set up with his friend S.Z.A. Akbar. Noriega's imbroglio came at a good time for Awan; according to a later indictment, he would bring the general along with him to Capcom, but not before he laid a paper trail that would confuse anyone who tried to follow it.

Armed with a withdrawal letter from General Noriega dated July 26 and, the government would later claim, acting under the direct authority of Swaleh Naqvi, the acting BCCI president, and Dildar Rizvi, the treasurer, Awan started his shell game. (The date, probably phony, was crucial. It was two days before the U.S. Senate subpoenaed Noriega's BCCI bank records.) Awan transferred nearly $12 million from BCCI-Luxembourg to an account at the Bank Deutsch Sudamerikanische in Hamburg, Germany. A like amount went to the Union Bank of Switzerland in Zurich. Although Noriega later claimed fervently that these were his personal funds, the accounts were registered in the name of the Banco Nacional de Panama. The use of Panama's central bank helped screen the funds, to hinder any auditors the U.S. government might set on the trail, but several years later it allowed the new government of Panama to lay its own claim to the money. The accounts were soon emptied, however. In early August, Awan met with S.Z.A. Akbar at the London office of Capcom Financial Services. Syed Akbar allegedly offered a list of accounts that could be used to hold Noriega's money. Awan chose one under the name of Finley International. He then flew to Panama to brief Noriega, taking the long way around through Spain, as Naqvi directed, to avoid going through the United States.

In early September, the $23 million from the two accounts merged again, as the funds were transferred to a Banco Nacional de Panama account at the Middle East Bank in London. A week later, the government claimed, Akbar moved the money to the Finley International Ltd. account, still at Middle East Bank. The funds sat there long enough to attract the attention of Capcom's auditor, Arthur Anderson & Co. The auditors started asking who owned the Finley millions, and Capcom wouldn't tell them. Akbar had to get the money away from this unwanted scrutiny. So, in a breathtaking display of the principle that the best place to hide things is in plain sight, Akbar moved the deposit to the last place American authorities would think to look. He allegedly put it in a Capcom account in New York City. There were no fancy code names. The account was labeled MAN Trust, the initials of Manual Antonio Noriega. The bold maneuver succeeded brilliantly. Over the next six months, according to the government indictment, more than $20 million filtered out of the New York account, completely undetected by the international effort to freeze Noriega's assets. The authorities still don't know where the money went.

As soon as Noriega's money was in motion, Awan had flown to Washington, where he met with the bank's lawyers who were fighting the Kerry subcommittee's subpoenas for bank records. It was a frustrating and frightening time for Awan, and he brought it up with Bob Mazur when he returned to Miami.

"I don't know if Akbar mentioned it to you," said Awan as he and Mazur sat in Awan's office on August 17. "We're going through a bit of a problem these days. We think there is another investigation going on. I've been with the lawyers for the last couple of days, trying to sort some things out."

"Why are there grumblings?" asked Mazur.

"Senate committee again," replied Awan.

The banker tried to seem unconcerned about the inquiry. And a few minutes later, Bilgrami too downplayed the investigation. "It doesn't concern you," he assured Mazur. The American agreed that it was no doubt a general inquiry involving many banks and nothing to worry about.

However, the bankers and the agent were concerned that the Senate investigation would disrupt their relationship, but for different reasons.

Awan and Bilgrami did not want to spook a lucrative customer. Mazur did not want to spook his key targets.

The overtones were more serious the next time the issue arose. Mazur and Awan were having drinks at the Grand Bay Hotel, their favorite haunt in Coconut Grove, on September 9, a Friday.

"Let me tell you what's happened, Bob," said Awan. "Ah, I'm in a bit of a poop right now."

As Mazur sipped his Scotch and water and Awan seemed to gulp his Corona beer, the banker said that he had been back and forth to Washington and London several times in recent weeks.

"What I've learned is not very pleasant," Awan said. "And, ah, I wanted to talk to you personally and tell you about it. What's happened is that we were served with a subpoena last month. The bank was and Mr. Shafi our general manager was. I was supposed to have been served also, but with their normal efficiency they opened the phone book and there's some poor Awan who works for Rockwell International."

The bank's lawyers in Washington, led by Clark Clifford and Robert Altman, had so far refused to turn over the documents sought by the committee. More important to Awan, the investigators had singled him out as General Noriega's banker and were demanding to talk to him. He described himself as the only person in the bank who knew all about Noriega's accounts and business.

"On a personal level, last Friday I was told that our lawyers, Mr. Altman was there, and he suggested to the bank that I should be immediately transferred from the United States to Paris. So, they duly transferred me Friday to Paris," said Awan. (In sworn testimony before the House Banking Committee, Altman said he had advised the transfer for Awan's safety.)

"Ah," said Mazur.

Awan said that the bank had wanted him out of the country by Monday—four days ago. He was determined not to go, and he was angered at the order.

"I was extremely upset at that," he said. "You know, I'd been planning to leave [the bank] anyway, but that was just the last straw. So I came back Friday and Monday night I flew out to Washington and Tuesday morning I met with the counsel to the Foreign Relations Committee who is doing all this."

"You mean on the other side?" asked Mazur, who was really starting to worry that his prime target was about to bolt.

"The other side, yeah," replied Awan. "Because I'm not too, too happy on what our attorneys are telling us to do. I think that they're doing a very stupid thing."

The undercover agent was in for another shock, when he asked what the Senate lawyers had said to him. Awan replied: "They said, 'We're going to get this bank. We know that this bank is the biggest money launderer in the world. They're doing this and they're doing that.' And I said, 'No, that's not the truth. You know, I've been in Panama. I know exactly what's happened. That's not true.' They said, 'Well, we have a lot of information. So it'll all come out in the hearing.' Ah, they do not have any information. That I know. They may have some circumstantial evidence, which is not going to stand up either. But it seems that there is a distinct disdain against BCC."

Mazur said that he thought the bank's backers in Washington had neutralized the Senate probe.

"Well, our attorneys are, they're heavyweights," said Awan. "I mean, Clark Clifford is sort of the godfather of the Democratic Party. . . . He's been in the White House since the time of Truman. He was Truman's legal counsel. He's like eighty years old, but he's all there. That's a very heavyweight firm."

Awan had his own dark suspicions about what was occurring. He thought that Clifford and Altman might be maneuvering to remove BCCI from ownership of First American Bankshares, the Washington holding company.

"We own a bank based in Washington," he said. "It's called First American Bank. The holding company is in Washington and there are five banks actually. First American of New York, First American of Washington, D.C., First American of Virginia, Maryland, Tennessee, and Georgia. There's six banks. Six large banks. Bought out by BCCI about eight years ago. . . . And BCCI was acting as adviser to them. But truth of the matter is that the bank belongs to BCCI. Those guys are just nominee shareholders.

"Clark Clifford and his law partner Bob Altman are the chairman and capital holders. I personally feel it would suit them if BCCI withdrew."

Awan added that Altman was very ambitious. "He has political aspirations," Awan said, "apart from being married to Wonder Woman." (Awan referred to Altman's wife, actress Lynda Carter, who had played the character in a television series years before.)

"I wouldn't at all be surprised if, you know, if they're totally screwing BCCI to take over this bank," said Awan, who was angrier than Mazur had ever seen him. Awan said he had cleaned out his files at the bank.

"If it doesn't work out," asked Mazur anxiously, "where would you go? Back to Pakistan or where?"

"It doesn't suit me to do that, Bob," said Awan. "I mean, they really don't have anything on me, and I, I feel I haven't really done anything wrong."

Awan's stubborn side was thoroughly aroused. ("He's a Pathan,"

Abdur Sakhia, his supervisor, later explained. "They're very stubborn, like your Scots.")

"I'm going to ride it out," Awan went on.

As the waiter brought them another round, Awan's thoughts took a morbid turn.

"I don't fancy going to Panama and spending the rest of my days there," he said, "however long it may be. I don't know how long."

"That would be the last place I'd think I'd want to go, if I were you," said Mazur.

"No, it's a great place," said Awan. "But I mean my protection would be this man. And when he's gone, I'm gone too. And what sort of protection would that be, anyway. I mean, he knows that I know everything. So he might well decide . . ." Awan let the thought trail off.

"He might not want you around," prompted Mazur. "Do you think he would get that rough?"

"Who knows?" replied Awan, who was still in the middle of hiding Noriega's $23 million. "It's a question of money. And I know exactly where he has what."

Awan suggested that Mazur close his accounts at BCCI in the event the bank was forced to turn over information. In the meantime, he promised that Mazur would get maximum protection from any investigation. The agent thanked him politely, and cheered him up by turning the talk to his approaching wedding.

Gifted with hindsight, some in Congress and the press would say that Mazur's supervisors should have relayed the information about BCCI's secret holdings in First American to top-level banking regulators in Washington.

This was the third time the BCCI–First American connection surfaced in one of Awan's conversations with Mazur, and it was far more explicit, but the revelation came at a critical time in Operation C-Chase. The agents were moving at a frantic pace to keep the investigation from coming unglued before they could nab the bad guys. Nonetheless, Mazur took the time to write several memos to his supervisors suggesting that the connections to Clifford and Altman should be examined, but nothing happened.

"As managing supervisor, it just wasn't something that I wanted to pursue," said Bonni Tischler later. "There was nothing there for us to pursue. Our case was complicated enough in trying to sink the bank."

Gregory Kehoe, who became first assistant U.S. attorney in Tampa after the bust, was blunter: "We had to get the guys in our gunsights first."

Indeed, before the investigation was closed down at the wedding in

October, Mazur wanted to net another banker or two. And he wanted to make sure that Awan did not flee to some foreign country where he could not be extradited. Even with Awan's worries about Noriega, the possibility that the banker might run to Panama was a substantial threat, given the state of relations between Noriega and the United States government at the time.

One of the other BCCI bankers on the target list was Saad Shafi, the Pakistani who was the country manager in Nassau. Mazur had had a brief telephone discussion with Shafi about moving funds through two corporate shells Mazur had bought in the Bahamas. On August 25, 1988, he and Kathy Ertz took the short flight from Miami to Nassau and the next afternoon they met with Shafi at the bank's offices in the bustling downtown, where tourism and offshore banking were the biggest industries.

Saad Shafi explained that he and Awan were old friends. They had worked together at the Bank of Montreal until Shafi left in 1976 to take a job with BCCI. Awan followed two years later. He said that the Nassau branch had opened in 1986. For two years before that, however, it had been a phantom branch. It was run by a lawyer in Nassau and the books were kept in the Miami office.

Now, however, Shafi was getting good business for the Nassau branch and he was anxious to work out an arrangement with Mazur. He had made a reservation for dinner at the Cafe Martinique, one of the city's best restaurants. It would be, he told Mazur and Ertz, at the bank's expense. They agreed to meet forty-five minutes before dinner to discuss business at Mazur's hotel, the Britannia Towers on Paradise Island.

The pitch was rote by now, down to the comparison to Lee Iacocca. When Shafi arrived in his room, it was almost like turning on a tape recorder. Describing his web of front companies and cash pickups, his need for security and professionalism, Mazur said: "Lee Iacocca sells cars in the United States. My clients, for their own reasons, sell cocaine in the United States and what they do is their business. What I do is my business and I'm a wall between them."

"Sure, sure," replied Shafi, who seemed nervous at the mention of drugs and tried to steer the conversation in other directions.

For instance, the banker praised Bahamian Prime Minister Lynden Pindling for resisting U.S. efforts to break down the bank secrecy laws that had turned the island into an offshore tax and banking haven.

Shafi suggested that Mazur gradually increase the volume of money he moved through the Bahamas to avoid attracting attention. But he also said that big deposits in December would make Shafi look good at the end of the bank's business year.

The discussion closed with plans to wire $382,000 to Mazur's account at BCCI-Nassau from Crédit Suisse bank in Zurich.

The coke bust in Detroit, the blown surveillances in Houston and New York, Armbrecht's suspicions, and the drying up of the drug cash—all had contributed to the decision to close down Operation C-Chase.

It was a decision that seemed prescient on August 30. Wiretaps placed on the telephones of Roberto Baez Alcaino had revealed that a shipment of cocaine was bound for Philadelphia from Argentina. The conversations indicated that it was a major shipment, possibly several tons, hidden in a shipment of canned anchovies.

There was never a question about what would happen once it arrived. Customs agents would board the ship and seize the cocaine. This was a record haul. No chance of this one slipping through, C-Chase or not.

When the freighter *Colombus Olivious* arrived in port on August 30, Customs agents swarmed over it. A containerized shipment of anchovies was hauled off the ship and taken to the U.S. Customs House at the port. There agents began to search through the 1,000 cartons of anchovies. And they found anchovies.

Then a sharp-eyed agent noticed that some cartons were heavier than others. The cans inside the heavy cartons contained cocaine. Additional inspection revealed that each cocaine carton had a pin-sized hole punched just above the importer's trademark. By the time they finished scrutinizing every carton and the remainder of the ship, it was September 7. The Customs agents had discovered more than twelve tons of cocaine, with a wholesale value of nearly $30 million.

Customs officials kept the bust secret for another week. Then, on September 15, an indictment was returned against Alcaino. At a press conference in Philadelphia, Customs and DEA officials said that Alcaino appeared to be a high-level narcotics dealer.

Suddenly the clock was ticking faster. The undercover agents needed to nail down the last of the targets and keep their fingers crossed until October 9, the date set for the phony wedding.

One of the eleventh-hour targets was Syed Ziauddin Ali Akbar, the former BCCI treasury head who had formed Capcom. At the suggestion of Awan and Bilgrami, an account had been opened by Mazur with Akbar's trading firm. Mazur and Erickson flew to London and met with him on September 19, 1988.

The trip began with an embarrassment. Mazur had been traveling for more than two years on a passport that listed him as Robert Musella as part of the total security that he tried to maintain while undercover.

However, this time something in the passport raised an alarm when he arrived at Heathrow Airport. The FBI had forged a visa using an outmoded stamper. British immigration took Mazur into custody and hustled him off to an interrogation room. Mazur maintained his cover, protesting that he was an innocent businessman while the British authorities wondered if they had nabbed a drug trafficker or even a terrorist. They searched Mazur down to his underwear and took him into London, where he was jailed. He took the risk of telephoning his U.S. Customs Service contact in London for help. The next day, Mazur's jailers received unexplained orders to release their mysterious catch. Mazur, unflappable, had spent the night playing charades with his cellmate, an Australian aborigine.

Mazur and the C-Chase agents knew little about Syed Akbar. An interesting character who looked far younger than his mid-forties, he had left BCCI in 1986 after the dispute with the London management over massive losses in the bank's trading portfolio. When he left, he took with him computer disks containing thousands of pages of internal documents that described what was essentially a bank within the bank. The material described how BCCI had used cash from deposits world-wide to cover up holes in its balance sheet created by trading losses as well as by suspicious and just plain lousy loans. Accountants would later claim that some of the customer deposits had gone to conceal nearly $1 billion in losses that the bank had sustained while Akbar was head of its trading unit. Nonetheless, he remained on friendly terms with BCCI, and only the month before he had helped the bank by taking $23 million in Noriega's money.

Mazur and the Customs Service were unaware of his potential importance to their investigation. When he picked up the two undercover agents at the Dorchester Hotel in London for dinner, they figured he was just another medium-sized fish, a friend of Awan and Bilgrami.

Over dinner and in meetings over the following two days, Akbar described his trading operation and the ways that Mazur could launder cash through his account with Capcom. When Mazur launched into his Lee Iacocca speech, the financial trader was skittish. He did not want to hear about the source of cash.

"We are not the need to know," he stammered in poor English. As soon as Mazur left, Akbar telephoned Akbar Bilgrami in Miami and complained about the American's bluntness.

Mazur didn't know it, but he was becoming notorious throughout BCCI. During his visit, a somewhat naive senior bank officer called an assistant manager in the Panama branch to warn that Mazur was moving drug money. His account should be closed, the senior officer said. "If you do that," replied the local manager, "BCCI might as well shut down the entire Panama branch."

Again Mazur had pressed Awan to set up a meeting with Naqvi. Again the agent had been frustrated in his attempts to move higher into the bank. And time was running out.

From London, Mazur and Erickson hopped across the English Channel to visit with Nazir Chinoy, Ian Howard, and Sibte Hassan. Most of this trip was social, including a cocktail party at Chinoy's apartment on Thursday, September 22.

There were a hundred people at the party in the elegant apartment on the Right Bank. Among them were BCCI officers, businessmen, and diplomats. During the party, Chinoy informed the BCCI contingent that he had just been told that Amjad Awan would soon be joining the Paris office.

The bankers in Paris were pleased to see their American friend. Chinoy told him that arrangements had been made to handle $20 million a month for him through BCCI-Paris and the other branches in France.

Mazur said that he and Ertz were being married in two weeks and he invited all three bankers to attend the wedding. Howard and Hassan accepted eagerly, but Chinoy was uncertain about whether he would be able to attend.

It turned out that he couldn't. Around October 3, Naqvi himself vetoed the trip. BCCI general managers, he said, should not become too visible with these types of accounts.

The trip's only sour note came on September 23. Sibte Hassan showed Mazur new documents for the Nicesea Shipping account that had been opened back in May. On Rudy Armbrecht's instruction, Mazur had been removed as a signatory on the account and it had been transferred to a BCCI branch in Colombia.

The change shocked Mazur. Armbrecht had been drifting away. There had been no more pickups of drug money from Don Chepe's distributors, but Mazur had not been prepared for being secretly cut out of the Nicesea account. Now, he thought, they would be lucky to get Rudy to the wedding.

In Washington, Customs Commissioner William von Raab was eager to bring down his agency's longest-running undercover operation. The timing looked perfect to him.

Von Raab had been Customs boss throughout the eight years Ronald Reagan was president, but with a new administration coming into office, he was hoping for a bigger post. He wanted to be drug czar in the new administration of George Bush. And he figured that a major drug bust involving an international bank, a month before the presidential election, was a good way to get noticed as a doer.

The Customs agents assigned to C-Chase had mixed feelings about taking down the operation. In recent weeks, they had uncovered intriguing new evidence about the bank. There appeared to be accounts at BCCI branches for organizations and front companies tied to Abu Nidal, the Palestinian terrorist responsible for dozens of murderous attacks around the world. The CIA seemed to be using BCCI to finance some of its global covert operations. And there was the bank itself. How much higher could they go, given more time?

The agents recognized the dangerous line that they were walking since the series of mishaps that had created suspicions among the Colombians. One false step there could be fatal, so they understood the justification for bringing down the operation.

Mazur, however, was frustrated and angry that the operation was being shut down. He had written memos and harangued Tischler and others to devote more resources to C-Chase. He wanted to expand the investigation and devote more time to it, no matter what the risks, because he sensed it would be possible to move far higher in the bank. Almost from his first meeting with Awan and Bilgrami, Mazur had been convinced that BCCI was corrupt from top to bottom.

The fear of Mazur and some of the others that politics were at play in scheduling the takedown was fed by the fact that Bonni Tischler was so close to Von Raab, so seemingly attuned to the commissioner's political agenda.

"Did politics play a role in the timing? I really couldn't say," said one of the federal agents involved in Operation C-Chase much later. "I wouldn't doubt for a minute that it did. We all sort of figured that much. But we all knew that there were damn good reasons for closing down the operation when we did."

In fact, the Customs agents had political considerations of their own. The DEA's rival Operation Polarcap was expected to be rolled up in late fall or at least by the end of the year. The C-Chase team did not want to get overshadowed by that investigation. They had heard it would include indictments of major figures in the Medellín cartel and the laundering of far more money.

Too, strains were showing within the C-Chase team. The long months of tense undercover activity had left nerves frayed, and angers normally kept in check were surfacing in what would turn out to be lasting animosities.

Bonni Tischler, who had spent much of her career encouraging the advancement of women in federal law enforcement, had taken Kathy Ertz under her wing when the younger woman was brought into the operation. She had even encouraged her to transfer to Tampa from Miami. But Ertz's flirting with Rudy Armbrecht, vital as it had seemed in keeping the Colombian's suspicions at bay, had grated on Tischler's tough-talking persona. In the same way, Tischler had been irritated by the submissive role that Ertz assumed with the Pakistani bankers, though that was clearly what the Muslim culture dictated for women. By this time, the two women were barely speaking.

For his part, Mazur was having problems with both women. Ertz played her role as his girlfriend too enthusiastically. It was a joke on her part, but one that Mazur did not find amusing, particularly given the inevitable strains on his marriage created by the months of minimal contact with his wife. As for Tischler, Mazur viewed her as too political, someone who had pushed from the start to close down the investigation. By this point, Tischler regarded Mazur with a high degree of skepticism, too. Her view, forged during her brief stint undercover in Operation Greenback years earlier, was that undercover agents had to be kept on a tight leash by supervisors who had a broader view of the case. On top of that, she simply thought Bob Mazur had become a prima donna. C-Chase was shutting down none too soon, as far as Tischler was concerned.

Amjad Awan stepped onto the thick beige carpet of the suite's living room. In front of him were sliding glass doors leading to a porch that overlooked a winding path bordered by lush hibiscus, azaleas, and oleanders. Towering above were cypresses and pines.

It was almost five o'clock on the afternoon of October 8, 1988, another sunny Saturday in Florida. The Awans had arrived at Tampa International Airport an hour earlier, after a short flight up from Miami. They had been met by a limousine for the thirty-five minute drive to the Innisbrook Resort, a thousand acres of golf courses, swimming pools, and luxurious suites northwest of Tampa. Now Awan and his wife Sheereen needed to hurry. Checking into their suite, they found an invitation waiting: Please join the other guests beside the swimming pool for a cocktail party to kick off a weekend of festivities surrounding Sunday's wedding of Bob Musella and Kathy Erickson.

At the pool, the trim Pakistani banker eyed the crowd of guests. A few faces were familiar, colleagues from various branches of BCCI. There was Akbar Bilgrami, his partner in Miami who had come up with his wife on an earlier flight. Syed Hussain, round-faced and friendly, had flown up from Panama. Sibte Hassan had come all the way from Paris. So had Ian Keith Howard. The bankers exchanged greetings.

Slowly, Awan met some of the other guests. They seemed to fall into two distinct categories, both a world apart from the realm of international banking where Awan and his colleagues dwelled. Some of them were conversing loudly in Spanish. Among them was a man Awan vaguely remembered. It was Gonzalo Mora, Jr., who had barged into his office months before to see Mazur. In the other group were hale and hearty Americans, who kept insisting that Awan's plastic glass always be brimming with Scotch. One of them, who said his name was Mike Miller, seemed particularly keen on befriending Awan. On balance, the Latinos and the Americans seemed to be men of action, rather than of finance.

Amjad Awan was looking for some relief this weekend. Pressure was still coming from the bank to leave the country, and he was resisting. At the same time, he had provided a sworn statement to Senator Kerry's investigators and he feared that General Noriega might order him killed if he learned of the betrayal. His best shot, Awan believed, was remaining in the United States and hoping that the investigation would blow over.

As the party around the pool progressed, word began to circulate that there was going to be a bachelor party at a restaurant in Tampa. It was the Americans who murmured tantalizing suggestions about the blowout. Men only, of course.

The sun was beginning to drop by the time a line of black Cadillac and Lincoln limousines pulled up the drive at Innisbrook to pick up the would-be revelers. It was shortly after seven o'clock. As he crawled into a limo, Gonzalo Mora, Jr., joked in Spanish to Emir Abreu.

"We're going to get fucked tonight," laughed Mora.

"You better believe it," replied Abreu.

Awan was less eager, but he had been assured by Mike Miller that they would be back in time for a late dinner with their wives. As Awan and Akbar Bilgrami started to get into the same car, Miller stepped between them and said there was another car assigned to Bilgrami. Miller then crawled in with Awan.

As the limousine started to pull away, Miller asked the driver to stop outside one of the clusters of rooms. Apologizing to Awan, he said that he had to get the gag gift he had left in his room. Miller ran back to his suite and grabbed a gift-wrapped box. Inside were a gun, badge, and handcuffs. They belonged to Bob Mazur. Taped to the box and sealed in an envelope was a card. On it, Miller had scrawled, "The jig is up!"

The party was planned for MacBeth's, a restaurant on top of the NCNB Tower in downtown Tampa. The first seven stories of the building were a parking garage. As the limousines drove onto the second floor of the garage, a man was waiting with a smile and a clipboard. The cars would pull up, a few minutes apart, and he would stick his head inside each one.

"This is the Musella party?" he would ask, scanning the faces of the passengers and asking for their names.

Checking the names off his list, the attendant would open the door and ask the guests to take the elevator to the seventh floor. There, he said, they would switch to another bank of elevators and go to the top floor for the party.

It was a party they never attended. When the elevator doors glided open on the seventh floor, the guests were greeted by a bevy of mostly middle-aged men wearing dark blue Windbreakers. On the back of the jackets, in white capital letters, were the words CUSTOMS, DEA, IRS, and FBI.

"Welcome to Tampa. You are under arrest," the federal agents told the stunned arrivals as they snapped handcuffs around their wrists and read them their Miranda rights. The limousines had been driven up to the seventh floor and the men were put back in the same cars and whisked a few blocks away to the Federal Building on Zack Street. There, they were photographed, fingerprinted, and interrogated.

The reactions to the arrests were as varied as the men. Akbar Bilgrami shook his head and thought to himself that he had seen signs that the cops might be after Mazur. He protested to the arresting agents, saying he had never done anything illegal. He claimed that Mazur must have done something, but he said he had no idea what it could have been.

Sibte Hassan had been to a fabulously ribald bachelor's party in Paris not long before where prostitutes dressed as police had handcuffed the guests and stripped them as part of the fun. His initial thought was that this was a replay of that elaborate hoax, particularly when he spotted a petite, blond woman among the crowd of men with guns.

"All right, let's party," shouted the handcuffed Hassan.

It took the agents several minutes to persuade the banker that this was not a repeat of Paris and that the blond woman was the chief enforcement officer for Customs in Tampa, Bonni Tischler.

Amjad Awan was shocked when he saw the armed men. "Don't do anything stupid like trying to run," Mike Miller ordered as he pulled Awan's hands behind him and put on the cuffs. Slightly tipsy from the Scotch and the shock, Awan was taken to an office inside the Federal Building where he signed a statement acknowledging that he had been read his rights and waived them. Then he was allowed to read the indictment against him and his colleagues, which had been returned secretly by a federal grand jury in Tampa a few days before.

Scanning the document, Awan realized that he had not been close to the truth about Mazur. Awan had thought that Mazur was a money launderer posing as a legitimate businessman, but inside that secret was another secret: Mazur was a federal agent posing as a money launderer pretending to be a businessman.

In another room, Operation C-Chase had set up a command center to orchestrate the climax of the largest and most successful undercover investigation ever conducted by the Customs Service.

As the Tampa suspects were booked and jailed, orders went out around the world to grab those who had skipped the wedding or had not been invited. Nazir Chinoy was arrested in London, where he was attending a BCCI board meeting. Also arrested in London were Syed Akbar of Capcom and Asif Baakza, one of the bank's mid-level officers there. Rudolf Armbrecht was arrested in Miami; he had decided to skip the wedding, but not the country. Simultaneously, authorities in the United States and Europe executed search warrants and began to scour the offices of the Bank of Credit and Commerce for documents about the worldwide money-laundering scheme.

The wedding ruse did not give the Americans the corner on ingenuity. In Paris, an inspector with French customs had wanted to get an advance layout of the bank's office on the Champs Elysées, so that his men would know where to search for documents before they could be destroyed by employees. So, on October 4, he had gone to the office and told a security guard that there had been a bomb threat. A floor plan of the office was necessary, he explained, so that police could search for the bomb. When the inspector returned a few days later with the search warrant, the guard recognized him.

"Another bomb threat?" asked the guard.

"Not this time," said the inspector. With a theatrical flourish, he added, "I am zee bomb."

A real bomb turned up a short time later in connection with C-Chase, but it was a continent away from the Champs Elysées.

IRS agent David Burris had drawn the assignment of searching BCCI's offices in Miami on October 8. He drew up a forty-four-page summary of the evidence in the investigation and used it to obtain a search warrant from a federal judge in Tampa. After the arrests in downtown Tampa, Burris led a team of agents who gathered boxes of documents from the offices in Miami. (When they arrived at 6:30 A.M. on Sunday, they were astonished to find a local television camera crew staking out the building.) After several days of searching, Burris loaded the cardboard boxes on a U-Haul truck and returned to Tampa. The IRS investigations division was located several floors below Customs Enforcement in the North Lois Avenue office building. Burris had arranged for new office space for the documents, but no one had remembered to put locks on the door. Burris and his supervisor, George Scott, decided to stay in the room and guard their haul until the locks were installed.

They were sitting there a few days after the arrests when someone decided to strike back at C-Chase. On October 13, the Customs office received an anonymous call saying a bomb had been planted in the building. A quick search found a device in the stairwell between the sixth and seventh floors. It looked like a professionally made bomb but the explosive charge had been left out. The building was evacuated and a bomb squad was called to remove the device. No one thought to notify the IRS agents guarding the documents. Burris and a fellow agent did not learn about the danger until Burris left the room to get some coffee.

A few days later there was a threat against Bonni Tischler. Intelligence agents had picked up on the street that someone had put a contract out on her. Tischler maintained that she was unconcerned by the threat, but she was nonetheless saddled with what she dubbed "Bonni-guards" for six weeks.

The indictments behind the bachelor party bust had been returned on October 4, 1988, by a federal grand jury in Tampa under the direction of Mark Jackowski. They had remained sealed until the arrests occurred to avoid tipping off any of the targets.

Awan was the first defendant named in the main indictment. He was one of eleven BCCI employees named. The others were, in the order they appeared, Syed Aftab Hussain, Akbar A. Bilgrami, Nazir Chinoy, Sibte Hassan, Ian Howard, Saad Shafi, Iqbal Ashraf, and two employees in the bank's Panama offices, Surjeet Singh and Haroon Qazi, who were charged with assisting in money laundering there. Rudolf Armbrecht and Gonzalo Mora, Jr., also were charged in the main indictment, as was Syed Z. A. Akbar of Capcom Financial Services.

The corporate defendants were the parent BCCI Holdings in Luxembourg, the Bank of Credit and Commerce International in Luxembourg, the Bank of Credit and Commerce International in the Cayman Islands, the Banco de Crédito y Comercio de Colombia in Bogotá, and Akbar's Capcom Financial Services.

The bank and its employees were among the first defendants charged under the 1986 money-laundering act that made it a crime to transfer money known to have been derived from illegal activities. Since BCCI had not accepted cash from the drug pickups and the bankers never saw any drugs, it is highly unlikely that they would have been accused of violating the law under the old statutes.

In all, there had been 102 bank deposits of drug cash over a two-year period. They totaled $33,033,103. Of that total, $19,294,822 had been laundered by transfers through various branches of BCCI, from Panama to Geneva, Paris to London and Nassau.

A second Tampa indictment focused on the drug traffickers. Charged in it were Mora, Jr., his father, his brother Jimmy, Armbrecht, Javier Ospina, Santiago Uribe, and seven others. Among the others was a defendant identified as "John Doe, also known as Don Chepe." The agents were fairly certain that Don Chepe was Gerardo Moncado, but since the chances of extraditing him from Colombia were slim, they decided not to take the chance they were wrong.

Indictments also were handed down in Detroit, Houston, and New York. Those charges involved the money couriers and other people related to the drops. They brought the total number of individual defendants in Operation C-Chase to eighty-four.

In Washington, D.C., Customs Commissioner William von Raab had kept in touch with Bonni Tischler in the days leading up to the bust. Widely regarded as one of the premier publicity seekers in a town where few were shy about the press, he wanted maximum exposure on this case. He planned a nationally televised press conference to announce the charges.

As the weekend of the takedown approached, Von Raab had grown slightly anxious about the types of questions that might come up at the press conference concerning the bank, so he telephoned the CIA to see what they could tell him about the organization. Eventually he got connected with Robert Gates, the deputy director. What did Gates know about BCCI?

"Oh," replied the man who would one day be chosen by President George Bush to head the CIA, "you mean the Bank of Crooks and Criminals International."

Gates sent over the brief classified report that the agency had prepared on the bank in September 1986. The report described BCCI's role in money-laundering operations and said: "Many of BCCI's illicit banking activities, particularly those related to narco-finance in the Western Hemisphere, are believed to be concentrated in the Cayman Islands facility." It also confirmed and elaborated on what Amjad Awan had said in the C-Chase tapes: "In late 1981, BCCI made an unsuccessful attempt to acquire or gain control of Financial General Bankshares, a Washington, D.C.–based multi-state bank holding company; BCCI achieved its goal half a year later, although the exact nature of its control is not clear."

According to the distribution list on the report, it had been routed soon after it was written to the Treasury Department, the Commerce

Department, the State Department, and several intelligence agencies within the U.S. government. But somehow it apparently had not gotten to the Federal Reserve, the independent agency that regulates banking companies.

From Von Raab's viewpoint, the CIA report merely confirmed his conviction that this was a dirty bank.

On Tuesday, October 11, Von Raab made the evening news with the announcement that eighty-four people and one of the world's largest private banks had been indicted on drug conspiracy and money-laundering charges. Curiously, at the press conference no mention was made of General Manuel Noriega, probably the most notorious drug criminal in the world in the eyes of the American public at the time, no mention that BCCI had handled millions of dollars for the dictator, or that the sting had snared Noriega's personal banker. That would have been even bigger news.

Later, Von Raab would explain that he did not want to take away from the hard work and long hours of his Customs agents by muddying the water with Noriega's name. He denied it when asked if he had wanted to avoid mentioning Noriega because of the potential embarrassment to George Bush.

Embarrassment about the handling of the investigation of the Bank of Credit and Commerce International would come later and from other quarters. Bob Mazur and his crew had done stellar work in busting the bank, but they had only scraped the surface of what would one day be dubbed "the world's sleaziest bank."

PART THREE

Breaking the Bank

BCCI has an international reputation
for capital flight, tax fraud, and
money-laundering activities that
far exceeded the conduct charged in
the Florida indictment.

—Robert Morgenthau,
New York District Attorney

CHAPTER EIGHTEEN

Roadblocks

Jack Blum, who suspected everyone's motivation save his own, was running John Kerry's investigation into Manuel Noriega's ties to the American government when he came across the Bank of Credit and Commerce International in early 1988, ten months before the indictments in Tampa. Jose Blandon, the former Panamanian diplomat turned ardent enemy of Noriega, told Blum that BCCI was the general's favorite bank. In pursuing that connection with inspired doggedness, Blum would confront overt and covert obstacles that made him leery of anyone not one hundred percent committed to his vision. For all intents and purposes, it was Blum's stubborn suspicion that fanned the dying embers and eventually fueled the firestorm that engulfed BCCI.

He is a lawyer and a sometimes government official who does not really like working for government, an intense and intelligent man whose curiosity and instinct made him an excellent sleuth. He is a big, jug-eared man, with a hearty appetite for food and conspiracy theories.

Soon after graduating from law school at Columbia in New York City in 1965, Blum had gone to work as an investigator for a Senate antitrust subcommittee. He stayed twelve years in government, moving on to the Senate Foreign Relations Committee and working on such big international investigations as the Lockheed foreign bribery scandal, oil-price fixing during the Arab embargo, ITT Corporation's efforts to rig elections in Chile, and the financial acrobatics of Robert Vesco.

It was on the Vesco investigation that Blum caught a glimpse of the intricacies of international finance. Vesco pillaged hundreds of millions of dollars from mutual fund investors and used front companies to funnel the cash through banks in the Bahamas and Luxembourg. Assisting him at every step of the way were accountants, attorneys, and bankers. Years after Vesco fled to asylum in Costa Rica, government lawyers were still trying to unscramble the labyrinth of transactions into which between $250 million and $450 million had vanished.

"What I learned was that there is a cynicism in banking circles," Blum explained later. "Bankers say, 'We just move money. We don't concern ourselves with the business of our clients.' But that begs the question. They are knowingly soliciting the proceeds of all sorts of crimes. Bankers the world over wink at what I call the 'legal illegal' money. Tax evaders, exchange-restriction avoiders, the Marcoses, the Baby Doc Duvaliers. The banking world makes a judgment that that's okay. But it then becomes easy for the banker to make the leap from that to drug money. And as long as the traffickers are treated like gentlemen in some corner of the world, they are going to continue to deal drugs."

Blum spent the late 1970s and early 1980s in private practice. Many of his clients had international business, particularly oil business. He made a good living and built a splendid house outside Annapolis, Maryland, overlooking a creek near the Chesapeake Bay. But every time a major financial scandal broke in the newspapers or a friend in law enforcement described an interesting case to him, Blum got itchy.

In early 1987, he received a telephone call from Senator John Kerry, the freshman Democrat from Massachusetts. Kerry was a member of the U.S. Senate Foreign Relations Committee and he wanted to take a look at the relationship between drug dealers, money laundering, and U.S. foreign policy. Someone had recommended Blum to him as a lead investigator.

Kerry himself was an interesting senator. A tall, handsome graduate of Yale University, he had won three Purple Hearts, a Silver Star, and a Bronze Star in two tours of duty with the Navy in Vietnam. He had returned home, graduated from Boston College Law School in 1976, and spent six years as a state prosecutor in Boston. After two years as lieutenant governor of Massachusetts, he was elected to the Senate in 1984 at the age of forty. He wanted to be liked by his colleagues, to join what was known as the most exclusive club in the world, but he was given to fits of speaking his mind, of rocking the boat in ways that caused his colleagues distress and upset the constant march toward consensus that characterizes the Senate. Some of his colleagues found Kerry to be a headline hunter, the paramount Senate brat, but the young senator retained a prosecutor's habit of following clues in any direction.

In early 1986, Kerry staff members began an investigation of allegations that the Nicaraguan Contras were getting some of their arms money by trafficking in drugs, possibly with the knowledge of the U.S. government. The inquiry raised questions in Kerry's mind about whether the Reagan administration was willing to overlook drug trafficking in favor of the administration's perceived national security interests. However, he did not have the staff resources to pursue the issue.

When Kerry got the chairmanship of a Foreign Relations subcommittee called Terrorism, Narcotics, and International Operations later in 1986, he wanted to use the panel as a vehicle to expand his Contra inquiry into a full-blown examination of U.S. foreign policy and drug dealers. To do so, he had to get permission from Senator Claiborne Pell, the Rhode Island Democrat whose patrician demeanor symbolized the Senate to many people. Pell granted the request, but he did not like the sound of it. Foreign Relations was a policy-making committee, a place where senior government officials and renowned academics testified on a grand scale. Not since former Senator Frank Church had gone after the CIA in the early 1970s had Foreign Relations been regarded as much of a watchdog. It was, in Pell's view, no place for hooded witnesses surrounded by armed U.S. marshals.

It was Kerry's investigation that Blum was hired to head. The first hearings were held in the summer and fall of 1987 and focused on the Bahamas, Cuba, and Costa Rica. After that, Blum and his small staff had turned their attention to Panama and General Manuel Noriega. As he was preparing for hearings on Noriega in early 1988, Blum learned that Jose Blandon, Panama's ambassador to the United Nations, was ready to blow the whistle on the general's dealings with the Medellín cartel. Blum arranged immediately to interview Blandon and he got an earful. Blandon even described a trip he had taken with Noriega to Cuba, where Fidel Castro had mediated a dispute between Noriega and the cartel after Panamanian soldiers had raided a cocaine laboratory. Great material for a Senate hearing.

Blum's interest had also been piqued by the defecting diplomat's description of Noriega's relationship with BCCI. Blandon said that the bank was a favorite of Noriega's, and that the general moved his own money through it and referred associates to the bank. Soon after that initial session with Blandon, marijuana smuggler Leigh Ritch had mentioned BCCI to Blum in a similar pretestimony debriefing. Late that same month, Ritch's partner, Steven Kalish, had testified about the bank at a hearing before another Senate committee. It was an accumulation of information that Blum could not ignore.

Jack Blum was not unfamiliar with BCCI. While Blum was in private practice in 1985, one of his clients had wanted to do an oil deal with Attock Oil, the Pakistan-based company whose shareholders included Kamal Adham and Ghaith Pharaon. The client's primary bank was Mellon Bank in Philadelphia and it was asked to approve some financing arrangements on the deal that would be done through BCCI.

"We won't accept a BCCI letter of credit. We don't do business with them and we advise you not to," a Mellon officer had told Blum and his client.

Blum was astonished. Here was a major American bank refusing to do business with one of the largest international banks in the world. He was smart enough to know that big banks keep blacklists. He wondered to himself what BCCI had done to earn a spot on Mellon's list. He was not in the investigative business at the time, so he did nothing more than walk his client away from the transaction with Attock and BCCI, but the incident stuck with him. When Blandon, Ritch, and Kalish all mentioned BCCI, Blum set out on the trail of the mysterious bank.

Jose Blandon testified before Kerry's subcommittee in February of 1988 about Noriega and the cartel. Among the charts that he used to illustrate the general's dealings with the drug cartel was one that mentioned BCCI. After the hearing, Jack Blum put out feelers among his contacts in the banking and petroleum worlds. He wanted to learn more about the bank.

Blum's grapevine worked. Near the middle of March, he got a telephone call from a former client with ties to the U.S. intelligence community. The former client said that he had been in contact with a BCCI executive who was fed up and leaving the bank. Blum got the name, Amer Lodhi, and phone number in BCCI's agency office in New York.

"I'm on my way out the door," Lodhi, a lawyer who had worked years for the bank and for Ghaith Pharaon, told Blum. "I didn't know what I was getting into when I came here. This place is a cesspool."

Lodhi described the bank's enormous, worldwide network of branches as little more than a cover for handling hot money. He said the bank had strong relationships in China and extensive political ties in Pakistan and elsewhere. He said the bank often flew favored clients to London on its planes for medical treatment at hospitals there. Among the clients receiving special treatment, he said, were Third World dictators, arms dealers and terrorists, and Colombian drug traffickers.

"The real purpose of the branch system is to create the climate to attract large personal customers who want their money moved out of the country and want the funds managed discreetly and free from prying eyes," Lodhi explained to Blum.

Since Agha Hasan Abedi's heart surgery, he said, the bank's management had been in disarray and there had been a power struggle to replace the ailing founder.

Asked about Noriega, Lodhi identified several people within the bank who were aware of the general's secret accounts. The main banker on it, he said, was named Amjad Awan and the records of Noriega's accounts and others were kept in Miami. But he advised Blum to hurry with a subpoena if he wanted to get the Noriega account records. The bank and Awan were hiding Noriega's assets within the mega-branch system in a scheme to "rewrite the history" of its relationship with the Panamanian leader since his February indictment.

Senate subpoenas must be authorized by a full committee. On March 25, a week after Blum's conversation with the BCCI executive, Senator Kerry asked the Foreign Relations Committee for subpoena power in the BCCI investigation. The committee authorized issuing subpoenas to BCCI and two officers demanding the records of its dealings with Noriega and other accounts in Panama. About the same time, Blum checked with federal prosecutors in Miami. The Noriega indictment there was less than two months old. Maybe they knew something about the bank. There was the danger that the subcommittee subpoenas would set off a document-destroying frenzy within the bank that could damage the criminal prosecution of Noriega.

Dick Gregorie was the Miami prosecutor who had assembled the case against Noriega there. He and Blum had clashed in late 1987 when the Senate subcommittee wanted testimony from some of the witnesses in the grand jury investigation of Noriega and Gregorie had refused. He was a professional prosecutor protecting his case, and Blum had understood. This time, Gregorie told Blum that Tampa was working on a big case involving BCCI. He advised him to call there.

In early April 1988, Blum spoke with Joseph Magri, the first assistant U.S. attorney in Tampa. Blum said that he was examining the relationship between Noriega and BCCI. He had received authority to subpoena bank records but wanted to check first with the prosecutors. Magri was alarmed, both by the investigation itself and at the prospect of a subpoena. He urged Blum to back off, telling him that a sensitive undercover investigation could be jeopardized if anything was done to spook the bank. Blum was reluctant at first. Too often, he had found, the Justice Department and other agencies tried to hide under the blanket of ongoing investigations.

When Magri talked with Mark Jackowski about Blum's call, he learned that Amjad Awan had mentioned the Senate investigation to Mazur in a conversation less than a month earlier. It seemed that BCCI had a source close to the committee who had learned a little about it. Awan had not seemed too worried, but the prosecutors agreed that they did not want Blum's probe to get higher profile with the bank.

So Magri arranged a conference call for Blum with the lead Customs supervisors on the undercover case, Bonni Tischler and Steve Cook. The idea was to impress upon him the need for backing away completely. By this time, Blum had decided not to issue the subpoenas. He did not want to endanger the lives of the undercover agents, but he did want to use the conference call to alert the Customs agents to the type of operation they were investigating.

The agents on the other end of the line were never identified to Blum. They listened and Magri did most of the talking as Blum explained that he had a source inside the bank who had identified Awan as the bank officer who handled the Noriega account. Blum described the outlines of the widespread corporate-instituted corruption relayed by the BCCI executive. Two of the unidentified Customs officials echoed Magri's deep concern that the Senate postpone its investigation. Without providing any details of the undercover operation, they pleaded, "Please don't serve your subpoenas." Blum told them that he had already decided to hold off, at least for the time being.

By July 1988, Kerry's hearings were over and the investigation was winding down. Jack Blum was busy writing the final report, but the Bank of Credit and Commerce International was still in the back of his mind as he waded through page after page of testimony and evidence to compile the voluminous report. What he really wanted was another crack at uncovering the institutional corruption at BCCI described by his source.

The chance came on July 26. Early that Tuesday morning, a woman called Blum at his office on the fourth floor of the Senate's Dirksen Office Building. From the connection, Blum assumed it was an international call. From her voice, she seemed to be British.

"I understand you are investigating BCCI," the woman said.

"Who are you? Where are you calling from?" asked Blum.

"That doesn't really matter," she said. "There's someone in London you ought to talk to."

The woman then gave him the name and telephone number of Syed Z. A. Akbar at Capcom Financial Services. As soon as she hung up, Blum dialed the number in London and got Akbar on the telephone.

"I've just been told that you have information about BCCI and I'd like to talk to you," said Blum.

"Send me a letter inviting me to come over and talk to you and I'll come to your office," replied Akbar.

Sometimes it's better to be lucky than smart. This appeared to be a gift from heaven. In instances like this, investigators often stop to consider the motives of the person who is volunteering information, for it helps to understand the context of the material. Blum figured he was dealing with a disgruntled former employee, often an investigator's best source.

Blum, of course, had no way of knowing the depth of Akbar's grudge against BCCI or the complicated motives driving him. Akbar felt he had been mistreated when he had been forced to leave the bank. For Akbar, this was an opportunity to work through someone else to get back at BCCI. He might even hand over the computer disks that would blow the lid off the bank. Or he might threaten to do so and see what the bank offered in return.

On July 26, Blum telefaxed a letter to Akbar formally inviting him to meet with Blum and one of his colleagues on the investigation, Kathleen Smith. "We would prefer meeting you here in Washington, although we are prepared to meet you elsewhere in the United States or in London," it said.

Akbar was not certain when he would be able to meet with them. He wanted to do it in the United States, and he expected to have some business there soon. Spurred by the possibility of mining Akbar for information, Blum and Kathleen Smith decided to make another push for information about BCCI and Noriega. There was still time to get it in the final report, or even hold a new round of public hearings. The authority to issue subpoenas was still in effect.

Blum contacted the Department of Justice in Washington to see if it was okay to demand the bank's records. He was given the green light at main Justice. This would later turn out to be a bureaucratic mistake on the part of the Justice Department, since the C-Chase undercover operation was still going on. But on July 28, with the department's okay, four subpoenas were issued: one each for BCCI in Luxembourg and the Cayman Islands, one for S. M. Shafi, the manager of its Miami office, and one for Khalid A. Awan.

The two demands for the bank records were sent to the bank's lawyers, Clark Clifford and Bob Altman. Shafi's was served at the office on Brickell Avenue in Miami, but the Awan who got the last subpoena was an aerospace engineer with Rockwell International in Miami. Because the information about Awan was sketchy, Blum had relied on telephone records in Miami. Awan's subpoena had gone to the wrong guy. The deadline for complying with the subpoenas was August 11.

In early August, Syed Akbar walked through the door of Jack Blum's cramped office in the Dirksen Building. It was only days after Akbar had allegedly agreed to accept the $23 million from Noriega's accounts at BCCI. That information would have been of enormous value to Blum and the Senate investigation, but Akbar had no intention of giving it up, at least not yet. He was in Washington on a fishing expedition to find out how much Blum really knew about BCCI and his friend Awan.

To Blum, Akbar appeared to be someone off the pages of GQ, the men's magazine. He was handsome and trim, wearing an elegant suit and a wry grin.

"All BCCI does is launder money and Noriega is only the beginning," said Akbar. "The bank is extremely nervous about your investigation. I know you are trying to talk to Awan. He is being advised to leave the country by the bank's lawyers. But he would like to cooperate with you if he can do so."

Akbar hinted that he had documents that could be helpful to Blum, but he was not interested in giving them up just yet. It seemed to Blum that Akbar was sniffing around to see how much Blum knew about BCCI. When Akbar volunteered to talk to Awan about cooperating, Blum accepted happily and crossed his fingers.

A few days later, Blum flew to New York and met Akbar at the Inter-Continental hotel, where he bought the Pakistani an expensive lunch. The tab was too much for his Senate per diem, so he had to put it on his own credit card. It was a small price to pay. Akbar told him that Awan had agreed to talk and would be in touch the next time he was in Washington. Akbar then got on a plane to return to London in plenty of time to accept Noriega's $23 million into an account at Capcom, as a later indictment charged.

After Akbar's promise to deliver Awan, Blum had spoken confidentially about the pending interview with some of his friends in law enforcement. Several of them warned him not to talk with Awan at his house. The bank's clients were a rough bunch and who knew what Awan might pull.

"You're taking a great risk," one of the agents warned Blum.

The bank's friends also were a smooth bunch. In early August, Clark Clifford had contacted his old friend Claiborne Pell, the chairman of the Senate Foreign Relations Committee. Clifford told the senator that the bank was having difficulty complying with the subpoenas. The records were spread around the world and there were lots of them. Pell had suggested that Clifford contact the staff director of the full committee, Geryld Christianson. When Clifford explained his case to Christianson, the staff director agreed that there were valid reasons for extending the deadline. Christianson telephoned Dick McCall, Kerry's senior foreign policy aide, who agreed that the deadline would be pushed back a month since Congress was in recess and Blum was out of town for several days.

It was a frantic time for BCCI officials. Clifford, Altman, and bank employees were making repeated trips back and forth between London and Washington in an effort to decide what to do about the Senate investigation. Awan was deeply involved in these discussions and was spending a considerable amount of time in Washington.

For his part, Blum was angry about the delay in getting the documents demanded by the subpoenas. Anger turned to outrage when Blum heard allegations that BCCI documents were being destroyed instead of turned over to the subcommittee. Former employees of First American and BCCI, he said, had provided him with reports that the Noriega documents had been flown to Washington from Miami and were being shredded at the First American offices. The reports claimed that Swaleh Naqvi, the acting head of the bank, had supervised the destruction of documents. Blum had confronted Altman with the allegations, but the lawyer denied that any material was being destroyed. And Blum never received any proof of the claims.

These concerns, however, convinced Blum that he had to interview Awan as soon as possible. He was willing to ignore the advice of his friends in law enforcement.

Monday, September 5, 1988, was Labor Day. As they sat in Blum's living room in front of a wall of glass, Amjad Awan and Jack Blum watched sheets of rain sweep across the creek and woods outside.

On the day of the meeting, it was Awan who seemed nervous and guarded. He described his background briefly, his father's role in Pakistan's intelligence service, his own years as an international banker. He explained that he had been introduced to Noriega by one of his superiors in London several years earlier and had cultivated Noriega when he was transferred to Panama. He talked about the loan to Ricardo Bilonick and his dealings with other Noriega associates, such as Enrique Pretelt and Cesar Rodriguez.

Surprising details were revealed about the Noriega account. Awan told of how it had been opened with a cash deposit of about $200,000 and how checks and cash had raised the balance into the millions over the years. He described handing out money to politicians on Noriega's orders.

"Have you ever been approached to launder drug money?" asked Blum.

"Never," Awan assured him. "BCCI had a conscious policy of avoiding drug money."

Blum sensed that he was not getting the full story from Awan. It certainly did not fit with the information he had received from Blandon and others, but he also had the feeling that Awan was there to cut some sort of deal. Clearly, here was someone who was intelligent and sophisticated. Perhaps the banker thought that he could give Blum a little and avoid having to testify in public.

Blum decided to scare him. Not with what the Senate could do, but with what Noriega might do if he thought Awan was better off unable to spill his secrets. The logic was to persuade Awan to tell everything at a public hearing and thus eliminate the reason for Noriega to harm him. So Blum had showed him testimony from Floyd Carlton Caceres, Blandon, and others who described Noriega's violent streak and made allegations that the general was involved in voodoo and homosexuality. Blum told him of uncorroborated evidence that Noriega brutalized women and had ordered Hugo Spadafora tortured and beheaded.

"Listen," Awan interrupted, trying to control his agitation. "I've known him now for about ten years. I've been with him on occasion for two weeks traveling with him, been with him in Panama and, you know, day and night. And if there was anything of this sort, I would have known something about it. But listen, he's like you and me, you know."

When Awan said that the bank's lawyers did not want him to testify before the subcommittee, Blum suggested that he hire his own lawyer. Awan's interests and the bank's were not necessarily the same in this matter, he said, writing down the names of three law firms that specialized in representing witnesses before Congress. He also promised Awan the full protection of the subcommittee.

After six hours of mixing truth with lies and omissions, Awan left Blum's house. His hope was indeed that he could avoid a formal appearance before the subcommittee. His fear was that what Blum had told him about Manuel Noriega was true. So, as he told Bob Mazur a few days later back in Miami, he had cleaned out his office and dropped out of touch with the bank until he could figure out what to do. In the meantime, he hired a lawyer.

Blum wanted Awan at the witness table in front of the committee before the end of September. And he wanted to do so without letting Clark Clifford and Robert Altman know any further in advance than necessary. He felt they were stonewalling the subcommittee on its request for documents. Awan's allegations about being instructed not to testify increased his suspicions.

But Blum could not get a hearing date. The congressional session was coming to a close, there was the usual crush of last-minute business, and everyone's eyes were on the presidential and congressional elections in November. Members wanted to get home. So he had to settle for a formal deposition. At least that would put Awan on the record.

After getting Awan's address in Coral Gables, Blum had a new subpoena served on him. Awan was to appear before the subcommittee counsel and staff for a sworn statement on September 30. A few days before the appearance was scheduled, Blum wrote a memo to the staff files about his earlier conversation with Awan. Across the top, he wrote:

"Warning. The contents of this memo are committee sensitive. Disclosure of the contents or the fact of Mr. Awan's cooperation with the committee could endanger his life."

At one point in this period, Blum had asked Altman about the prospects for questioning Awan. "Maybe you can see him if you travel to Paris," said Altman. While Blum interpreted this remark as confirmation of Awan's story that Altman and the bank's other lawyers were trying to keep the banker from testifying, Altman told a different story.

Much of Awan's story to the bank's lawyers had been the same as the version he had told Blum. He maintained that he knew nothing about any money laundering at the bank, that Noriega's accounts had been handled legally, if secretly. For that reason, Altman would say later that he was eager for Awan to testify before the Kerry committee. The hang-up, he said, was Amjad Awan's own fear that Noriega would have him killed.

In Altman's version, the bank management had suggested transferring Awan to Paris in hopes he could assume a lower profile within the bank, but only after Awan had cooperated with the Senate investigators. "There was no effort to prevent Mr. Awan from testifying," Altman would say in sworn testimony before the House Banking Committee in September 1991.

But Awan had conveyed a different interpretation to both Mazur and Blum. He saw the transfer as part of a scheme to silence him.

Clark Clifford had made his first appearance in Senator John Kerry's office near the end of September in 1988. The two men sat in armchairs in the office, which was far smaller than Clifford's expansive office downtown. In his deep voice, Clifford had promised politely that the bank wanted to cooperate in any way possible with the subcommittee's inquiry.

"I want you to understand," he told Kerry. "We are prepared to cooperate. We want to be helpful."

His hands folded in trademark steeple-fashion in front of him, the lawyer assured Kerry that he knew of no documents regarding General Noriega that were in the possession or under the control of BCCI, apart from a small number already turned over, but if any such documents were uncovered, they would be turned over to the subcommittee in accordance with the subpoena.

Kerry wanted to believe this. He did not want to buck Clark Clifford and all that he symbolized. So far, however, the bank had been less than cooperative. Some documents had been provided, but they were of little relevance. Some travel records for Shafi and Awan had been turned over, but Blum and the other key staffers on the investigation, David McKean and Jonathan Winer, were telling Kerry that critical records were being withheld and possibly destroyed. The senator did not challenge Clifford. Nor did he ask about Amjad Awan's claim that First American was owned by BCCI. Here was a man who deserved the benefit of the doubt. Instead, he assured the lawyer that he was happy that the bank was cooperating.

Why did John Kerry not confront Clark Clifford? After all, it was Kerry who was insisting on keeping the investigation of BCCI going. One explanation lies in Kerry's own character. He tends to operate in bursts, pushing relentlessly on a subject and then seeming to lose interest in it. Also, Kerry was learning the Washington game and beginning to think of himself as possible presidential timber down the road. That meant that certain people were not attacked, at least not until all the evidence was in.

By this time, Kerry had become chairman of the Democratic Senatorial Campaign Committee. Known by the shorthand DSCC, the committee was one of the key fund-raising mechanisms for the party's senators and a big step on the path to power in Washington.

Political campaigns cost millions of dollars these days, mainly because they rely on expensive television advertising. As a result, members of the House and Senate spend a great deal of their time raising the campaign money necessary to keep them in office. And they succeed, with more than nine out of ten congressmen winning reelection. To raise the funds, most of these politicians tap the special interest groups affected by the legislation they handle. The clearest example of the dangers of this system was the savings and loan disaster, in which campaign contributions by thrift owners gained them access to the highest levels of U.S. government.

In addition to personal contributions, the special interests contribute millions of dollars through political action committees, or PACs. Much of both the individual donations and PAC money is channeled through the DSCC and its counterpart organizations for Republicans and House members. So Kerry's new job put him at the center of power and meant that he would rub shoulders with the movers and shakers who were financing the Democratic Party.

One of these men was David Paul, the owner of CenTrust Savings in Miami and a pal of Ghaith Pharaon. On July 20, 1988, Kerry hosted a reception honoring Paul, one of the largest contributors to the DSCC, and later the senator used Paul's private jet to fly to a DSCC leadership meeting. He was one of forty select guests at a $122,000 dinner thrown by Paul in Miami that December. Ghaith Pharaon was guest of honor. Later, Paul would boast that he had derailed Kerry's investigation. It was not true. But the senator's rising political profile grated on Jack Blum in the summer of 1988 because of some of the people it put Kerry next to.

Four days after Clifford's call on Kerry, Amjad Awan appeared for his deposition shortly after ten on the morning of September 30 in an office in the Capitol.

Awan was accompanied by his own lawyer, a former Senate legal counsel named John Grabow. Awan had hired him following his long session with Blum. Grabow had told Altman and Clifford that he was representing Awan, so the bank's lawyers were aware of the deposition. Attending with Blum were Jim Lucifer, the top Republican staffer on the Senate Foreign Relations Committee, and two of Blum's associates— Kathleen Smith and Jonathan Lichtman. Also present as testament to Awan's fears were two guards from the congressional security office, Alvin Romanowski and William Cochran.

There were no surprises. Awan's sworn testimony essentially tracked what he had told Blum three weeks earlier on that rainy day in Annapolis. He stuck steadfastly to his story that BCCI was not involved in any illegal money laundering, so far as he knew.

The deposition had been taken just in time. On the following Friday, October 7, Jack Blum learned of the impending climax of Operation C-Chase. The investigator was told that the arrests of Awan and several other BCCI bankers on money-laundering charges were expected to start the following day. Apart from informing Kerry, Blum was urged to keep the information secret.

He sat on the material until after the arrests, but then played a game the C-Chase agents would have trouble understanding when they learned about it months later. Whether on his own initiative or at the direction of Senator Kerry, he called Clark Clifford's law office on Monday and asked for an urgent meeting. On Tuesday afternoon, after the Customs Service announced the arrests to the press, John F. Kovin, a partner at Clifford & Warnke, and Robert A. Altman himself met with Jack Blum at the Kerry subcommittee's office. Blum handed over the packet he had received from Customs the week before, without reading it: the packet included a draft press release that was never meant to go further than the Customs Service headquarters. Blum said that he sought the meeting to show the lawyers how deeply BCCI was implicated in the case. The packet later surfaced at the Tampa trial, in a filing by one of the defense lawyers. It may not have had any effect on the case, but the incident showed just how much access Clifford & Warnke still had to the Senate staffers attempting to investigate BCCI.

The arrests occurred on Saturday as planned. On Tuesday, Customs boss William von Raab held his televised press conference on Operation C-Chase. He warned banks around the world that they had better know their customers or face the same sorts of charges.

BCCI responded with a press release asserting that it was the victim of "a malicious campaign" and had never been involved in laundering money from drug trafficking. "BCC has a strong belief in the legal processes of the United States of America and is confident of a satisfactory outcome," said the statement distributed to news organizations around the world.

The next day, the sting and the arrests were big news in newspapers around the world. But hard as he looked, Blum could find no mention of Manuel Noriega and the dictator's connection to the bank and Awan. He decided that Von Raab was playing politics with the case. Noriega had been left out because the bank's tie to him would reawaken questions about relations between the Panamanian and the CIA under George Bush. With a month to go before the presidential election, such questions could prove embarrassing for Bush.

So Blum went to Kerry and persuaded the senator that this was a connection that should not be swept under the rug until after the election. Kerry authorized the release of a transcript of Awan's deposition detailing some parts of his relationship with Noriega. It generated another round of news stories, more to Blum's satisfaction. And then the story died.

The only blip on the screen related to BCCI was a story in December in *The Boston Globe*. In a deposition to Kerry's subcommittee, Aziz Rehman, the one-time gofer at BCCI in Miami, had described dragging around bags full of cash. The story said that Rehman had gone to the IRS with his allegations and there had been no follow-up investigation.

The criminal case in Tampa put an effective lid on the subcommittee's efforts to obtain more bank documents from Clifford and Altman. The Justice Department had demanded the same records, and their request took precedence. Blum spent the remainder of the fall working with Dick McCall, David McKean, and Jonathan Winer of Kerry's staff to draft a massive report from the hearings in 1987 and 1988.

Blum kept after BCCI information, however, mining his network of sources for information and hoping that the subcommittee could hold hearings on the bank sometime in 1989. Kerry, too, remained interested in the bank. Blum's contract as special chief counsel for the subcommittee expired in December, but Kerry had persuaded Senator Pell to authorize the additional money to keep Blum on a monthly basis until the subcommittee report was published. In March the Rhode Island senator said that the investigation had gone far enough and there would be no more money since the report on the investigation was done and scheduled to be published in April. Blum would be out of a job on March 31, 1989.

By the spring of 1989, Jack Blum was in too deep to let go of BCCI just because his job had ended.

In early March, Blum's old friend with the intelligence ties, the one who had put him in touch with Amer Lodhi a year earlier, sent him a memorandum in which a man identified as a BCCI executive boasted that the bank's lawyers had succeeded in quashing the Senate subcommittee's investigation of BCCI. Blum was angered by the allegation and fired off a memo of his own to Kerry complaining about it. He also decided to try to get the Operation C-Chase investigators to take a broader look at the bank.

A week after getting the boastful memo, Blum persuaded Amer Lodhi to meet him in Miami to talk about the bank's operations again. Since the C-Chase indictment, Blum had gotten to know Steve Cook, David Burris, and some of the other Customs and IRS agents assigned to the case. He contacted them with a promise of new information on the case and they arranged to record the meeting without Lodhi's knowledge.

The meeting was set for late March at the Embassy Suites hotel near Miami International Airport. The hotel had been selected because all of the rooms were suites, which meant that Blum and Lodhi could sit and talk comfortably in the living room. In a smaller room, Lodhi might have wanted to have the conversation in the hotel lobby or another more comfortable place.

Two suites were rented, side by side. The plan was for the Customs technicians to drill through the wall between the suites and insert a tiny microphone to pick up the conversation. Agents would sit in the next room and monitor the meeting. What they did not count on was that the hotel was built of poured concrete, a substance that does not take well to drilling. They did not want to alert hotel authorities, so the technicians could only drill when there was an airplane passing overhead to cover up the sound. Still, they could not get through the wall. Finally, in frustration, they ran the wire out the window of the listening room and into the other suite. They ran it under the carpet and stuck the microphone behind the couch.

For several hours over the course of three days, Blum pumped Amer Lodhi for specific information. Again, Lodhi described corruption on a global scale: insider loans to major shareholders, the use of front men to acquire banks in the United States, money laundering and capital flight, massive trading losses covered up with fake loans. A laundry list of accusations.

On the third day, Blum spent two hours persuading Lodhi to cooperate with Tampa prosecutors in the BCCI case. Lodhi protested that he feared for his life, that the bank would think nothing of having him murdered. In the end, with assurances of confidentiality, he agreed, and that day he and Blum were flown to Tampa to meet with the BCCI prosecutors.

By this time, Mark Jackowski had been joined on the case by Michael Rubinstein, another assistant U.S. attorney in the office. The Customs agents, who seemed interested in the allegations, wanted the prosecutors to hear firsthand what the witness had to say. The question in the agents' minds was whether the information was relevant to the pending case against the bank and its employees.

Armed Customs agents accompanied Blum and Lodhi on a USAir flight from Miami to Tampa. They were supposed to be met at the airport by other agents and taken to a hotel suite for a meeting with the prosecutors. For security reasons, they did not want to take Lodhi to the federal building downtown, but it turned out that all the suites in local hotels were booked. Blum, Lodhi, and their Customs guards wound up driving from hotel to hotel trying to find a suite large enough for their meeting. Finally, after the agents said they had no luck at a Howard Johnson's motel, Blum stomped out of the car and into the registration office. When he came back, he had rented a conference room for the session.

Lodhi was nervous and frightened. Before saying anything, he elicited a promise that his name would be kept confidential. He also was cagey as he began to repeat the highlights of his story for several Customs agents and Mark Jackowski.

Mike Rubinstein was late, but he arrived with a splash. Rubinstein is a voluble man, one whose loose talk sometimes caused Jackowski and others to wince or motion for him to keep quiet. Walking into the room, he asked, "Are you the guy we taped in Miami?" Lodhi did not quite hear what the prosecutor said and Rubinstein was hustled out of the room by one of the Customs agents. In the hall, the agent explained that Lodhi did not know he had been taped and was already plenty nervous.

Over a couple of hours, Lodhi provided a more cautious version of what he had told Blum. He told everyone that he did not want to be a witness, that he was providing this information only as leads, a road map for the investigators and prosecutors to follow. He said that he feared for himself and his family if he went public with what he knew about BCCI. Amer Lodhi did not want to appear in court, and he constructed his story and his answers to the questions from Jackowski and Rubinstein in a way that seemed designed to avoid having to testify.

Basically, only a witness with firsthand knowledge of criminal activity can testify in a trial. Rumors and information passed on by someone else fall into the category of hearsay and are rarely admissible in court. Lodhi was careful to couch his information in terms of secondhand knowledge or general rumor within the bank. For instance, when Jackowski asked him how he knew about huge insider loans to bank shareholders, Lodhi said, "Everybody knew that."

While Blum thought that Jackowski and Rubinstein seemed excited at the new information, the prosecutors really saw little that they could use. Their indictment, by its nature and the demands of law, was focused tightly on what had occurred during the undercover operation. The case would rest on the taped conversations and the testimony of Bob Mazur. It was a complicated piece of prosecution to begin with, since the jury would be asked to follow the money through the banking system. Plus, the entire team was devoted to complying with the barrage of motions being filed by defense attorneys. More than 2,000 taped conversations had to be transcribed and the top fifty or so selected for use at the trial.

The information from Lodhi was deemed too tangential to pursue as a new case. It was possible that Lodhi might be called as a witness in the case against BCCI to show that the bank was corrupt from top to bottom, but there were two problems from the point of view of the prosecutors. One was Amer Lodhi's obvious reluctance to testify in court. The other was Jack Blum.

According to Jackowski and Rubinstein, at one point during the questioning of Lodhi, Blum had taken them aside. Explaining that his job with the Kerry subcommittee was ending that month, Blum offered to continue helping the criminal investigation. However, he wanted to be paid. He would not go on the payroll. Rather, he proposed that he be paid out of funds available to confidential informants.

In characteristically blunt language, Mark Jackowski later described the incident this way: "Blum wanted to become a paid snitch."

The request was rejected immediately by the two prosecutors and it changed their perception of Jack Blum. In their view, his motives were suddenly tainted. They decided that this was a guy who should be kept at arm's length. (Blum denies ever seeking money from the prosecutors, saying later: "It is absolutely untrue. I never brought up the subject of money.)

Despite what they said were their misgivings about Blum, in early April the prosecutors and agents went through a similar process with a former BCCI executive whom Blum had persuaded to meet with him in Miami. This time, the agents chose the Hilton Hotel near the airport since it was deemed to have more accommodating walls. A day-long interview in which the banker provided a similar story to that of Lodhi was climaxed with another trip up to Tampa for a session with the prosecutors.

As the days passed after these two sessions, Jack Blum began to believe that the prosecutors and agents in Tampa were not following up on the information his sources had provided them. The sources had not been contacted by any government authorities. Other avenues for pursuing the information appeared to be untrodden. When Blum telephoned Steve Cook, the case agent on C-Chase, he often could not get through and his calls were rarely returned.

It is possible that the reaction of Jackowski and Rubinstein to Blum's supposed request for money had so colored their view of the information provided by his informants that it was not given proper consideration. Even if Blum never asked for money, there was another explanation for the apparent unwillingness of the prosecutors to pursue the broader allegations at that point in the case.

In the spring of 1989, the prosecutors were immersed in the legal complexities of preparing the BCCI case for trial. They were working on a new, broader indictment of the bank and its employees as well as responding to dozens of motions filed by a small army of top-notch defense attorneys. In addition, Jackowski and Rubinstein both had a full load of other cases. Another factor at play was the basic strategy of the prosecution, one that is followed in virtually every U.S. attorney's office around the country.

"Convict the people that are in your gunsights," explained Gregory Kehoe, who had replaced Joe Magri as the first assistant U.S. attorney. "You take the case you have and you win it. You get the bank and you get the employees. Then you get them to cooperate and you move up. That is the traditional way of operating at the Justice Department, and it is the strongest way of operating."

Mark Jackowski has a more colloquial way of explaining the process: "It's like a dinner with a number of courses. Your mother tells you that you have to eat what's on each plate before you get the next course. So we ate all the food on all the plates. But we didn't forget about dessert."

Despite his years of investigating complex crimes and his righteous indignation over the apparent crimes of the Bank of Credit and Commerce, Jack Blum had never been a prosecutor. His experience said that he should charge ahead.

So, near the end of April, Jack Blum decided to take matters into his own hands. If the feds were not going to move fast enough on the BCCI trail, he would find someone who would do so.

By this time Blum was off the Senate payroll and Kerry's investigation into the bank was being handled chiefly by David McKean and Jonathan Winer. One afternoon, Blum took McKean aside and said that he planned to take the information that he and the subcommittee staff had learned about BCCI to Robert Morgenthau, the district attorney in New York City. If a state prosecutor started raising hell about BCCI, Blum explained, then the Feds would have to follow. He asked McKean to tell Kerry of his decision, and the senator later gave his blessing to the mission.

The U.S. attorney in Manhattan from 1961 to 1970 and the district attorney for New York County since 1975, Bob Morgenthau had a reputation for unstoppable integrity and enough sophistication to handle a major financial investigation. He also had preached that a critical step in fighting the drug problem was stopping the suppliers from getting their money out of the United States. Indeed, Morgenthau had been the very first witness at the same February 1988 subcommittee hearings at which Jose Blandon had mentioned BCCI. And he had railed against the billions of dollars in money taken out of the United States by the drug barons, calling it a "contemporary Marshall Plan."

Not only did Blum expect Morgenthau to be receptive to going after a money-laundering bank, he thought he might have a way for the district attorney to gain jurisdiction. First American Bankshares owned a New York bank. If Amjad Awan was right and BCCI controlled First American, it would be a way into the case for the New York district attorney's office.

In late April, Blum had three or four prospective law clients to see in New York, so he made an appointment for late one afternoon with Morgenthau and wound up sitting in the district attorney's memento-filled office in the south wing of the massive Criminal Courts Building in lower Manhattan.

"Look, this is why I'm here," said Blum. "I stumbled upon this problem. It's enormous. Maybe the biggest bank fraud ever. It was with the Feds in Tampa, but Tampa doesn't have the will or the resources to follow up on it. It may be a giant Ponzi scheme with drug money. The bank appears to be built on air. Loans to shareholders are counted as capital. Noriega is involved and who knows who else. The U.S. attorney's office in Tampa has reached the end of the road. Senator Kerry's mandate to hold hearings has expired. And we couldn't get the interviews we wanted."

Morgenthau nodded as Blum explained how his office might have jurisdiction through First American Bank of New York. The district attorney summoned John Moscow, the deputy chief of his fraud division, to the office and introduced him to Blum. Moscow then took Blum to his office one floor below, where Blum described what he knew about the BCCI network in far greater detail for Moscow and two financial crimes investigators who worked for him. He also said he would contact the two potential witnesses and help persuade them to cooperate with the new investigation.

Walking out of the district attorney's office, Jack Blum felt a sense of relief. He was confident that nobody could stop Robert Morgenthau. Finally, he believed, someone was going to go after the Bank of Credit and Commerce International in earnest.

CHAPTER NINETEEN

Cracks in the Facade

Bob Morgenthau was destined to speed up everything from the day Jack Blum walked into his office. The initial going, however, was slow and sometimes frustrating. Unraveling a fraud as byzantine, sophisticated, and long-standing as that executed by officials at the Bank of Credit and Commerce presented an enormous challenge to his office. From the outset, Morgenthau's vision of the bank was shaped by Jack Blum's description of it as a gigantic Ponzi scheme.

Over the years, a Ponzi scheme has come to describe any swindle in which the original investors are paid off with money that comes from new groups of investors. The phrase originated, however, in a specific scheme in Boston that began in 1919. That was the year that Charles Ponzi, an Italian immigrant and convicted forger, formed Securities Exchange Company and promised customers a fifty percent return on their investment in forty-five days, double their money in six months.

Ponzi said he bought International Postal Reply coupons, a type of international postage, in countries with low exchange rates. He then claimed to sell the coupons in countries with high exchange rates, collecting the difference as his profit. He started with 15 customers and $870 and, within six months, had lured nearly 20,000 investors and $10 million into the scheme. The new funds were used to pay lavish returns to earlier investors and thus persuade more people to give Ponzi money. Ponzi was a hero in Boston, cheered wherever he went.

In 1920, however, a Boston newspaper disclosed that Ponzi had never bought the coupons. Instead, he had used the money to finance his own high living and pay off investors. By the time the hoax was uncovered, the money was gone. Ponzi served three years in a federal prison and eventually died a pauper in Brazil.

In the case of BCCI, the original investors were the Arab backers who bought the first shares in the bank. They were paid off with loans that they never had to pay back. The funds for the loans came from the deposits of customers in Third World nations and rich countries alike. Later, the deposits were used to provide loans to nominee shareholders as the bank acquired hidden interests in American banks and to cover the huge expenses of the bank's global expansion. When the bank sustained massive trading losses in 1985 and its portfolio of loans soured, more deposits were needed to paper over larger and larger holes in the balance sheet and maintain the appearance of a profitable institution.

The peril of a Ponzi scheme for its operators is that a single tear in the fabric of respectability can bring down the entire operation. It was desperation to retain the appearance of profitability that drove the bank to push its employees to gather more and more deposits.

Sketching the broad outlines of this scheme was far easier than uncovering the details essential to making a criminal case out of it. The bank, after all, had been constructed to avoid exactly the type of scrutiny that would reveal the underlying artifice. And Agha Hasan 'Abedi and his crew of executives were far craftier than Charles Ponzi.

Approaching his seventieth birthday in the spring of 1989, Robert M. Morgenthau was the dean of American district attorneys. He was the direct successor to such legends as the racket-busting Thomas Dewey and the upright Frank Hogan. Morgenthau's office walls reflected three generations of distinguished public service. A plaque from the American-Armenian Society expressed gratitude for the role of his grandfather, Henry Morgenthau, Sr., in exposing the Armenian massacres of 1915, a task that cost him his position as U.S. ambassador to the Ottoman Empire. There was an autographed 1928 photograph of Franklin Delano Roosevelt, then governor of New York, who had hired Henry Morgenthau, Jr., as his secretary of the U.S. Treasury Department when he became president. Next to it hung an autographed draft of an Irving Berlin ditty advertising war bonds. On an adjoining panel hung a series of photos commemorating Morgenthau's own service aboard the destroyer USS *Harry Bauer* in World War II.

As district attorney for New York County, Morgenthau was committed to the war on drugs. His office prosecuted thousands of drug cases every year. The courts were flooded with pushers and traffickers and users. Morgenthau had long known that the solution to the drug problem included attacking the flow of money out of the country. His office had drawn up the original draft of the federal Bank Secrecy Act of 1970, which required the currency transaction reports that formed the basis for the first money-laundering cases. Pursuing numerous white-collar crimes, Morgenthau had gone after Swiss bank accounts and tried to pierce secrecy laws in offshore havens worldwide. Crime in the suites is as important as crime in the streets, he was found of saying.

So Morgenthau had indeed been predisposed to accept the challenge of the complicated case when Jack Blum walked through his door. And the pattern of the BCCI investigation quickly assumed the shape of countless other white-collar cases in his office.

"Every investigation goes through three phases," Morgenthau explained one day in his office. "In the first phase, you have allegations and suspicion. You look at the case and try to understand its merits. Then, you say, 'Hey, I know there is a case here. Can I prove it?' In the third phase, you're trying to prove it."

Morgenthau knew a bit about BCCI before Blum arrived. He had read the thick green report prepared by Kerry's subcommittee a few months earlier and remembered being struck by Amjad Awan's deposition about the bank, but there was little more with which to work. After that first meeting with Jack Blum, John Moscow summed up the case this way: "We have one sentence to go on. Here's a dirty bank and the Feds won't touch it."

John Moscow, a Harvard Law School graduate and lifelong prosecutor in his mid-forties, sat in an office a floor below that of his boss. If Morgenthau's digs were far from palatial, Moscow's were positively spartan. He shared half of a duplex with another attorney. The reception desk was unoccupied due to unending budget woes. There was a coffee machine and several cracked communal mugs. His bookshelf was dominated by volumes of the New York Penal Code. On any given day his desk was littered with documents related to dozens of cases at various stages of investigation. Occasionally peeking from under a stack would be a copy of The New York Times, where Moscow's father, Warren, had been a well-known political reporter.

Looming outside his window was the Family Court Building, where every day he could watch the procession of broken families that was yet another legacy of the cocaine problem enveloping the city's poor neighborhoods. In the last five years, the number of child abuse cases in Family Court had almost quintupled to 29,000 annually. Officials attributed almost all of this terrible increase to drug use among parents.

Over the years, Moscow had developed a reputation as a no-nonsense, independent-minded prosecutor. He had the appearance and some say the demeanor of a veteran prize fighter, with a square jaw, Roman nose, and powerful chest.

Moscow first made his name in the middle 1970s with his tenacious prosecution of a case against what was known as the Washington Square Park Eleven. The case, a favorite of the tabloid press, involved a group of teenagers who went on a gay-bashing rampage.

Over the years, Moscow's black hair had turned salt and pepper as he moved to the prestigious financial fraud division and rose through the ranks, honing his skills against the corruption on Wall Street. He was a crusader, and his style occasionally led to clashes, even with those arguably on the same side. A former federal prosecutor who had worked alongside Moscow on a couple of big cases referred to his style as "combat prosecution." Anything that got in the way of Moscow's charge was knocked aside or buried.

Right from the start, the BCCI investigation had some pluses. Morgenthau had learned that British authorities were sponsoring a conference on money laundering in early July 1989 at Cambridge. BCCI was on the printed agenda. So he sent Moscow and two other lawyers from the office to see if they could get a jump on the investigation. When they arrived, however, Moscow was told that BCCI had been removed from the conference schedule after protests from the bank itself. In fact, BCCI had sent lawyers of its own to the meetings to make sure it would not get back on the agenda. The incident aroused Moscow's curiosity even more. The BCCI lawyers could not stop the people at the conference from talking informally about the mysterious bank and the fallout from its indictment the previous year in Tampa.

The problem of jurisdiction had been solved early in the investigation, as far as Morgenthau and Moscow were concerned. The taped conversation in which Amjad Awan described BCCI's ownership of First American Bankshares to Bob Mazur was mentioned in court documents filed along with the indictment in Tampa. First American Bank of New York had forty-three branches in the state. Said Morgenthau, "You can stand on the steps of the Capitol Building in Albany and see two branches of First American down the street." This meant that First American filed annual financial statements with the New York State Banking Department, which also regulated its operations in the state. Court documents in the Tampa case also indicated that some of the money laundered through C-Chase had passed through First American in New York.

The district attorney's investigators also were gathering public information about the structure of the bank. They quickly discovered that it was a weird one. First American Bankshares was the holding company for banks in six states and the District of Columbia. In turn, First American was owned by Credit and Commerce American Holdings. Between them were two additional holding companies. To Morgenthau, these layers of legal entities gave him the feeling that someone was trying to hide something. He also was struck by the use of the words *credit* and *commerce*.

As Morgenthau was learning about BCCI, he went to a friend who was a professor at the Yale University School of Business and Public Administration and an expert on banking and insurance. When the prosecutor described the structure of BCCI and First American, the professor asked, "Why don't you talk to the Federal Reserve?"

Following up the suggestion, Morgenthau's investigators got copies of the April 1981 hearing on the application of CCAH to acquire Financial General Bankshares, the predecessor to First American. They also learned about the 1975 efforts of Agha Abedi and BCCI to acquire Chelsea National Bank in New York and the 1982 state hearings on the CCAH acquisition of Financial General. The records of these hearings provided more details for the investigation, but it was still slow going.

Similar attempts to obtain bank documents from the Bank of England, such as audits of BCCI by Price Waterhouse, were unsuccessful. The British regulators said that they were bound by their own bank secrecy laws, which prohibited disclosure of such material. Likewise, the Price Waterhouse affiliate in Britain, Price Waterhouse U.K., said it was not permitted under British law to disclose audit results without authorization from the Bank of England.

Price Waterhouse Luxembourg had certified the audit of BCCI's financial statement filed with the State of New York for its agency office in New York City. Morgenthau suspected the statements were not accurate. When his office asked the auditors for the records supporting the profit and loss calculations, it was told that they were maintained by Price Waterhouse U.K. and the records were thus unavailable.

It was just as Sidney Bailey had feared. Back in 1981, the Virginia banking commissioner had opposed the sale of Financial General to the Arab investors because it would be beyond the reach of regulators. The bank's financial statements were certified by auditors who were also beyond the reach of American law enforcement. There was no way for authorities in the United States to determine the accuracy of the audit reports. And no way for Bob Morgenthau and John Moscow to examine them for evidence of the widespread fraud that they suspected was there.

In another day, Clark Clifford and Bob Morgenthau might have been friends. They might have been seated on the same dias at some big Democratic fund-raiser, two esteemed white-haired lawyers whispering and nodding. But this time they were on opposite sides.

The indictment of the Bank of Credit and Commerce International and its officers in Tampa had taken Clifford by surprise. All of his efforts had been concentrated on heading off the Senate investigation, which could embarrass the bank and damage its reputation, if not worse. Whether or not BCCI had done anything wrong in its handling of the

Noriega business, Clifford was well aware of the tendency for congressional hearings to turn into public floggings for the benefit of television cameras.

The criminal charges brought a new urgency to his work on behalf of the bank, and he and Altman quickly organized the best team of defense lawyers that the bank's millions could buy. They hired lawyers not only for the bank itself, but also for the individual bank employees charged in the scheme.

Altman had the best contacts among the city's white-collar defense bar. Many of the top lawyers were his age, in their early forties. While he had spent his career earning millions at Clifford's side, they had risen through the ranks in the U.S. attorney's office in Washington or New York and then embarked on careers in private practice.

None of them had attained Altman's exalted status. He and his actress-wife Lynda Carter were stars in a town that thirsts for glitter. Not long after their marriage in 1984, *Washington Post* columnist Chuck Conconi referred to them as "that couple seen everywhere around town." At their $3.5 million, 20,000-square-foot mansion in the exclusive suburb of Potomac, Maryland, white-gloved servants attended to guests at dinner parties where the entertainment crowd mixed with power brokers from Washington's political and legal circles.

On less formal occasions, Altman and his lawyer pals gathered around the television at the house to watch the Washington Redskins when they were playing a game out of town. The regulars included Larry Wechsler, a former federal prosecutor who had joined a big Washington law firm, and Larry Barcella, who had left the federal prosecutor's office after his highly publicized prosecution of Edwin Wilson, the renegade spy.

Wechsler and Barcella became the nucleus of the defense, representing the bank along with another Altman friend and top lawyer, Ray Banoun. John Hume, who spent fifteen years as a federal prosecutor in Washington, was hired to represent Amjad Awan. Peter Romatowski, who had worked on the prosecution of insider-trader Dennis Levine in New York and put *Wall Street Journal* reporter R. Foster Winans in jail for his role in a widely publicized insider-trading scheme, was hired as Nazir Chinoy's lawyer.

For Clifford and Altman, protecting the bank was a professional responsibility and a personal one. More was at stake than simply defending another client. BCCI had funneled millions of dollars in legal fees to the firm of Clifford & Warnke over the years, as much as $4 million one year. From their positions as chairman and president of First American, Clifford and Altman sat atop a significant power center in Washington. The advantages had been most evident to them just a few months earlier, when the two lawyers had reaped enormous profits from an unusual deal involving BCCI and stock in First American's holding company.

It was a deal with the usual BCCI trademarks. The bank had loaned $18 million to the two lawyers in July 1986 so they could buy 8,168 shares of stock in Credit and Commerce American Holdings, the parent company of First American Bankshares. None of the lawyers' money was at risk and the sole collateral for the loan was the stock itself. They paid $2,204 a share, an insider's price and less than half the cost to another investor a few days earlier. Clifford and Altman received warrants that carried the low price and had been provided for them by another shareholder, the Mashriq Corporation. The Federal Reserve later identified Mashriq as a front for the BCCI management.

Four days after Clifford and Altman bought their block, a group of companies controlled by the Mahfouz banking family of Saudi Arabia paid $6,000 a share. The Mahfouz family was injecting $150 million into the bank to cover for the trading losses discovered earlier by Price Waterhouse. As part of its agreement, the family acquired stock in both BCCI and CCAH with the understanding that BCCI would buy back the stock at the same price at any time.

Eighteen months later, Clifford and Altman had sold sixty percent of their CCAH stock at the highest price it ever commanded, $6,800 a share. The buyer was another corporate entity identified by the Federal Reserve as a BCCI front. They paid off their entire BCCI loan from the proceeds and pocketed a total profit between them of $9.8 million. They also retained debt-free ownership of the remaining forty percent of the original stock block. Along with their executive roles at First American, both men also were on the four-member board of CCAH, which approved the stock purchases and the pricing. For its role, BCCI received $4.2 million in fees and interest.

The deal was unusual in many ways. First, banks rarely make loans equal to 100 percent of the collateral; they like to keep a safety margin, similar to requiring a homeowner to make a down payment. Second, there was no risk to Clifford and Altman; all they stood to lose was the stock itself, not any of their own money. That meant the bank took all the risk. Third, the Federal Reserve Board had been promised at the 1981 hearing and in documents related to the acquisition of First American by CCAH that there was and would be no financial relationship between CCAH and BCCI. While the loan for the stock purchases was not a direct relationship between BCCI and CCAH, using the stock as collateral put BCCI in a position to acquire an interest if Clifford and Altman defaulted.

The entire transaction was a private one. Because the shares of BCCI and CCAH were held privately, the stocks did not trade on any public exchange. When word of the loans surfaced eventually in 1991, Clifford and Altman would defend them as legal and proper. A spokesman for the two men would say that the transactions were conducted at arm's length, the Federal Reserve was notified, and the CCAH board approved the deal.

In the weeks following the Tampa indictment, the defense lawyers got their first look at the government's case against BCCI and the individual defendants. There were two general reactions.

Jay Hogan, one of Miami's toughest and most colorful defense lawyers, was hired to represent Aftab Hussain. When Hogan came up to Tampa for a meeting with his colleagues on the defense team, he expressed his surprise: "You know, I got the call and I thought, 'Great, this is going to be a big huge case with high visibility.' It has high visibility all right. But when I read the indictment and saw $32 million, I couldn't believe it. This is the smallest money-laundering case I've been involved in in years."

There was general agreement among the lawyers that this case was not about money laundering per se. It was not even about going after major drug dealers, since even Rudy Armbrecht was not a major figure in the trafficking world and Gonzalo Mora, Jr., was a small fry. This case was about going after a major international bank. And that provided the basis for the second general reaction.

John Hume is low-key and analytical, not given to outbursts in court or outside of court. After examining the evidence and listening to some of the taped conversations between Bob Mazur and his client, Amjad Awan, Hume had a blunt reaction.

"Unless we're at Our Lady of Lourdes, we are only going through the motions with a trial," Hume told Awan candidly. "It will take a miracle to win this one."

The defendants' own words on the conversations picked up by the James Bond briefcase would be compelling evidence against them. Each of the defendants had a clear understanding that the man they knew as Bob Musella derived his money from clients who were drug dealers. Many times the jury would hear the agent's masterful Lee Iacocca analogy.

There was another problem, too. It is an unpleasant subject, but one that the defense lawyers had to address at the outset. BCCI was a shadowy bank run by Pakistanis and financed by Arabs. Its clients in this case were Colombian drug dealers and their money launderers. The bankers on trial were Pakistani and Muslim. Plus, there was a very real chance that evidence would be introduced linking the bank to Manuel Noriega, a big-time bogeyman to the American public.

Winning a case against strong government evidence, particularly taped conversations, demands that a jury be given some reason to want to acquit the defendants, some justification, however flimsy or emotional, for overlooking the hard facts. The odds as well as the evidence seemed stacked against these defendants.

"Here you had an Arab-owned, Paki-run bank with no overt constituency to take their side," explained Barcella in analyzing the strategic problem posed by the racial and religious overtones. "When we were discussing going to trial, I explained to the bank officials the difficulty of taking their case to a jury in Tampa. You were going to have a bunch of little dark men with funny accents facing a bunch of old people."

So, naturally, the talk turned early to the possibility of a plea bargain. Cutting a deal with the government for the bank meant paying a fine, since a corporation cannot be put in prison. Many reputable banks had paid fines and continued to operate. A plea bargain for BCCI would be a business proposition, a negotiation like so many others: How much money will it cost?

Cutting a deal for the bankers was a dicier proposition. Obviously, they could go to prison. Indeed, it seemed certain that many if not all of them would do some time. The key question would be how much. Maybe three years. Maybe five. John Hume, Jay Hogan, and the other lawyers for the individual defendants felt initially that they could get away with fairly light terms. The money involved was small by most standards. None of the bankers had taken a bribe for handling the transactions. None had a previous record. The money-laundering statute was a fairly new law that many bankers did not understand fully. They had not even handled any cash. They were part of a corporate culture that encouraged aggressive banking.

"The BCCI bankers had a more European attitude," explained Peter Romatowski, whose client Nazir Chinoy was fighting extradition from London to Tampa. "There is a lot of winking and nodding and looking the other way on flight capital, whether it is evading currency restrictions or even criminal problems. The prevailing attitude is, 'Where the money comes from is none of my business.' The European view, shared by the bankers at BCCI, was that we are authoritarian, puritanical, and too eager to stick our nose in other people's business."

But this strategy for leniency ran smack into the prosecutorial locomotive of Mark Jackowski. The tough-minded lead prosecutor and his partner, Mike Rubinstein, had a much different view of what had transpired in Operation C-Chase. Jackowski signaled early that he was not interested in a slap on the wrist for the bank or the bankers. Partly this stemmed from the strength of the government's case. Mostly, however, it grew out of his personal conviction that money laundering is an integral element of drug trafficking and deserves equivalent punishment. That was one of the reasons that the first count of the indictment accused all of the defendants of conspiring to distribute cocaine, which carried a twenty-year sentence.

"My view is that these guys are bankers who traffic in narcotics proceeds," Jackowski told Hume and the others late in 1988. "My personal view is that they are no different than dopers themselves. There is absolutely no way that these guys are going to plead to five years."

At the outset, Jackowski insisted on guilty pleas to the overall drug conspiracy charge in the indictment. It was a count that carried a maximum prison term of twenty years. The judge could impose less, but that would probably require statements from the government that the defendants had cooperated and provided significant information about crimes by other people. The defense attorneys viewed Jackowski as unreasonable, unwilling to negotiate a fair deal, but it was a clear-cut case of might makes right. They had to deal with him if they wanted a plea bargain.

Jackowski's intention was to go up the ladder within BCCI. He also was looking for help on the two Noriega cases still pending in Tampa and Miami. He believed that Awan in particular could provide invaluable assistance in those prosecutions, but even the most extensive cooperation was not going to translate into five years for him.

There was another hitch. The policy of the U.S. attorney's office in Tampa on plea bargains was firm: No deals would be cut without a written statement from the defendant outlining the information that he or she would provide in cooperation with the government. These statements, called proffers, were crucial to any deal. But the defense attorneys refused to provide them, maintaining that their clients were innocent and therefore knew of no wrongdoing that they could describe to the government.

Nonetheless, plea negotiations occurred at regular intervals. Sometimes they were downright acrimonious. Often, Bob Mazur sat in on the sessions, but he said little. Usually the meetings were confusing to the defense lawyers.

"What do you want from us?" Hume would ask. "What do you think my guy knows?"

"He knows," Jackowski or Rubinstein would reply and then demand a proffer.

Although the talks would continue right up to the trial and even after it started, it became apparent early that the chances of a plea bargain for the individual clients were slim, so the defense was crafting a joint strategy against the charges.

A central element of this strategy was to challenge the government's case, accuse Mazur and the government of misconduct in targeting BCCI, of selective prosecution. It was a risky move, one that was debated extensively among the defense lawyers in late 1988. If the judge agreed that there had been misconduct, he could take the highly unusual step of throwing out the case. It was a long shot. And merely leveling the accusation was sure to anger the prosecutors, for it impugned their ethics and integrity. That would make any future plea negotiations tougher.

In January 1989, the defense filed a motion seeking dismissal of the indictment on grounds of outrageous government misconduct. The motion, prepared by Akbar Bilgrami's attorney, Bennie Lazzara of Tampa, accused the government of manufacturing a criminal enterprise to ensnare the bank and its employees. These were people, said the motion, who otherwise would not have committed any crimes. They were targeted unfairly by the government.

"The question arises why the defendants were singled out and whether it was because BCCI is largely owned and operated by foreigners—Arabs and Pakistanis—who are not particularly popular or influential in this country," said the motion. "This question raises the distinct issue of selective prosecution."

Similar allegations had been made in other sting operations, most notably by former United States Senator Harrison Williams (D.-NJ) after he was caught up in the Abscam investigation and convicted of taking bribes from FBI agents posing as Arab sheiks. But the trial judge and appeals courts had rejected Williams's charge and, in fact, the rules regulating government conduct in undercover operations remained vague.

The accusations by Lazzara and the other defense attorneys angered the prosecutors and the agents, as expected. The government's immediate response was to suggest that the judge wait until all of the evidence was in at the end of the government's case and then evaluate the allegation. But what the prosecutors really did was decide to play a little rougher.

On May 4, 1989, the federal grand jury in Tampa returned a new indictment of BCCI and the same individuals. Such a document is called a superseding indictment, and it generally followed the same lines as the original charges. New, however, were far broader charges about the bank's activities in laundering drug money and general allegations that what had occurred during C-Chase was an example of overall corporate policy. The previous laundering activity in Panama for convicted drug smuggler Steven Kalish was a central allegation; it rebutted the defense claim that the bank was not predisposed to money laundering.

Far from being lured into illegality by government agents, accused the superseding indictment, BCCI and its officers followed "a corporate strategy for increasing BCCI's deposits by encouraging placement of funds from whatever sources, specifically including 'flight capital,' 'black market capital,' and the proceeds of drug sales, in conscious disregard of the currency regulations, tax laws, and anti-drug laws of the United States and other nations.

"It was also part of the conspiracy, and in the furtherance of BCCI's corporate strategy to pursue deposits from any and all sources in disregard of United States and foreign law, that BCCI . . . did knowingly offer a full range of services to co-conspirator drug importers, suppliers, and money launderers."

This broader language set the stage for introducing evidence at trial of similar crimes committed by the bank and its employees beyond those uncovered directly during Operation C-Chase. The accusation was that the bank itself was corrupt. The trial could turn into a full-blown exposé, provided the judge would allow the evidence to be presented to the jury.

Because the indictment accused the defendants of a drug conspiracy, they stood a real chance of spending the long pretrial months in prison. Drug crimes allow federal prosecutors to bypass normal bail procedures. The concept of bail is that a suspect puts up enough cash to ensure that he or she will appear for trial. With drug lords, however, money is so plentiful that courts have allowed suspects to be held without bail under preventive detention. This is most often used with foreigners who are deemed likely to flee to a country from which they cannot be extradited. Defense lawyers argue that such measures are extreme and unconstitutional, the result of overzealousness in the guise of fighting the war on drugs.

In the case of the individuals indicted, the government sought preventive detention on the grounds that the bankers and Colombians were likely to flee. However, U.S. District Judge William Terrell Hodges, the Tampa judge in charge of the case, agreed to an unusual provision for the bankers. Rather than jail, each would get his own apartment in a condominium complex outside Tampa. Each would wear an unremovable electronic bracelet that would allow federal agents to monitor their location constantly. Off-duty Tampa policemen would be hired to guard the bankers twenty-four hours a day. The bank, of course, would pay for this special treatment.

There were some, such as Jack Blum, who viewed the arrangement as coddling, an effort by the bank to shield the individual defendants from the reality of prison life and make them less likely to accept a government plea bargain that would require them to implicate higher-ups in BCCI. A more reasonable interpretation seems to be that these were not hardened criminals and there was little reason to subject them to prison life for the months and months it would take to get ready for trial.

The fate of the bank officers from Miami made a deep impression on Abdur Sakhia, who for a while had been their supervisor. From time to time, he had warned about the way things were heading, even threatening to resign after Akbar A. Bilgrami's coup in expanding into Colombia. He flew to London in early 1989 to try to escape the impending disaster.

"If a government takes over in Panama that's friendly to the U.S.," he told senior executives, "the entire BCCI office will go to jail." But headquarters wasn't impressed. "The United States isn't the rest of the world," the officers replied. They did, however, give Sakhia an escape from his North American duties. "Would you like a transfer to London?" they asked. "Thank God!" he replied, and leaped at the relocation, even though it meant leaving his ailing wife alone with their fourteen-year-old son.

Why didn't he just leave the bank? he later mused. His lawyers advised him to hang on, he answered himself. Not only would he lose his medical benefits and legal coverage if he left, he would become an immediate target of prosecutors, as the most senior officer to bail out of BCCI. Besides, warnings were coming from Swaleh Naqvi's office that the bank could easily implicate him in wrongdoing, if it wanted to. Sakhia stayed on and found ways later to appease the prosecutors.

Another former bank employee also made his peace with the prosecutors. Daniel Gonzalez, the Panama branch's emissary to the Medellín cartel and handler of some of its dirtiest accounts, had dropped from sight after he had been forced to resign in 1985. Unknown to the bank, he had been located by the C-Chase investigators and brought to Tampa. As the government prepared for trial, Gonzalez put his lurid story on paper. He wrote a book in Spanish called *The Kings of Money Laundering* that later appeared in Panama with no identification of the publisher. Many in Panama thought the U.S. government was behind it, in part because of Gonzalez's flattering description of Customs agent Kathy Ertz in a bikini. Even without a publishing house to plug it, the book became a runaway best-seller.

Response to the indictment of BCCI and its officers had been fast, if not particularly effective, at the Federal Reserve Board in Washington.

BCCI had a handful of agency offices in the United States that took no domestic deposits but did business for international clients. These offices were in New York City, Los Angeles, Tampa, Miami, and Boca Raton, Florida. They were supervised and regulated by state authorities. With help from state banking authorities, the Fed examined the limited books and operations of those offices. At the New York and Boca Raton offices, examiners discovered cash deposits in excess of $10,000 that had not been reported to the IRS as required under federal law. The cash came from foreign nationals, the only people who could make deposits at an agency office, and appeared to represent new money-laundering activities by the bank. In October and November of 1988, the details were passed on by banking authorities to the Justice Department and the IRS for possible criminal action. The Fed never heard back.

The examinations also revealed that internal controls and lending practices at the agency offices were poor. The Federal Reserve, as the main regulator of U.S. branches and agencies of foreign banks, began preparing a civil order requiring BCCI to clean up its operations and enforce compliance with the cash-reporting requirements of U.S. law.

The first the Federal Reserve Board heard of Amjad Awan's claims that BCCI controlled First American and other U.S. banks was on December 27, 1988, when IRS agent David Burris, who was part of the C-Chase team, telephoned William Ryback, a supervisor at the Federal Reserve in Washington. Burris had talked with Ryback several times since August about various BCCI matters. This time, the IRS agent was looking for a copy of the transcript from the April 1981 hearing on the acquisition of First American.

During the conversation, Burris explained that a BCCI employee had claimed in taped conversations that BCCI controlled First American and a bank in Georgia. Burris offered to provide the Fed with five or six witnesses who could testify about BCCI's secret ownership of First American Bank. While Burris couched the offer as what he called a "hypothetical instance," he felt certain that he conveyed to Ryback that he could produce the witnesses.

The bank regulator's response was disappointing. He told Burris that he would need documents to corroborate any testimony before the Fed could take action. Burris did not understand why the evidence he had offered, which might have been sufficient for charges in a criminal case, was of so little interest to the Federal Reserve.

Slightly more than a month later, Burris and his IRS supervisor, Maurice Dettmer, flew to Washington to pay a visit to Ryback. It was February 1, 1989. The chief mission of the IRS agents was to gather additional background material on BCCI for the criminal case in Tampa. Again Burris mentioned briefly to Ryback the possibility of witnesses who would link BCCI and First American. Again, the regulator was uninterested.

After the Tampa indictments the previous October, the Federal Reserve had opened a special inquiry into the possible relationship between BCCI and First American. At the time, First American had an application pending to acquire a small bank in Pensacola, Florida, which had been foreclosed by its Georgia subsidiary. The inquiry was conducted under the auspices of that application by the Federal Reserve Bank of Richmond, Virginia, which had jurisdiction over First American Bankshares, but it was only cursory. Each of First American's subsidiary banks was asked to report on any transactions with BCCI, and the CCAH management was asked whether any relationship existed with BCCI.

In its report to the Fed board in Washington on February 8, 1989, the Richmond bank said it had found no evidence of irregular or significant contacts between First American and BCCI. The auditors found that the common ownership between CCAH and BCCI had increased. This was principally a recognition that the Mahfouz family now owned thirty percent of CCAH and about twenty percent of BCCI. However, repeating the promise they had made in 1981, Clark Clifford and Robert Altman assured the Fed that BCCI exercised no control or influence over CCAH.

So a week later, ignoring the leads provided by David Burris, the Federal Reserve approved First American's acquisition of the Bank of Escambia in Pensacola. In a letter to Altman announcing the approval, the Fed said that "a recent inspection and investigation by the Federal Reserve System indicate that applicants have adhered to their original commitments to the board" that BCCI was not involved in First American's operations. There was no indication in the record that Ryback had ever talked to Burris and Dettmer.

Concerns remained at the Fed. Officials were frustrated with their inability to pierce the regulatory secrecy that concealed BCCI's true operations. By-the-book bank examiners insisted on documentary evidence of the links to First American, not rumors and allegations. And no documents were available.

It was not until late in 1989 that the facade of secrecy erected in front of the Bank of Credit and Commerce International began to crack. Even then, the truth was still a long way off.

At the time, BCCI was regulated in a most unusual fashion. The long-standing concerns of the Bank of England and other jurisdictions over the lack of a single regulator for the bank had led to a novel step in 1988. Officials of Britain, Switzerland, Luxembourg, and Spain had formed an informal college of regulators to try to monitor the affairs of BCCI. Later, the group was expanded to include the Cayman Islands.

The concerns of the regulators were heightened by the bank's indictment in Tampa in late 1988. By the middle of 1989, the anxiety had deepened as the bank continued to provide only partial financial information to the regulators. So that fall, the college of regulators had insisted that Price Waterhouse conduct an immediate audit of BCCI's Luxembourg and Cayman Islands operations and that the bank provide the results to the regulators. Reluctantly, the bank had capitulated.

This agreement might not have been made if Agha Hasan Abedi had still been in control. He had never wavered in his devotion to secrecy, but with Abedi sidelined by serious illness, Swaleh Naqvi still in tenuous command, and the Tampa case about to go to trial, the bank had agreed to provide the regulators with a first-ever look at the worldwide financial operations of the Bank of Credit and Commerce International.

Price Waterhouse had first examined the bank as a whole in 1987, after Ernst & Whinney quit in anger over the near collapse of the bank from the trading losses. Since then, Price Waterhouse had given the bank an unqualified report each year. But all that changed with the audit demanded by the regulators.

Dated November 17, 1989, the audit said that the bank had performed reasonably well over the past nine months in light of the repercussions from the American criminal charges. Some business had been lost, but the bank also had attracted new business. Senior management had told the auditors that they anticipated a year-end profit of $220 million to $240 million. Price Waterhouse thought the estimate was high, but agreed that the bank appeared headed for another profitable year.

The major problem at the bank seemed to be its concentration of huge loans to a handful of customers. The risk in such a concentration was that the collapse of one customer could ripple through an institution and topple the entire structure.

The largest concentration that Price Waterhouse found was $856 million in loans to the shareholders of Credit and Commerce American Holdings, the parent company of First American Bankshares. From the audit, it was apparent that Price Waterhouse had raised a similar alarm about the concentration the previous year. Since then, however, the audit found that loans to CCAH had increased by $113 million.

It was this concentrated lending that was the basis for questions about the loans. There was no evidence in the report that BCCI actually controlled the CCAH shares. The side agreements were not shared with the auditors. Indeed, the auditors raised similar questions about the high concentration of loans to other clients, such as the Gokal brothers and their shipping companies and Ghaith Pharaon.

Still, when the college of regulators went over the audit, one of the regulators knew that the CCAH loans would be of interest to the Federal Reserve Board in Washington. The regulator knew that the board had been investigating ties between First American and BCCI for nearly a decade.

Bank secrecy laws in Britain and Luxembourg prohibited the regulator from passing on a copy of the audit or even describing its contents to outsiders, but in December 1989, the regulator contacted William Taylor, the chief of bank supervision at the Federal Reserve. Taylor was told that an audit had uncovered extensive loans from BCCI to Kamal Adham and other CCAH shareholders. The audit did not indicate whether there were any links between the loans and control of CCAH stock, but Taylor was told that more information might show up in later audits.

The Federal Reserve immediately wrote a letter to Robert Altman asking for information on any loans that BCCI or its affiliates had made to the shareholders of CCAH. The response came from Swaleh Naqvi, who assured the Federal Reserve that BCCI had not financed the First American acquisition and that the loans to CCAH shareholders were unrelated to that transaction. Kamal Adham sent a personal assurance that his CCAH shares had not been financed by BCCI. Indeed, Adham maintained steadfastly that he, and he alone, was the owner of about thirteen percent of the shares in First American's parent company. Later, through his Washington lawyer and in communications with the Federal Reserve, he denied that he was a nominee of any sort for BCCI.

The Kerry subcommittee was not faring much better than the Fed in trying to get the full story on BCCI. Attempts to schedule public hearings on the bank were stalled. By the Justice Department. By the Senate. By the failure of BCCI's lawyers to provide key documents.

After Blum's departure, the BCCI investigation had fallen primarily on the shoulders of two young lawyers on Kerry's personal staff, David McKean and Jonathan Winer. In weeks of negotiations with BCCI's lawyers, chiefly Ray Banoun by this point, the staffers had been unable to obtain internal bank records related to the Noriega account and other overseas activities by the bank. In their defense, the bank's lawyers were concerned first with complying with similar demands from the prosecutors in Tampa. At one point, Banoun referred the request for records to the Tampa prosecutors and Kerry's subcommittee was told that its access would have to wait until after the trial. Banoun and Robert Altman also continued to maintain that they were relying on Amjad Awan's assertion that there were no Noriega records in the bank's files.

John Kerry was finding little support within the Senate. Congress as an institution does not move easily into arenas of great controversy. Usually it is forced to confront a scandal by the press, with daily page-one stories and network broadcasts goading publicity seekers and prodding well-meaning legislators to hold hearings.

"There was no appreciation in this institution for the tentacles of BCCI and not a lot of appetite for upsetting the apple carts," Kerry lamented later. "There is a role of accountability and oversight that Congress must play in these situations. But sometimes it is easier to avoid it."

In early 1990, Kerry joined the Senate Banking Committee and immediately tried to interest its chairman, Senator Donald Riegle of Michigan, in funding a full-scale investigation of BCCI under the banking panel's jurisdiction. The idea was to examine whether BCCI violated U.S. banking laws in purchasing other institutions and whether the Federal Reserve had regulated the bank properly. The requested budget for the year-long investigation was $135,000. However, the Senate Banking Committee, like Foreign Relations, is more of a lapdog than a watchdog, and Riegle's attention was riveted understandably on his own political survival. He was one of five senators under scrutiny for helping Charles Keating stave off regulators who had tried to shut down his California savings and loan.

CHAPTER TWENTY

Bagging the Bank

The trial of the Bank of Credit and Commerce and the individual defendants was scheduled to start in the middle of January 1990 in Tampa, Florida. The bank's lawyers had been unable to negotiate a plea agreement, and they had essentially given up trying. Lawyers for the individual bankers also had little hope of getting what they deemed a reasonable agreement from Mark Jackowski, though they continued to discuss pleas. Then everything changed.

The cause was an order issued by Judge Hodges on December 5, 1989. The judge threatened to dismiss the drug conspiracy charges against the bank and the bankers. The government is put on notice, said Hodges, that it cannot convict BCCI or the bankers as drug conspirators solely on evidence that the bank and its employees may have laundered drug proceeds. The judge said that Congress had made money-laundering a separate crime in 1986 and that was the statute under which he felt the bank and its employees should be prosecuted.

Faced with the first major victory for the defense, the government suddenly had to reevaluate its position on a plea bargain with the bank. Certainly the prosecutors had ample evidence to support the money-laundering charges, but the drug count was a different matter, for neither the bank nor the bankers had been linked directly to drugs.

The ramifications of the ruling were important: The prosecutors had used provisions of the law attached to the drug count to freeze $14 million of BCCI's money and seek its forfeiture. If the drug count was dismissed, as Hodges was threatening, the money would be freed. Even if the bank were convicted of the other charges, the likelihood of a $14 million fine was slim. To date, the highest money-laundering fine against a bank was $5 million, and that case involved a bank that had laundered about $300 million. Further, Hodges did not have a reputation as a judge who handed down tough penalties against white-collar criminals.

Gregory Kehoe, second in command at the U.S. attorney's office in Tampa, was adamant that the bank not get a single penny of that money back. The solution was to reach a plea bargain with the bank that would allow the government to retain the $14 million as a forfeiture. Also at play was the consideration that a corporate defendant could not be put in jail; the worst that could happen was a fine.

A few days after Hodges's critical ruling, the prosecutors sat down with the bank's lead lawyers, Larry Wechsler and Larry Barcella, and began to talk about a deal. The judge's order had brought the prosecutors back to the table and also cleared the way for Wechsler and Barcella to reach a bargain. Their instructions from the bank's management had been explicit: Do not plead guilty to a drug charge. The money laundering could be explained away, for many banks were guilty of that, but the publicity of a drug conviction was far more serious.

The ruling did not have the same impact on negotiations with the individual bankers. Even if Hodges dismissed the drug count against each of them, they still faced up to twenty years in jail on the other charges. Plus, the prosecutors did not have the same financial incentive to strike a deal with the individual defendants, since their potential forfeitures were nowhere near the bank's $14 million.

Many believe that another event in December made a plea bargain with the bank more palatable to the government. Shortly after one o'clock in the morning on December 20, 1989, a battalion of U.S. Army Rangers parachuted onto the runways of Omar Torrijos Airport on the outskirts of Panama City, Panama. It was the first wave of the U.S. invasion of Panama. Within days, the tiny nation's armed forces were vanquished. Its leader, General Manuel Noriega, was flown out of the country under armed guard and escorted to a tiny prison cell beneath the U.S. District Courthouse in Miami to await trial on drug and conspiracy charges.

The Noriega cases in Miami and Tampa had lain dormant for months. Prosecutors had little expectation that the Panamanian strongman would be brought to the United States for trial. When those expectations were proven wrong, prosecutors in two cities and at main Justice in Washington had to scramble to prepare for Noriega's trial. Because the Miami case was much broader and far sexier, it was decided that Noriega would be tried there first.

The surprise invasion and capture of Noriega meant that the Bank of Credit and Commerce International now was an important potential source of documents for his trial. Its records could help corroborate the government's charges that Noriega had taken payments from the drug cartels and been involved with traffickers at various levels. Securing access to his account records and interpreting them would be far easier with BCCI's help. In addition, as the lead lawyer on the Tampa case against Noriega, Jackowski's own case against the general rested heavily on the testimony of Steven Kalish. Bank records could support Kalish's claim that he opened an account at BCCI on advice from Noriega's cronies.

The BCCI prosecution team remains unanimous in arguing that the Noriega arrest had no effect on their case. They contend that the sole motivation was the prospect of losing the frozen $14 million when the drug charge was dismissed. Given the incredible pressure within the Justice Department to convict Noriega at all costs, it seems hard to believe that BCCI's potential cooperation did not come into play in the plea talks. Yet Jackowski and Kehoe point out that they showed no willingness to soften their position on a plea by the individual bankers, even though Amjad Awan was a strong potential witness against Noriega.

Two weeks after Noriega was taken into custody in Panama, Operation C-Chase bagged its bank.

Tuesday, January 16, 1990, was the eve of jury selection in Tampa for the trial of the bank, the bankers, and Rudy Armbrecht and Gonzalo Mora, Jr. At mid-morning, it was announced in Tampa that BCCI Holdings in Luxembourg and the Bank of Credit and Commerce International in the Cayman Islands had admitted laundering millions of dollars of cocaine profits. They were pleading guilty to every count of the indictment except count one, which charged them with a conspiracy to aid in the distribution of cocaine. As part of the settlement, the bank agreed to forfeit the $14 million in frozen funds plus about $800,000 in interest.

The bank also agreed to cooperate with federal authorities in other investigations, which were not identified. In exchange for its cooperation, the bank was promised that the U.S. attorney's office in Tampa would not charge BCCI or any affiliates with other federal criminal offenses "under investigation or known to the government at the time of the execution of this agreement."

The eleventh-hour settlement was hailed by the Justice Department as "the largest cash forfeiture ever." It was denounced by Senator John Kerry. He called it a "sad commentary on a country that is supposed to be taking money laundering extremely seriously." Added Kerry, "When banks engage knowingly in the laundering of money, they should be shut down."

Kerry's opposition, which received considerable attention in the press, angered the Tampa prosecutors and C-Chase agents. It also put the

Justice Department on the defensive. Top Justice officials defended the plea, arguing that the $14.8 million, while short of the $28 million maximum fine, was three times greater than the largest money-laundering fine paid to date. Too, they pointed out, Judge Hodges already had indicated that he intended to throw out the drug conspiracy count, the only charge to which the bank had not pleaded guilty.

In response to Kerry's criticism that the bank should have been shut down, the Justice Department said the money-laundering statute contained no provision for closing down a bank convicted of money laundering, whether it was American or foreign. Kerry responded by drafting and introducing, in a matter of weeks, legislation to require regulators to revoke the operating charter of any bank convicted of money laundering. It was a Draconian piece of work, immediately dubbed "the death penalty" by the American Bankers Association. Nonetheless, the measure was approved by the Senate Banking Committee and probably would have won passage in the full Senate had it not been for a Republican attack led by Senator Orrin Hatch. The Utah Republican went to the floor of the Senate and denounced Kerry's legislation and praised BCCI as a good corporate citizen.

The most sweeping part of the bank's plea bargain was the clause that prohibited the U.S. attorney's office in Tampa from charging BCCI with other crimes. The Justice Department maintained that the prohibition was restricted to Tampa and to crimes known or under investigation at the time of the plea. It also did not cover any individuals. This seems a reasonable interpretation, and one that was later endorsed by a staff report prepared for Representative Charles Schumer, a New York Democrat who was highly critical of other aspects of the government's handling of C-Chase. However, the net effect of the agreement was far more significant than what was written on the paper.

In effect, BCCI switched sides. No longer were the bank and its top officers adversaries of the government. They were cooperating witnesses, seemingly key players in the far larger effort to nail Noriega. Certainly other federal jurisdictions could start their own investigation, but the chances of that seemed slim. If Tampa was not going to proceed, no one else in the Justice Department was likely to do so, at least not without some strong outside pressure. Jackowski and Rubinstein had to be content to prosecute the remaining case and hope that they could develop another case against other BCCI officials once it was over. In the meantime, they took a pasting in the press and in Congress.

Sentencing for the bank was set for February 5, 1990. The only choice for Judge Hodges was to ratify or reject the plea agreement, since there was no sentencing provision for the corporation. Kerry was joined by five other Democrats in a letter urging the judge to reject the agreement and impose the full $28 million fine. By this point, Hodges was a week into the trial of the individual bankers. He also had accepted a guilty plea to all counts by Gonzalo Mora, Jr. Mora's lawyer, Joel Rosenthal, said his client wanted to avoid sitting through the lengthy trial. On February 5, Hodges accepted the settlement with the bank as well.

The Bank of Credit and Commerce International forfeited a record $14.8 million. Far more significantly, the bank was transformed from an enemy to an ally within the Justice Department. For instead of shutting down BCCI, as John Kerry urged initially, the Justice Department had a secret plan to keep BCCI open. The argument was that the government wanted to try to monitor the activity in a number of other suspect accounts, although anyone using BCCI for criminal purposes after the plea bargain would have to be a fool.

Nonetheless, on February 13, 1990, Charles Saphos, the head of the Justice Department's narcotics section, wrote to the state comptroller of Florida, Gerald Lewis, asking him to allow the bank to remain open. The bank's license to operate in Florida expired on March 14, 1990, and Lewis had indicated that he was not willing to renew it because of the guilty plea. But Saphos said that the Justice Department wanted to keep the institution open to monitor certain unidentified accounts. Saphos offered to meet with Lewis to discuss the matter.

The letter offered Lewis a heaven-sent opportunity to posture and distract attention from his own ambiguous record as a regulator. As the head of all bank and savings and loan regulation in Florida, Lewis had presided over a series of supervisory lapses, many involving fund-raisers for his own campaigns. Now, this impolitic letter from the Justice Department let the Florida comptroller pose as the man who shut down BCCI in spite of interference from Washington.

Lewis fired off a cold reply to Saphos. The Florida official indicated little willingness to come to attention because the Justice Department had called, though he did offer to meet with Saphos if he could be in his office on February 19. In a curt reply, Saphos apologized to Lewis for any indication that the Justice Department might be trying to influence his decision on BCCI's future. And he said the matter would be dropped. That was fine with Lewis, who went ahead and shut down BCCI's operations in Florida.

Similar letters had been sent to state regulators in California and New York. Saphos telephoned officials in those states, too, and offered his apologies for appearing to try to interfere with their jobs.

To Amjad Awan and the others facing trial, the bank's guilty plea was the second major action that had gone their way, coming on the heels of the dismissal of the drug conspiracy charge.

There had been plenty of setbacks. Judge Hodges had refused to suppress the incriminating statements made by Awan after his arrest, despite his claim that he was slightly drunk from too many Scotches pushed on him by Mike Miller. He had refused to bar conversations recorded by Bob Mazur in France without proper consent, agreeing with the government that U.S. constitutional safeguards do not apply on foreign soil.

Most significantly, Hodges had rejected the defense contention that the bank and its employees had been lured into the scheme by the undercover agents. In a ruling on the defense motion in December 1989, Hodges said: "Examining the totality of the circumstances in this case, the government's conduct falls far short of the outrageous conduct necessary to constitute a constitutional violation." The ruling was not unexpected. The issue could still be raised at the trial, but it seemed unlikely that a jury would find it any more credible than the judge had.

The pretrial motions worked out better for Iqbal Ashraf, the head of BCCI's Los Angeles office. The day before the trial was to start, the government dismissed the charges against Ashraf, tacitly acknowledging that the banker had been contacted improperly by Mazur on October 5. It was a key move by the government to protect its larger case.

The indictment against BCCI and the bankers had been returned on October 4. Federal policy prohibits undercover agents from having contact with defendants following an indictment. Yet on October 5, Mazur met with Ashraf in Los Angeles and discussed the transaction to launder $500,000 of Roberto Alcaino's money in the apartment complex. Ashraf's lawyer, Sandy Weinberg, accused the government of misconduct. Jackowski and Rubinstein were adamant that Mazur, who was still undercover, was unaware that the indictment had been handed down. His mind was focused on gathering as much evidence as possible before the arrests planned for October 8.

But the prosecutors faced a risk in allowing Ashraf to go on trial. Weinberg would bring up the issue, possibly raising doubts about Mazur's credibility in the minds of the jury. Rather than take the risk that their star witness would seem less than 100 percent truthful, Jackowski and Rubinstein agreed to drop the charges against the Los Angeles banker.

For the remaining bank defendants, the BCCI plea was a bright spot because it created the appearance of a major injustice to offer the jury. The primary defense strategy was to claim that the employees were pushed into accepting the C-Chase deposits because the bank was overaggressive and its policy was to encourage turning a blind eye to the sources of money. Yet here was the bank wriggling off the hook. The defense could play on the jury's sympathy and also attack the bank for failing to train its employees in the specifics of the new U.S. money-laundering law. They were, as John Hume later told the jury, "guinea pigs" under the new statute.

Had the bank's lawyers been sitting at the defense table, they would have claimed that bank policy was against money laundering. The defendants, the bank would argue, were overzealously trying to advance their own careers.

Even without the bank at their table, the defense was doing little more than going through the motions, as Hume had phrased it. None of the lawyers held out much hope for an acquittal. Their expectations would turn out to be quite realistic. The bank's belief that the $14.8 million forfeiture had put its troubles to rest, however, would turn out to be one of the world's most wrongheaded cases of wishful thinking.

It took nearly a year for Robert Morgenthau's team to gather enough information to begin making presentations to a New York grand jury, the first and most secret step in obtaining a criminal indictment.

The standards for taking a case to a New York grand jury and getting subpoenas for testimony and documents were higher than those for a federal grand jury. For John Moscow to put a witness before the county grand jury, he had to be sure that the testimony was firsthand and would pass the same tests of law required for it to be admissible in a trial. With a federal grand jury, secondhand information, known as hearsay, is admissible, although in most cases it could not be entered in court.

This meant that Moscow could not put a single investigator before the grand jury to describe what the investigation had uncovered so far and then seek subpoenas, as could his counterparts in the Justice Department. He had to assemble a series of firsthand witnesses.

The issue of immunity also was a minefield. A witness before a New York grand jury is granted automatic immunity unless he specifically waives it. This is a broad form of immunity that prohibits prosecution of the witness for any crimes connected with the actions covered in the testimony. Some of the first witnesses scheduled for the BCCI grand jury were former employees of BCCI, including Amer Lodhi. They were disgruntled and cooperative. But Moscow had to be careful not to put someone before the panel who would turn out to be a major player in the eventual scheme.

The first grand jury testimony was taken in the spring of 1990 and the first subpoenas to the bank for documents went out in May of that year. At this point, the investigation was focused on whether BCCI was behind the takeover of Financial General. If it could be proven that it was, filings made with New York banking regulators could be fraudulent. Simultaneously, a fuzzy picture was emerging in which the bank appeared to be in far poorer financial condition than it had reported in its financial statements. That, too, might constitute fraud.

Thus, as the subpoenas went out, Morgenthau and Moscow had met the test of the first phase of an investigation. They had uncovered the allegations and were beginning to understand them. The next step would be finding a way to prove them.

In this initial phase of Morgenthau's inquiry, the Federal Reserve in Washington and New York as well as the Justice Department in Tampa were fairly cooperative, although it had come as a complete shock to the prosecutors in Tampa when Morgenthau's office first called and said it was investigating BCCI. Jack Blum had never told Mark Jackowski or Mike Rubinstein that he was going to Morgenthau.

Nonetheless, the Tampa prosecutors had briefed their New York counterparts on their case against the bankers and provided them with access to all of their documents. However, as Moscow started his grand jury in the summer of 1990, the prosecutors in Tampa really were not paying much attention to what was going on in New York. They were focused on the trial nearing its conclusion in the ceremonial courtroom on the first floor of the old courthouse in downtown Tampa.

Every weekday morning for six months, Amjad Awan, Akbar Bilgrami, Ian Howard, Sibte Hassan, and Aftab Hussain left their condominiums and headed for the Tampa federal courthouse. Sometimes there would be television cameras waiting on the steps of the building. Most often, they walked in with their lawyers unmolested. Inside the courtroom itself, they were watching their lives blown away by the testimony of Customs agent Robert Mazur. And by their own words, repeated on dozens of tape recordings played over headphones for the jurors.

The defense strategy held few surprises. It was basically two-tiered. The government had unfairly targeted the bankers and lured them into a criminal scheme, and the bank itself had failed to train them properly in the complexities of the new U.S. money-laundering statute. The tapes themselves seemed to belie the contention that these were innocent bankers ensnared unwittingly in a government net. In recorded conversations with each of the defendants, the jurors heard Mazur compare his clients to Lee Iacocca, explaining that they sold cocaine instead of cars. And as anyone who watches television crime shows knows, ignorance of the law is not a defense, but there was little else available to the defense lawyers.

Which is not to say that the trial was without drama. Bob Mazur spent fifty-four days on the witness stand. He recounted the key meetings in the indictment and interpreted the tape recordings. His testimony was so complex that Mazur used a script. It was a 300-page, color-coded computer printout that summarized each recorded conversation introduced into evidence by the prosecution.

At each step, Mazur was challenged by defense lawyers. They tried to shake his credibility, jar his recollection of events, cast doubt on his interpretation of the taped conversations. Bennie Lazzara, who had written the original motion accusing the government of misconduct, was especially combative in his cross-examination of Mazur. But the agent was as cool on the witness stand as he had been operating undercover for more than two years.

Mazur seemed to lose his temper only a few revealing times. When a defense attorney addressed him as Mr. Musella, the agent, flushed with anger at the thought he had lost his own identity, shot back, "The name is Mazur." A second time he reacted angrily when a line of questioning threatened to endanger his family by revealing details of his background.

The day after Mazur stepped down from the witness stand the government rested its case. John Hume sought a meeting with the prosecutors. He wanted to cut a deal for Amjad Awan.

Hume and Mike Rubinstein sat down in a conference room in the Federal Building, a block from the courthouse. Rubinstein repeated that the first step in a plea bargain would be a proffer from Awan outlining what he could provide to the government on other cases. As he had at the outset of plea talks months before, Hume balked at the idea of laying out what his client knew before a deal was promised. Rubinstein countered that Hume could draft a document, leaving Awan free to denounce it if they failed to reach agreement. Still Hume refused.

Exasperated, Rubinstein asked why and Hume said, "I don't trust you, Mike. I don't know that you would go ahead and deal and not just use the information." Rubinstein exploded in a string of expletives. That was the last plea discussion, and the case went to the jury when the defense completed its case a few weeks later.

When the twelve jurors began deliberations on July 18, 1990, they had access to the exhibits introduced as evidence in the trial. Among them was an address book seized from Rudy Armbrecht's briefcase the night he was arrested. Using Armbrecht's phone book, one of the jurors undertook an unusual initiative. He made several telephone calls to people in Colombia whose names had come up in the trial as associates of the Medellín cartel and whose numbers were listed in the book. The juror mentioned the calls to at least five of his fellow jurors. One of them told her husband about the incident when she went home one night and he contacted the FBI. The FBI alerted the U.S. attorney's office, which related the incident to Judge Hodges.

Because of the publicity, the judge had told the jurors specifically that they were to base their decision only on the evidence produced during the trial. They were told to avoid any outside information. Judges habitually warn juries not to discuss the case with relatives, and to avoid reading newspaper stories or watching television broadcasts about their trial. But the thought that a juror would launch his own investigation was totally bizarre and unprecedented.

There was a flurry of meetings between the lawyers and the judge. Defense attorneys sought a mistrial. Hodges decided to put the juror on the witness stand and assess the damage. The last thing he wanted was to retry a six-month case. On the stand, the juror acknowledged making the calls and said he was acting out of "simple curiosity." Hodges dismissed the juror from the panel and ordered the eleven remaining jurors to continue their deliberations.

On Sunday, July 29, 1990, the remaining jurors filed back into the courtroom. Filling the front-row pews were relatives of the defendants, many of whom had come from Pakistan for the verdicts. Awan's wife, Sheereen, and his two children sat in the front row alongside her father, the elderly Asghar Khan, former air marshal of Pakistan.

As the jury foreman read the verdicts, the courtroom erupted in wails and cries. All six defendants—the five bankers and Armbrecht—were convicted of conspiring to launder $14 million in proceeds from cocaine sales. As threatened, Hodges had dismissed the drug distribution charge during the trial, but the defendants were also convicted of various individual counts of money laundering, ranging from a low of three for Sibte Hassan to a high of twenty for Aftab Hussain and Akbar Bilgrami. Exotic Asian laments filled the courtroom and spilled out onto the steps of the courthouse as U.S. marshals cleared the building. The relatives mobbed anyone who looked official. An elderly woman stood face to face with Customs supervisor Steve Cook, yelling curses at him in Urdu, and was later charged with threatening a federal officer.

The convictions carried prison terms of up to twenty years for each of the defendants with fines that could run into millions of dollars, based on the amount of money laundered. Hodges revoked the unusual bail arrangements and the bankers joined Rudy Armbrecht in regular cells at Hillsborough County Jail. Sentencings were set for the following week, but there would be months of delay before that chapter of Operation C-Chase was written.

From the London headquarters of BCCI came a press release expressing "sympathy to the families" of the bankers. It also said that the crimes were "contrary to express, written policies of BCCI" and had taken place without the knowledge of the bank's management or board. Privately, the bank cut off all financial assistance and legal aid to the bankers when they were convicted. By that time, BCCI had spent at least $10 million on defense attorneys in the Tampa case. The bank was not interested in spending any more. It was having troubles of its own.

In March 1990, Robin Leigh-Pemberton, the governor of the Bank of England, had received a new audit report that had been performed for BCCI by Price Waterhouse. Problems were much more serious and practices far more questionable than had been described in the November 1989 report. Clearly, the financial condition of the bank was sorry indeed.

The problems, said Price Waterhouse, centered on insider loans to shareholders and others with close affiliations to the bank. Payments had not been made on many of these loans for years. Some of the borrowers denied ever receiving the loans. As much as $2 billion had been loaned to associates of the bank and major customers, often with little or no documentation and security.

For instance, the accountants said that bank records showed Kamal Adham owed BCCI's Luxembourg subsidiary $313 million at the end of 1989. Yet the auditors said they found no valuations for the property in Saudi Arabia that the former Saudi intelligence chief had put up as security for some of the debts. There were no written loan agreements. In addition, the audit said that the property itself was dubious security because Saudi law probably prohibited the bank from seizing it in a foreclosure action.

Adham was only one of the shareholders in CCAH who had apparently borrowed extensively from the bank. When combined with his loans, CCAH shareholders now owed BCCI $856 million, according to the audit. The list of CCAH shareholders with loans was a long one and it included Faisal al-Fulaij, A.R. Khalil, and the rulers of the tiny Arab emirates of Fujaira and Ajman.

Far more significant, the audit spelled out for the first time the true arrangements behind those loans. It said that BCCI held at least sixty percent of the shares in CCAH as security for the loans and that it had held the shares since at least 1984. With the loans in default, the bank effectively had majority ownership of the parent company of First American Bankshares. Indeed, the audit said that in past years BCCI officials had told Price Waterhouse that they held all the CCAH shares.

Here was the smoking gun that the Federal Reserve had been trying to find for a decade. But they would not get it so easily. Bank secrecy laws in Britain and Luxembourg prohibited the regulators from sharing the audit with or describing its findings to anyone else, even their counterparts in other countries. This was a clear and concrete example of the dangers in allowing banks that are located in secrecy havens to operate in open countries, such as the United States.

The ownership of the American bank was not the top priority for the British and Luxembourg regulators anyway. As the leaders of the college of regulators trying to keep a rein on BCCI, they were far more worried by the concentration of loans shown in the audit and its potential impact on the health of the bank. BCCI had loaned huge amounts of money to a handful of customers and virtually none of the loans to these favored few appeared to be documented properly or have a satisfactory repayment schedule. If the loans were marked down as the losses they appeared to be, the bank's capital would be wiped out and it would be insolvent.

The biggest single borrower was the Gokal shipping family. Companies associated directly with the three brothers owed BCCI $405 million. Seventy-one other companies apparently owned by the brothers had borrowed an additional $300 million. All of the transactions had gone through the bank's Cayman Islands subsidiary and many of them were shrouded in secrecy.

For instance, Price Waterhouse listed these seventy-one companies as owned by the Gokals, but the accountants acknowledged in the audit that they were uncertain of the true ownership. The companies were registered in offshore havens, ranging from the Bahamas and Cayman Islands to Liberia and Uruguay, and the real owners were concealed behind secrecy laws in those countries.

According to the accountants, the offshore companies apparently grew up in response to questions in previous audits about heavy lending to the Gokals. When bank limits were reached on loans to one entity, another was created to receive new loans. The audit said that the offshore companies also appeared to have helped their owners evade currency restrictions in Pakistan and India. Other than $65 million worth of ships under mortgage, Price Waterhouse said it found no tangible security for the loans to the offshore companies.

Another example of the bank's favorable treatment for insiders involved the Mahfouz family. Since injecting $150 million in new capital into the bank in 1986 to stave off its collapse from the trading losses, the Saudi Arabian banking family had borrowed $152.5 million from the bank without loan agreements or security, said the audit.

Another sometime BCCI shareholder, Ghaith Pharaon, owed the bank a total of $288 million at the end of 1989. The major collateral was an eleven percent stake in BCCI held by his brother, Wabel Pharaon. As with the other major borrowers, Price Waterhouse found no loan agreements or correspondence to support the Pharaon loans and provide a means to recover them.

The Price Waterhouse report of March 1990 was a stunning indictment of insider dealing and questionable practices at the Bank of Credit and Commerce International. And it was an indictment with a price tag.

Millions of dollars in depositors' money had been loaned to bank shareholders and cronies with little prospect of repayment. The money was simply gone. A month after providing the report to the bank, Price Waterhouse had followed up with a letter to the directors of BCCI that detailed the price of these practices. The accountants said that $1.78 billion in new funding was required to restore the bank's financial health. While the entire amount would not be necessary immediately, a substantial chunk of the new cash was needed fast. In spite of the findings, the auditors issued unqualified statements for the bank, an amazing contradiction that later put the accountants' own reputation in question.

When the regulators in Britain and Luxembourg got a look at the Price Waterhouse report completed that March, they convened an emergency meeting. They hauled in acting BCCI president Swaleh Naqvi, chief financial officer Masihur Rahman, and other bank officials. The bankers agreed that an infusion of cash was needed. They said they were already trying to arrange a bailout from Abu Dhabi. They also agreed to form a task force of senior management, as proposed by Price Waterhouse, to begin restructuring the bank.

For the immediate cash to keep the bank running, Naqvi turned to Sheik Zayed and the Abu Dhabi Investment Authority. Naqvi flew to Abu Dhabi immediately after meeting with the regulators and pleaded for more money. The sheik agreed to pump in $600 million. He also bought out the shares held by the Mahfouz family, increasing the stake held by his government and family to seventy-seven percent from twenty percent. His representatives demanded greater control over the bank's affairs. Its operational headquarters would be moved to Abu Dhabi, and Swaleh Naqvi and other top managers would come along. The government set up its own investigative committee to begin poring over the internal documents of BCCI and reconstructing for itself what had happened. And layoffs would begin immediately in an attempt to restore profitability.

The layoffs were the most stunning news when the bailout agreement was announced to the public. Hundreds of employees who had signed on with a family, not a bank, suddenly found themselves out of work. Twenty branches in Britain were closed, and offices were shut down in many other countries, too. On advice from his financial advisers, Zayed was cleaning house at BCCI. But it did not stop the momentum carrying BCCI toward ruin. Zayed's $600 million bought more time for the world's largest Ponzi scheme, but the fabric of respectability had been torn and the saga was headed toward its climax.

Price Waterhouse continued its examination of the bank's books. In October 1990, the accountants told British regulators of broader financial mismanagement at BCCI.

The new audit, done with the bank's cooperation, disclosed that the previous BCCI managers may have colluded with major customers and shareholders to misstate or disguise the underlying purpose of millions of dollars worth of the questionable loans and other transactions described in March. This was a step beyond the previous report. The accountants were suggesting that top bank officials may have been involved knowingly in a massive fraud. This time around, said the audit, at least another $400 million would be needed to keep the bank afloat.

The second negative audit had a dramatic effect on the bank's management. The report was delivered to the Bank of England on October 3. The following day, Swaleh Naqvi and Agha Hasan Abedi resigned from the Bank of Credit and Commerce International. Abedi had not been involved in day-to-day operations for more than two years, but now, he and his right-hand man were severed officially from the bank they had founded nearly two decades earlier.

Abedi was still at his home in Karachi, struggling to recuperate from his heart ailment. Naqvi was in Abu Dhabi and the government there decided to keep him as an adviser. However, he was confined to a hotel and many believed that he was a virtual prisoner. If he was a prisoner, the tall, gaunt Naqvi also was a witness. For months, he had been helping the Abu Dhabi investigating committee try to unravel BCCI's internal finances from the thousands of files and hundreds of bogus accounts created over the years in a desperate attempt to hide the bank's losses. The man in charge of the investigation for the royal family was Ghanim Faris al-Mazrui, who a decade earlier had ferreted out the losses sustained by Abdullah Darwaish's ill-advised commodities trading scheme.

This October Price Waterhouse report and the existence of Abu Dhabi's investigative committee were kept secret. There was no news conference on the reasons for the management changes at BCCI. Indeed, the scope of the Price Waterhouse findings from March and October 1990 remained a closely guarded secret within the Bank of England. That was what British law demanded. It also was vital to avoiding any sort of panic and a possible run on the bank.

At the Bank of England, Robin Leigh-Pemberton and his chief deputy, Eddie George, decided that they still had insufficient evidence to take any stronger action against BCCI. The Price Waterhouse reports described mismanagement and probably fraud, but the British regulators judged the questionable transactions to be individual acts, not systemic fraud that warranted dismantling the entire bank. Sheik Zayed and Abu Dhabi had promised to make another contribution of cash to bolster the bank's capital. Abedi and Naqvi were gone, and a general restructuring was in the works.

"If we closed down a bank every time we had a fraud, we would have rather fewer banks than we have," Leigh-Pemberton said later.

Bank regulators the world over are notoriously reluctant to shut down troubled institutions. They fear that dramatic closings threaten the stability of the banking system. In the case of BCCI, its biggest base of deposits and customers was Britain. There were about 120,000 customers with $404 million in accounts at BCCI. Many of them were Pakistani immigrants and Asian owners of small businesses who depended on the bank. Closing the bank would make them victims of BCCI because all would lose at least some of their funds. Britain's Deposit Protection Fund provides for compensation equal to only seventy-five percent of even the smallest bank deposits. And the maximum payout is limited to about $25,000, a quarter of the amount protected at insured institutions in the United States, where customers can recoup 100 percent of their money up to $100,000.

On top of the inevitable outcry over the losses, closing the bank would require the Deposit Protection Fund to come up with $100 million or more to pay off depositors. The fund maintains no cash reserves, so Britain's banks would have to be assessed fees to pay for reimbursing BCCI's depositors. The good banks, many of which had avoided dealing with BCCI because of its reputation, would wind up paying for its actions anyway. So the best tactic seemed to be to delay the closing in the hopes that the mess could be sorted out without more government intervention. It was very similar to the logic that was employed by American regulators in permitting the savings and loan industry to try to grow itself out of dire troubles in the 1980s. And the results were destined to be similar, too.

Further complicating the task of the British and Luxembourg regulators was the fear that shutting the bank in a few countries would send ripples through the international banking community, possibly leading to runs on other BCCI branches worldwide, possibly setting off a financial panic.

So the Bank of England was reluctant to close the bank in October

1990. With Sheik Zayed pumping in new money, there was still a sliver of optimism that the bank could be salvaged.

In the meantime, Leigh-Pemberton instructed Price Waterhouse to conduct yet another examination of BCCI financial records. This was a different, more serious audit. It would be carried out on behalf of the Bank of England under special powers of investigation granted to the regulators under British banking law. Soon, accountants from Price Waterhouse were flying to Abu Dhabi, the Cayman Islands, and other countries in search of the true financial condition of BCCI. It was an investigation marked by great urgency and great secrecy. The bank itself was code-named Sandstorm by the accountants.

A month after the Bank of England sent the accountants after BCCI in earnest, the final chapter was written in the U.S. criminal case that had started the unraveling of the world's greatest Ponzi scheme.

On November 30, 1990, the defendants in the BCCI case had appeared before Judge Hodges in Tampa for sentencing. Dozens of friends and influential people, including Pakistan's former ambassador to the United States, had written letters pleading for mercy for the bankers. Awan's wife Sheereen had sent the judge a mournful letter expressing fears over the impact of losing their father on the couple's two teenage children. Awan himself had written a letter expressing remorse for his actions. All of the bankers, said the letters, were upstanding men with no prior criminal convictions. None of them had profited personally from their crimes.

Awan was the first to be sentenced that Friday morning. Hodges said he had taken into account Awan's lack of a criminal record and the fact that he had not profited personally. That was the reason, he explained, that he was not imposing the full sentence of fifteen to nineteen years called for by federal sentencing guidelines. But there would be no slap on the wrist, and Hodges offered an epitaph for dirty banks.

"The use and abuse of cocaine is a scourge of this country today and has been for at least a decade," said Hodges. "It has produced enormous sums of money, which have served to corrupt many of our institutions in a way that was unknown and unthought of twenty years ago."

Hodges sentenced Awan to twelve years in federal prison and fined him $100,000 for his role in the C-Chase money-laundering operation. It shocked the bankers and their lawyers. Sheereen Awan wept in the courtroom.

Akbar Bilgrami, whose suspicions of Bob Mazur had been overcome by the prospect of big new business, got twelve years, too. Syed Aftab Hussain, the trainee who had first proposed a better way for Mazur to launder his funds, was sentenced to seven years and three months in prison. Ian Howard, whose involvement had consisted of a handful of meetings in Paris, got four years and nine months, and Sibte Hassan was sentenced to three years and a month. Rudolf Armbrecht, the Colombian pilot whose career revolved around cocaine trafficking, received only a slightly tougher sentence than Awan and Bilgrami. He got twelve years and seven months, plus a fine of $200,000.

CHAPTER TWENTY-ONE

The Critical Event

The restructuring of BCCI and the resignation of Agha Hasan Abedi had sent new waves of anxiety through the bank's 14,000 staff members worldwide. The godfather was gone. So was his heir apparent, Swaleh Naqvi. In their place was a Pakistani named Zafar Iqbal. His previous post as BCCI country manager in Abu Dhabi meant he was close to Zayed and the royal family. The bank's senior employees feared that his loyalties were to the rulers of the tiny sheikdom, not to BCCI and its family of workers. Such anxieties seemed justified when the layoffs began.

This was not the only rude awakening. The bank employees had always been told that they were major shareholders in the bank through International Credit and Investment Company, or ICIC. The company was registered as a trust in the Cayman Islands and was supposed to hold the twenty percent of BCCI shares set aside for employees, but the restructuring under the Abu Dhabi ruling family had raised questions about the status of the trust. Rumors were spreading within the bank that ICIC held no stock for the employees, that somehow it had been mixed up in a giant fraud.

By late fall of 1990, John Moscow and his investigators had questioned many current and former BCCI employees. Among the witnesses had been Amer Lodhi, the lawyer with ties to the bank who had first talked to Tampa prosecutors at Jack Blum's urging, and Abdur Sakhia, the BCCI manager in Miami and New York who had finally left the bank earlier in 1990. Out of the October turmoil at the bank came a new level of assistance for the investigation from BCCI employees.

"A lot of them were angry," said Robert Morgenthau. "They had been told they were shareholders. They were going to get their share through ICIC. Then they found out they weren't."

The discontent was a gold mine. And one of the nuggets represented a major defection.

Masihur Rahman first learned of Abedi's dream in 1972 when the two men were colleagues at United Bank in Pakistan. Since 1975, he had served as BCCI's $200,000-a-year chief financial officer. But Rahman said it was not until he had become chairman of the bank's internal review committee in the spring of 1990 that he got a view of the bank's financial picture that was unobstructed by deception and manipulation. What he saw disturbed and angered him. The more Rahman learned, the more he became convinced that his only recourse was to quit, for he, the man in charge of the finances, had been deceived.

As soon as the internal report was finished, Rahman told the bank management that he was resigning. His fellow executives tried to persuade him to stay. They even asked his American wife to plead with him to remain, but Rahman was adamant and, on August 1, 1990, he resigned from the bank. In the days following his resignation, anonymous telephone callers threatened Rahman, his wife, and their two young children. The police in the London suburb of Guildford where the family lived set up special patrols in the neighborhood and hooked up an alarm system tied directly to the police station. About the same time, Rahman learned from another former BCCI executive, John Hillbery, that a shot had been fired through a window at Hillbery's home. Early that fall, the Rahmans pulled their children out of school and eventually the family fled to the United States.

Late in October, Rahman stepped forward. Through an intermediary, he contacted Morgenthau's office and arranged to be questioned informally. He provided a bombshell: two Price Waterhouse audits described BCCI's hidden ownership of First American Bankshares through a series of sham loan transactions with shareholders of CCAH. They had been given to the Bank of England in November 1989 and March 1990. While the prosecutors did not receive copies of the documents immediately, Rahman provided enough information for Morgenthau to ask the Bank of England for them.

Based on information from Rahman and other present and former BCCI employees, a new round of subpoenas was issued by the New York County grand jury in October and November of 1990. Equally important, Morgenthau instructed John Moscow to share the information with the Federal Reserve regulators in Washington.

For Fed counsel Virgil Mattingly, Jr., and William Taylor, the director of bank supervision, this was the second time that fall they had heard about the Price Waterhouse reports. Earlier, a regulator in Luxembourg had passed on word informally about the findings, but the detailed description provided by Morgenthau's office was far more substantive.

The Fed was finally getting confirmation of what some there had suspected for a good while. Although Rahman was not identified to the Fed initially, the two regulators sensed that Morgenthau's informant was speaking with authority when he said that BCCI had made substantial loans to CCAH shareholders and the loans were secured by CCAH shares. It also matched what the Luxembourg official had told them.

The disclosure meant that BCCI could be the owner of First American Bankshares, the exact arrangement that the Fed had feared since 1981 and which had been denied repeatedly by the bank and by its American lawyers, Clark Clifford and Robert Altman. After a decade of inquiries and examinations by the regulators, after a two-year investigation by the U.S. Customs Service, this potential breakthrough was handed to the Fed by the district attorney for New York County.

Immediately, the Fed staff requested access to the November 1989 and March 1990 Price Waterhouse report from BCCI officials in the United States. The request was relayed to Price Waterhouse in London, where the accountants initially refused to permit the reports to be delivered to the Federal Reserve or examined by Fed staff members because of British laws. The Fed found a way around the laws, however, by demanding that BCCI itself provide them with access to the report. This time the demand came at the right time, for the bank's new management was eager to clean house and restore good relations with the regulators.

On December 10, 1990, a senior staff member of the Federal Reserve arrived at BCCI's plush headquarters on Leadenhall Street in London, where he was allowed to examine the auditor's reports from 1989 and 1990. As Morgenthau's source had said, the Price Waterhouse audits confirmed the existence of long-standing loans by BCCI secured by the shares of CCAH. The total was staggering—more than $1 billion. And the loans were only part of the horrors described in the audits.

The Fed staff member then met with Zafar Iqbal, the bank's new chief executive. Ordered by Sheik Zayed's representatives to cooperate, Iqbal confirmed that the loans to CCAH shareholders had not been paid off. Indeed, there had never been any payments on any of them, except in the form of new loans from BCCI. The loans appeared to be window dressing for the bank's ownership of First American.

Within days, there was more progress. When Abu Dhabi took over the bank, new defense lawyers were hired in Washington to replace the team assembled by Clifford and Altman and represent the institution in its dealings with the Federal Reserve. The lawyers were from the Washington firm of Patton, Boggs & Blow. As Agha Hasan Abedi had turned to a politically powerful firm for help in another era, so did the new owners of BCCI select influential legal advisers. The lead partner in the firm was Thomas Hale Boggs, Jr., the son of the late House Majority Leader Hale Boggs of Louisiana, and regarded widely as one of the most powerful lobbyists in town. But this time the strategy was dramatically different than the one employed by the earlier lawyers.

On December 21, Patton, Boggs partner Caffey Norman and some of his associates met with Virgil Mattingly and his staff lawyers at the Fed. The BCCI lawyers had requested the meeting. Norman described how the Abu Dhabi ruling family had invested a large sum of money in BCCI the previous spring in an attempt to correct its capital deficiencies. As a result, he said, the rulers now held seventy-seven percent of the bank's stock. A substantial amount of the stock in CCAH had been pledged to BCCI as collateral for hundreds of millions of dollars in loans to certain CCAH stockholders. Chief among them was Kamal Adham. Payments had never been made on some of the loans, said Norman, and BCCI had thus gained control over the CCAH shares pledged as collateral. It was confirmation of the audits, and of the years of deception.

The Abu Dhabi government and Sheik Zayed, explained Norman, had hired Patton, Boggs & Blow to help conduct a special inquiry into the relationship with CCAH shareholders and other matters. They had been instructed to cooperate with the Federal Reserve's inquiry into the relationship between BCCI and First American's parent company.

Based on the Price Waterhouse audits and the cooperation of BCCI's new owners, the Fed had enough information to open a formal investigation into whether BCCI controlled First American and other U.S. banks. On January 4, 1991, the Federal Reserve Board voted to initiate the inquiry into how BCCI had gained control of CCAH. It asked whether false or misleading statements had been made to the board during the 1981 application process and subsequently. The Fed has no power to bring criminal cases. It can only initiate civil actions, levy fines, and ban individuals from participating in banks doing business in the United States. It can, however, pass on information it obtains to the Department of Justice for possible criminal prosecution.

The grand scale of the BCCI deception was still unknown. The pieces of the puzzle were only beginning to fit together. But, based on what the Fed staff had seen in the past six weeks, enough had been revealed to move on the criminal front, too. On January 22, a criminal referral was sent to the Justice Department proposing possible prosecution of people who had misled the board in describing the relationship between the bank and CCAH with regard to control of First American. Eight days later, the Federal Reserve Board assembled for a final vote on a proposed cease and desist order against BCCI in connection with its First American holdings. The vote was approved with one abstention. Chairman Alan Greenspan said that he was not voting because he had socialized several times with Robert Altman, First American's longtime president and BCCI's longtime lawyer. Nonetheless, the board sent the proposed order to BCCI's new lawyers requiring the bank to sell the shares of CCAH that it controlled.

With the cooperation of BCCI's new owners, the Fed began to uncover the most extensive covert penetration of the U.S. banking system in history. The $856 million in secret loans and other agreements that gave BCCI control over First American's parent company meant that the very institution regulators had fought to keep out of the country had held controlling ownership from the start. And First American turned out to be only the first of BCCI's secret expansions in the United States.

Led by a former federal prosecutor named Rick Small, the banking investigators discovered evidence that they said showed that BCCI and its banking affiliate in the Cayman Islands, International Credit and Investment Company, had financed the initial acquisition of Financial General. The two entities had advanced most, if not all, of the money used by the original shareholders to buy the bank, said the investigators.

For instance, Small's team determined that BCCI had loaned some of the CCAH shareholders the entire amount that they invested in the company. The Federal Reserve would charge that the loans were subject to secret side agreements in which the investors were not liable for paying the money. In exchange, the Fed inspectors said, the shareholders signed blank agreements under which BCCI controlled the shares. It appeared to be a classic case of using front men.

Initially, the bank appeared to have obtained control over 25.78 percent of CCAH's shares in this way, just over the level constituting a controlling interest under banking law. The documents showed that the figure had risen to at least fifty-eight percent by July 1986, when Clark Clifford and Robert Altman had been allowed to buy the stock in CCAH that netted them nearly $10 million in profits when they sold it eighteen months later.

In another example, the original application to buy Financial General in 1981 said that $50 million of the purchase price was coming from a loan from Banque Arabe et Internationale d'Investissement. However, the Fed said the new documents showed that BAI I had never assembled a syndicate to handle a loan that big, so BAI I accepted personal guarantees from Kamal Adham and Faisal Saud al Fulaij for the loan and accepted a $30 million deposit from Adham as a form of collateral. But, the Fed charged, the $30 million deposit was in fact a loan from ICIC at the direction of BCCI that Adham was assured in writing he would not have to repay. In addition, on the date in 1982 that the Federal Reserve approved the purchase of Financial General, both Adham and Fulaij allegedly received written notices from BCCI that they were not liable for the personal guarantees on the BAII loan, according to a later Fed report.

All of this was just becoming clear when the Fed approved the proposed cease and desist order. The order became the starting point for negotiations with the new management of the bank. As the fine points were being discussed in confidential sessions, word of the talks leaked to the *Wall Street Journal.* On February 25, the newspaper reported that a tentative agreement had been reached for BCCI to divest itself of its First American stake and cooperate in the continuing investigation. Along with First American, regulators were delving into allegations that BCCI had similar arrangements that had given the bank control of the National Bank of Georgia before it was sold to First American. The story was the same at Independence Bank, a medium-sized institution in Encino, California.

On March 4, 1991, a Monday, the Federal Reserve Board announced that the Bank of Credit and Commerce International had agreed to divest itself of its secret control over Washington's largest bank. The bank also agreed to begin closing down all operations in the United States through its agency and representative offices. It was the first time that the regulators had kicked a foreign bank out of the country. The order required the bank to submit a plan to sell the CCAH stock and close its offices within sixty days. The bank's owners agreed to the order without admitting or denying wrongdoing.

In a statement, First American's management said that if BCCI controlled shares of its parent company, the bank supported the divestiture order. The statement said that the operations of the $11 billion institution would not be affected by the Fed's order and added, "BCCI hasn't ever directly or indirectly controlled the actual management or operations of First American."

Rather than marking the end, the order was the real beginning of the most extensive and exhaustive investigation in the history of the Federal Reserve Board. Investigations of this nature are complex under the best of circumstances. There are no bodies, and clues are hidden in reams of paper and on computer disks, but BCCI had achieved stunning levels of duplicity and concealment, and then scattered the evidence all over the world. The Fed officials in charge of the inquiry, Bill Taylor and Rick Small, were certain that BCCI had deliberately structured transactions to conceal the relationship with CCAH for more than a decade. What else had the rogue bank done?

* * *

The Federal Reserve's declaration that BCCI owned a controlling interest in First American put Clark Clifford in an awkward position. A man who had built himself into a legend of probity, a man presidents from Truman to Carter had turned to in a crisis, suddenly faced the dilemma of a lifetime: Either he had to admit that he had lied to the regulators for a decade or tell the world that he had been fooled.

"I have a choice of either seeming stupid or venal," he told a reporter from The New York Times in his handsome paneled office with its view of the White House.

He chose the former route, although the wording selected by Clifford and his partner Robert Altman was that they had been "duped." It was kinder than saying they were stupid. Central to their argument, as it unfolded in some early press interviews and later in testimony before the House Banking Committee, was the contention that Clifford and Altman had been fooled in the same manner that the Federal Reserve System and the Bank of England had been fooled. Those guys at BCCI, they were just too crafty by half for all of them.

Indeed, Altman would later say that he had launched a major investigation into the ownership relationship after receiving a copy of the transcript of the conversation in which Amjad Awan boasted to Bob Mazur that BCCI owned First American. There were several conversations in which he confronted BCCI's top management with the accusations and always their denials were as adamant as they had been back in 1981, said Altman. Even Price Waterhouse had told one of First American's lawyers, in a private conversation, that there were no documents substantiating Awan's claim, according to Altman.

The matter was also taken to First American's shareholders. In July 1990, Altman flew to London and met with Kamal Adham and another major shareholder, El Sayed Jawhary. Both men, he said, told him emphatically that the allegations of BCCI ownership of First American's parent company were untrue, and Altman said that he believed the shareholders.

Over the years, Clifford had traveled to London twenty-six times to discuss First American business with Agha Hasan Abedi, but Clifford said it never occurred to him that Abedi was any more than the financial adviser to First American's Arab shareholders. One of the primary reasons that Clifford provided for never assuming that Abedi was actually in control of Clifford's bank tells a great deal about both men.

"In dealing with the shareholders, Mr. Abedi was deferential almost to the point of being obsequious," said Clifford. "His whole attitude was that of a man who was in contact with his superiors."

Clark Clifford, the confidant of presidents, a man treated as a true celebrity in Washington and deferred to at every juncture within government, could not imagine that the quiet, unassuming Abedi was any more than an employee of the wealthy sheiks and rulers with whom Abedi dealt.

Plenty of people derived satisfaction from the Fed's order on March 4. Among them was Senator John Kerry, who felt that he had traveled a long, often lonely road on the trail of the bank. Stonewalled by the Justice Department and BCCI's former lawyers, scoffed at by colleagues in the Senate, vacillating at times in his own commitment to the investigation, finally Kerry believed that he was no longer the senator who cried wolf.

By the spring of 1991, Kerry had been trying to get approval for public hearings on BCCI for nearly two years. Senator Claiborne Pell had resisted the effort in the Foreign Relations Committee, arguing with some logic that it was a banking matter, not a foreign policy issue. Senator Donald Riegle, chairman of the Senate banking committee, was still mired in the Keating Five ethics charges and was not inclined to focus attention on another banking scandal.

In April 1990, Kerry had gone clandestine. He had enlisted Republican Senator John Heinz of Pennsylvania in an effort to persuade the banking committee to conduct an investigation into the whole savings and loan fiasco. They wanted a special select committee appointed. Although Kerry told no one outside his staff, the special committee was a Trojan horse. His plan was to use the panel to finish up the investigation into BCCI. Creating a select committee required approval of the Senate leadership, so Kerry and Heinz took the idea to Senate Majority Leader George Mitchell. At a meeting with several Democratic leaders in the Capitol, it turned out that there was no more enthusiasm for delving into the savings and loan mess than there had been for examining BCCI. Too many Democrats had already turned out to be vulnerable to charges of favoritism and worse in connection with the $500 billion S&L scandal. Kerry figured he would have to find a way to go public through his subcommittee on terrorism and narcotics after all.

Kerry's staff had sensed a turning point in their long battle in May 1990. On May 15, the bank had turned over 775 pages of its records on the Manuel Noriega accounts. According to a later indictment, the accounts traced $23 million of Noriega's funds through various BCCI branches and into another institution, the Middle East Bank in London. Some of the money also appeared to have passed through Syed Akbar's Capcom Financial Services.

In providing the documents that they had denied existed for months,

BCCI attorneys Robert Altman and Ray Banoun explained to David McKean and Jonathan Winer of Kerry's staff that the bank had not discovered the material earlier because it had relied on Amjad Awan's assertion that there were no more documents. Only when the lawyers had gone to London themselves did they discover the Noriega documents. It was an argument that did not play well with the two young Senate investigators. After all, almost exactly a year before, NBC investigative reporter Brian Ross had aired a report in which he described some of the very documents that were only now being turned over to the Senate in response to 1988 subpoenas.

McKean, a Duke University law school graduate who had become Kerry's most trusted investigator on BCCI since Jack Blum's departure, sensed that turning over the documents was a watershed moment for the bank and for Robert Altman personally. For months and months, Altman had been cocky and almost insolent in his dealings with Kerry's staff. On the afternoon of May 15, McKean had the strong impression that some of the starch had been knocked out of Clark Clifford's protégé.

Kerry and his staff continued to be frustrated in attempts to obtain additional overseas BCCI records through the Justice Department. The Tampa prosecutors had refused to share the material and bucked the matter up to main Justice in Washington. There the subcommittee was stonewalled. A schedule had been drawn up for four days of hearings in the summer of 1990. The extensive public sessions would examine the bank's covert acquisition of U.S. banks, its money-laundering practices, its relationship with Noriega, and whether the January 1990 plea bargain with the bank had served the interests of justice. Among the witnesses would be Clark Clifford, Robert Altman, and Ray Banoun. Somehow, Kerry's staff thought, they would get Pell's permission. On July 24, the Justice Department wrote to Kerry that it would not participate in the hearings because they would deal with matters that were under litigation. At the time, the jury in Tampa was deliberating and the verdict was returned five days later, so there were no Senate hearings that summer.

There had been little appetite for a full-scale investigation of BCCI from the start. Some people believed it was partly the result of Clark Clifford's soothing assurances to political and governmental leaders that there was nothing wrong with the bank. Then Clifford emerged as a potential principal in the scandal, rather than simply a lawyer. The result was a new level of resistance in the Senate and elsewhere in Washington. And somewhere within the Senate a spy was passing secrets to BCCI's lawyers.

Along with a star-studded team of Washington lawyers, the bank employed Holland & Knight, one of the leading law firms in Miami. On

September 24, 1990, a lawyer at the firm named Roma Theus II, a specialist in white-collar crime, wrote an extraordinary memo in which he recounted meeting with a "highly reliable, confidential source." According to the memo, the source said that Altman and Banoun had called in "political markers" and expected to quash subpoenas that the Kerry committee had issued for their testimony.

In the three-page memo, the lawyer's unidentified source proved to have extremely detailed knowledge of the inner workings of the Kerry investigation. The source said that Kerry's staff believed that false representations had been made about bank documents and that the staff was deeply concerned about the overlapping ownership between BCCI, First American, and other institutions. "The source stated bluntly that the Kerry Committee is on a 'crusade,'" wrote Theus.

The memo said that the source emphasized that the matters he was revealing were extraordinarily sensitive and confidential. Accordingly, Theus did not give any hints about the identity of his confidential source. It was clear from the source's extensive knowledge that a spy was lurking somewhere in the Senate. However, the memo itself was not discovered until the middle of 1991 and the identity of the source remained a secret.

Testifying before a Senate committee was the last thing that Clark Clifford or Robert Altman wanted to do in the fall of 1990. Clifford was just completing work on his monumental memoir of his years at and near the center of power in Washington. He wanted the adulation he felt he had earned over the past four decades, not a challenge to his reputation in a public forum. Already, his public role in the BCCI scandal had been altered by one bout with bad press.

In May 1990 a lengthy article about possible ties between First American and BCCI had appeared in *Regardie's*, a slick business publication in Washington known for its irreverence and investigative zeal. The article, by free-lancer Larry Gurwin, detailed the backgrounds of the Arab investors who owned First American's parent company and their links to BCCI as customers and borrowers. It raised the specter of Clifford as a front man for BCCI's interests, witting or unwitting. But it stopped well short of accusing Clifford of any wrongdoing. Nor did it charge that BCCI owned the city's biggest banking company.

Editor Brian Kelly and the magazine's owner, Bill Regardie, had published the article despite an all-out campaign by First American, Clifford, and Robert Altman to squelch it. Soon after Gurwin had started work on the piece in the fall of 1989, one of the bank's lawyers had written to him and Kelly warning that they would find no basis to allege that BCCI owned or controlled First American. Many other letters from lawyers followed. Near the publication date, former Democratic Congressman Michael Barnes, then a lawyer with Ray Banoun's firm, had telephoned Bill Regardie to express concerns about the upcoming article. But it was all to no avail. The article ran as scheduled, with an ominous picture of Sheik Zayed on the cover.

The opposition John Kerry ran into was more subtle. No one had suggested to Kerry that he stop his investigation of BCCI and its links to First American. However, there were snide comments about the attacks on Clifford and digs at Kerry for questioning the word of the august lawyer. Despite his age, Clifford remained a power in Washington and he would not be brought low easily. Part of the power stemmed from his access to political contributions. He was a close friend and adviser to Pamela Harriman, a major fund-raiser for Democrats. And Clifford and the partners in his law firm contributed to politicians in both parties. Even Kerry had received a $1,000 contribution from Clifford.

All Kerry would say later about the remarks was that it was an uncomfortable period for him, yet the Massachusetts senator never called off McKean and Winer. And then in March, the Fed's order added new vigor to his pursuit of BCCI and once more Kerry began to press for Senate hearings on the broadening bank scandal.

The Fed's order had a different effect on the investigation being conducted by Robert Morgenthau's office. Suddenly the Justice Department stopped its cooperation with the New York prosecutor.

In January 1991, Moscow had gone to Washington for meetings with senior officials at the Justice Department. He offered to share information being gleaned from his grand jury investigation. He knew that the Justice Department had started work on the criminal referral from the Federal Reserve and, in exchange, he wanted some of the information being dug up in Washington. Morgenthau's office often cooperated with federal agencies, so the request did not seem extraordinary, but the department refused to cooperate. They wanted no information from Morgenthau's office. They would provide none to the New York prosecutors.

"As we went along, the federal government grew less and less helpful," explained Morgenthau. "Maybe because they saw we were getting somewhere."

Although they report to the Justice Department, United States attorneys have a measure of freedom and independence. Over the previous year, the U.S. attorney's office in Tampa had shared a substantial amount of information with Moscow and his investigators. Mark Jackowski and Mike Rubinstein had provided copies of records and transcripts. The prosecutors and the Customs supervisors had discussed avenues for New York to pursue within its jurisdiction and relations were generally cordial.

Snags had cropped up at various points. Jackowski had refused to share a computerized index of the 2,000 tape recordings and other evidence that he prepared, claiming it was confidential. And Rubinstein had been caught in a well-intentioned lie about the existence of the Amer Lodhi tapes. When Morgenthau's office first asked for the sixteen hours of tapes that had been made with Jack Blum's assistance in March of 1989, Rubinstein had said there were no such recordings. The New York investigators were stunned because they had been told of the tapes by Lodhi himself. Yet Rubinstein believed that he was honoring the commitment of confidentiality to Lodhi. Even when Moscow provided a written release of the tapes from Lodhi, Rubinstein resisted because the name of another confidential informant was mentioned several times on the tapes.

The Tampa prosecutors also had refused to allow Morgenthau's men to interview Amjad Awan or any of the other convicted bankers. The feds said that they had not interviewed the bankers yet, and they were not about to have investigators from another jurisdiction in there first. There were good legal reasons for this, but there was also an element of turf protection.

Despite the refusal to share the convicted bankers with Morgenthau, the Tampa prosecutors were still sharing other information with them, and relations between the two offices remained cordial. As recently as March 6, 1991, Richard Preiss, an assistant district attorney in New York, and Andrew Finan, a senior investigator, had interviewed Bob Mazur for several hours in Tampa about other leads he had picked up during Operation C-Chase.

A week later, the cooperation ended. In a one-paragraph letter dated March 15, Mike Rubinstein told the New York prosecutors that any requests for information on the BCCI case had to go through the fraud section at the Justice Department in Washington.

"We called the Feds," said Morgenthau. "They told us to call Tony Leffert. We called for three weeks with no answer. Finally, we faxed him a letter asking him to answer his phone. He called back and said he would take the letter under advisement."

Clearly the order had come down from main Justice, although no one would acknowledge it. Rubinstein did not provide a reason for shutting off cooperation, and Morgenthau could get none out of Justice. The answer may be found, however, by examining the timing of the letter.

Before March 1991, the BCCI case remained a sleeper as far as the world's press was concerned. There had been isolated articles in the U.S. press, such as the May 1990 *Regardie's* article and a page-one story in *The Wall Street Journal* a few days later.

All that had changed after the Federal Reserve ordered BCCI to sell its hidden stake in First American. Suddenly, the case was getting serious attention in the world press, including the paper read by all the top U.S. officials. After the Fed order, *The Washington Post* had done a major front-page story reconstructing how the Justice Department had allegedly dragged its heels on following up additional leads about the bank. At the same time, the Fed had focused new attention on Clark Clifford and stories appeared in every major newspaper in the country questioning his role with BCCI and First American. Stung by the criticism and always turf conscious anyway, the Justice Department had no intention of allowing a New York County prosecutor to take the lead in what had become the most highly publicized banking case of the new decade.

Along with questioning Clark Clifford's assertion that he was unaware of any secret ownership of his bank by BCCI, the press began asking why the Justice Department had seemingly failed to follow up on the allegations uncovered about BCCI's links to First American during C-Chase. Suddenly, the Justice Department got very interested in talking to Amjad Awan, Akbar Bilgrami, and their compatriots.

"My client had sat for months and been shifted from prison to prison and no one wanted to interview him about cooperation," maintained John Hume, who had taken on Awan's appeal without pay.

Then the ex-bankers found themselves back in Florida, undergoing extensive questioning by federal prosecutors. Not only were they answering questions from the Tampa prosecutors, they were talking to federal prosecutors from Washington who were investigating the Federal Reserve criminal referral regarding the secret ownership of First American. And they were interviewed by prosecutors handling the federal investigation into the collapse of CenTrust Savings in Miami.

Mark Jackowski had transferred to the United States attorney's office in Denver. For Mike Rubinstein and his new partner in Tampa, William Jung, the questioning of the bankers covered ground first plowed during Operation C-Chase. Clues that the money-laundering scheme was countenanced higher up in BCCI had surfaced during Mazur's original undercover operation. Indeed, he had written numerous memos begging for help to follow the trail in the many different directions it seemed to head. Only now, with extensive help from Awan and Bilgrami, were Rubinstein and Jung able to begin assembling the evidence that would lead to the highest reaches of BCCI.

Awan was describing meetings with Swaleh Naqvi and other BCCI officials at which transfers of Manuel Noriega's money and various drug accounts were discussed. It was not as good as having Bob Mazur and his James Bond briefcase on the scene, but the information that Awan was providing could be corroborated with the evidence obtained during the undercover probe.

Gregory Kehoe, the first assistant U.S. attorney in Tampa, maintained that the intention was always to go after other bankers and drug dealers with the cooperation of the convicted bankers. Backed by Jackowski and Rubinstein, Kehoe said they were simply waiting for the right time. Kehoe said he wanted the ex-bankers softened up and ready to tell everything in the hopes of getting out of jail sooner. No longer condo convicts, permitted to lounge in their own apartments, they were doing hard time. Separated from their friends and facing up to twelve years in jail, Kehoe reasoned the defendants would be more willing to tell everything they knew.

Other evidence indicates that the BCCI investigation was accorded a low priority in the U.S. attorney's office in Tampa and virtually no priority within main Justice. Only after the wave of publicity surrounding the Fed's order against BCCI on First American did the Tampa prosecutors and their counterparts from other jurisdictions begin seeking the cooperation of Awan and the others. And then there was the matter of Bob Mazur's resignation from the Customs Service.

In March 1991, Bob Mazur decided to quit. He quietly arranged to go over to the Drug Enforcement Administration and then, on April 3, sent an explosive letter of resignation to Carol Hallett, the Customs commissioner in Washington. In that letter, Mazur complained that the federal government in Washington, primarily his own agency, had been too slow to follow up on leads about BCCI generated during C-Chase. Had more resources and a higher priority been given to the investigation, he maintained, indictments would have reached far higher into the bank. He said that his many requests for additional help, including the suggestion of an international task force, had been rejected at every level. Further, said Mazur, his supervisor had taken his repeated complaints personally and responded by harassing him and threatening to transfer him.

It was a bitter missive, one that Bonni Tischler later rejected as totally unfair and untrue. She maintained that she had provided Mazur and C-Chase with all the resources necessary. Within days of his resignation, Bob Mazur, the man who had brought off the biggest undercover case in the history of the Customs Service, was in a training program to become a Drug Enforcement Administration agent and hoping to go undercover again.

The resignation climaxed frustrations that had been experienced by

Mazur, the other Customs agents, and Mark Jackowski since the conviction of the bankers. They had expected to resume investigating the bank with renewed vigor, and with lots of help. On January 30, 1991, Jackowski had written a "road map" for other prosecutors on how to continue pursuing the leads that had come out of C-Chase. Critical to the next phase, said the memo, was a thorough examination of all the BCCI records seized in the October 1988 raids. Pressed by the trial and a shortage of agents, boxes of bank records had never even been examined. But Jackowski also expressed serious reservations about whether the Customs Service would support a continued investigation. Jackowski then transferred to the U.S. attorney's office in Denver, citing personal reasons.

Mazur's resignation and Jackowski's transfer seemed to point to what at least those two veteran law enforcement agents felt was a federal failure to pursue the BCCI case. It was a failure that was remedied, but only after the Justice Department was forced to act in response to criticism in the press and rising concern in Congress. And in finally moving to claim the BCCI case as its own, the Justice Department stopped its help to Robert Morgenthau at a critical moment in the New York County prosecutor's investigation.

In the spring of 1991, Morgenthau, Moscow, and their investigators were ready to move to the third stage. They had determined that a broad scheme of fraud could be proved. Now they needed to find more witnesses and documents to prove it. It would have helped to talk to Amjad Awan. The effort would have been speeded up with Amer Lodhi's tapes as a guide to corruption inside the bank, but they had gone ahead without that assistance.

For nearly two years, Moscow had been presenting evidence to the grand juries that met regularly for thirty-day sessions. Now he needed a longer session so that the jurors could grasp the complexity of the scheme and understand the crimes that Moscow felt he could now prove. So in April 1991, he was granted authority by a New York judge to empanel a special grand jury to investigate BCCI for as long as it took to make a case.

By this juncture, John Moscow was confident, even cocky in private moments as he contemplated the emerging criminal case, with or without federal assistance. He had seen the Price Waterhouse audits describing the bank's hidden ownership of First American and they had pushed him well into the second phase of the investigation. Material was flowing into the office from many sources. Much of it helped; some just boggled the mind. In the latter category was a fifteen-hour tape recording of a BCCI annual conference.

"Absolute mind rot," Moscow called it after sampling an hour of Abedi's rhetoric. "This is a cult, not a bank."

Moscow sensed some intimidation of his sources. He had learned that a 1981 article from the liberal British journal *New Statesman* was circulating among current and former BCCI employees. The article described the beating and rape of a BCCI banker by a group of Pakistani soldiers after the man had left the bank and threatened to disclose adverse information about it to authorities.

When he was more naive about BCCI, Moscow had asked one of its employees how the bank made money.

"By taking deposits," replied the banker.

"But how can you make money just by taking deposits?" asked Moscow. He found, in his words, that "the conversation deteriorated rapidly after that." But by the spring of 1991 the prosecutor had found out for himself.

Often he and some of the investigators on the case would slip out for hurried lunches at basement restaurants in nearby Chinatown. The conversations over Szechuan beef and twice-cooked pork invariably turned to BCCI.

"What is a bank?" Moscow asked one day. "You give it your money. It pays you interest and it makes loans at a higher interest. That's how it makes money. But BCCI doesn't make long-term loans."

As the outlines of the Ponzi scheme became clearer, Moscow's ruminations became more pointed. "Why do you target central bank deposits?" he would ask, referring to the large cash reserves available from government banks in many countries. "Because they're the only ones with enough money to keep you going."

Analyze the structure of the bank, he said. Ask what it is for. You are offshore to everybody. Sure, you can hide accounts from law enforcement and from tax collectors. But you can also hide bad assets from your own auditors. Two legally separate holding companies, each based in an offshore banking haven, each with separate auditors. The more he learned, the more certain Moscow became that this was the world's biggest financial scandal.

"Take the largest single savings and loan fraud," he said one day. "This is ten times bigger."

"Ten times two billion?" asked a companion incredulously.

Moscow just grinned.

With the new grand jury, Moscow and Richard Preiss were delving into evidence that bribes were paid to officials of Peru's central bank in exchange for $250 million in deposits in 1986 and 1987. At that time, Alan Garcia was president of Peru and more than a quarter of the nation's cash had been deposited in a secret account at BCCI's Panama branch. The government believed money was placed in BCCI as part of a scheme to hide the country's hard currency after foreign banks threatened to seize Peru's assets when Garcia stopped paying the country's foreign debt.

Such large deposits, Moscow believed, were vital to BCCI because they helped cover the trading losses and bad loans that were threatening to topple the Ponzi pyramid. The bank apparently was so desperate for money that it had been willing to pay substantial bribes to Peruvian officials to obtain the deposits.

On May 23, 1991, John Kerry finally got a public hearing on the Bank of Credit and Commerce International. He had persuaded Senator Riegle to approve a limited session before a banking subcommittee. The official subject matter was proposed legislation to grant the Federal Reserve Board new powers to regulate foreign banks operating in the United States. The real topic was the regulatory oversight of BCCI and the behavior of the Justice Department.

Sidney Bailey, the Virginia banking regulator, was the first witness. When asked why he had opposed the takeover of Financial General in 1981, he responded with blunt country humor: "You can't send the sheriff after them." He also testified that he felt too much of what was being said by Clark Clifford and others was accepted at face value by the decision makers in Washington.

"A lot was being taken because if he says it's so it must be so," drawled Bailey in his gravelly voice.

Virgil Mattingly and William Taylor testified about the lingering suspicions about BCCI and First American and the difficulty in gaining access to records that showed the true relationship. They said there had been a concerted effort to keep information from the agency for years and such concealment was the subject of an ongoing investigation and criminal referrals to the Justice Department.

Among the criminal referrals was information regarding the true ownership of Independence Bank in Encino, California. Just three weeks before the Kerry hearing, the Fed had issued an order demanding that BCCI sell off its shares of Independence Bank. The Fed said it had uncovered evidence that Independence had been acquired by BCCI through Saudi tycoon Ghaith Pharaon. A Fed official said that the acquisition had been pulled off through a series of loans and other transactions similar to those arranged with the investors in First American. While Pharaon protested adamantly that he owned 100 percent of the California bank, BCCI agreed to the order without saying whether it did or did not actually control the institution.

It was late in the afternoon of the all-day hearing when the star witness moved to the witness table in front of Kerry and the two other senators in the room, Democrat Alan Dixon of Illinois and Republican Alfonse D'Amato of New York. The witness was Robert Morgenthau. Seated behind him, in the first row of the audience, was John Moscow. Near the back of the room sat Jack Blum.

Morgenthau's prepared remarks addressed the proposed new powers for the Federal Reserve. He praised the legislation and urged its passage as a way of piercing the bank secrecy laws that had protected BCCI and other banks. This was a mild appetizer for the entree.

Under gently prodding questions from Kerry, Morgenthau said that the Justice Department had refused to cooperate with his investigation into BCCI. He said that his progress had been slowed by the Justice Department's refusal to grant him access to key witnesses and its rejection of his offer to share information.

"We run many cooperative investigations with federal agencies," Morgenthau testified. "This is the exception, not the rule."

Paul Maloney, a lawyer at the Justice Department who had no background in the BCCI investigation, followed Morgenthau to the witness table. He had the unenviable task of persuading Kerry that the department had not impeded Morgenthau's probe or tried to slow Kerry's own investigation. He said the department was willing to cooperate with Morgenthau and other agencies.

"There are, however, some procedural matters that may prevent a full exchange of information, at least at this time," he said.

Maloney did not go into any details, but he said that the Justice Department was pursuing additional investigations of BCCI through several U.S. attorneys' offices. Seated beside him at the table was Robert Genzman, who had replaced Bob Merkle as U.S. attorney in Tampa. Genzman assured Kerry and the other senators still in the room that his office was investigating more BCCI leads stemming from Operation C-Chase. But neither man found a sympathetic ear.

Senator Kerry's anger at the Justice Department was evident. His investigation had been stonewalled by the department, he complained. He found it hard to imagine that the department was pursuing BCCI aggressively. Morgenthau himself was convinced that the Justice Department had been uninterested in ferreting out the entire BCCI story since the indictments in October 1988. Perhaps it was the focus on Noriega. Perhaps it was that no one cared much about a complicated bank fraud case. Certainly at that point, no one could see the true extent of the corruption and the potential global impact, although Jack Blum had had a pretty good eye for the scope of the scandal more than two years earlier.

By the time of Maloney's testimony in late May of 1991, the Justice Department was beginning to take the BCCI case more seriously. Investigations were being conducted by federal grand juries in Washington, Miami, Tampa, and Atlanta. After months of lingering in cells, Awan and Bilgrami were being questioned extensively by prosecutors and federal agents. But it was late and, as the scope of BCCI's corruption began to emerge, criticism mounted that the Justice Department and other federal agencies had ignored obvious leads about the bank until forced to act.

CHAPTER TWENTY-TWO

A World of Unreality

On Friday, June 28, 1991, the Bank of England notified the Federal Reserve Board that a new Price Waterhouse audit had been received. The audit virtually forced the authorities in Britain, Luxembourg, and the Cayman Islands to take control of the principal banks in the BCCI group. Alerting the Federal Reserve was vital. The seizure of a global bank operating around the clock in seventy countries would have to be executed with great care to avoid disrupting the banking world on an international scale.

The decision to begin planning the global shutdown of BCCI had been made that morning in London by the two top officials of the Bank of England, Robin Leigh-Pemberton and Eddie George. There had been consultations with officials in Luxembourg and the Cayman Islands. The new report by Price Waterhouse made the shutdown a foregone conclusion unless a massive new infusion of cash could be arranged secretly and immediately from Abu Dhabi. Price Waterhouse had been working for the Bank of England as its examiners under special provisions of British law. This new inquiry into the bank had been authorized by the regulators after the results of Price Waterhouse's October 1990 report. The latest and most startling findings had been turned over to the regulators on June 27. That night, Eddie George, the deputy governor, had taken the report home with him when he left work. What he had read was a regulator's nightmare, and George had not slept well.

Ordered by the regulators to perform a full audit and permitted far broader access to records by the bank's new owners, the accountants had discovered what they referred to in the report as a secret "bank within a bank." They found evidence of massive and complex fraud at BCCI. There were huge losses. Perhaps $5 billion. Perhaps twice or even three times that amount. It was so hard to tell because the losses had been systematically covered up for years through an endless array of accounting tricks and outright fraud. There were fictitious deposits and loans, thousands of unrecorded transactions, falsified records.

Years of financial manipulations at the Bank of Credit and Commerce International constituted what Price Waterhouse described as "probably one of the most complex deceptions in banking history" in service of an effort to conceal "total losses of several billions of dollars."

In all, more than 6,000 documents were uncovered and attributed to the secret bank within the bank. According to the report, Swaleh Naqvi himself had held these files, and the auditors said it appeared that he had done little more for years than manage the hidden bank. Deposits were taken in but not recorded on the books. The funds were then used to cover up losses in bad loans and trading operations. When customers wanted to withdraw the unrecorded deposits, further deposits were taken and went unbooked. The potential spiral was endless. From the books, Price Waterhouse said it appeared possible that the bank had never earned a profit in its nineteen-year history. Yet it had grown enormously and reported robust earnings until the late 1980s—$108 million in 1982, $136 million in 1983, $234 million in 1984. The report's assertion that these may have been the result of manipulating the books was a classic description of a Ponzi scheme, only on a grander scale than any such swindle in history.

The Price Waterhouse report of June 1991 itself was an unusual document, for it went beyond the usual dry rhetoric and numbers associated with financial audits. An attempt was made to explain how Agha Hasan Abedi's dream of building the world's biggest bank had gone so far astray.

The report placed the blame on Abedi and Swaleh Naqvi, accusing them of making the strategic decisions to manipulate accounts and ordering other employees to carry out their plans. Price Waterhouse said the scale and complexity of the deception was so vast that most senior managers were or should have been aware of at least certain elements of what was going on.

The report proposed several answers to the question of why bank officers had not blown the whistle on the manipulations at BCCI. Many of them, it said, received substantial loans from the bank that were not repaid so long as they remained with the bank. Others had been paid off in different ways. The report charged that Syed Akbar had taken secret documents detailing the fraud within the bank when he left in 1986 and it said he was later paid $32 million in hush money. As for the board of directors, the accountants said that they served mainly as a rubber stamp for Abedi and Naqvi, taken in by trust and loyalty.

"Many simply followed instructions they should have questioned," said Price Waterhouse. "Failure to do so appears to have arisen from a blind loyalty to Abedi and Naqvi brought about by the cultural background where it was unthinkable to question."

In the end, Price Waterhouse concluded, the fraud was so widespread that determining the total loss was impossible: "There is insufficient information available with which to re-create the bank's accounts with the knowledge that is now available. But on the basis of the losses which have been concealed, it would appear that the bank has generated significant losses over the last decade, and may never have been profitable in its entire history."

Later, Ian Brindle, the senior partner in the Price Waterhouse office in London, would describe the task that confronted the auditors in reconstructing BCCI this way: "It was like doing a huge jigsaw puzzle where you don't have the picture, just the pieces sitting there, thousands of pieces. Over time you get an idea of what the picture looks like, but it gets ever more difficult. You are dealing with deception and manipulation of information both inside and outside the company."

When Eddie George telephoned Bill Taylor, the top banking regulator at the Federal Reserve in Washington on June 28 with word of the audit, Taylor had promised to be on the first plane to London.

Leaving Fed general counsel Virgil Mattingly, Jr., to handle the American end of preparations for the shutdown, Taylor and a small team of Fed officials from Washington and New York had flown to London for a series of meetings with their counterparts at the Bank of England. On July 2, a Tuesday, the Americans and British sat down at Bank of England headquarters on Threadneedle Street with officials from the Cayman Islands, France, Luxembourg, Spain, and Switzerland to discuss how to wind down the operations of BCCI.

The session lasted all day. At the start, there was talk of approaching Sheik Zayed bin Sultan al-Nahayan of Abu Dhabi for another massive cash infusion to bail out the bank. One of the world's richest men, Zayed had already pumped $1 billion into BCCI since becoming its principal shareholder in 1990 in an effort to salvage it, but the fraud described by the latest Price Waterhouse report was deemed so pervasive that there was no hope of eradicating it. The remainder of the day was spent discussing the timing and strategy for bringing down the bank.

This in itself was no small matter. BCCI's tentacles extended to every corner of the globe and the massive step being planned would ripple through the world's financial system in a matter of minutes. This was the era of twenty-four-hour stock markets and global dependence and that system was about to get a major test.

319

The Federal Reserve was concerned about the potential for disrupting the U.S. banking markets and the dollar-based payment and clearing systems around the world. While BCCI's banking activities in the United States were minimal at this point, a large portion of its dealings worldwide were conducted in dollars. The Fed wanted the seizure to occur when American banks were closed and accounts among institutions dealing with BCCI had been settled for the day.

Another danger was that the seizure would set off a run on other banks in the Persian Gulf, where BCCI was a major player and tied to the royal families of several nations. The regulators felt that the herd mentality of bank customers had been demonstrated countless times over the years. Officials worried that declaring BCCI insolvent could spark fears about all Gulf banks. Many of these banks maintained major operations in London, Paris, and New York, which meant their troubles could ricochet through Western financial capitals.

Over the course of Tuesday and Wednesday, the regulators determined that the best time to close the bank was at the close of business in the United States on Friday, July 5. It would be night in Europe and the bank would simply be stopped from opening over the weekend.

On Wednesday night, Bill Taylor flew home to brief Mattingly and top officials at the U.S. Treasury Department and the Office of the Comptroller of the Currency. He left a senior regulator, Steve Schemering, behind to work with the special unit of officials from all seven countries that would coordinate the action from London.

A career regulator who had been consumed by the BCCI investigation for months, Taylor was at his desk in Washington on the Fourth of July when he got word from Schemering that the seizure could not wait until the end of business in New York on Friday. The BCCI management was meeting July 5 in Luxembourg and the regulators wanted to act before they offered up a new restructuring that might force a delay. With just hours until the deadline, Taylor contacted Fed officials in New York and Los Angeles and informed them of the new schedule.

There would later be criticism that the international regulators had acted prematurely and should have waited for a new proposal from the Abu Dhabi government, but the Price Waterhouse report had convinced everyone who had read it that closing the bank was inevitable and urgent.

The coordinated shutdown of the Bank of Credit and Commerce was announced at eight-thirty in the morning New York time on July 5, 1991. BCCI's remaining American offices in New York and Los Angeles were taken over by bank examiners. Many of BCCI branches in Britain had been closed in recent months as part of the layoffs and restructuring ordered by Abu Dhabi. At one o'clock in the afternoon London time, Bank of England officials walked into the bank's remaining twenty-five branches, most of them in the London area, and ordered employees to leave.

The actions of the seven countries set off a chain reaction. By the end of the weekend, BCCI's operations had been closed in eighteen countries around the world and operations were placed under close supervision in dozens of others. The effect of the seizures was to place the assets and liabilities of BCCI banks and branches worldwide under protective control of the regulators and, in some cases, the courts. Bank accounts large and small were frozen. Receivers would be appointed to sort out the scrambled finances of the bank and eventually dole out what remained to thousands of creditors.

For nearly two decades, BCCI had fed off the illusion that a bottomless reservoir of Arab wealth stood behind the bank. Now that illusion was being shattered.

Two days after the coordinated swoop on the bank, the British ambassador to Abu Dhabi relayed a request from the Bank of England. The British wanted the sheikdom to cover the losses suffered by the bank's depositors worldwide. The normally friendly relations between Britain and Sheik Zayed had been strained by the abrupt seizure. Abu Dhabi's first reaction to the takeover was an attack on the regulators for not consulting them in advance. Had the regulators permitted the bank's restructuring to continue, including the infusion of a planned $5 billion, "no depositors' money would have been lost," said the government's statement.

As if to thumb its nose at the British regulators, Abu Dhabi kept open the seventeen branches of the Bank of Credit and Commerce–Emirates, which was forty percent owned by BCCI and served customers in all seven of the tiny city-states comprising the United Arab Emirates. The possibility was that the bank there would form the nucleus of a regrouping effort for the entire bank. And there seemed no doubt that Sheik Zayed, a proud ruler known for generosity to his citizens, would make sure that no customers in the Gulf lost money in the collapse. Efforts also were planned by Abu Dhabi to salvage the bank's three branches in Pakistan.

On July 8, top banking officials from Abu Dhabi arrived in London for consultations with the Bank of England and other international regulators over what would happen to the Bank of Credit and Commerce International. The Abu Dhabi officials wanted an explanation for the decision to seize the bank's assets without prior consultation with them.

When a reporter for London's *Financial Times* asked one of them whether Abu Dhabi would continue supporting the bank worldwide, the reply was, "What is there to support now that the Bank of England has moved in?"

Anger was in evidence elsewhere, too. BCCI employees in Britain staged demonstrations outside the court hearing the Bank of England's request for permission to liquidate local operations of BCCI. They accused the regulators of moving too swiftly and of ignoring equally pressing problems at British banks. The most violent outbreak occurred in Hong Kong, where BCCI customers clashed with police.

In Pakistan, the events of July 5 were perceived as part of a Western conspiracy against BCCI in particular and the Third World in general. Had it been an American or European bank, they believed, the difficulties would have been worked out quietly behind closed doors.

"The West never wanted a Muslim bank to grow so big because most of the big banks are run by Jews," Asif Ali, a retired engineer waiting outside the Karachi branch, told a reporter.

Another Pakistani, construction company owner Jashed Omar, described his reaction to another reporter by saying: "Shutting down BCCI was a classic case of overreaction. This bank gave Pakistanis a sense of participation in world finance. I think BCCI was a threat to some powerful people outside this country and it was singled out unfairly."

Others saw ghosts of conspiracies. Still, the questions that they asked should not be ignored.

"If there was a problem with drug money, it is the same problem that is found at every other big bank," said Rais Khan, an automobile dealer in Karachi. "What about Swiss bank accounts? Don't you think drug money, Mafia money, finishes up in Swiss banks? Isn't there money laundering in American banks?"

Not far from downtown Karachi was the guarded, walled compound on a dusty road where Agha Hasan Abedi was still struggling to recuperate from his heart attacks and a stroke. It was not the home of a man who exhibited great wealth. There was a large house flanked by two cottages, one of which was home to Abedi's aged mother.

The Sunday after the seizure of the bank, two Pakistani newspapers ran stories about the reactions of a man who was viewed there as a victim, not a victimizer. The articles portrayed Abedi as a man in failing health, unable to remember many events about the bank, unable to speak in full sentences. Abedi was able, however, to deny any responsibility for what had happened to his bank.

"God knows better," he told one of the reporters.

There was reason not to believe the worst about Abedi and BCCI in

Pakistan, neighboring Bangladesh, and other poor countries in Asia and Africa.

Over the years, BCCI had been a banker of last resort to businessmen and others who were ignored by the established international banks. BCCI's employees understood the local culture and customs and seemed willing to take risks based on a common bond of trust and belief in Third World development. The bank cultivated the image of a visionary bank. It used charitable organizations and respected figures to create a model for the dreams of developing nations and their citizens. When the collapse came, it was these customers and those nations that lost the most. As with the unquestioning employees cited in the last Price Waterhouse report, trust and loyalty were betrayed.

For Abedi, there was to be more bad news a few weeks later. And again, it would come from the West.

Word was leaked first to the television stations. They needed the extra time to arrange for camera crews, so they were alerted about eleven o'clock on a Sunday night in late July that something big was on tap for eleven the next morning at the offices of New York District Attorney Robert Morgenthau.

Throughout the morning of Monday, July 29, 1991, camera crews loaded their videocameras, sound packs, and cables into the creaking elevator and rode up to the eighth floor. They hefted the tools of their trade down the dingy marble hallway, past photographs of 200 years' worth of glaring district attorneys. Inside the narrow office of the district attorney, more than fifty journalists and technicians jostled for position as the bright TV lights bathed the cluttered desk in harsh light.

At eleven o'clock, Robert Morgenthau walked into the room and sat down at his desk. With him, dressed in their best suits, were the men who were leading his investigation into BCCI. John Moscow wore a shiny blue-gray suit and electric blue shirt. Andrew Rosenzweig, a former private investigator turned chief of investigations for the DA, wore a conservative brown suit. Alongside him was the bulky senior investigator, Andrew Finan, in a well-cut suit.

"A New York County grand jury has returned an indictment that charges that the Bank of Credit and Commerce International, its related entities, and two of its founders engaged in a multibillion dollar scheme to defraud its depositors, falsified bank records to hide illegal money laundering, and committed larcenies totaling more than $30 million," Morgenthau said, reading from the prepared press release.

"This indictment spells out the largest bank fraud in world financial history," he continued. "BCCI was operated as a corrupt criminal organization throughout its entire nineteen-year history. It systematically falsified its records. It knowingly allowed itself to be used to launder the illegal income of drug sellers and other criminals. And it paid bribes and kickbacks to public officials."

The long-awaited other shoe had dropped. The indictment charged BCCI, Agha Abedi, and Swaleh Naqvi with crimes far broader than those contained in the federal indictment in Tampa nearly two years earlier. The seizure of the bank worldwide had provided Morgenthau with the last piece of evidence he needed for his charges, for the seizure had demonstrated that BCCI customers were going to lose huge sums of money as a result of the years of fraud and deception.

The top charge in the twelve-count indictment accused Abedi and Naqvi of grand larceny in defrauding customers by misrepresenting the bank's ownership and financial condition. Among the victims listed was American Express Bank, which stood to lose $30 million of its money that was on deposit with BCCI when the bank was seized on July 5. A key section of the charge supplied Morgenthau's jurisdiction. It said that the bank and its officials had provided false statements on its financial condition to the superintendent of banks for the State of New York.

The bank also was accused of paying $3 million in bribes to senior officials of the central bank of Peru to obtain $250 million in deposits in 1986 and 1987. The indictment did not name the officials, but in his press conference Morgenthau identified them as Hector Neyra, the central bank of Peru's former general manager, and Leonel Figueroa, former head of the central bank's board of directors. Abedi and Naqvi were accused of instructing bank employees to open a bank account with a Swiss bank in Panama to transmit the bribes and kickbacks to the Peruvian officials.

And the grand jury accused the bank's New York agency office of failing to report cash deposits in excess of $10,000 on each of at least eight occasions. This last charge, said the indictment, constituted money laundering. Americans were not allowed to deposit money at the agency office, but it could conduct transactions for foreign nationals. Whoever deposited the allegedly dirty dollars was not identified.

"This largest of Ponzi schemes is over," said Morgenthau. "But we have much yet to discover about this bank, and much to do in reforming international banking practices. The key to the scheme was that BCCI was structured in such a way so that no single central bank was able to monitor its activities. No foreign bank should be permitted to operate in the United States unless it is supervised by a single, strong central bank and is not protected by bank secrecy laws of another jurisdiction. Without these reforms, the potential for massive worldwide bank fraud remains."

In response to a reporter's question, Morgenthau estimated that his investigation was only twenty to twenty-five percent done, but he declined to speculate on what remained to be covered.

Morgenthau thanked the staffs of the state banking superintendent and the Federal Reserve in Washington and New York for their assistance. He even had kind words for the Bank of England, saying that once they found a way to do so legally, the British regulators had shared important information. Missing from the list of those thanked was the U.S. Department of Justice.

In Washington, Assistant Attorney General Robert Mueller III, the Justice Department official who had taken over the federal investigations into BCCI in July, issued a statement saying that the department had "fully supported" the work of Morgenthau and provided substantial information. Yet shortly before, senior officials at Justice had tried to stop the Federal Reserve from coordinating a major announcement of its own with Morgenthau's indictment. The Fed, however, had refused.

So at the same time Morgenthau was unveiling his indictment, the Federal Reserve Board in Washington released the charges resulting to date from its massive investigation into BCCI. They were as stunning and far-reaching as those of Morgenthau. And they were detailed in a hundred-page catalog of surreptitious actions that provided the public with the most detailed look yet into the clandestine workings of BCCI in the United States.

The Fed's notice of charges alleged that BCCI controlled about sixty percent of First American's holding company through a series of secret arrangements. The regulators portrayed the Washington banking operation as BCCI's stepping-stone to other U.S. financial institutions, such as the National Bank of Georgia and CenTrust Savings. All of this was concealed, the Fed claimed, because BCCI itself could not get necessary approvals to buy a bank in the United States. The notice also laid out a pattern of hiring decisions at First American and the National Bank of Georgia in which Abedi and Naqvi either provided candidates or were consulted.

A record $200 million fine was assessed against BCCI by the Fed and the regulators sought to bar permanently nine people associated with the bank from any involvement with a U.S. banking organization. Along with Abedi, Naqvi, and Pharaon, the Fed asked that the ban be imposed on Hasan Mahmood Kazmi, the former general manager of ICIC, the bank's affiliate in the Cayman Islands; Khusro Elley, manager of BCCI's New York office; and the four major investors in CCAH who were accused of serving as fronts for the bank's control of First American. They were Kamal Adham, Faisal Saud al-Fulaij, Saudi businessman A. R. Khalil, and El Sayed Jawhary, an adviser to Adham.

* * *

The twin blows drove the staggering bank to the canvas. By week's end, lawyers for its British-appointed liquidators were in U.S. Bankruptcy Court in New York to seek protection from the regulators and investigators zeroing in on the bank.

The day after the joint Morgenthau-Fed actions, the High Court in London agreed to a four-month delay in the Bank of England's attempt to liquidate BCCI. Abu Dhabi was granted the extra time to explore possibilities for reviving the shattered institution. In exchange, the Gulf nation's representatives revealed a plan for about $80 million in compensation for depositors in Britain and pay for BCCI employees.

In a proceeding just before the close of business on Friday, August 2, a federal bankruptcy judge in New York City approved a temporary order stopping the bank from paying the $200 million fine imposed by the Federal Reserve and freezing the production of bank documents in a host of criminal and civil court cases involving the bank.

These were holding actions, capable only of delaying the inevitable. Trust is the essence of banking, and trust in BCCI had been shattered by disclosures worldwide. Agha Hasan Abedi's invisible bank was stripped of its cloak of secrecy. And still the blows came.

In Tampa, federal prosecutors were nearing the completion of another major criminal indictment of bank officials and the bank itself. It was based on the cooperation of Amjad Awan and the other bankers convicted the year before.

In Karachi, Pakistan's finance minister acknowledged that local BCCI branches may have been used to launder money from the country's heroin trade. Later, he claimed he had been misquoted.

In London, Ghassan Qassem, the manager of BCCI's Sloane Street branch, went on BBC-TV and described taking Abu Nidal on shopping sprees and allowing the world's most virulent terrorist to use the branch as an office when he was in town.

In Washington, stung by allegations about the CIA's relationship with the bank, one of William Webster's final acts before retiring as CIA director was to order a full review of the agency's dealings with BCCI. In a rare public statement, the deputy director of the CIA, Richard Kerr, admitted to an audience of high school students that the agency had used BCCI for years to pay for covert operations and had passed on information about corruption in the bank to other U.S. agencies since the early 1980s. But he said there was nothing illegal about the CIA's involvement.

"We, CIA, used it as anyone would use a bank, not in any illegal way and not in any way that the bankers knew the objective of," Kerr told the students. "You probably don't move the quantities of money for the purposes that we do, but nevertheless, the same point is you use it merely as a transfer point."

The BCCI scandal had reached such heights that George Bush entered the debate, calling the widening charges about BCCI "a very serious matter" during a press conference. "This bank apparently was doing very bad things," said the President of the United States.

The day of Bush's remarks, August 1, Jack Blum and former Customs boss William von Raab appeared together before Senator John Kerry's Subcommittee on Terrorism, Narcotics and International Operations. Nearly one hundred journalists jammed the ornate hearing room and listened as the two men vied for top honors in villifying the bank and accusing the Justice Department of failing to respond aggressively to the long-standing allegations about it. Some of the charges sounded far-fetched.

But the sharks were circling the bloodied bank, and the scandal seemed so bewilderingly vast that almost any accusation was given instant credibility. There was a conspiracy theory to fit any point of view, and shenanigans enough to lend at least temporary credibility to most of them.

Around the world, investigators from the Justice Department, Scotland Yard, the New York district attorney's office, and various regulatory agencies were trying to discover how many billions of dollars had been stolen from the bank depositors, how it had been pulled off, and where the money had gone. They faced the same arduous task that confronted Price Waterhouse in trying to re-create the Bank of Credit and Commerce International puzzle from a jumble of pieces carved by years of deception and manipulation.

As Ian Brindle of Price Waterhouse said after his accountants turned in the audit that ultimately forced banking regulators around the globe to act: "Wherever you turn, whatever you are looking at, all is unreal. You are living in a world of unreality."

Epilogue

Could it happen again? Even now, is another financial institution bending and breaking the rules in the service of its own grand enterprise, robbing the poor and giving to the rich?

The answer must be yes, for history is replete with swindlers large and small. The schemes vary from person to person, age to age, but since Jesus threw the money changers out of the temple, we have been victims of those who would transform the world's financial institutions into a den of thieves.

There is some truth in the argument of BCCI's defenders that the bank was only engaging in activities pursued by many other big international banks. Indeed, as sophisticated bankers the world over channel money through a maze of bank secrecy havens and front companies with the push of a computer button, opportunities for corruption on a world scale are almost endless. The great lesson of this scandal lies in the surprising vulnerability of international banking regulations. And its lasting value depends on recognizing exactly where those weak points are located and how they can be strengthened, if not eliminated.

The vulnerabilities exploited by the Bank of Credit and Commerce begin with the bank's very structure. Whether driven by a deep desire to avoid another nationalization or by a criminal design, Agha Hasan Abedi set up a bank that was located everywhere and regulated nowhere. This is the most glaring regulatory failure exposed by the BCCI scandal. Global financial systems have been constructed without the global coordination and laws needed to keep them honest. The existing patchwork of financial regulation is decades behind the times—and the crooks.

As Justice Louis Brandeis used to say, sunshine is the best disinfectant. At the very least, the world's leading nations must establish uniform standards for banks that do business across borders. Most important among these requirements must be home-country supervision in which a single regulatory authority has the information-gathering tools to supervise an institution's activities worldwide. BCCI played a shell game with regulators, shifting its financial data from jurisdiction to jurisdiction without detection because no single country had responsibility. As a result, BCCI was able to extend its Ponzi scheme by drawing in larger and larger quantities of fresh cash and concealing its deteriorating condition. The Bank of England knew for years that there was fraud inside BCCI, but the regulators believed the incidents were isolated and could be resolved because they never saw the whole picture.

In America, the Federal Reserve Board and Congress already have taken a step in the right direction, with legislation establishing standards for entry and expansion of foreign banks within the United States. The heart of this reform is the demand that every bank have consolidated home-country supervision. No foreign bank could do business in the United States unless its books and records were open to full inspection by regulators in the country where it is based. With foreign bank operations controlling more than a fifth of the banking assets in the United States, this legislation is essential.

Another element is necessary for this step to be effective: Complete and accurate financial information must be shared with regulators in other countries where international institutions are operating. There will always be countries that refuse to participate in such international accords. Those banks and other entities that choose to shroud themselves in the secrecy laws of these inevitable offshore havens must be recognized as pariahs and their activities restricted severely. The BCCI affair has heightened the awareness of regulators and politicians in major countries to the necessity of such cooperation and to the steps that must be taken against those who shun participation.

The most charitable interpretation of the federal government's reaction to the massive evidence accumulated during Operation C-Chase is that it was a monumental case of miscommunication and interagency bungling. The Customs Service failed to provide the additional resources requested over and over by Bob Mazur and his team, so more than 100,000 documents seized from the bank went unexamined for critical months. In testimony before John Kerry's subcommittee in November 1991, Mazur said that "literally hundreds of leads" about additional allegations of wrongdoing by the Bank of Credit and Commerce International went uninvestigated for precious months. "It was a costly time-out," said Mazur.

In addition, the Justice Department failed to recognize the scope of the BCCI case in the early days. This was in part due to the system of decentralized control established within the department during the Reagan era. Local U.S. attorneys around the country were granted enormous power over their own cases and, as a result, main Justice in Washington was often ill-informed about the true scope of a case and reluctant to get involved.

There are signs of hope at the Justice Department. In testimony at his confirmation hearings in November 1991, incoming Attorney General William Barr acknowledged that the BCCI case had not been handled in the best way between the indictments in 1988 and July of 1991, when the department finally began to coordinate its investigations of the bank. And Barr promised that the problems would lead to a reexamination of the policy of decentralization within the Justice Department.

As for the Federal Reserve System, its primary failing in the BCCI case was the inability to discover the true ownership of First American Bank and to detect BCCI's clandestine takeovers of other American financial institutions. That, too, may be on the mend. In testimony before congressional committees in the fall of 1991, top Fed officials said that more money would be spent to hire and train criminal-type investigators and better use would be made of the Fed's subpoena power in the future.

Bank regulators and law enforcement cannot be expected to prevent fraud altogether, but it is clear that the Bank of Credit and Commerce International should have been closed far sooner. With adoption of proper standards and new coordination among regulators and law enforcement authorities, there is a chance that the next BCCI will not be so devastating to unsuspecting customers and to faith in government institutions.

A few minutes before ten o'clock on the morning of September 11, 1991, a Wednesday, Clark Clifford walked slowly into a crowded hearing before the House Banking Committee, clutching an old gray fedora and struggling to salvage the reputation he had built over fifty years as a man of probity and honesty.

Clifford sat at the long witness table, with partner and protégé Robert Altman at his side, and told the congressmen that he and Altman had clear consciences. At no time did they know that BCCI owned the controlling stock in First American Bankshares. Never did BCCI have a say in management decisions at the Washington bank. He and Altman were entitled to the millions they made by purchasing stock in First American's parent with money borrowed from BCCI.

"My judgment is questionable," Clifford conceded, spreading his hands in a theatrical gesture. "I guess I should have learned it some way. I've been in this business a long time. It's been a very active life. You learn a good deal from government. I guess I should have some way sensed it. I did not. I would have given anything if I could have avoided this past year. Still, I have to face it. In the process, I'm going to work as hard as I can in an effort to try to preserve my good name."

For eighty minutes, rarely referring to notes, Clifford described how he had gotten involved with BCCI and later First American, how he and Altman had maintained contact with Abedi because they thought BCCI and its president were the financial advisers to the stockholders in First American. For five more hours, after a two-hour break for Clifford to rest, he and Altman answered questions from members of the banking committee. Altman answered most of the questions. He described diligent efforts by himself and other lawyers to investigate allegations that BCCI controlled First American's stock, explaining that they had come up with no evidence, only steadfast denials from First American's shareholders.

Never did Clifford or Altman give an inch in the face of the ill-informed, skeptical questioning from the congressmen. Republicans were the most hostile, led by Representative Toby Roth of Wisconsin, who said to Clifford: "Others may believe your statement, but I don't believe a word of it." Democrats seemed more sad than angry, as illustrated by the comment of Representative Jim Bacchus of Florida, to Clifford: "Sir, I've admired you for many years, and I've looked forward to the day that I would have an opportunity to meet you. I regret that it's today in these circumstances."

It was evening before the 84-year-old Clifford shambled out of the hearing room, his wife, Marny, holding his hand. Trailing them, and absorbing most of the television lights, were Altman and his actress-wife Lynda Carter. Echoing behind them was a eulogy delivered by Representative Charles Schumer of New York, who had told Clifford: "My heart wants to believe you. My head says no. There is just too much of a nexus between BCCI and First American to believe that the two aren't inextricably linked."

POSTSCRIPT

On December 19, 1991, the Bank of Credit and Commerce International agreed to plead guilty to federal and state criminal charges and to forfeit a record $550 million to help repay foreign depositors and shore up the two struggling American banks that it controlled secretly, First American Bank in Washington, D.C., and Independence Bank in Encino, California. The plea agreement was reached with the Department of Justice and the New York district attorney's office by the court-appointed liquidators for BCCI in Britain, Luxembourg, and the Cayman Islands. In addition to pleading guilty to an array of criminal charges, the liquidators pledged to open the bank's books and records to investigators pursuing cases against former BCCI officials and others who used the bank for criminal purposes.

NOTES AND SOURCES

Research for this book started in the spring of 1990, as the trial of the BCCI bankers in Tampa was unfolding. Before the end of the reporting in November 1991, the story of the Bank of Credit and Commerce International had reached truly global proportions. As a result, the search for the truth spread across three continents and encompassed well over 150 interviews with people who have firsthand knowledge of the bank and the characters involved in the story. These interviews were augmented by tens of thousands of pages of records. The range of records themselves was extensive—internal records from BCCI and its chief auditor, Price Waterhouse; the complete record of the five-month Tampa trial of the BCCI bankers, including transcripts of 148 conversations taped as part of Operation C-Chase and thousands of pages of investigative files; more than 1,400 pages of material from the Federal Reserve dating back to 1981, most of it the result of a Freedom of Information Act request; files from more than twenty other civil and criminal cases across the country; and much more.

These interviews and records form the core of the research for the book. But a tale of this breadth cannot be reported by two people alone, and the work of dozens of journalists around the world contributed to our understanding of the story and was integral in our ability to explain it in as complete and cohesive a style as possible. The names of all the publications and journalists whose excellent work was invaluable comprise too long a list for this space, although an attempt has been made in the accompanying source notes to be as thorough as possible in apportioning proper credit. As usual on a story involving finance, The Wall Street Journal proved an excellent source for both detailed information and stories that put the operations of BCCI in perspective. The Financial Times of London also was essential daily reading, particularly with its massive coverage after the July 5 shutdown of the bank.

The book is written in a narrative style that attempts to place the reader as close as possible to the major events and players in the story. No part of any conversation was made up. The sources were either firsthand participants in the conversation or those who were in a position to have direct knowledge of what took place. In the section on the undercover investigation, every conversation between the agents and their targets is drawn from transcripts in the resulting court case. A more detailed description of the sources follows.

Notes and Sources

PART ONE

Building the Bank

Chapter 1: A REVERSE ROBIN HOOD

3 At one o'clock in the afternoon . . . The chronology of the shutdown of BCCI came from interviews with banking regulators in the United States and London, including William Taylor of the Federal Reserve, the testimony of Taylor and J. Virgil Mattingly, Jr., of the Federal Reserve before the Senate Foreign Relations Committee's Subcommittee on Terrorism, Narcotics, and International Operations (hereafter the "Kerry subcommittee") on August 1, 1991, and from numerous newspaper stories.

4 "Fraudulent conduct on a worldwide scale . . . "European, U.S. Authorities Seize Scandal-Ridden BCCI Bank," Jean-Claude Ernst, Reuters, July 5, 1991.

4 What had been . . . There has been considerable confusion in the press over how large BCCI was at its peak. Annual reports, however, indicate that at one point in 1988 the bank was operating in seventy-three countries and had 400 branches, so that is the figure used here.

4 "Under State Bank of Pakistan . . . "Illness Mutes the Founder of BCCI," John Bussey, The Wall Street Journal, July 16, 1991.

4 That Friday a county prosecutor . . . Interview with John Moscow, July 1991.

5 That same day . . . Interview with William Taylor, July 1991.

6 Estimates of profits . . . The figure $110 billion is generally accepted by the U.S. Treasury Department's Financial Crimes Enforcement Network, the leading agency on money laundering in the United States.

6 Topping the list . . . The existence of Abu Nidal's account at BCCI was first revealed on BBC-TV's Panorama program on July 23, 1991. Information about that account and BCCI's extensive dealings with Abu Nidal and other terrorists came from various sources, including interviews with Ghassan Qassem, the BCCI branch manager in London who handled the terrorist's account, and documents obtained from the CIA and the State Department's counterterrorism division.

6 "The bank of crooks and criminals . . . This phrase was first attributed to Robert Gates, at the time the second-ranking CIA official, by William von Raab, former commissioner of the U.S. Customs Service, in an interview in May 1991. Von Raab also provided the same information to other journalists, who used the phrase in several news articles.

7 In the tiny, impoverished . . . "BCCI Debacle Leaves an African Country All the More Troubled," Craig Forman, The Wall Street Journal, August 6, 1991.

8 "At that moment, I thought . . . "Watching the Ground Open Up Beneath 20-Year-Old Business," Neil Buckley, Financial Times, July 9, 1991.

8 "The garment trade was already . . . " 'Tragedy' for Asian Traders," Neil Buckley, Financial Times, July 8, 1991.

8 Not just businesses . . . "A Slam Heard 'Round the World," Steven Mufson, The Washington Post, July 23, 1991.

8-9 The Western Isles Council . . . "Council Reinstates Finance Director," James Buxton, *Financial Times*, July 18, 1991.
9 Shipments around the world . . . "BCCI Seizure Halts Cargoes at World Ports," Allanna Sullivan and Peter Truell, *The Wall Street Journal*, August 8, 1991.

Chapter 2: TRUE BELIEVERS

10 Abedi was born in 1922 . . . Biographical information about Agha Hasan Abedi was collected from many sources, including interviews with associates, bank publications and documents, and newspaper and magazine reports. Among the most helpful articles was "BCCI Founder: 'These Things Happen'," Najam Sethi, *The Wall Street Journal*, July 29, 1991.
12 For Muslims . . . A description of Muslim banking practices is set forth in *The Arabs*, David Lamb (New York: Vintage, 1988).
12 While at Habib Bank . . . Interviews with S. M. Fayyaz in June and July, 1991.
12 For five centuries . . . The history of Pakistan and the partition of India was drawn from several sources, including *Politics in Pakistan*, Khalid B. Sayeed (New York: Praeger, 1980), and *Can Pakistan Survive?* Tariq Ali (London: Schocken, 1984).
13 Habib Bank moved . . . Fayyaz interviews.
13 One day in 1956 . . . "BCCI Founder," Sethi.
14 "These were hardly profitable . . . Ibid.
14 "New management is needed . . . Interviews with the man who met with Abedi and spoke on the condition that his name be withheld.
14 Abedi was fixated on expansion . . . Various sources described Abedi's rise within the banking world, including but not limited to an investigative report obtained by the authors and numerous newspaper and magazine articles.
14 Bearing a finely made carpet . . . "BCCI Founder," Sethi.
14-15 (After he was replaced . . . "The Oil Monarchs," Lewis Grossberger, *New York Post*, January 16, 1974.
16 "Will you work hard? . . . "A Tragic Figure of Destiny," Bernard Weinraub, *The New York Times*, April 5, 1979.
16 This was a watershed event . . . This section on the ideas from which BCCI was forged is drawn largely from the testimony of Masihur Rahman on August 8, 1991, before the Kerry subcommittee.
17 His guest was Roy P. M. Carlson . . . Interviews with Roy Carlson in May and June 1991, in which Carlson provided extensive details of the early history of the BCCI-Bank of America relationship.
19 Bank of America was started . . . An excellent history of the Bank of America and the culture that led to its embrace of BCCI is *Breaking the Bank*, Gary Hector (Boston: Little, Brown and Company, 1988).
20 "Before we could consider . . . Carlson interviews.
20 As expected . . . Interviews with Carlson and Alvin C. Rice, former vice chairman, Bank of America, May 1991.
21 In June 1972, Abedi arrived . . . Carlson interviews and interviews with two former BCCI officials.

Notes and Sources

Chapter 3: THE GO-GO YEARS

23 Like Abedi, the Gokals . . . The long relationship between Abedi and the Gokals was described in numerous interviews and documents, including Price Waterhouse audits of BCCI. Most helpful among the news articles was "Family Shipping Firm Is One Reason BCCI Lost So Much Money," Marcus W. Brauchli and Peter Truell, *The Wall Street Journal*, August 15, 1991.

24 "We gave our all . . . "Chastened Retreat to Mid-East Roots," Richard Donkin and Victor Mallet, *Financial Times*, June 11, 1990.

24 Abdur Razzak Sakhia . . . Interview with Sakhia, July 1991.

24 "You didn't make calls . . . Carlson interviews.

25 In 1973, when Egypt attacked Israel . . . *Saudis: Inside the Desert Kingdom*, Sandra Mackey (New York: Signet, 1990).

26 In the words of Khalid Abu Su'ud . . . "Banking: Who Gets the Petromoney?" Geoffrey Smith, *Forbes*, May 15, 1978.

26 A new unit was formed . . . "Rogue Bank: BCCI Took Deposits from Drugs, Noriega, and Now Is in the Red," John J. Fialka and Peter Truell, *The Wall Street Journal*, May 3, 1990. This practice also was described in internal BCCI documents obtained by the authors.

27 "If you want five hundred thousand pounds . . . "Chastened Retreat to Mid-East Roots," Donkin and Mallet.

27 One of Abedi's lieutenants . . . "Banking: Who Gets the Petromoney?" Smith.

27 Zayed reportedly had fourteen wives . . . Interview with a Pakistani banker with extensive Middle Eastern business dealings in the 1970s who saw firsthand the delivery of cash on one occasion and said it was explained to him by BCCI officials on other occasions.

28 "Mr. Abedi's dream . . . "BCCI Founder's Aides Tell Another Tale," Mark Fineman, *Los Angeles Times*, July 30, 1991.

Chapter 4: THE ODD COUPLE

31 Bert Lance was a country boy . . . Biographical information on Lance is drawn from several sources, chiefly *The Bankers*, Martin Mayer (New York: Ballantine Books, 1977), pp. xiii–xxi; transcripts of interviews with Lance by *Los Angeles Times* reporters Paul Houston, Robert L. Jackson, and John Medearis in February and May of 1991; "Lance Chronology," Associated Press, May 24, 1979; and Lance's own testimony before the Kerry subcommittee on October 23, 1991.

32 First, Lance's stock-purchase loan . . . "Bankers Say Lance Never Revealed Collateral Already Was Pledged," Charles Campbell, Associated Press, April 1, 1980; "FBI Agents to Testify in Bert Lance Trial," Charles Campbell, Associated Press, April 2, 1980.

33 The U.S. Comptroller's Office . . . "Lance Chronology," Associated Press.

33 On Labor Day, 1977 . . . "Reversal of Fortune," Harry Jaffe, *The Washingtonian*, June 1991.

34 At a Washington hotel . . . Lance interview with Houston and Jackson; "Who Owns First American Bank?" Larry Gurwin, *Regardie's*, May 1990; Lance testimony before Kerry subcommittee.

34 Holley had met Abedi . . . "Washington Dateline," James H. Rubin, Associated Press, April 9, 1979.
34 As 1977 was drawing to a close . . . Annual Report for 1977, Bank of Credit and Commerce International; "Banking: Who Gets the Petromoney?" Smith.
35 To attract deposits . . . "A Capital Scandal," Jonathan Beatty and S. C. Gwynne, *Time*, March 4, 1991.
35–36 A jade-encrusted Chinese screen . . . "Chastened Retreat to Mid-East Roots," Donkin and Mallett.
36 Muzaffar Ali Bukhari . . . "BCCI Founder's Aides Tell Another Tale," Fineman.
36 "You have lost everything . . . Rahman testimony before Kerry subcommittee.
37 "The extraordinary success . . . Copy of a speech to employees by Agha Hasan Abedi, undated but described by BCCI employees as having been delivered in the mid-1970s.
37 In *hundi* . . . "Long Before BCCI, There was 'Hundi,'" Marcus W. Brauchli, *The Wall Street Journal*, August 15, 1991.
38 Alvin Rice was one . . . *Breaking the Bank*, Hector, pp. 101–110.
38 Rice often traveled . . . Interview with Alvin Rice, May 1991.
38 The swiftness with which . . . Interview with Carlson.
39 "It is meaningless . . . Ibid.
39 One of BCCI's senior executives . . . Interview with Sakhia.
39 Nonetheless, this was . . . Rice interview.
40 Concerns within Bank of America . . . Memo from Alvin Rice to Scudder Mersman, Jr., senior vice president, dated May 10, 1976, which includes a description of Tony Tucher's memo of April 27, 1976.
40 "On the subject . . . Memo from Rice to Mersman.
41 In a conversation with Abedi . . . Memorandum to Files, Alvin Rice, May 26, 1976, recounting conversation with Abedi.
42 "We felt that they were . . . Amjad Awan and Robert Musella, taped conversation, January 11, 1988.
42 By 1977, the Bank . . . Affidavit by Douglas M. Kraus, August 29, 1978, which included a summary of the loan examination report.
42 For instance, Kamal Adham . . . Adham's loans were described in Price Waterhouse audits on November 1989 and March 1990 obtained by the authors. In addition, they were detailed in several news stories, most expertly in "How BCCI Took from Depositors, Gave Billions to the Rich," Peter Truell, *The Wall Street Journal*, July 12, 1991. Adham, through his Washington lawyer, has denied any wrongdoing and denied the later accusations by the Federal Reserve Board that he was a nominee shareholder in the parent company of First American Bankshares.
43 Armacost dispatched one of his . . . Unpublished interview with Armacost by Tom Furlong of the *Los Angeles Times*, August 1991. The Bank of America was under no legal obligation to report the problems at BCCI to the authorities and the California bank has never been accused of wrongdoing in its association with BCCI.
44 Abedi arranged . . . Interview with Ghaith Pharaon, May 1991, in which he said he had bought the Bank of America's shares in BCCI. It was the first time that the purchaser of that stock was ever identified. ICIC was identified later when Price Waterhouse audit reports were obtained.

Notes and Sources

47   Chelsea National Bank . . . Testimony of John Heimann before the Senate Banking, Housing, and Urban Affairs Committee on May 23, 1991. The section on the Chelsea affair is drawn largely from Heimann's written and oral testimony that day, plus press accounts that identified Abbas Gokal as the person who tried to acquire the bank on behalf of BCCI.

48–49 In November 1977 . . . Interview with Bert Lance by John Medearis of the *Los Angeles Times*, May 1991, and author interview with Ghaith Pharaon, May 1991.

49   Pharaon was the son of . . . Robert Lacey, *The Kingdom* (New York: Harcourt Brace Jovanovich, 1981), pp. 251–52.

49   "There were so many opportunities . . . "The Richest Man in Georgia," Kenneth Cline, *Atlanta Business Chronicle*, April 27, 1987.

50   "In America . . . "Bank's Buyer: Arab's Hunt for Bargains Spans the World," Paul J. Lieberman, *Los Angeles Times*, October 8, 1985.

51   Agha Hasan Abedi already . . . While bits and pieces of the Attock Oil story were found in various publications and described in several interviews with the authors, the most complete account was provided in "The 'Concept' That Controls Governments," *New Statesman*, October 1981. Information about Attock Oil also came from an interview in April 1991 with Jack Blum, the former counsel to the Kerry subcommittee.

52   A former secretary to Bhutto . . . "Area Bank Cites Abedi Payments," Jerry Knight, *The Washington Post*, September 14, 1978.

53   The stock price was never disclosed . . . Transcript of taped conversation between Robert Mazur and Nazir Chinoy in Paris, May 24, 1988.

53   Five days before Christmas . . . "Lance Chronology," Associated Press.

53   The deal was completed . . . "Bankers Say Lance Never Revealed Collateral Already Was Pledged," Campbell.

54   After Carlson had left . . . Interview with Carlson.

55   Lance had known . . . The general scenario of the first attempt to take over Financial General Bankshares is contained in the extensive records of *Securities and Exchange Commission v. Bank of Credit and Commerce International* et al., Case No. 78–0469, the SEC civil action against BCCI, Lance, Abedi, and others. In addition, information also was obtained from the records of *Financial General Bankshares v. Lance* et al., the civil lawsuit brought by the bank's management in 1978. Further material related to this critical event was drawn from an extensive article by John F. Berry and Jerry Knight, "The Lance Role and Other Moves as Factions Dispute Battle for Control," which appeared in *The Washington Post* on April 2, 1978. Lance described how he brought Financial General to the attention of Abedi in his testimony before the Kerry subcommittee.

55   The investor was . . . *SEC and Financial General v. Lance* case records.

56   The weekend after Thanksgiving . . . Ibid.

56   On January 30, 1978, Sami . . . A copy of the telex was obtained by the authors.

57   Aligned with Middendorf . . . SEC and civil case files plus "The Lance Role and Other Moves as Factions Dispute Battle for Control," Berry and Knight.

57   In late January . . . Testimony of William McSweeny in *Financial General v. Lance* et al.

Notes and Sources

58 "BCCI always wants control . . . Affidavit of B. F. Saul, February 16, 1978. In an affidavit sworn the following day, William Middendorf said his recollection was that Lance said that BCCI "usually wants control." Lance disputed having made either statement.
58 Middendorf asked . . . Memorandum to Files, M. S. Thaler, Financial General attorney, February 7, 1978. In this memo, written on the day of the luncheon, Thaler put down the events and remarks as told to him by Middendorf and Saul. Considerable weight can be attached to this version since the memo was written immediately after the crucial meeting.
58 Right after the lunch . . . Court records, *Financial General v. Lance.*
59 As often happens . . . Settlement agreement of SEC case against BCCI *et al.*
59 Bert Lance's dream . . . Lance was indicted on May 23, 1979, on federal charges of conspiracy and violations of banking laws. In 1980, he was acquitted of most of the charges and the jury was unable to reach a verdict on the other charges, so they were dismissed.

Chapter 6: DANCING ELEPHANTS

61 "You can't do anything . . . Versions of Kennedy's remarks have appeared in numerous publications, including *The Washington Post* and *The New York Times.* The quotes are sometimes different, but the meaning is consistent. The version used here was drawn from Clifford's memoir, *Counsel to the President,* Clark Clifford with Richard Holbrooke (New York: Random House, 1991). Additional biographical material concerning Clifford was drawn from the book plus an excellent two-part series on his life by Marjorie Williams, published in *The Washington Post* on May 8 and May 9, 1991. Also helpful was "Clark Clifford, Symbol of the Permanent Government, Is Faced with a Dilemma," Neil A. Lewis, *The New York Times,* April 5, 1991.
62 To each, when . . . *Counsel to the President,* Clifford with Holbrooke.
62 Years later . . . "Cliffhanging," Jonathan Alter, *The Washington Monthly,* June 1991.
63 "I didn't want to retire . . . Clifford testimony, House Banking Committee, September 11, 1991.
63 Some of his former . . . "Reversal of Fortune," Jaffe.
64 On October 19 . . . The history of the Federal Reserve investigation and hearing is contained in hundreds of pages of material obtained under the federal Freedom of Information Act. In addition, J. Virgil Mattingly, Jr., general counsel to the Federal Reserve Board, provided a thorough synopsis in testimony before the Senate Banking, Housing, and Urban Affairs Committee on May 23, 1991. The report accompanying Federal Reserve case 91–043 against BCCI Holdings *et al.* also provides a detailed analysis of how BCCI acquired Financial General.
66 "These are honest . . . Sidney Bailey testimony before Senate Banking Committee, May 23, 1991.
66 That did not mean . . . It was disclosed at the Federal Reserve public hearing that up to $50 million of the purchase money would come from a bank, but the name was not disclosed. BCCI corporate records, sources close to the U.S. investigation of BCCI, Federal Reserve case 91–043, and private detectives in Europe provided information concerning the name of

the bank and its relationship to BCCI, including Yves Lamarche's position on both boards.

67 The solution was a complicated one . . . The loan transaction involving Adham and Fulaij is spelled out in Federal Reserve case 91–043. Adham has denied any wrongdoing or acting as a front through his lawyer, and Fulaij has never been reached for comment.

68 There was a curious omission . . . Testimony of William Taylor, staff director, Federal Reserve Board, at Senate Banking hearing on May 23, 1991.

69 At nine-thirty . . . Information and quotations from the Federal Reserve Board hearing on April 23, 1981, were obtained from a 182-page transcript of the hearing.

70 A man who knows . . . "Clark Clifford: The Rise of a Reputation," Marjorie Williams, The Washington Post, May 8, 1991.

71 Adham was gracious . . . Information on Kamal Adham's background came from several published sources, including "Who Owns First American Bank?" Gurwin; The House of Saud, David Holden and Richard Johns (London: Holt, Rinehart and Winston, 1981); and The Kingdom, Lacey.

72 Reflecting on the day-long . . . Bailey testimony, Senate Banking Committee.

72 Manfred Ohrenstein . . . Press release from Senate Minority Leader Manfred Ohrenstein, February 10, 1982.

73 Clifford responded . . . "Rogue Bank," Fialka and Truell.

73 There also was a threat . . . "State Clears Bank Sale," Karen W. Arenson, The New York Times, March 3, 1982.

73 "I've never seen so much . . . Ibid.

74 As DPA head since 1975 . . . Court records in Financieria Avenida v. Refco Inc., United States District Court, Chicago. The lawsuit was ultimately dismissed because Sheik Zayed refused to provide testimony, asserting his sovereignty as a foreign head of state.

74 The day after the article . . . Michael Bradfield letter to Clark Clifford, August 10, 1982.

74 In language . . . Clifford letter replying to Bradfield, August 16, 1982.

75 The bulk of the information . . . Affidavit of Khalil Fooladi contained in files of Chicago federal court case.

75 Also, during the time . . . Decree on January 28, 1981, by Khalifa bin Zayed al-Nahayan, Crown Prince of Abu Dhabi, naming Abedi to the board of the Department of Private Affairs.

Chapter 7: NORIEGA'S FAVORITE BANK

76 On September 22, 1983 . . . Testimony of Steven Kalish before the Permanent Subcommittee on Investigations, Senate Committee on Governmental Affairs, January 28, 1988. Kalish also testified before the Tampa federal grand jury that indicted BCCI and various bankers. Information about Kalish also came from "Drug Informants Hold Key to Prosecution of Noriega," Robert L. Jackson, Ronald J. Ostrow, and Douglas Frantz, Los Angeles Times, January 26, 1990. Questions were raised among defense lawyers in the BCCI case and elsewhere about the truthfulness of Kalish's

testimony before the Senate. However, U.S. Customs Agent Laura Sherman testified before the same subcommittee that Kalish was telling the truth, and there was substantial documentation to back up his assertions about his relationship with Noriega and with BCCI. For instance, Kalish produced a Panamanian diplomatic passport that Noriega had provided to him and records of his account at BCCI. The claims about BCCI also were supported by the subsequent Senate testimony of one of Kalish's convicted drug-smuggling partners, Leigh Ritch.

77 A one-time drug pilot . . . Information about Cesar Rodriguez came from several sources, including interviews with Richard Gregorie, the original Noriega prosecutor in Miami, and such books as *Divorcing the Dictator*, Frederick Kempe (New York: G.P. Putnam's Sons, 1990), and *Our Man in Panama*, John Dinges (New York: Random House, 1990).

77 When Kalish explained . . . Kalish Senate testimony.

77 "Oh, it's for you . . . Ibid.

78 "The general wants . . . Kalish Senate testimony and interview with his lawyer, Samuel Buffone, in January 1990. In addition, former Panamanian diplomat and Noriega confidant Jose Blandon testified before the Kerry subcommittee on February 8, 1988, that BCCI was the general's favorite bank and that Cesar Rodriguez often referred customers there. "It is a very famous bank in Panama," Blandon testified at a time when few in the United States had heard of BCCI.

78 Amjad Awan was born . . . Deposition of Amjad Awan, September 30, 1988, Kerry subcommittee, and confidential memorandum prepared for the subcommittee files by Jack A. Blum, dated September 24, 1988. The memo was based on an informal debriefing of Awan by Blum in advance of the sworn deposition. Later evidence showed that Awan lied at various points in both statements and efforts have been made not to use anything that was contradicted by later information. Additional information about Awan's personal history was obtained from letters filed with the sentencing judge in Tampa on his behalf by friends and relatives, including his wife, two children, father, and father-in-law.

78 "I need you . . . Transcript of taped conversation between Awan and Robert Mazur, January 11, 1988.

79–80 "He can talk . . . Author interviews with John Hume, Awan's lawyer, June and July, 1991.

80 When Panamanian President . . . Awan deposition and memo by Blum.

80 Noriega was . . . *Divorcing the Dictator*, Kempe, p. 109.

80 During the Panama Canal . . . Interviews with prosecutors and defense lawyers in the Miami prosecution of Noriega, as well as court documents in that case.

80 BCCI was trying . . . Awan deposition and confidential Senate memo by Blum.

82 "This will be a secret . . . Blum memo.

82 Noriega became . . . *Divorcing the Dictator*, Kempe, pp. 113–125.

82 He began to telephone Awan . . . Awan deposition and Blum memo.

83 One day in 1983 . . . Ibid. Bilonick later pleaded guilty to drug-related charges in the Noriega prosecution in Miami.

83 "I can only conjecture . . . Awan deposition.

84 "The businessman would deposit . . . "The Bank That Liked to Say Yes," David Lascelles and Richard Donkin, *Financial Times*, July 8, 1991.

84 Steven Kalish had returned . . . Federal indictment of Amjad Awan *et al.* in Tampa and Senate testimony of Kalish.

85 In his testimony before . . . Testimony of Ramon Milian-Rodriguez before Kerry subcommittee, February 11, 1988.

85 One day in the fall of 1984 . . . Circumstances surrounding the loss of the $3.7 million are described in Awan's deposition and Blum memo. In those two sessions, Awan also described Noriega's efforts to keep him in Panama.

Chapter 8: FEELING THE FORCE

87 One of BCCI's London managers . . . "The 'Concept' That Controls Governments," *New Statesman.*

88 A Pakistani named Aziz . . . Deposition of Aziz Rehman to Kerry subcommittee staff, October 24, 1988. Rehman's claims have been disputed by BCCI officials and were never part of any criminal complaint against the bank or its employees. Nonetheless, he seemed a credible witness, providing extensive detail in his recollections and delivering to the subcommittee written and computerized BCCI records concerning many of the transactions he described.

89 In April 1984 . . . Details of the failure of the IRS to follow up on Rehman's information are contained in Subcommittee Staff Report Regarding Federal Law Enforcement's Handling of Allegations Involving the Bank of Credit and Commerce International, September 5, 1991, House Judiciary Committee Subcommittee on Crime and Criminal Justice.

89 This branch was the BCCI office . . . Interviews with Ghassan Qassem.

90 At one point, he used . . . BBC-TV *Panorama* and interviews with Qassem.

90 The contact carried . . . Interviews with Qassem and declassified version of "The Abu Nidal Terror Network," U.S. State Department report, July 1987.

91 The organization run by Abu Nidal . . . "The Abu Nidal Terror Network," U.S. State Department.

93 In the eighties . . . Reports of these violations are contained in many newspaper accounts, most notably "How BCCI Grew and Grew," *The Economist,* January 27, 1990.

93 In Kenya . . . "The Bank That Liked to Say Yes," Lascelles and Donkin.

93 In Colombia, the bank . . . "Documents Link BCCI to Slain Medellín Cartel Leader," Douglas Farah, *The Washington Post,* August 19, 1991, and "BCCI Honed Bank-Buying in South America," Guy Gugliotta, *The Washington Post,* August 1991.

94 Despite its limited public presence . . . "Drug Cash Laundering Crackdown," Ronald Koziol, *Chicago Tribune,* September 5, 1986.

94 The links between the operations . . . Internal BCCI documents describe the April 24, 1985, meeting.

94 Afridi had served as . . . Records in Federal Reserve case 91–043.

95 By this point, BCCI had . . . Ibid. (This control has been denied both by some of the alleged nominee shareholders in First American's parent company and by Pharaon.)

95 This was a familiar pattern . . . Ibid.

96   "Management is providing a purpose . . . A full transcript of Abedi's address to the Miami conference was obtained by the authors.

97   "What can you do sitting in London?" . . . Rahman testimony before Kerry subcommittee.

97   So when a new division . . . Syed Akbar's trading operations at BCCI are described in numerous newspaper and magazine articles as well as court documents contained in his 1991 federal money-laundering indictment in Tampa, Florida. Rahman also described the activities in his testimony before the Kerry subcommittee. Akbar, who was convicted of money laundering in connection with BCCI by a British court in 1990, asserted that he was a scapegoat who had done nothing wrong in his trading operations in "Man Who Says He Is a Scapegoat," Richard Waters, *Financial Times*, August 12, 1991.

98   In January of 1986, accountants from . . . Rahman testimony to Kerry subcommittee and internal documents from Price Waterhouse.

98   After Rahman broke the news . . . Rahman testimony.
      Indeed, soon after that, one . . . Details of the Bin Mahfouz investment and the family's relationship with BCCI are drawn from audits of BCCI performed by Price Waterhouse in November 1989 and March 1990 and from a report on significant problem loans by an internal BCCI task force in March 1990. The family has not been accused of any wrongdoing in its dealings with the bank.

PART TWO

Busting the Bank

Chapter 9: THE LEGACY OF AL CAPONE

103   Enter Meyer Lansky . . . *Hot Money and the Politics of Debt*, R. T. Naylor (New York: Simon & Schuster, 1987), pp. 19–22.

104   ICB, as it was called . . . Ibid. pp. 21–22.

105   In Senate testimony . . . Testimony of David Wilson, Senate Foreign Relations Committee, September 27, 1989.

106   The probe's initial success . . . *Kings of Cocaine*, Guy Gugliotta and Jeff Leen (New York: Simon & Schuster, 1989), p. 68.

106   Early in 1981 . . . Ibid.

106   Another Greenback target . . . Information about the Robert Walker case came from interviews with Customs agents Bonni Tischler and Dennis Fagan plus numerous published articles and testimony of Customs agents before the House Banking Committee on January 28, 1985.

107   "He was a sucker for women . . . Fagan interview.

107   "He was just an unattractive . . . Tischler interview.

107   "So what you have . . . Transcript of conversation with Walker taped as part of a Greenback undercover sting.

107   "One thing about Panama . . . Ibid.

108   The bust of Robert Walker . . . This section is drawn from interviews with Tischler and Fagan.

110 "It is a money business . . . Senator Donald Riegle before Senate Banking Committee, November 1, 1989.

110 "Sometimes it was . . . "Washington Not Putting Its Money Where Its Mouth Is," Justin Gillis and Jeff Leen, *The Miami Herald*, February 13, 1990. This account was part of an excellent three-part series on money laundering by Gillis and Leen.

110 "I can hide money . . . Testimony of William Mulholland, Standing Committee on Banking, Trade, and Commerce, Canadian Senate, October 2, 1985.

111 The place is called . . . One of the authors visited the New York Clearing House Association in May of 1991 and its operation was described in detail by officials there. In addition, a good account of how CHIPS works is contained in "Launderers Disguise Drug Profits Through Electronic Transactions," Justin Gillis and Jeff Leen, *The Miami Herald*, February 14, 1990.

112 The importance of . . . "Launderers Disguise Drug Profits Through Electronic Transactions," Gillis and Leen.

112 Consider the case . . . Ibid.

112 Lee estimates . . . Interview with John Lee, May 1991.

113 Loan sharks and racketeers . . . *Hot Money*, Naylor, pp. 288–290.

114 The Treasury Department, which includes . . . "Money Laundering: The U.S. Government Is Responding to the Problem," U.S. General Accounting Office, May 1991. This report also provides information about the impact of the 1986 money laundering law and efforts by law enforcement to crack down on the growing problem.

Chapter 10: ABREU AND MAZUR

115 According to legend . . . *Pirates and Buried Treasure*, Jack Beater (St. Petersburg, Florida: Great Outdoors Publishing Company, 1959), pp. 7–17.

116 The Tampa money-laundering . . . Interview with Customs agents Steve Cook and Bob Moore, October 1990.

117 For two years, Mora . . . Indictment in Case No. 88–329, U.S. District Court, Tampa, *U.S. v. Gonzalo Mora, Jr.*, et al. (hereafter, Mora *et al.* indictment) and related court documents.

117 Ambitious and greedy . . . Characterizations of and background on Gonzalo Mora, Jr., were obtained from interviews with Cook and Burris and voluminous court records in the federal cases against Mora and the BCCI bankers in Tampa.

117 In July of 1986 . . . Sentencing Memorandum of Defendant Amjad Awan, Indictment No. 88–330, U.S. District Court, Tampa, *U.S. v. Amjad Awan* et al. This document (hereafter, Awan sentencing memo) from court records contains an extensive summary of the significant actions in the course of Operation C-Chase and is based on thousands of other pages of documents and testimony in the six-month trial of Awan and the other BCCI employees. This was only one of hundreds of documents, including transcripts of hundreds of recorded conversations, relied upon in reconstructing the chronology of Operation C-Chase. For instance, a fifty-eight-page affidavit by IRS agent David Burris listed by date and place a summary of every significant event that occurred in the investigation. (Hereafter, Burris affidavit.) In addition, thousands of

pages of other court documents and extensive testimony were reviewed by the authors, and interviews were conducted with more than a dozen of the direct participants in C-Chase. The most critical testimony was that of Bob Mazur, who recounted every significant step in the case during fifty-four days on the witness stand.

118   For his initial tip . . . Awan sentencing memo plus closing argument of his attorney, John Hume.

118   The plan was hatched . . . Interviews with Paul O'Brien and David Burris.

118   It was Mazur who pointed out . . . Ibid.

119   "We would ask . . . Interview with Moore.

119   At the age of sixteen, Emir Abreu . . . Testimony of Abreu at the trial of Awan et al. in Tampa in 1990.

119   The meeting occurred on July 14 . . . Mora et al. indictment.

120   Nine days later . . . Ibid., plus Awan sentencing memo.

120   On August 1, Uribe and Abreu . . . Abreu trial testimony and transcript of taped conversation, August 1, 1986.

121   The following month . . . Abreu trial testimony.

122   Mazur heard the noise . . . Interviews with Cook and Moore, October 1990.

122   Over the next several months . . . Mora et al. indictment.

123   "Bob Mazur is . . . Interview with John Hume, July 1991.

123   "He is the best agent . . . Interview with a top federal law enforcement official who asked that his name be withheld.

123   "Undercover could be . . . Interview with Cook.

123–24   In his college days . . . Transcript of conversation between Mazur, Amjad Awan, and Akbar Bilgrami, February 1, 1988.

124   When Operation Greenback . . . Interviews with Fagan, Customs agent Bill Rosenblatt, and Burris.

125   In August 1981, officers . . . Interview with Burris and trial records in Tampa case.

125   After three months . . . Internal IRS memo on the Taylor case and Justice Department press release, December 2, 1983. The sentence was reported in "Defendant Sentenced to 10 Years," Linda Haase, Tampa Times, December 3, 1983.

126   Broun's basic laundering . . . Justice Department press release, August 4, 1983, accompanied by indictment of Broun and Perlowin.

126   "I'm a very intuitive person . . . "California Connection," Stephen Cain, The Ann Arbor News, February 6, 1984. Broun and Perlowin were eventually convicted and sentenced to prison on federal racketeering and conspiracy charges connected to the money-laundering operation.

Chapter 11: SETTING THE HOOK

127   "I've been led to believe . . . Transcript of taped conversation on December 2, 1986. These transcripts, which were part of the court record in the trial of Awan et al. in Tampa in 1990, coupled with testimony from prosecution witnesses, form the basis for virtually every conversation recounted in Part Two of this book.

128   As the partnership progressed . . . Numerous transcripts of tapes from December 1986 and early 1987.

128 The following day . . . Mazur testimony in Awan *et al.* and transcript of conversation of December 3, 1986.

129 Customs had put up Mora . . . The trip to New York is described in numerous conversations taped during the trip and in court files, such as the Burris affidavit.

130 "It's important for us . . . Transcript of taped conversation, December 5, 1986.

131 Shortly after Mora returned . . . Mazur's actions were described in his trial testimony and in court documents.

132 "Bob Mazur is the most careful . . . Hume interviews.

132 This task was a pressing one . . . Mazur testimony.

133 Argudo was extremely helpful . . . Argudo's involvement is described in court documents, such as the Burris affidavit, and in transcribed conversations with Mazur. Argudo left BCCI for another Tampa bank in the summer of 1987 and was never charged with any wrongdoing.

134 "It's the dumb people . . . Transcript of taped conversation, April 3, 1987.

134 However, the Bank of Credit and Commerce . . . The authors were shown the CIA report on BCCI. In addition, acting CIA director Richard Kerr described the agency's many reports on BCCI in testimony before the Kerry subcommittee on October 25, 1991. He said that some of those reports were circulated to the Customs Service and other law enforcement agencies, including the September 1986 report.

136 Another example of this desperation . . . The bribery allegations are contained in the indictment of BCCI, Agha Hasan Abedi, and Swaleh Naqvi in New York State Court on July 29, 1991.

137 When Bob Mazur first mentioned . . . Transcript of taped conversation, April 7, 1987.

137 Argudo and Mora hit it off . . . Transcript of taped conversation, April 8, 1987.

138 But Mazur wanted another piece . . . Awan sentencing memo, Burris affidavit, and Mazur trial testimony.

138 "First, though, I have to see . . . Transcript of taped conversation, April 14, 1987.

139 Here was a man who enjoyed . . . "Drug Indictments Show Intricate International Links," Eric Wilhelmus, Jeffrey Miller, and Ashley Dunn, *Los Angeles Times*, October 16, 1988.

140 The first major cash from . . . Affidavit by Stanley Jacobsen, FBI agent, which is part of the court record in the Awan *et al.* indictment (hereafter, Jacobsen affidavit).

140 A week later, the process . . . Ibid.

140–141 That day, Alcaino listened thoughtfully . . . Transcript of taped conversation, April 15, 1987.

141 On May 6, 1987, U.S. Attorney General . . . Justice Department press release and various news articles.

142 Since 1982 at least . . . "The Secrets of a Dictator," Douglas Frantz and Robert L. Jackson, *Los Angeles Times Magazine*, July 21, 1991, and court records in the prosecution of Noriega in U.S. District Court in Miami, Florida.

142 The second worry was more immediate . . . Interviews with O'Brien, Cook, and Moore.

143 So on May 20, when . . . Transcript of taped conversation, May 20, 1987.

Notes and Sources

144 When Mora next met Mazur . . . Transcript of taped conversation, August 31, 1987.
145 Budgets of undercover operations . . . Interviews with Cook and Moore.
145 "The likelihood of betrayal . . . Interview with Cook.
146 A credit card was the source . . . Interviews with Cook and Moore.
147 During a demonstration . . . Ibid.

Chapter 12: A FULL SERVICE BANK

148 On November 24, 1987 . . . Mazur trial testimony and Burris affidavit.
149 His replacement, Dayne Miller . . . Transcript of taped conversation, June 18, 1987. Miller was never accused of any wrongdoing.
149 The first step was picking up . . . Burris affidavit and trial testimony of Mazur and Abreu.
150 It was a Saturday morning . . . Transcript of taped conversation, December 5, 1987.
151 "What type of service do you want . . . Ibid.
153 "Here was this guy laying . . . Cook interview.
153 On December 8, word came . . . Burris affidavit and Mazur trial testimony.
154–55 Shortly before nine o'clock . . . Transcript of taped conversation, December 9, 1987.
155 "This drug-related money . . . Ibid.
156 Later in December . . . Burris affidavit and Awan sentencing memo.
156 "Amjad Awan is on the team" . . . Transcript of taped conversation, December 22, 1987.
156 Since moving to BCCI's representative office . . . The account of Awan's relationship with Noriega is drawn from his deposition to the Kerry subcommittee, the Blum memo, his testimony at Noriega's trial, and numerous documents from the Noriega account, such as hotel bills from the Helmsley Palace and various limousine services.
157 Marijuana smuggler Steven Kalish . . . Kalish Senate testimony and bill of sale for the airplane.
157 When Noriega stepped off the jet . . . Awan deposition.
157 In March of 1986, the corpse . . . "The Secrets of a Dictator," Frantz and Jackson; and Divorcing the Dictator, Kempe, pp. 240–241.
158 Although Noriega made use of . . . "The Secrets of a Dictator," Frantz and Jackson, and testimony of Luis del Cid at Noriega trial in Miami.
158 And $500,000 worth of checks . . . Copies of the actual checks were provided to the authors by Senate investigators.
159 Amjad Awan and BCCI were always . . . Awan deposition.
159 Independence Bank was a medium-sized . . . In May 1991, the Federal Reserve accused Ghaith Pharaon of acting as a nominee for BCCI in the acquisition of Independence Bank, and the transactions surrounding the deal, including a reference to the November 1984 letter to Abedi, are included in documents provided by the Federal Reserve in connection with that case. Pharaon has maintained in an interview and through his lawyer that he was not acting as a front for BCCI and that he owned all of Independence Bank.
160 Not until much later . . . May 1991 Federal Reserve case against Pharaon.

160 For his part, Noriega . . . *Divorcing the Dictator*, Kempe, pp. 215–216, and Awan deposition.

161 "Awan was a very free-spirited person . . . Sakhia interview.

161 "Sir, I'm not the fellow . . . Awan deposition.

Chapter 13: THE AMERICAN SECRET

162 Abedi made his plans clear . . . Minutes from BCCI managers' meeting in New York City, September 30, 1987.

163 Portions of the strategy . . . Memo to Agha Hasan Abedi from Abdur Sakhia, October 22, 1987.

164 A month later, Sakhia wrote . . . Memo to Agha Hasan Abedi from Abdur Sakhia, November 15, 1987.

165 The biggest of these catches . . . Lance interview by Jackson and Houston of *Los Angeles Times* and Lance testimony before Kerry subcommittee.

165 The primary vehicle . . . "Carter Donors: Questionable Givers?" Elizabeth Kurylo, *The Atlanta Constitution*, April 14, 1991.

165 The project was bankrolled by . . . *Selling Out*, Douglas Frantz and Catherine Collins (New York: Contemporary Books, 1989), pp. 80–83.

165 Over three years . . . Donation figures were taken from partial IRS Form 990 tax returns filed by Global 2000 and from various newspaper accounts. The figure of $6 million is drawn from the IRS returns; the $8 million was mentioned in "Seized Bank Helped Atlanta's Ex-Mayor and Carter Charities," Ronald Smothers, *The New York Times*, July 15, 1991.

165 For instance, in late June 1987 . . . "Former U.S. President Carter Honored at Beijing Banquet," Xinhua General Overseas News Service, June 29, 1987.

166 The climax of the visit . . . "Zhao Ziyang Meets Former U.S. President Carter," Xinhua General Overseas News Service, June 29, 1987.

166 A similar artificial limbs factory . . . "Global 2000 to Help Kenya Produce Artificial Limbs," Xinhua General Overseas News Service, August 15, 1988.

166 In Bangladesh, Carter and . . . "Former U.S. President Carter Arrives in Dhaka," Xinhua General Overseas News Service, November 1, 1986.

166–67 During his two terms . . . "Seized Bank," Smothers.

167 "I saw them . . . Ibid.

167 "We don't have . . . "Carter Donors: Questionable Givers?" Kurylo.

167–68 In 1983, the Carters were among . . . "People in the News," Associated Press, June 21, 1983.

168 In the spring of 1987 . . . "The Richest Man in Georgia," Kenneth Cline, *Atlanta Business Chronicle*, April 27, 1987.

168 Back in June 1986 . . . "How a Saudi Helped BCCI Scandal Spread from Miami to Encino," Peter Truell, *The Wall Street Journal*, June 13, 1991.

168 In reality, Abedi had been . . . Interview with Carlson, who readily acknowledged that Abedi was involved in the negotiations with First American. He maintained, however, that Pharaon had been the sole owner of National Bank of Georgia and that the sale of the bank was an arm's length transaction. Lawyers for Pharaon, First American, and Clifford and Altman also said that the transaction was conducted at arm's length. Bert

Lance also maintained that he always thought Pharaon was using his own money and that Abedi played the role of a financial adviser.

169 Even the timing of the sale . . . The disposition of the proceeds from the sale are described in documents related to Federal Reserve case 91–043. Price Waterhouse's concerns over the loan were repeated in BCCI Holdings (Luxembourg) SA, "Interim Report on Results and Operations," 17 November 1989, by Price Waterhouse.

170 In August 1987, four months after . . . "CenTrust Announces Receipt of Schedules 13D Filing," *Business Wire*, August 12, 1987.

170 At the time, CenTrust . . . "CenTrust, the Saudi, and the Luxembourg Bank," Gail DeGeorge with Tim Smart, *Business Week*, August 27, 1990. Numerous other publications have written extensively about the rise and fall of CenTrust and David Paul. Among the best articles have been those appearing in *The Wall Street Journal* and the *Miami Herald*.

171 In May, Ghaith Pharaon . . . Office of Thrift Supervision, Criminal Referral for 366, Number 00060, undated. This document reflects the analysis of the deals between David Paul and Ghaith Pharaon by the federal regulators who did the postmortem on CenTrust. It was most likely written near the end of 1989. A federal grand jury was convened early in 1990 to investigate the collapse of the savings and loan. In case 91–043, the Federal Reserve also raised questions about the CenTrust-BCCI bond transaction and accused BCCI of violating federal banking laws by taking a controlling interest in CenTrust through Pharaon's acquisition, which the Fed said was financed by BCCI.

171 "It is highly likely . . . Ibid.

Chapter 14: A CLEAR RELATIONSHIP

172 "They'll ask you who . . . Transcript of taped conversation, January 11, 1988.

173 "Why don't you invite him . . . Ibid.

174 "I have a fiancée who lives . . . Ibid.

175 At the end of January . . . Mazur testimony at trial of Awan *et al.*

175 The reference to a fiancée . . . Interviews with Cook, Moore, and O'Brien.

176 Mazur himself had learned . . . Interviews with Burris and Cook.

176 Early in the C-Chase investigation . . . Interviews with Burris, Cook, and Moore.

176 The solution was Kathy Ertz . . . Interviews with Cook and Tischler.

177 Occasionally Mazur strayed from the path . . . Interview with O'Brien.

177 A foolproof alternative had been . . . Transcript of taped conversation, January 6, 1988.

178 On January 25, 1988, Mazur returned . . . Transcript of taped conversation, January 25, 1988, and Mazur trial testimony.

178 "First American is a bank which . . . Transcript of taped conversation, January 25, 1988.

178–79 "I'm not concerned further than that . . . Ibid.

180 "My friend is in deep trouble . . . Transcript of taped conversation, February 1, 1988.

181 There was the matter of the ouster . . . *Divorcing the Dictator*, Kempe, pp. 145–156.

Notes and Sources

181 The atmosphere was tense when Mazur . . . Transcript of taped conversation, February 2, 1988, and Mazur trial testimony.
182 One day earlier, on February 1 . . . "The Secrets of a Dictator," Frantz and Jackson.
182 "It was an undercover operation . . . Interview with a federal law enforcement official who spoke on the condition that his name be withheld.
183 The biggest worry for the Customs agents . . . Interviews with several Customs agents and other federal authorities, including Cook, Moore, and Tischler.
183–84 However, agents in Los Angeles . . . Ibid.
184 In one instance, in late January . . . Ibid.
184 Had C-Chase been under the control . . . Extensive management problems within the Customs Service were described in a report issued in August 1991 by a blue-ribbon panel headed by Frank Keating, a former assistant secretary of the treasury for enforcement.
185 There was little trouble . . . The February meeting of law enforcement officials from around the country was described in interviews with several of the participants, all of whom asked that their names be withheld.

Chapter 15: PRECIOUS FRIENDS

187 On February 8, Emir Abreu . . . Burris affidavit.
188 "The most important thing . . . Transcript of taped conversation, February 17, 1988.
189 Nonetheless, BCCI executives . . . Transcript of taped conversation, February 24, 1988, in which Awan described what happened in London to Mazur.
189 "As far as we're . . . Ibid.
190 The subpoena demanded . . . Ibid. Additional details about the Khashoggi account were obtained from an interview with a member of the staff of Lawrence Walsh, the independent counsel investigating the Iran-Contra scandal, and from records provided by the Kerry subcommittee.
190 "For the moment what we feel . . . Transcript of taped conversation, February 24, 1988.
191 The strategy adopted . . . Minutes of marketing meetings held by BCCI Group–Panama from May 1987 through June 1988.
191 The exodus of money . . . Details about the efforts of Panamanian exiles to declare Noriega's an outlaw government and the resulting freeze on assets are drawn primarily from *Divorcing the Dictator*, Kempe, pp. 263–272. Attempts by Awan and Hussain to recover Mazur's funds were described in several taped conversations with Mazur. The $725,000 was eventually released in September 1988.
192 The DEA agents . . . Affidavit of Albert Latson, special agent of the DEA, in *U.S. v. Eduardo Martinez*, U.S. District Court, Atlanta, Georgia. Martinez later pleaded guilty to money laundering and was sentenced to six and a half years in prison. Perez was arrested in possession of a major quantity of cocaine by French authorities.
193 One of the drug suppliers . . . Affidavit of David Panek, special agent of the DEA, in *U.S. v. Pablo Emilio Escobar-Gaviria* et al., U.S. District Court,

Atlanta. A full description of the La Mina investigation can be found in "Gold, Drugs, and Clean Cash," Evan Lowell Maxwell, Los Angeles Times Magazine, February 18, 1990.

193   The C-Chase team was generally . . . Interviews with several Customs and IRS agents assigned to C-Chase.

193   During the same period . . . Interview with James F. Dougherty II, an attorney in Miami, who investigated the BCCI-Bilbeisi relationship for years on behalf of Lloyds, the London insurance underwriters. Additional information was obtained from records in the civil lawsuit filed by Lloyds against BCCI and a report prepared for BCCI on the Bilbeisi accounts by the Miami law firm of Holland & Knight and Phil Manuel, a private investigator.

193   Bilbeisi was a full-service . . . Testimony of Dougherty before the Kerry subcommittee, October 16, 1991, and records from the Miami civil case. Bilbeisi was indicted in August 1991 by a federal grand jury in Miami on charges of tax evasion in connection with profits from the coffee scheme that were moved through BCCI on his behalf. He remains a fugitive.

194   Another letter of credit . . . "Businessman Convicted in Pakistani Nuclear Plot," Michael R. Gordon, The New York Times, December 18, 1987, and interview with Jeffrey Miller, Pervez's lawyer.

194   That was not BCCI's only connection . . . "BCCI Avoided Huge Tax Bite in Pakistan," Mark Fineman, Los Angeles Times, August 9, 1991.

194   Awan's house was in . . . The description of Awan's house and its price came from legal records in Miami and a 1991 sales listing with the Kendall-Perrine Board of Realtors. Michael Y. Cannon, president of AREEA, a Miami real estate investment firm, provided some of the legal information. Awan described the tennis court incident in a taped conversation with Mazur.

195   "So, the intelligent . . . Transcript of taped conversation, March 9, 1988.

196   Two days later . . . Transcript of taped conversation, March 11, 1988.

196   Arriving in Los Angeles . . . Burris affidavit and Jacobsen affidavit.

196–97   Before his plane left . . . Burris affidavit.

197   On March 28 . . . Burris affidavit.

198   The former president had . . . "Influence and Intrigue in BCCI Chief's Illness," Douglas Frantz and William C. Rempel, Los Angeles Times, September 21, 1991. Additional details of the circumstances surrounding Abedi's transplant were provided in an interview with Dr. Charles Rackley, chief of cardiology, Georgetown University Hospital.

198   Cromwell, the largest private . . . The ownership of Cromwell Hospital was described in audit papers of BCCI prepared by Price Waterhouse.

198–99   "An issue like that . . . Interview with Frank Vogel, Harvard University.

199   "I think that I have a better . . . Transcript of taped conversation, March 28, 1988.

199–200   In testimony in January . . . Testimony of Steven Kalish, U.S. Senate Permanent Subcommittee on Investigations, January 28, 1988.

200   Just four days after . . . Testimony of Leigh Ritch, U.S. Senate Subcommittee on Terrorism, Narcotics, and International Operations, February 8, 1988, and testimony of Jose Blandon before the same panel, February 9, 1988.

200   A former prosecutor, Kerry was . . . Interview with Senator John Kerry and records of the Kerry subcommittee.

200 In a conversation in late March . . . Transcript of taped conversation, March 28, 1988.

201 However, the matter did not go . . . Interviews with federal prosecutors involved in BCCI case and "Handling of BCCI Case Arouses Deep Suspicions," Dean Baquet, *The New York Times*, September 6, 1991.

201 Tischler was no political innocent . . . Interviews with Tischler.

201 In fact, Tischler was already kicking . . . House Judiciary Committee Subcommittee on Crime and Criminal Justice staff report, September 5, 1991.

Chapter 16: LEE IACOCCA WITH A TWIST

204 "I would suggest you don't tell . . . Transcript of taped conversation, May 12, 1988.

205 Mazur and Abreu flew by . . . Burris affidavit.

205 The next morning, Mazur and . . . Transcript of taped conversation, May 19, 1988.

205 Mazur said that he hoped . . . Transcript of taped conversation, May 20, 1988, and Mazur trial testimony.

206 "If some of your clients have . . . Ibid.

207 At Chinoy's apartment the following . . . Transcript of taped conversation, May 21, 1988, and Burris affidavit.

207 "Let's get to the point . . . Transcript of taped conversation, May 22, 1988.

208 On May 23, in the lobby . . . Mazur trial testimony and transcript of taped conversation, May 23, 1988.

209 He later told Mazur that Uribe . . . Trial testimony of Abreu and Mazur plus interviews with Customs agents Cook and Moore.

210 Yes, said Mora . . . Transcript of taped conversation, May 24, 1988. Don Chepe was later identified as Gerardo Moncado, a member of the Medellín cartel, and he was indicted in Tampa federal court in September 1991 on money-laundering charges. Indicted with him were Santiago Uribe and several BCCI bankers, including Swaleh Naqvi. Moncado and Uribe remain fugitives.

210 "I am having a very good impression . . . Transcript of taped conversation, May 24, 1988.

211 "Any friend of yours . . . Transcript of taped conversation, May 25, 1988.

211 "What we need to accomplish . . . Transcript of taped conversation, May 27, 1988.

212 "I heard you mention my client's . . . Transcript of taped conversation, June 6, 1988.

213 "The system is like a merry-go-round" . . . Transcript of taped conversation, June 6, 1988.

214 "They're not using that truck . . . Interview with a Customs supervisor who requested that his name be withheld.

215 The Customs SAC called him . . . Ibid.

215 Word of the fracas . . . "Customs Fumbled on Big Drug Cargo, DEA Says," Michael Hedges, *Washington Times*, August 15, 1988.

216 Ian Howard solidified his place . . . Transcript of taped conversation, June 9, 1988, and Mazur trial testimony.

216 On June 30, 1988, Awan and Bilgrami . . . Transcript of taped conversation, June 30, 1988.

217 "Yes, that's what we're . . . Ibid.

217 No one would remember . . . Interviews with Cook and Moore.

Chapter 17: CLOSING DOWN C-CHASE

218 On June 27, 1988, Emir Abreu . . . Burris affidavit and Abreu trial testimony.

218 "The lady was nervous" . . . Transcript of taped conversation, June 29, 1988.

219 Gonzalo Mora, Jr., was summoned . . . Transcript of taped conversation, July 14, 1988.

219 Mazur was meeting Roberto Alcaino . . . Interviews with Cook, Moore, and Broun.

221 "Little things are adding up" . . . Transcript of taped conversation, August 4, 1988.

222 "I will give you an encouraging . . . Ibid.

222 According to Bilgrami's story . . . Transcript of taped conversation, July 21, 1988.

223 Awan was already planning . . . The circumstances surrounding the transfers of Noriega's money are described in the September 1991 federal indictment in Tampa of Naqvi, Rizvi, Akbar, and Capcom Financial Services, along with Moncado and others. Awan was identified in the indictment only as a BCCI employee, but his attorney, John Hume, confirmed the role that Awan played in the money transfers in an interview. Efforts to recover the $23 million were recounted in "Money in Panama Dispute Is Frozen," Steven Prokesch, The New York Times, September 3, 1991.

224 "I don't know if Akbar mentioned . . . Transcript of taped conversation, August 17, 1988.

225 "What I've learned is not . . . Transcript of taped conversation, September 9, 1988.

225 "On a personal level . . . Ibid.

226 "Well, our attorneys are . . . Ibid.

227 "As managing supervisor . . . Interviews with Tischler.

227 "We had to get the guys . . . Interview with Gregory Kehoe, first assistant U.S. attorney in Tampa.

228 The pitch was rote by now . . . Transcript of taped conversation, August 26, 1988, and Burris affidavit.

229 When the freighter Colombus Olivious . . . Circumstances surrounding the seizure of the drug shipment and indictment of Roberto Alcaino are drawn from the federal indictment to which he pleaded guilty in New York, interviews with Customs agents involved in the investigation of Alcaino, Mazur's testimony at the Tampa trial of Awan et al., and "A Ton of Drugs Is Seized," Linda Lloyd, Philadelphia Inquirer, September 16, 1988.

229 The trip began with an embarrassment . . . Interviews with Cook and Moore.

230   "We are not the need . . . Transcript of taped conversation, September 21, 1988.

231   There were a hundred people . . . Mazur trial testimony.

231   The trip's only sour note . . . Transcript of taped conversation, September 23, 1988.

232   The Customs agents assigned . . . Interviews with several Customs agents and Mazur's April 1991 resignation letter provided information about the attitudes of the C-Chase team members about the shutdown. In addition, the authors viewed several memos that Mazur had sent to superiors throughout the C-Chase investigation asking for more resources and more time to go higher up in the bank and pursue what Mazur said in one memo were "literally hundreds of leads." Similar findings were reported in the September 1991 report by the House Judiciary Committee Subcommittee on Crime and Criminal Justice.

232   "Did politics play a role . . . Interview with a federal law enforcement official involved in the prosecution of the C-Chase case.

232–33   Bonni Tischler, who had spent . . . Interviews with Tischler and other Customs agents.

233   For his part, Mazur . . . Mazur's April 1991 resignation letter describes his difficulties with Tischler. Other Customs agents on the case related his other frustrations during interviews.

233   It was almost five . . . Motion to Suppress Post-Arrest Statement filed in Tampa in the Awan et al. case by Awan, and testimony by Awan at a hearing to suppress the statement.

234   They seemed to fall into . . . Memorandum of interview of Awan, U.S. Customs Service, October 8, 1988.

234   "We're going to get . . . Interviews with Cook and Moore.

234   Awan was less eager . . . Awan testimony at hearing to suppress post-arrest statement.

234   As the limousine started to pull . . . Interviews with Cook and Moore.

235   Akbar Bilgrami shook his head . . . Memorandum of interview of Bilgrami, U.S. Customs Service, October 8, 1988.

235   Sibte Hassan had been . . . Cook and Moore interviews and "Joyride for Bankers Turns to Nasty Surprise," Ron Bartlett, Tampa Tribune, October 12, 1988.

235   "Don't do anything stupid . . . Testimony by Customs Agent Mike Miller and Awan at hearing to suppress post-arrest statement.

235   Slightly tipsy from the Scotch . . . Awan claimed in court papers that Agent Miller had induced him to drink heavily at the pool party. He also said Miller had frightened him by brandishing his gun during the arrest at NCNB Tower. As a result, Awan and his lawyer, John Hume, tried to suppress Awan's post-arrest statement. The government produced a waiver of rights signed by Awan the night of his arrest. Miller denied brandishing his gun, though he said it was in plain sight at least twice, and he denied pushing liquor at Awan. The judge permitted the statement to be used as evidence.

236   The wedding ruse did not . . . Interviews with Cook, Moore, and O'Brien.

237   They were sitting there . . . Interview with Burris.

237   A few days later . . . Interview with Tischler.

237   The indictments behind the bachelor . . . Names and details are taken directly from the indictments themselves.

238   "Oh," replied the man . . . Interview with William von Raab.
238   "In late 1981, BCCI made . . . The authors reviewed the CIA memo.
239   Later, Von Raab would explain . . . Interview with Von Raab.

PART THREE

Breaking The Bank

Chapter 18: ROADBLOCKS

244   "What I learned was that . . . Jack Blum was interviewed on numerous
       occasions in 1990 and 1991. In addition, he was the subject of two major
       newspaper profiles, "A Crusader Driven by Outrage," Michael Wines, *The
       New York Times*, August 20, 1991, and "The Lawyer Who Broke Open the
       Bank," Phil McCombs, *The Washington Post*, August 13, 1991. He also
       testified before the Kerry subcommittee on August 1, 1991.
245–46 "We won't accept a BCCI . . . Blum interviews and Senate testimony.
246   "I'm on my way out the door" . . . Blum interviews. Lodhi's role also was
       discussed in "Handling of BCCI Case Arouses Deep Suspicions," Baquet.
247   In early April 1988, Blum spoke . . . Interviews with Blum and Joseph
       Magri.
248   "I understand you are investigating . . . Blum interviews and Senate
       testimony.
248   "Send me a letter . . . Ibid.
249   Blum contacted the Department . . . Blum interviews and interview with a
       top-ranking federal prosecutor.
249   "All BCCI does is launder money . . . Blum interviews.
250   "You're taking a great risk" . . . Blum interviews and Senate testimony.
250   In early August, Clark Clifford . . . Interviews with Blum and Kerry staff
       member David McKean.
251   Monday, September 5, 1988 . . . Blum interviews and Blum memo to files
       of Kerry subcommittee.
251   "Never," Awan assured him . . . Ibid.
252   "Listen," Awan interrupted . . . Ibid.
253   In Altman's version . . . Testimony of Robert Altman before House Bank-
       ing Committee, September 11, 1991.
253   "I want you to understand" . . . Interview with Kerry.
254   One of these men was . . . Records of Kerry's relationship with David Paul
       include Paul's diaries, a report by Senator Orrin Hatch on CenTrust in the
       summer of 1991, and a lawsuit filed against Paul by the Resolution Trust
       Corporation.
255   Four days after Clifford's call . . . Transcript of Awan deposition and
       interviews with Blum and McKean.
255   On the following Friday . . . Blum memo to files of Kerry subcommittee
       and Blum interviews.
256   So Blum went to Kerry . . . Interviews with Kerry and Blum.
257   In early March, Blum's old friend . . . Blum interviews.
257   The meeting was set for late March . . . Blum interviews and Senate
       testimony.

258 Lodhi was nervous and frightened . . . Interviews with Blum and federal prosecutors.

258 "Are you the guy we taped . . . Blum interviews.

259 While Blum thought that . . . Interviews with Blum and federal prosecutors.

259 According to Jackowski and Rubinstein . . . Interviews with Gregory Kehoe and other federal prosecutors. Kehoe and Mark Jackowski also told the same story to Kerry staff members in the summer of 1991 and in Senate testimony—November 1991. Blum denied ever asking for money and claimed that the allegation was part of a government effort to discredit him. New York District Attorney Robert Morgenthau and his staff said Blum never asked them for payment after he took his information to them.

260 "Convict the people that are . . . Interview with Kehoe.

260 By this time Blum was off . . . Interviews with Blum and McKean and the testimony of Robert Morgenthau before the Senate Banking Committee on May 23, 1991.

261 "Look, this is why I'm here" . . . Interviews with Blum and Morgenthau.

Chapter 19: CRACKS IN THE FACADE

263 Over the years, a Ponzi scheme . . . Such schemes are described in "Heirs of Original Ponzi Scheme Can Still Fleece the Unwary," David Clark Scott, *The Christian Science Monitor*, March 24, 1986, and "Charles Ponzi: A Pyramid of Postage," Stephen Labaton, *The New York Times*, December 7, 1986.

264 In the case of BCCI . . . The comparison to a Ponzi scheme draws on several documentary sources describing the original loans that helped finance the start of BCCI and the relationship between the bank and those first shareholders over the years. Among the most important sources were the Federal Reserve case 91–043, Price Waterhouse audits of BCCI from November 1989, March 1990, and June 1991, and sworn Senate testimony of Masihur Rahman. As with Ponzi's original investors, the comparison does not suggest that the original shareholders of BCCI were part of the conspiracy, although some were later accused by the Federal Reserve of serving as nominees for the bank in its secret purchase of First American Bankshares in Washington.

265 "Every investigation goes . . . Interview with Morgenthau.

266 Moscow was told that BCCI . . . Interview with Moscow.

266 The problem of jurisdiction . . . Interviews with Morgenthau and Moscow.

266–267 As Morgenthau was learning . . . Morgenthau interview.

268 The criminal charges brought . . . Interviews with numerous defense lawyers involved in the BCCI case.

268 None of them had attained Altman's exalted . . . Numerous press accounts appeared about Altman and his life-style in 1991. The best was "Reversal of Fortune," Jaffe.

269 It was a deal with . . . The existence of the stock deals for Clifford and Altman was first disclosed in *The Washington Post* by reporters Jim McGee

and Joel Glenn Brenner in May 1991. After that, there were numerous press accounts of the transactions and they were the subject of testimony by Clifford and Altman before the House Banking Committee on September 11, 1991, and the Kerry subcommittee on October 24, 1991. The chronology of the transactions was laid out in documents provided by Clifford and Altman. There were no allegations that the loans were illegal, although they were viewed by some banking officials as unusual.

270 "You know, I got the call . . . Interview with John Hume, who heard Hogan's remarks.

270 "Unless we're at Our Lady . . . Ibid.

271 "Here you had an Arab-owned . . . Interview with Larry Barcella.

271 "The BCCI bankers had a more . . . Interview with Peter Romatowski.

272 "My view is that these guys . . . Interview with Hume.

272 "What do you want . . . Ibid.

274 There were some, such as Jack Blum . . . Blum was most notable in this group, but his views were supported by other critics of the bank.

275–76 At the New York and Boca Raton offices . . . Examination reports are contained in Fed documents obtained through Freedom of Information Act requests and were described in testimony by Virgil Mattingly and William Taylor before the Senate Banking Committee on May 23, 1991.

276 The first the Federal Reserve Board . . . Mattingly described this conversation as extremely brief in his May 23, 1991, testimony. However, federal law enforcement sources said in later interviews that Burris provided Ryback with a more extensive explanation of what had been uncovered. In addition, the House Judiciary Committee Subcommittee on Crime and Criminal Justice report noted that Burris had offered to provide Ryback with witnesses with knowledge of BCCI's alleged control of First American. Further, IRS travel records also showed that Burris and Dettmer flew to Washington in February 1989.

277 In its report to the Fed board . . . This finding is described in a February 13, 1989, letter from the Federal Reserve Board to Robert Altman approving First American's acquisition of Bank of Escambia.

277 The concerns of the regulators . . . The chronology of events leading up to the eventual shutdown of BCCI is drawn from many sources. Chief among them are the Senate testimony of Virgil Mattingly and William Taylor in May, August, and September of 1991, copies of Price Waterhouse audit reports and accompanying letters and documents from 1989 and 1990, the Senate testimony of Masihur Rahman, and many published articles. The best coverage of these events was provided by the *Financial Times* and *The Wall Street Journal*.

278 Dated November 17, 1989 . . . A copy of the report was obtained by the authors.

279 Bank secrecy laws in Britain . . . Taylor's August testimony before the Kerry subcommittee and an interview with Taylor.

279 The response came from Swaleh . . . A copy of the Fed letter to Altman and Naqvi's response were obtained by the authors.

279 In their defense . . . Interviews with McKean and Jonathan Winer plus internal files from the Kerry subcommittee.

279–80 "There was no appreciation . . . Interview with Kerry.

Notes and Sources

Chapter 20: BAGGING THE BANK

281 The cause was an order . . . Gregory Kehoe said in an interview that the December 5, 1989, order by Judge Hodges altered the government's entire posture toward a plea bargain with the bank. Defense attorneys agreed that the ruling was a major motivator for the government to reach an agreement.

283 Tuesday, January 16, 1990, was the eve . . . Details of the plea agreement are drawn from the document itself.

283 It was denounced by Senator . . . Interview with Kerry and numerous press accounts of his reaction.

285 Nonetheless, on February 13 . . . A copy of the Saphos letter was obtained by the authors, as was a copy of the Lewis response.

287 The issue of immunity also was . . . Interviews with Moscow.

288 In this initial phase . . . Interviews with Morgenthau and his Senate testimony on May 23, 1991.

289 Hume and Mike Rubinstein sat down . . . Interviews with Hume and Mike Rubinstein.

289 When the twelve jurors . . . The matter was made part of the record of the trial when it occurred.

291 The problems, said Price Waterhouse . . . Price Waterhouse audit of BCCI and accompanying documents, dated March 14, 1990.

291 For instance, the accountants said . . . Ibid.

291 Far more significant . . . Ibid.

292 The biggest single borrower . . . Ibid.

292 Another example of the bank's . . . Ibid.

293 When the regulators in Britain . . . Rahman Senate testimony and press accounts.

293 Naqvi flew to Abu Dhabi . . . Ibid.

294 The new audit, done with . . . Taylor testimony to Senate on August 1, 1991, and press accounts, such as "How the Bank Within a Bank Failed to Keep Records," *The Times* of London, July 20, 1991.

295 "If we closed down a bank every time . . . "Major Knew of BCCI Problems Two Years Ago," Peter Norman, Richard Waters, and Ivo Dawnay, *Financial Times*, July 24, 1991.

Chapter 21: THE CRITICAL EVENT

298 "A lot of them were angry" . . . Morgenthau interview.

299 Masihur Rahman first learned . . . Rahman Senate testimony.

299 For Fed counsel Virgil Mattingly . . . Senate testimony of Mattingly and Taylor on May 23, 1991, and interview with Taylor.

300 Immediately, the Fed staff . . . Senate testimony of Mattingly and Taylor on August 1, 1991.

300 On December 10, 1990 . . . Ibid.

301 On December 21, Patton, Boggs . . . Ibid and interviews with attorneys involved in the discussions.

301 On January 22, a criminal referral . . . Senate testimony of Mattingly and Taylor on August 1, 1991.

302 The $856 million in secret . . . The figure was obtained from the March 1990 Price Waterhouse audit. The conclusion that the transactions gave

BCCI control over First American came from the Senate testimony of Mattingly and Taylor on August 1, 1991, and from the Federal Reserve case 91–043 against BCCI and various shareholders.

302   The loans were subject to secret . . . Federal Reserve case 91–043.

302   In another example, the original . . . Ibid. (The Fed case lays out this transaction and many others in great detail; Adham, through his Washington lawyer, Plato Cacheris, denied that he was a front for BCCI and maintained that he invested his own money in First American.)

304   "I have a choice of either . . . "Clark Clifford, Symbol of the Permanent Government, Is Faced with a Dilemma," Lewis.

304   Indeed, Altman would later say . . . Altman testimony before House Banking Committee on September 11, 1991.

304   Over the years, Clifford . . . Clifford testimony before House Banking Committee on September 11, 1991.

304   "In dealing with the shareholders . . . Ibid.

305   In April 1990, Kerry had gone . . . Interview with Kerry.

305   Kerry's staff had sensed a turning point . . . Interviews with McKean and internal staff memo prepared by Winer.

306–07   On September 24, 1990, a lawyer . . . The authors obtained a copy of the Theus memo.

307   Editor Brian Kelly and . . . Interviews with Brian Kelly and Larry Gurwin and copies of letters from the files of *Regardie's*.

308   However, there were snide comments . . . Interviews with Kerry and staff.

308   Even Kerry had received . . . Federal Election Commission records.

308   "As we went along . . . Interview with Morgenthau.

309   Snags had cropped up . . . Interviews with Kehoe and Rubinstein.

309   "We called the Feds" . . . Morgenthau Senate testimony.

310   "My client had sat . . . Hume interviews.

311   In March 1991, Bob Mazur decided . . . A copy of Mazur's resignation letter was reviewed by the authors. Additional information came from the House Judiciary Committee Subcommittee on Crime and Criminal Justice report and "Bureaucratic Snags Blocked BCCI Inquiry in '88," Dean Baquet, *The New York Times*, August 13, 1991. Tischler's response came in the Judiciary report and interviews with the authors.

312   On January 30, 1991, Jackowski . . . House Judiciary Committee report.

313   "Absolute mind rot" . . . Moscow interview.

314   "A lot was being taken . . . Testimony of Sidney Bailey before Senate Banking Committee on May 23, 1991.

315   "We run many cooperative . . . Morgenthau Senate testimony.

315   Maloney did not go into any details . . . Testimony of Paul Maloney before Senate Banking Committee on May 23, 1991.

Chapter 22: A WORLD OF UNREALITY

317   On Friday, June 28, 1991 . . . Taylor interview and testimony before Senate on August 1, 1991.

317   The latest and most startling . . . Information about the Price Waterhouse 1991 audit and reaction to it came from several sources, including interviews with participants, Senate testimony of William Taylor on August 1, 1991, portions of the audit itself, and numerous press accounts.

Among the best articles were "The Bank That Liked to Say Yes," Lascelles and Donkin, which included the information that Eddie George did not sleep well; "How the Bank Within a Bank Failed to Keep Records," *The Times* of London; "Secret Bank Inside BCCI Disguised Huge Losses," David Lascelles, Richard Donkin, and David Waller, *Financial Times*, July 8, 1991; "Abu Dhabi 'Knew of BCCI Fraud,'" David Lascelles, Peter Martin, and Richard Waters, *Financial Times*, August 3/4, 1991; and "Unrecorded Funds from 'Islamic Banks' Concealed Losses at BCCI, Report Says," Peter Truell, *The Wall Street Journal*, August 6, 1991.

318 Years of financial manipulations . . . "Fraud Reaches BCCI's Top, Bank of England Head Says," Nicholas Bray and Peter Truell, *The Wall Street Journal*, July 24, 1991, and "Audit: BCCI Used D.C. Bank Funds," Mark Potts, *The Washington Post*, August 6, 1991.

318 Swaleh Naqvi himself had held . . . Ibid.

318 The report placed the blame . . . "Blaming the Bank of England," *The Economist*, July 20, 1991; "1st American Role in BCCI Documented," Jim McGee and Steven Mufson, *The Washington Post*, July 24, 1991; and "Major Knew of BCCI Problems," Norman, Waters, and Dawnay.

319 "Many simply followed instructions . . . Quote from Price Waterhouse report comes from "Abu Dhabi 'Knew of Bank Fraud but Stayed Silent,'" Sonia Purnell, *The Daily Telegraph*, August 3, 1991.

319 "It was like doing a huge jigsaw . . . "BCCI's Marathon Man," Robert Tyerman, *The Daily Telegraph*, July 14, 1991.

319 Leaving Fed general counsel . . . Taylor's Senate testimony on August 1, 1991, laid out a detailed chronology for the events leading up to and immediately following the shutdown of the bank as well as the concerns among regulators over the potential impact of the shutdown. It was augmented by an interview with Taylor and numerous press accounts.

321 Two days after the coordinated . . . "Abu Dhabi Urged to Aid Depositors," Alison Smith and Victor Mallet, *Financial Times*, July 8, 1991.

322 When a reporter for . . . Abu Dhabi Asks UK to Explain BCCI Closure," David Lascelles and Alison Smith, *Financial Times*, July 9, 1991.

322 "The West never wanted . . . "Pakistan Rallies Behind BCCI," Philip Shenon, *The New York Times*, August 5, 1991.

322 Another Pakistani, construction company owner . . . Ibid.

322 "If there was a problem with drug money . . . Ibid.

322 "God knows better" . . . "Illness Mutes the Founder of BCCI," John Bussey.

323 At eleven o'clock, Robert Morgenthau . . . Morgenthau press conference, indictment, and press release.

325 "This largest of Ponzi schemes . . . Morgenthau press conference.

325 The Fed's notice of charges . . . Federal Reserve case 91–043.

326 In Karachi, Pakistan's finance minister . . . "Pakistan Admits CIA Used Local BCCI Branches," Christina Lamb, *Financial Times*, July 24, 1991. Two days later, Sartaj Asis, the finance minister, issued a statement denying that he made the remarks to the *Financial Times*. Other persons interviewed who are familiar with BCCI's operations in Pakistan, however, say that the bank was used by the CIA as a conduit for money to Afghan rebels.

326 "We, CIA, used it as anyone . . . "CIA Probed, Used BCCI, Official Says," George Lardner, Jr., *The Washington Post*, August 3, 1991, and "Agency

Used BCCI, Intelligence Official Says," Elaine Sciolino, *The New York Times*, August 3, 1991.

327 "Wherever you turn . . . "Billions in Losses Led to Seizure," Steven Mufson, *The Washington Post*, July 9, 1991.

Epilogue

330 A few minutes before . . . Appearance and testimony by Clark Clifford and Robert Altman before the House Banking Committee on September 11, 1991.

331 "My heart wants to believe . . . Statement by Representative Charles Schumer at House Banking Committee hearing, September 11, 1991.

INDEX

A

Abdul-Aziz, King (Saudi Arabia), 49
Abedi, Agha Hasan, ix
  and Altman, 331
  and Attock Oil Corporation, 51–53
  and Amjad Awan, 78, 96, 161, 189
  in Bangladesh, 166
  and BCCI in America, 94, 95–96,
    162–64
  and BCCI shutdown, 322–23
  and BCCI treasury losses, 98
  and Jimmy Carter, 7, 34, 165–67,
    198
  and central bank of Peru, 136
  and Chelsea National Bank, 48,
    267
  in China, 165–66
  and Clark Clifford, 7, 59–60, 164,
    304–05, 331
  early career, 10–14
  and early growth of BCCI, 23–28,
    34–38
  and External Marketing Plan,
    190–91
  and Financial General Bankshares,
    54–60, 71
  and founding of BCCI, 16–22
  heart surgery on, 197–99, 246
  indicted, 324, 325
  and Lance, 34, 48–49, 53–54
  and National Bank of Georgia,
    168–69
  and 1991 audit, 318–19
  and Noriega, 86
  in Panama, 80
  and Pharaon, 48–49, 52, 53–54,
    159–60
  resignation from BCCI, 294, 298
  and Young, 166–67
  and Zayed, 14–15, 75, 98, 164
Abreu, Emir, ix, 143
  and Alcaino, 139–41
  and beginnings of C-Chase, 118–22
  and cash pick-ups, 131, 145–46,
    149, 153, 183–84, 187
  and C-Chase arrests, 234
  with Mazur in Europe, 203, 205,
    207, 209–10
  and Medellín cartel, 218–19, 221
  and Gonzalo Mora, Jr., 127–29,
    137–39, 176, 211
Abscam investigation, 273
Abu Dhabi
  and BCCI shutdown, 3, 4, 317,
    320–21, 326
  takes control of BCCI, 293, 296, 301
Abu Dhabi Investment Authority, 293
Adham, Kamal, ix, 245
  and Altman, 304
  BCCI loans to, 42–43, 279, 291, 301

Index

9 780671 729127

29570613R00250

Made in the USA
Middletown, DE
24 February 2016